THE GREAT LIQUIDATOR

THE GREAT LIQUIDATOR

by
JOHN V. GROMBACH

DOUBLEDAY & COMPANY, INC.

GARDEN CITY, NEW YORK

1980

No copyright is claimed on any United States Government material quoted in this book. Declassified information and/or material obtained from or by the Secret Intelligence Branch of the War Department General Staff (1942–47) later transferred to the Foreign Service of the State Department (1947–55) was used in this book as well as material obtained from its penetrations into the police and intelligence services of both friendly and enemy sources. The author as director of the branch during its thirteen years was able to obtain information and documents and material on Dr. Petiot unavailable to most researchers.

ISBN: 0-385-13271-9
Library of Congress Catalog Card Number: 77-12862
Copyright © 1980 by John V. Grombach
All Rights Reserved
Printed in the United States of America
First Edition

Contents

Acknowledgments

The author acknowledges, with thanks, the personal and sometimes confidential assistance of the following in the preparation of this book over a period of over thirty years. As a result of the length of time, many of the persons listed are now deceased.

Fernand Laurent, prewar Acting Mayor of Paris, one of the French agents of the Special Service Branch (WDGS) of the U.S. Army who, later, working for the U.S. State and War departments, accomplished the surrender of Martinique without loss of life after all other means had failed; Judge Marcel Leser, District Attorney Pierre Dupin, Maître (attorney) Pierre Veron, Jacques Yonnet, Mme. Pavie de Saint Lorette, Maître Louis Monard, Dr. Trocme, Ugo Papini, J. Gilbert, Andy Schwedersky, Jean Millet, Henri Fournier, Mme. Nezondet; lawyers, doctors, psychiatrists and witnesses who requested that their names not be listed; Dr. W. I. Taylor, CIBA, other experts on narcotics, intoxicants, and hallucinogens, Professor Edouard Rougement, Europe's greatest graphologist, the doctors and technicians at the Paris Morgue and the Institut Médico-Légal, the Paris police and its many retired personnel; the police and gendarmerie of Villeneuve-sur-Yonne, Auxerre, Gambais, Tessancourt, Montargis, Versailles, Seignelay, Quimper, Dijon, Lyon, Marseille; lawyers and brokers, real estate agency personnel, tenants, superintendents and concierges of the many Petiot properties, offices, apartment buildings, hotels, houses, farms, vineyards, and cafés (fifty-one); the many other installations involved in the Petiot story and those adjoining; Paris printers, public stenographers, and newspaper reporters who helped recoup documents and facts; Dr. André Lemaître, who later lived and practiced medicine from the Petiot mansion in Villeneuve; the French War Department General Staff and its archivists, the French Army hospitals for access to their records, former members of the Gestapo and the Abwehr, the German Occupational authorities of Paris, Paris druggists, the Prison de la Santé guards, Laboratoire de Recherches Thérapeutiques, court attendants, jurymen, and spectators at the various trials of Dr. Petiot; Dr. S. Dérobert, Dr. Paul (Paris coroner), Dr. René Piedelievre of the Institut Médico-Légal; the families of the victims who requested that their names not be listed; the maids of the Petiot families, especially one who later became a nun; members of the F.F.I. and DGER, the guillotine staff members and personnel, the many persons interviewed who were witnesses, acquaintances, friends, enemies, patients, or scouts of Dr. Petiot (or Dr. Eugène or Dr. Valéry or Dr. Wetterwald), particularly Edmond Pintard (Francinet); the Ivry Cemetery personnel; a former French Intelligence General who desires to remain unnamed; Russian General Alexander Barmine, who defected from Soviet Intelligence in Paris in 1937 and served both the U.S. War Department Secret Intelligence, the OSS, and the USIA; Professor Louis Rougier of the University of Besancon, secret emissary of Pétain to Churchill before the fall of France. (I was assigned to study documents submitted indicating a double cross of Pétain by Churchill for the WDGS received by the President); Dr. E. Gross, forensic medical expert and Chief Medical Examiner, State of Connecticut; the Department of Sewers of the city of Paris, the personnel of the Usine de Clichy, the 1944 personnel of the Caserne Reuilly; the authors of a number of French books which were suppressed, withdrawn, or no longer available, and, most important, the U.S. secret agents in Paris during the Occupation and thereafter who were my original scouts and got much of the original basic data but who cannot be named, and, more than anyone else, two Paris police officials: one a high-level officer of the Paris police in charge of the Petiot case and the one man with a strange but intimate rapport with Dr. Petiot and the only man in whom the doomed man confided with the promise that some one American be given his notes and summary of his conversations to write a book in the U.S. that would make him, Petiot, famous. Only six persons contacted by me refused to be interviewed; among these were Dr. Petiot's brother, Maurice Petiot, who threatened my life and who died of cancer shortly thereafter, Mrs. Marcel Petiot, defense counsel René Floriot, and Dr. Heuycr, a psychiatrist who testified that Dr. Petiot was not responsible for stealing gasoline as mayor of Villeneuve but who later testified that Petiot was fully responsible for the murder of twenty-seven persons at his final trial. The defense lawyer carefully avoided an interview without actually ever refusing one . . . perhaps for a very good reason.

Although unable to break down the French Government's 1947 suppression and sequestration of all government records and several books, many of which I had already secured, I owe the U.S. State Department and the U.S. Embassy in Paris thanks for their repeated efforts to obtain access for me to the official Petiot records. The following State Department personnel tried hard: Hugh Fullerton, Cecil Lyon, Glenn G. Wolfe, at various times U.S. consuls general at Paris, Graham Martin, later the last U.S. Ambassador to Vietnam, Robert Murphy, then Deputy Under Secretary of State, David Linebaugh, Special Assistant to the Secretary of State, Counselor John R. Wood. I also want to thank Niles Bond, U.S. Consul General in South America, and Ambassador Elbridge Durbrow for their help. I owe thanks to Mickey Ladd, a deputy director of the FBI and my liaison as director of the S.I. Branch of the War Department and the State Department— together we co-operated in spotting enemy agents in the U.S. and feeding them false information as controlled agents. Credit is also due to Brigadier General Thomas King, JAG-USAF, for legal advice not only to me as director of the S.I. Branch in its friendly termination in preference to its being taken over and integrated into the CIA in 1955, but in helping me in the preparation of this book.

I admit having been encouraged to write this book by J. Edgar Hoover and General Walter Bedell Smith who believed it could discourage innocent administrators and legislators in the future from handicapping the prevention of subversion and espionage by the FBI and CIA. Last but not least I owe a great deal of credit to Major General Charles G. Stevenson, my executive officer in World War II, Colonel John Bakeless, Colonel Walter D. O'Brien, Fletcher Pratt, Colonel Harry Ryan, Colonel George Converse, Colonel Donald Foster, Herbert O. Yardley, Rosario

Candela—all members of the Secret Intelligence Branch, which I directed from January 2, 1942, to January 1, 1955, for the War and State departments and to my family physician, Dr. Eli Bauman, for his help and to my wife, Olga, for her patience and help with this book.

Preface

On August 20, 1944, during the Battle of Normandy, Nazi Reichsführer of the SS Heinrich Himmler sent a ciphered radiogram to Vichy Minister of Justice Gabolde. The message, classified "Top Secret," demanded immediate and complete information on a Dr. Marcel Petiot—the so-called mass murderer of Paris.

> IS THIS MAN, KNOWN AS DR. PETIOT, ASSASSINATING THE
> GESTAPO AND COLLABORATORS, OR IS HE LIQUIDATING
> MEMBERS OF THE RESISTANCE AND JEWS? URGENT THAT
> YOU INFORM US WHETHER HE IS WORKING FOR OR AGAINST
> THE THIRD REICH.

Himmler's query was intercepted and deciphered by Arlington Hall, the U.S. Dark Chamber or cryptoanalysis organization, later the National Security Agency (NSA). The clear text was read in Washington. The fast-spreading rumors of an "underground assassin," for or against the Nazis, had already been the subject of reports by U.S. secret agents in Occupied Paris. Several reports indicated that the killings could be the work of a Communist terrorist organization as they had begun after the Nazis attacked their Russian ally on June 22, 1941. (Twenty-one rue Le Sueur, later found to be the site of the murders, was purchased by Dr. Petiot shortly thereafter.)

Over two years before Himmler's query, completely unconnected with these reports, this same Dr. Petiot, in the Paris theatrical community, active in espionage (and with reported contacts

with Soviet Secret Intelligence, the German Gestapo, the German
Abwehr, and British intelligence), had furnished U.S. secret
agents with valuable information from a variety of sources, all of
great interest to the United States (as an insulated source—PC-P-
4 and, later, D-P-6). One report told of spies sent to the U.S. by
the German Abwehr headquarters in Paris (at the Hotel Lutetia)
to penetrate our Manhattan Project. They were to get vital information for the Kaiser Wilhelm Institute in order to win the atom
bomb race for Hitler. With the help of these reports the FBI converted the German spies into controlled agents. They were fed
wrong information—as can be proven by documentary evidence—
that delayed the Nazi atom bomb. This may well prove that a
strange Paris informer may have contributed to our winning
World War II.

The Petiot case was indeed the epitome of the sensational at
the time of the discovery of his mass murders, the all-out manhunt, and the final trial, conviction, and execution of "the Great
Liquidator." Strangely enough, or perhaps proving his sincerity,
there were only occasional references but no claims during all this
time that he was also involved in underground activities in intelligence work or in the planning of ways for Allied pilots, downed
over Axis Europe, to escape.

It was only natural that the confusion at the end of the war, the
atom bomb, the takeover of many countries by the Communists,
and the international problems attending the end of a world
conflagration completely overshadowed press reports in the
United States of Dr. Petiot's trial. Paris and European newspapers, although headlining the case, were pitifully short of news-
print paper and could give only limited space in their four-page
editions to the long and complex proceedings of the trial. All sub-
sequent attempts to give a full reporting of the case became almost impossible for a very real barrier was imposed thereafter—
the French Government dropped an official curtain of secrecy
around the entire Petiot case. It was apparent that de Gaulle and
especially his deputy, Communist Maurice Thorez, wanted no all-
out investigation or publicity on the case or on the violent liquidations of all anti-Communists as well as pro-Nazis during the liberation. Without the Communists, de Gaulle could not have gained
control of postwar France and there could be no doubt that Dr.

Petiot was a Communist, probably an insane one. All police records, evidence, and even the records of the public trial were sequestered; an old law was involved, namely, a fifty-year ban was put into effect insofar as the Petiot case was concerned and this is still in effect today—to be lifted in 1996. Then again there were evidences of de Gaulle's opportunism—great man that he was—in his frequent and open partnership with the Communists and his granting of amnesty to Thorez, a wartime deserter sentenced to death who had fled to Moscow but returned to Paris to become de Gaulle's number two man. (Dr. Petiot, in the twenties, knew both Thorez and another member of the French Communist Party, Ho Chi Minh, who, later, as is well known, became head of Communist North Vietnam.)

The backdrop for the story is wartime Paris. Like a shadow in the midst of the tangled intrigues of terrorists, spies, informers, collaborators, and double agents is the figure of a doctor playing many parts and all sides.

By great good luck, based on ceaseless and persevering investigation, I gained access to the equivalent of a start of an autobiography—the highly confidential story and a few notes by Dr. Petiot revealed to his favorite jailer in prison shortly before his execution plus certain other documents and facts given or relayed under certain conditions to me alone. In return, I was to write a biography or book to be published in the United States after the death of the parties responsible for the relay of this information and my lifelong promise never to reveal their names. The executed man had previously written a book in jail—in the period between his arrest and his trial—which was published, sold at his trial, and then suppressed by the French Government. I found every indication of an effort on the part of the about-to-be executed principal in his dream book and in his final story to try to find justification for his murders and to present a mysterious—if not heroic—self-portrait without attention, necessarily, to the true facts. Petiot desired to become a legendary character but without admitting any tie-up with the Communist underground, perhaps from loyalty or perhaps in fear for his family although there is every indication that he was involved with the Communists. There is no question that he hated the Nazis and all Germans, disliked the British, was confused by the breakup of the French, but had a strange respect and regard for the United States. It was this, incidentally, that made it possible for me, as an American, to get Petiot's last—or posthumous—notes.

So, in a way, as author of this book, I am another of the many guiltless and indirect accomplices of the master assassin that you will read about. I have a certain admiration for Dr. Petiot, a fascinating and extraordinarily intelligent man (who was twice mayor of a town founded before the Romans) whether he was merely a cunning paranoiac murderer for money or a mentally deranged Communist terrorist and would-be patriot. His cleverness and medical skill would have more than likely prevented him from being convicted by any Anglo-Saxon court for lack of positive evidence and some of his opinions and ideas were startlingly accurate and profound. As to his political and ideological thinking, it was, as he often admitted, purely selfish and power-seeking and an illustration of what many "have nots" see in a world revolution—the only possible way to come out on top! Yet he had the sound intelligence to see far beyond the present.

The lessons from this book—as requested for a listing by Dr. Petiot to be included in this book in return for his help—were that society must be ruthless and must exterminate dangerous and homicidal misfits and assassins, and man must become wise and not permit war or chaos or confusion that will make possible bloody and senseless periods of crime and disorder. That more and bigger wars have been caused by appeasement and compromise than by strong action to stop aggressors with hopes of world domination who often plan on the age-old cleavages of creed, race, ideology, and economics. That our major and most dangerous enemy today in dealing with aggressors, criminals, rioters, student agitators, radicals, and drones alike is permissiveness under the guise of liberalism. Based on a strange affection for Americans, Dr. Petiot had to voice his opinion that the United States' peace-making and naïve helping hand and almost unbelievable giveaways and alleged interest in other people's business, whether in the Far East or in the Near East or in Latin America or in Africa, were costly mistakes and not necessarily to the United States' credit. While no one would admit it, Dr. Petiot declared that the free world was financially in great trouble and charity should begin at home. Why, if communism was really the answer to the future, must the free world supply the U.S.S.R. with food, goods, and industrial know-how? That the most dangerous policy of the U.S. was to trust the Soviet Union and Red China in a détente that did not recognize that the Communist states wanted to bury the U.S. and end democracy, freedom, and the free enterprise system. Petiot strongly believed that the U.S. should have permanent compulsory military service to help the economy and to teach American youth patriotism, discipline, and service to their country. In doing this, the U.S. could also be more certain to remain the strongest nation in the world, for defense purposes only, even if the U.S. foolishly gave away the three-times-purchased Panama Canal Zone (in perpetuity) with millions already paid and still being paid to the Republic of Panama.

The Panama Canal giveaway if finally accomplished (as Petiot did not doubt it would be) is the direct result of its definite selection by the U.S.S.R. and Stalin as the first priority domino along with Cuba in the Communist play for world domination as far back as before 1942. It was definite Soviet direction, according to leaks from the German Abwehr in Paris and its Soviet penetrations, that was behind Dexter White's early pronouncement from the White House in Washington for a Panama giveaway and Alger Hiss's announcement at the UN that it was an occupied territory or an American colony and should be "liberated." Criminal subversion or naïve stupidity had begun in Washington. Still another worker preached the Panama Canal giveaway for the U.S.S.R. A reported Communist, Rudolfo Duran, an important if not the most important assistant to Nelson Rockefeller in President Roosevelt's good-will commission to Latin America, preached the Panama giveaway as a U.S. gift to Latin America although never denying his former relations with the Communists and his actual former connection with the Lincoln Brigade in Spain. His identity and his mission were also reported by Dr. Petiot in 1943. Duran was reported to have been recommended by the Rockefellers allegedly because of their extensive bank loans to Panama that would be protected if the Canal Zone and further cash payments would be given away by the U.S.

These were among the facts and opinions, strangely enough, reported by "the Great Liquidator" in connection with his espionage or former espionage activities in Paris. These were duly passed on to G2, the State Department, and the FBI, and were the subject of several meetings with A. A. Berle, Jr., Assistant Secretary of State, and with J. Edgar Hoover and his deputy, Mickey Ladd. Mr. Berle went to the President with regard to Alger Hiss but received a violent dressing down. It was also much later discussed with General Walter Bedell Smith, CIA chief. They all obtained a promise from me to write a book on some of my espionage activities exposing the criminal subversion in Washington, on the highest level prior, during and after World War II, in order to help preserve the unusual but necessary rights and special privileges of both the FBI and CIA and in order to preserve the security of the U.S. As a result of these promises and the disastrous limitations and handicaps placed on both the FBI and CIA by the Congress in the last twenty years, the problem of security is being projected in this Preface as well as in more detail in the text that follows. The opinions are based on the information, reports, and opinions later supported by true and provable facts first exposed or projected by an unusual informer with a love for the United States. His career and biography as a mass murderer alone are almost unbelievable but have been the subject of many books and may well become a fearsome legend. His espionage or informer activities are still shadowy and uncertain because as a mass murderer none of his secret sources or those to whom he relayed important information would admit any connection with him whatsoever. As discussed with J. Edgar Hoover and General Walter Bedell Smith, this story may well convince the U.S. public that subversion and clandestine and espionage activities cannot be controlled by normal, legal, and proper methods. The current limitations placed on both the CIA and the FBI would more properly fit a Boy Scout organization. According to some persons, including former Secretary of State Henry L. Stimson, "Gentlemen do not read each other's mail!" (interception of radio communications and the decipherment of the coded or ciphered messages)—even if a Pearl Harbor or an H-bomb attack is scheduled for next week!

THE GREAT LIQUIDATOR

CHAPTER I

"The Charnel House"
the story begins on Saturday,
March 11, 1944

Paris, during the German Occupation, seemed glassy-eyed and punch-drunk. Because of the crushing blitzkrieg and both an internal political conspiracy and a secret agreement* with an ally, Marshal Pétain had, on June 17, 1940, ordered all Frenchmen to lay down their arms, causing whole army divisions to quit against their will. This enabled the Germans to capture 1,500,000 men, a number unprecedented in history, almost as many men as France had lost in the entire four years of World War I. The fall of proud France was, therefore, so sudden and brutal that it stunned its citizens. Shops stood open and factories turned their wheels. In the Opéra district, prostitutes, still young and pretty, continued to promenade. There were still movies to attend, or the theater, but the busy taxis no longer dodged about as if by a will of their own, and there was no motor vehicular traffic. The Métro was only just alive. It was still crowded, even overcrowded, but half its trains had been suspended to conserve power and the remaining ones

* According to Professor Louis Rougier and documents secretly verified by the U.S. War Department G2 and the State Department, and used by them in sending Admiral Leahey as ambassador to Vichy in preparing for the invasion of French North Africa, Pétain made a secret pact with Winston Churchill with respect to surrender being the only way to save France and North Africa so they could return to the war at a later and strategically proper time and to save the French fleet and threaten the German rear and lines of supply. But Churchill later chose to forget the secret treaty. While de Gaulle never admitted it, Allied landings in North Africa and the full return of France in the war was due in part, to Marshal Pétain and the Vichy foreign service officers in Africa who served as our secret agents.

were meagerly lit and foul with air that had been breathed too often. The great hotels, which had once seemed to send pleasant chatter out over the sidewalks in a warm tide whenever the doors swung open, were as grim now as the field-gray uniforms that filled their lobbies, for most of them were open only to German military personnel. Many sidewalk restaurants, where girls in outlandish hats had made men turn and stare, were marked off by wooden barricades to make sure that none but Germans entered. The loving couples that once sauntered arm in arm along the boulevards were few, and nearly all were German military personnel in forage caps, some with muscular blond German girls, themselves severely clothed in field gray.

Here and there throughout the city, well-fed German soldiers in gray steel bucket helmets stood sentry in front of buildings that had become headquarters for German officials. Swastika flags, wide as sails, bellied down over many a building front. On every street there were shops whose windows had gone dead and where the dust of months had laid a film over the scanty window displays. Walking feet filled the avenues with an unusual clatter, for many shoes in wartime Paris had wooden soles. Traffic moved at bicycle pace, except when a German military vehicle, stuffed with silent men, roared past, but these were rare, and usually MPs for troop movements by-passed the city for security reasons. Frenchmen mostly pedaled along on bicycles, on rickshaw-type velo-taxis or *triporteurs* (three-wheeled affairs), or sometimes on bicycles with a trunk and two wheels in front or sometimes with a sort of trailer hitched to the rear—a cart large enough to hold furniture or trunks or laundry or fuel and food. After all, the absence of gasoline could not stop transportation in the city where a Parisian, Monsieur de Sivrac, invented the bicycle in 1690.

Even conversation in public places seemed curt and constrained. Who could tell which of one's acquaintances might not be an informer of sorts or might not be storing up bits of careless comment or opinion to be used against one in God knows what secret conclave? The job of Frenchmen was to stay alive. There was no imminent prospect of freedom, only a vague hope fed by rumors that were too often false, or by grim faith in the ultimate resurrection by another Chevalier Bayard, Joan of Arc, Napoleon, or Marshal Foch.

It was not a question of "collaborating." Entertainers kept the theaters and night clubs open for the Germans and men worked in factories that may have helped the Germans but also helped Frenchmen eat and be clothed. What would it avail, as one writer asked, to set a cemetery free? One did not love the Germans if one did not resist.

Above all, one did not poke into affairs that were none of one's immediate concern. There were all sorts of mysterious doings in the city; sudden death was nearly as commonplace as a minor illness. Bombs dropped at times—by mistake, it was said—having been intended for some factory in the suburbs. But they demolished homes impartially and killed good Frenchmen and bad Frenchmen without warning. Men and women were taken prisoner occasionally and cruelly questioned, even tortured, or carried off to some unmentioned destination to be done to death. There were bodies frequently found floating in the Seine or found by some dawn stroller in the Bois de Boulogne, or in an alley, or trussed and stuffed into some cellar, or in the famous sewers.

Thus it caused no alarm, and certainly no inquiries, when strange doings and strange sounds were noted from time to time in little rue Le Sueur, a shortcut and very short street from 30 avenue Foch to 61 avenue de la Grande Armée, not far from the Arc de Triomphe and close to the edge of the Bois de Boulogne. Rue Le Sueur was a sedate little street of comfortable apartments, rather like one of the East Sixties in New York, a row of quiet two- to five-story homes and apartments, snugly fitted together, with narrow sidewalks and a roadway the width of three European automobiles. Even in peacetime, it would have been unusual for anyone to be abroad on this street at midnight or for any loud cries to be heard here. During the Occupation, with the curfew, it was almost unthinkable. Yet, again and again, in 1941, 1942, and 1943, neighbors heard the slow and unaccustomed clop-clop of horses' hoofs and the grate on the pavement of the iron-rimmed wheels of an old-fashioned fiacre, always at night about eleven. And some, if they were wakeful and peering out from behind the blackout curtains, might see dark figures alight and enter number 21. Some, in the quiet of the night, were positive they heard screams, a voice calling "Au secour! Au secour!" and the sound of footsteps in flight. But whence all this sound came no one could determine at once and no one cared to try. Victor Avenelle, professor of Romance languages of 23 rue Le Sueur, testified to hearing muffled but terrifying cries for help on frequent occasions but always around 11:30 P.M. The cries always came from 21 rue Le Sueur and seemed to be repeated a few times, then stopped. Mr. and Mrs. Jacques Mercier at 22 heard, on a number of occasions, faint but desperate cries for help, always between ten and twelve midnight. These lasted only for short periods, then complete silence. Count Saunis, who lived at 23 rue Le Sueur, complained about horrible screams he heard coming from 21 rue Le Sueur during the night that prevented him from sleeping, but no one seemed to care to be too inquisitive. Most of the concierges of the neighborhood who had heard screams in the night thought that either the Gestapo were busy torturing secrets from resistants or that the building was a clinic for abortions and that, due to the shortage of medical supplies, the operations were performed without anesthetics. There was a small garage on the street, used by the German Army Supply Todt Service. A short way over the roofs was both a German Military Police and Gestapo headquarters, at 84 avenue Foch, where prisoners were sometimes hustled in, perhaps never to be seen again.† A few blocks away on rue Lauriston was the worst menace in Paris, the French Gestapo—cutthroats released from French jails by the Germans to help them fight resistants and steal for the Nazis. There, more murders were hatched or committed than anywhere else in Paris. Today, a plaque in front of 42 rue Bassano, which housed a branch of the same organization, also nearby, reads: "To the memory of the resistants tortured and murdered in this building during the Occupation, 1940–1944." The best policy in Occupied Paris was to hear nothing, see nothing, and mind one's business.

There was a nervous, dark-visaged man who from time to time went in and out of number 21. Sometimes he led or accompanied another person or two in, but no one in the neighborhood ever saw anyone go out but the dark man. Sometimes this man, riding

† It was here that the glamorous Noor Inayat Kahn, code name "Madeleine" (the Paris-educated daughter of an American woman and an Indian musician and mystic), a British spy, was imprisoned, escaped, and was recaptured to be executed with three other women at Dachau on September 13, 1944. Her recapture was due to a Frenchwoman who turned her in for a thousand francs ($60).

a green bicycle with a two-wheel trailer bumping along behind, would bring in furniture or paintings in ornate frames or, often, unidentifiable cargo covered by an old tarpaulin cover. At Christmastime, in 1941, there was hammering in number 21 until long after midnight and neighbors silently cursed the swarthy man, whoever he might be, for keeping them from sleep. But there was nothing sinister about this, nor about the man himself, at that time. About all that was strange about him was that he was a doctor.

A doctor! Often he did not look the part, wearing frayed shirts, unpressed clothes, and sandals instead of shoes, yet occasionally, especially on Sundays, he seemed immaculate and well dressed. But, on other days, he was seen carrying in furniture and pictures and unloading or loading all kinds of unidentified objects under a tarpaulin cover late at night or before dawn.

Later on, another man would appear on occasion, also dark, somewhat huskier and perhaps handsomer, but looking enough like the first man to be his brother. And that, indeed, is what he later proved to be. Sometimes the neighbors could not quite tell them apart, and once the concierge next door had gone up to the brother and given him a message meant for the doctor, and had not realized her mistake until the man turned and faced her.

Just what the doctor was up to during the long months of summer and winter in 1941 and 1942 none of his neighbors knew, not even the concierge at number 23, who was perhaps the only one of the neighbors who had ever seen the inside of number 21 since the doctor took it over. Once, in order to complete some repairs to the wall of number 23, it was necessary that workmen go in through the doctor's place and mount the stairs to the roof. The doctor freely offered the concierge a key to number 21 and she kept it for three weeks. There were neither strange sounds nor sinister movements in that time.

Then, in June 1943, the neighbors were fascinated to watch through their windows as a truck stopped before number 21 and either the doctor or his brother—the lady across the street could not be sure which—worked with the driver to load an unusual number of bags and suitcases onto the vehicle. There were forty-seven of them, said one of the neighborhood concierges. No, said another concierge, Mme. Pageot, there were forty-nine. She had counted them one by one. And it was a gray closed truck with a sign on it, "Avenue Daumesnil." But no one at this time, other than the neighbors, was counting suitcases or cared where the truck came from.

On Saturday, March 11, 1944, the headlines of the few Paris newspapers, all Nazi controlled, announced some epoch-making events, even though their ultimate import was hidden:

"The German and Russian armies are in a pivotal battle at Tarnapol." "U.S. and British planes bomb Toulon." "Marshal Pétain received Jacques Doriot." "The Atlantic Wall is reinforced against possible landings by Anglo-American and Free French Forces."

Although the news was censored and camouflaged, everyone knew that the tide of the war was finally turning against the Germans.

All was quiet, except on rue Le Sueur, where a heavy and nauseating smoke began to pour from the chimney of number 21—a famous smoke, for it marked the beginning, for the police, journalists, and for the authors of over twenty or more books, of L'Affaire Petiot (the Petiot case). It was a thick, heavy smoke, with a pestilential odor, penetrating, black as the smoke from an oven. It seemed to flow straight from the chimney stack to the fifth-floor windows of Mme. Marcais, who lived at number 22, on the other side of the street. The poor woman was at her wits' end. On March 6 this same smoke had bothered her and for several days thereafter. No matter what she did, she could not shut that foul smell out of her windows. Day after day, the smoke rose up and spilled across the street to her apartment, filling the rooms with a stench so foul that it took the appetite away. But on Saturday, March 11, it was worse and, since her husband was home, she asked him to go see what was wrong at number 21 and he walked over to ring the bell. There was a sign on the porte-cochere that said: "Gone away for a month. Forward mail to 18, rue des Lombards Auxerre." But it was dusk and M. Marcais probably did not see this. There was no answer to bell or to knock. Fearing a chimney fire, for the smoke was pouring out in increasing quantity, M. Marcais called the police. Two bicycle patrolmen responded quickly. It was after six now, the dark was growing deeper, but the smoke continued to rise, then as if too heavy, to roll down into the streets, thick, black, and all-enveloping.

M. Marcais could not tell the police who lived at number 21, so officers Joseph Teyssier and Émile Fillion sought the concierge next door, at number 23. The tenant, she told them (she did not know the owner), was a physician, a Dr. Petiot, who lived at 66 rue Caumartin. Telephone Pigalle 77-11. Officer Teyssier called the number. A woman's voice answered. Apparently Mme. Petiot. She would summon the doctor. Then the doctor's voice, cool but sharp.

"Have you gotten into the apartment?" he inquired.

"No."

"I will bring the keys at once. Fifteen minutes at the most."

The officers stood by. Neighbors peered from their windows, drawing the curtains aside to look into the dim street. Two or three idlers joined the police. Fifteen minutes passed. What could be keeping the man? It took only ten minutes to pedal from rue Caumartin to rue Le Sueur. Ten more minutes passed. Officer Teyssier would wait no longer. He called the fire department. The firemen, on the scene in a few minutes, quickly lifted a ladder to the second floor (*le premier étage* in France), raised a wooden shutter, knocked out a pane of glass, and made their way into the dark room. The fire-truck chief, Avilla Boudringhim, needed no guide to lead him and his men to the source of the smoke. By the light of their flashlights, they followed the now overwhelming stench down two flights to the basement into the furnace room, where two furnaces burned red-hot. Here the fetid odor was overwhelming. Fireman Roger Berody opened the door of the firebox of the smaller furnace and fell back in horror. In the door of the furnace sat a burning human skull, eyes and mouth agape. The whole firebox seemed full of human remains, seemingly packed in by the shovelful, broiling and bubbling in the flames. Deep inside, a torn, bloody, and shredded arm, the arm of a woman, with a delicate hand upraised, seemed to reach up to make a last grab at life. But there was no body attached to it. On the floor all about lay putrified and decomposed portions of other human bodies, arms, thighs, torsos, seemingly destined for tomorrow's fire. This was no work for the firemen. Nauseated and horrified, they

turned the job back to the police. On the way up the stairs, one of
the firemen leaned over the balustrade and vomited.

The police viewed the furnace room, holding their breath
against the smell of burning bodies and broiling human flesh,
then Officer Teyssier hurried out to a nearby call box to summon
his superiors of the Sixteenth Precinct (*Arrondissement*). Meanwhile, two other officers came by and set out to keep the growing
crowd, attracted by the fire engine, from intruding on the scene.
It was dark now, except for the muffled gleam of a single street-
light among many, all that the blackout permitted and hardly
enough even under it to show the sidewalk beneath. Neighbors
were pulling their curtains aside to look into the streets, sending
out shafts of yellow light. A few sharp blasts on a police whistle
and the curtains dropped back into place again.

Before Officer Teyssier returned from the call box, a tall man
on a green bicycle pushed his way through the crowd. He stood
his bicycle against the building wall and made his way to the
gate. The officer at the door stopped him, but the man looked
the officer straight in the eye and insisted on entering the court.
He was a dark man and wore a gray overcoat with a felt hat riding
on the back of his head. (Dr. Petiot almost never wore a hat, even
in the foulest weather, but some instinct may have prompted him
at this time to plop on a hat as a means of hiding his features or a
way to not be so easily identified.) He was out of breath and
sweat dripped from his cheeks and chin. He rubbed his hands together. "I am the brother of the owner," he said, and walked from
the court directly into the house. He started at once to mount the
stairs but the officer called to him: "No . . . downstairs!" Whereupon the dark man moved down to the furnace room. He opened
the door, took in the scene of horror at a glance, and closed the
door quickly, looking both disgusted and frantic.

"I am risking my life!" he exclaimed and started up the stairs.
At this point, Officer Teyssier returned. The tall man drew him
aside.

"Are you a Frenchman?" he demanded, in a low voice. The
officer recoiled slightly. A Frenchman? What a question!

"Certainly I am a Frenchman," said Teyssier. "What do you
mean by asking me such a question?"

The man gestured toward the basement. "What you see there,"

he muttered, "is all that is left of some Germans and some collaborators and traitors. Is there any way of hushing this matter up completely?"

"Impossible," said Teyssier. "I have notified headquarters and the police brass and also the Gestapo will be here any minute."

"Then it is a matter of great urgency," said the dark man, as he nervously rubbed his hands together. "My head and those of many others are at stake. I am the leader of a resistance group. Here." He showed Teyssier a paper which, in the dim light, the officer could not make out. Nor could Teyssier discern clearly the features of the man to whom he was talking, other than his burning, deep-set eyes. "I have three hundred identification cards of members of the Resistance at home," the man went on hurriedly. "I must destroy them at once, before they fall into the hands of the Germans as a result of the discovery of this place."

Teyssier nodded. "Go ahead," he said. He ushered him toward the door, where patrolmen Chanel, Choquart, Ciry, and Lafaysse were now busy keeping the crowd back. Teyssier waved the dark man on, as if he were just one more nosy intruder who had somehow gained entry into the house. The man, in his gray overcoat and pulled-down hat, pushed his bicycle through the crowd, then mounted it and sped away into the dark. It was not until much later, when he had seen pictures of the man, that Teyssier realized that this had been Dr. Marcel Petiot himself. (Some of the neighbors also had recognized him.) The man was long gone when the police brass arrived in the persons of the district captain, M. Deforeit, three commissioners, Laine, Gautherie, and Chevalier, soon followed by Commissioner Georges Massu, chief of the *Brigade Criminel* (Homicide Squad) of the famous Quai des Orfèvres, who brought his policeman son, Bernard, also on the Homicide Squad, along as his assistant. They arrived at 9:30 P.M. or, as the French call it, *Vingt-et-un-trente* (21:30). Officers of the German police and the German Gestapo headquarters from 11 rue des Saussaies arrived at 22:00. They saw flesh still burning in the furnace and the rotting remains on the floor—two heads, a corpse split down the middle, and other sections of dismembered bodies. On a landing outside the furnace room, they found a bulging cement sack. Inside it was the left side of a human body, with the leg attached but no foot.

Upstairs, the men found a house that looked like the gone-to-seed residence of some wealthy family that had fallen on evil days. Obviously, no one had tried to live here for years. On furniture and floor lay a thick coating of dust. Baseboards had come loose and wallpaper hung down in tattered strips. Furniture had been shoved into piles everywhere as if to await the junkman. But among the shabby and disjointed furniture lay a great number of pieces that were obviously very valuable—lovely oil paintings that might have been in museums, statuary, small antique tables, commodes, chests of drawers, desks, crystal chandeliers, imperial Chinese and Persian rugs, Sèvres vases, Wedgwood ware, and occasional chairs that might once have graced a palace. The first floor (our second floor) contained valuable antiques, objets d'art, and rugs of great value. The two upper floors had furniture, bric-a-brac, and all kinds of objects of no great value. There had been no error in classification, indicating that an expert controlled the seeming confusion. On all three upper floors even the police could discern the hand of someone who had loved rare antiques and fine possessions. They could see, too, the beginnings of the series of strange contrasts that marked the whole person and the whole life of Dr. Marcel Petiot. Below, in the basement, the police officials found a large and spotless kitchen, the floor scrubbed clean, with two sinks against the wall—one a deep laundry-tub type and the other a longer shallower sink, with a wooden table or drainboard between. The kitchen floor held a large drain that, strangely enough, was directly connected to the main sewer that emptied into the Seine via the Usine de Clichy, less than a mile away. A body could obviously be placed on the wooden board and eviscerated there, with the water from one sink washing across the board and into the other, carrying away and flushing off the blood before it could clot. This would account for the strange bloodlessness of the furnace room where the corpses were burned. The entrails and organs in the human rib cage could all be dropped through the large drain directly into the large sewer below. This seemed to explain the general lack of any blood with the corpses and the absence of any entrails or intestines or any strong odor of putrification.

The men moved out into the courtyard where several small, connected outbuildings stood, well concealed behind the wall, and opening only into the court. In one of these buildings, closest to the main apartment, they found the doctor's office. And how different from the house! Here the furniture gleamed with polish. Two comfortable tapestry-upholstered armchairs, in good repair, stood here. A neat, well-ordered desk, recently waxed. Two other chairs and a glass-front bookcase crammed with medical texts. A polished table held recent issues of medical and professional journals. One door of the office opened into a short corridor, rather feebly lit by a small fixture set into the ceiling. At the end of the corridor stood another door, opening inward, with a heavy chain dangling from the latch. The men walked through and found themselves facing another door, a few yards away, on the opposite side of a small triangular room. This was a double door, with ornate jambs and a bell button beside it, as if it might be the main entrance into roomier quarters or to the house next door. But this, the men found, was no door at all. The knob turned around and around. The bell gave no sound. The doors had been merely plastered to the wall, with no opening behind them.

The small triangular room was almost barren of furniture. There was a cot with a light cover on it such as a doctor might offer a patient he was examining. Carefully fixed to the wall with the false door and on the other side of the room from its entrance were several large hooks, such as a butcher might use to hang a half or a quarter of beef or lamb. But what was this little triangular room used for, this vestibule to nowhere? It could possibly have been a waiting room, but hardly an examining room, with only one small cot in it. Then the police discovered, set deep into the wall that formed the base of the triangle, a small aperture, and inside that, a Lumvisor (a patented lens device). Obviously, this was a viewer, such as some apartment dwellers have in their doors, to look out without being seen. Through this eyepiece a person outside in the stable could have watched—what? The death agonies of his victims? Or would he have just used it to make sure the victim was dead? Or could a doctor have used it to observe a patient under sedation? The room seemed completely soundproofed by being surrounded by rooms and walls so that a cry would hardly carry to the street.

The officers now went out back through the office and into the courtyard again. Farther in the court and with the entrance behind them to the right was a double door leading into a shed. This was a garage—once a carriage house. In here was a sodden heap of what looked first like broken plaster. But it turned out to be lime slaked by the weather and full of half-consumed bits of human flesh and bone. In the rear, a sliding door opened into what had been a stable. To the left, under a metal cover, they found a deep hole, perhaps an old storage pit for hay and later an abandoned site of a gasoline storage tank. Overhead was a pulley through which ran a cord with a running noose. A heavy chain was connected to the other end of the cord. Obviously, this could have been used to lower bodies into the hole or merely bales of hay for the horses once quartered in the stable. A fetid odor rose from the depths, but the light of flashlights held by police did not reveal what lay there. A ladder led down to the depths, however, and Commissioner Massu undertook to investigate. Down he went. Below him, a festering, bubbling mass almost caused him to strangle. He set a tentative foot on the heap at the bottom. It was quicklime, steaming foully as it devoured a measureless heap of human remains. This, then, was a real charnel house. There were many more bodies here than in the furnace room—and God only knew how many altogether. Already most of the flesh and bone was past recognition.

It was 10:30 P.M. now and Dr. Paul, the famous Paris coroner, had come. It would be his job, and that of his colleagues at the Institut Médico-Légal, to complete the gruesome jigsaw puzzle and tell how many bodies in all had been disposed of here and who they were. The men began at once the sifting out of the legs, torsos, heads, arms, and charred debris to determine if all these remains were human, how many, and how they had met their end. Most of the human debris, carefully marked, was sent to the laboratories of the Institut Médico-Légal, the first scientific and medical criminal detection organization and laboratory in the world. The lime refuse was carefully screened for human parts and bones by the personnel and technicians of the Passy cemetery. The police and Gestapo photographers had the easiest time.

This was the strangest of all murder investigations, the job being to learn not who the killer was but to work backward and find out who were the victims—and there were many. It was a time in history when men and women were being slain by the hundreds of thousands, many of them secretly, with no reports of their deaths and no one daring to seek after them. Still, these murders revolted even the men who had seen violent death every day. Here human bodies had been literally splattered about as if to signal an operation or to scare the discoverers, be they French or German. And the small, patented Lumvisor periscope, with the mirror inside, permitting the killer to look up and through and down upon his victims. Perhaps this was a device to make sure the victim was dead and safe to search, or perhaps only a device for a physician to observe a patient being X-rayed or reacting to medication.

But where was the murderer? The police could not connect the collector of antiques and the filthy abandon of the house with the neat and clean doctor's office on the court, or even less with the bodies, and human debris in the furnace, and the lime and remains of cadavers on the floor of the garage. Could the doctor be a resistant, killing Germans and collaborators? Who owned 21 rue Le Sueur . . . or was it rented out to one or several persons and did anyone live there? Or could a group or a French Communist terrorist organization have merely got rid of the bodies of their Nazi victims without any connection with the owner?

Massu lost valuable time running down the facts that the house once belonged to Princess Colleredo Mansfeld, born Maria Souit, that she had rented it and had her poor friends stay in it but had sold it to a Dr. Marcel Petiot on May 30, 1941, with title going to Dr. Petiot's son, Gerhardt, a minor. More time was lost by Massu in the confusion occasioned by the fact that a Petiot family, no relation to the doctor, operated a boardinghouse at 18 rue Le Sueur. There was a Mr. and Mrs. Eugène Petiot, age eighty-five and eighty-two, and four sons, one of them being another Marcel Petiot.

Then more time was lost by Massu, who, using an old police expression, "sat on his hands." Massu appears to have followed up every lead except going after the doctor, probably because he was half convinced that he might be chasing a resistant, busy killing collaborators and Germans. He had already had plenty of trouble with Communists when they were the allies of the Nazis. He was on their black list. Or, perhaps, on the other hand, the Paris police, after learning that the German Gestapo had released Pe-

tiot from an imprisonment where he was charged with conducting
an escape apparatus and therefore connected with the Resistance,
decided to tread very carefully. Some persons even told the police
that Dr. Petiot was a secret agent for the British; others claimed
he worked for the Free French Intelligence. Last, but not least,
many important people claimed the Germans had a hands-off sign
on Petiot. There was good reason to believe that the French Gestapo or the German Abwehr (military intelligence) actually were
connected with the building. Across the street was a German
Todt Supply Service building.

By this time, it should be understood, not only was Dr. Paul,
the coroner, there, along with most all of the Paris police principals, but the German police and Gestapo representatives as well.
A letter then arrived, addressed to the chief inspector. Massu read
it and found that the German authorities knew that Petiot owned
and frequented 21 rue Le Sueur, that he had been arrested on May
22, 1943, and held by them for many months but released on January 13, 1944, and that they stated he was not mentally responsible for his acts but should be arrested and held when found.
The Germans did not admit that he had been arrested as a resistant but many witnesses were ready to confide this information to
the Paris police. Well then, thought Massu, if he is a resistant, let
the Germans get him. He told his men to go around to Petiot's
place but only on the next morning. He and his son—who had expected this to be *one* night when they might get to bed early—
went home to sleep. Actually the Paris police records and the Gestapo records agree but do not support all of Massu's inter-
pretations and conclusions in the latter's book.

Meanwhile, Dr. Paul continued his labors. He was a painstaking man, as had been indicated when, during his investigation of *l'affaire Landru*‡ he had carefully burned a human head

‡ Landru, commonly called the "Modern Bluebeard," murdered some thirteen
of his wives or fiancées for money and burned their bodies in his stove. He
was happily married and had a young mistress whom he loved very much. A
host of books, plays, and movies, topped by Charlie Chaplin's *Monsieur Verdoux*, followed Landru's public guillotine execution at Versailles. The French
Government did not invoke the sequestration of all records for fifty years in
this case. He was arrested and executed as a direct result of the work of Dr.
Paul, the Paris coroner. Books on him were found in Dr. Petiot's collection of
crime books, especially on Jack the Ripper and the Crippen cases, both involving doctors.

in a stove to see how long it would take to destroy it utterly and how the ashes could be identified as human—a fact that broke the Landru case after World War I. He immediately sensed that as famous as the Landru case was then, this one, after World War II, would be much bigger. Now he endeavored bit by bit to find torso to match head, hand to match arm, foot to fit leg. After a time, he announced that there were, at the very least, twelve bodies in the charnel house. One fact bothered the painstaking expert: eleven pounds of hair were found at rue Le Sueur and eleven pounds of hair could not possibly belong to only twelve persons. But more important and disturbing was that many more cadavers found in the past and thereafter through the following days had to be ascribed to the same party who dismembered those just found and possibly connected with Petiot.

The records of bodies and parts of bodies that had been found in various parts of the city over the preceding three years, some floating in the Seine, some in trunks and suitcases, one in an alley near the Bastille, were carefully checked by both the Gestapo and the Paris police. A boatman had found two thighs, one male and one female, floating on the river. Dr. Paul also received hands, heads, a tibia, two torsos, half a torso—all, he said, had been dissected with the same skill and with an expert knowledge of human anatomy and great experience in the processes used. The shoulder and arm had been neatly separated, in many instances, from the body. With exquisite precision, the whole facial mask or face had been lifted off the skull so neither could be identified. This was a completely new development, indicating creative genius and unusual technical skill. All fingertips had been scraped free of prints with a sharp knife or scalpel so identification was impossible. According to both the Institut Médico-Légal and Gestapo records, eighty-six unidentified cadavers or bodies cut up into debris were found in the Seine as against 241 identified bodies between the time Petiot could have started operating in 1941 to May 1943 when he was arrested by the Gestapo. Most of these unidentified eighty-six bodies bore the very same characteristics of expert dissection and many more might have before the experts were alerted to any pattern. One other definite characteristic of most of the unidentifiable bodies were scalpel marks on the right thighs where doctors, professional dissectors, and medical students stab their scalpels or knives while resting, smoking, or stepping away from their chores to prevent having to pick up a gory or infected handle or the dangerous dropping of the sharp instrument. Later, more bodies and pieces of bodies were unearthed in trunks or in fields or deserted houses cut up by the same expert hand.*

It should not have been impossible, however, to pick up Dr. Petiot, for he had only a few minutes' start on the police. Had Massu understood that this was a criminal case and not a political one, he might have had his bird in a cage before the night was over. His record of 3,257 successful arrests was tarnished. But one walked carefully where the German authorities were concerned. Who could say if Petiot had really been a resistant? Or perhaps an agent of the French Gestapo of rue Lauriston? Or of the German Abwehr on avenue Henri Martin? Or an agent of the British? Many persons believed he was related to some espionage activities as an informer. It would be better to wait and see.

It was not until the next day, March 12, 1944, that the French police appeared at 66 rue Caumartin. They found the front door of the Petiot apartment ajar. "Why," Petiot, a frugal Frenchman, had evidently thought, "require the police to break down my door or force its lock? These things cost money." The Petiots, said the concierge, had been there at about half past eight and she was under the impression that they had spent the night there. A barman at the bistro next door had seen the Petiots leave the place at 21:05 (five minutes past nine). But the good doctor still had been granted time enough to pack up all his toilet articles and take a change of shirts. One thing the police did find was an extraordinary "arsenal" of drugs, including some crude peyote (mescaline) and 502 vials of morphine, worth a small fortune.

An alert was then sent out for the arrest of the Petiots, and the next day a poster, with the doctor's picture and that of his wife, was circulated throughout France. Wanted were Dr. Marcel André

---

* Allowing for parts of bodies never recovered because of the strong currents and unusual undertows of the Seine River and the rather large number of bodies recovered, Petiot's confidential admission to Dr. Paul of 150 liquidations (although he said he had lost count) was no exaggeration. Although he was charged with only twenty-seven murders and convicted of twenty-six, Petiot admitted under oath in court to sixty-three victims. These figures did not include the unpublicized murders committed in Villeneuve during his apprenticeship nor any liquidations during the liberation under the aliases of Dr. Valéry and Dr. Wetterwald under cover of the F.F.I.

Henri Felix Petiot and his wife, Georgette Valentine Lablais Petiot, with a green bicycle, license number 3866 RD 7. "Petiot," read the poster, "is considered very dangerous." The poster, however, was extraneous, for by this time the Paris newspapers, so long restrained from describing all the major horrors that the war had brought them, unable to dwell on the wholesale elimination of men, women, and little children in the Nazi death camps, or of the Gestapo tortures and secret executions that took place in Paris every day, and forced to suppress all news of the impending Allied invasion, could turn their fancies loose on the Petiot case. However, the newspapers seemed to avoid positively identifying Dr. Petiot as the murderer or as "Dr. Satan," or as "The Monster of rue Le Sueur." But not one word ever appeared about the fact that he had been arrested by the Gestapo, held and tortured by them for months as a member of the Resistance and the operator of an escape route from the Nazis!

Journalists, and the German censors, hungry for any story with no politics which might turn public attention away from the war the Nazis were beginning to lose, turned this case into a new and super Landru case. The police allegedly had found at 66 rue Caumartin four preserved sex organs—three male and one female. This was a complete fairytale, as were many other details the Nazi-controlled newspapers supplied. It succeeded in creating in the public mind a picture of some murderous sex fiend who tortured women to death. For the victims, according to the press, were all women. "A new Landru case," "Twenty-five to thirty women beaten to death and then burned" were the headlines, instead of reports that Germany was beginning to lose the war or that the bodies might be those of the Gestapo and collaborators—mostly men. And then, naturally, the grinning madman stood outside the death chamber—the triangular room that became the most infamous torture chamber in Paris—and gloated over the agonies of his victims. Some writers even reported that naked girls had been lowered alive into the pit of quicklime. And some purported to discover that living bodies, all or mostly women, had been hung on the eight or ten "meat hooks" in the triangular room, where they could be watched through a periscope. In fact, the hooks were not even in the line of sight from the Lumvisor, or periscope viewer.

Most newspapers were careful not to identify Petiot as the author of these crimes. In fact, the report was that an unknown tenant was responsible. Petiot was merely "the owner of the building." But his pictures, nonetheless, delighted the press for he would have been picked out of a crowd by a casting director to play the part of the mad doctor. There were the deep-set eyes that seemed to burn with their own fire. There was the generally disreputable air about him, his shabby clothes and dirty hands. And, contrasted with this, there was a strange sort of fascination, a face that could sometimes actually look handsome, and a glance so intense it was hard to turn one's eyes away. One could imagine Vincent Price being easily made up to look like Dr. Petiot . . . tall, handsome, but sometimes mad-looking, ingratiating yet menacing. So while the papers were careful not to identify the doctor as the fiend to protect themselves from libel, the public was not so squeamish and picked up the hint with relish. No mention was ever made in the Nazi-controlled press that he had been tortured and imprisoned as a French patriot or that many persons believed he was a spy for the British. Many people believed the bodies were those of Germans and collaborators.

The police, of course, knew better. They knew Dr. Petiot well and owned a fat dossier on him. The German Gestapo knew him too from having had him in custody for eight months. And so did the German Abwehr. Some of the better-informed but less straitlaced Paris police even acknowledged that Petiot had probably "knocked off a score or more persons" before the discovery of rue Le Sueur. They had even had some experiences to indicate Petiot had influence with the Occupation authorities or with the French Gestapo or with the Abwehr, the German Army Intelligence. There were also reports that he was a French resistant and a member of a French Communist terrorist organization. Why dig too deeply into what might develop into a political hornets' nest?

The Paris police, therefore, marked time by pursuing a few obvious lines of inquiry. They talked to the Petiot maid, Marie Leroux, and learned that Mme. Petiot frequently packed into suitcases or boxes large quantities of clothing that did not belong to the Petiot famliy and sent them away to Auxerre or Villeneuve or to Paris addresses of friends. (Another maid, Geneviève Cluny, who had become a nun, interviewed much later, was to tell a simi-

lar and more detailed and definite story.) There had been clothing
of every sort dug out of closets at 21 rue Le Sueur, none of it having ever belonged to the doctor or his wife. There was a black satin
dress with embroidered swallows, heavily perfumed and carrying a
label from Rose Silvy, dressmaker, rue Estelle, in Marseille. There
was a cute little lady's toque, a small brown flat hat with a feather
on the side with a label of the milliner Suzanne Talbot, 14 rue
Royale. There was a short lady's nightgown, marked "T." There
was a size forty man's shirt, gray with black and garnet pin stripes
and the initials K.K. over the pocket. One closet alone held
twenty-two pairs of ladies' shoes, twenty-six toothbrushes, thirty-
two flacons of toilet water, fifteen combs, fifteen powder boxes,
four umbrellas, and twenty-seven tubes of cosmetics, among other
miscellany.

Dr. Paul meanwhile had reported to Massu that many of the
bodies and parts of bodies fished out of the Seine or found elsewhere in Paris over the previous three years had definitely been
dissected by the very same expert hand that had cut up the cadavers found at rue Le Sueur. All of the cadavers and human
debris under question, both in the Seine and at 21 rue Le Sueur,
had another similarity. They could never be identified and
there was no sign of how the dead met their deaths—no trace of
poison, no signs of bullet wounds, knife wounds, or blackjack
marks. The coroner also called attention to the fact that the hair
and scalps found at rue Le Sueur were definitely from many more
than twelve persons. Altogether, from 1941 to May 1943, to reca-
pitulate, eighty-six unidentified bodies had been found in Paris—
fifty-one male and thirty-five female. Dr. Paul was satisfied that
many were the work of the same assassin or of the same disposer
of bodies and could represent not more than 50 per cent of an
overall total since many bodies and, even more so, parts of bodies
in the Seine were never recovered because of the strong currents
and undertows. Over a hundred murders might well be traced to
whatever was involved at 21 rue Le Sueur. These discoveries of
course tended to support the belief among many that a patriotic
or political organization was busy liquidating their opposition.

However, the directors of the General Information Service of
the Paris police reported that the bodies found at 21 rue Le Sueur
represented a criminal and not a political case and Massu was or-

dered to proceed with all diligence in the location and arrest of the missing doctor. And one of the first leads, of course, was that little card on the door at number 21 giving the address of 18 rue des Lombards in Auxerre. Then there were those forty-seven—or was it forty-nine?—or was it fifty-three?—suitcases the neighbors had seen carried away from number 21. It was simple enough, starting with the gray closed truck with a sign "Avenue Daumesnil" to dig up the trucker who had carried the suitcases. He had come from a garage near the Hôtel Alicot across the street from the Gare de Lyon and had dispatched the luggage to Auxerre. In wartime, however, one could not simply pick up a trail like that and chase after it. There were severe restrictions now on gasoline and on all sorts of transportation and the Germans put the needs of Occupied France far down on the list. Still, after two days, Commissioner Massu did manage to secure a car and special permission to use German gasoline to go to Auxerre. (There were only two trains a week to that town.) With his secretary, Canitrot, and his deputy, Battut, together with Inspector Schmidt, Massu left for Auxerre at eleven in the morning of March 14.

There were two places in Auxerre, in addition to 18 rue des Lombards, that the police meant to visit. One was the railroad station. It was routine for French police, anticipating an arrest in any locality, to cover the railroad station. The other address was that of Dr. Petiot's brother, Maurice, at 55 rue du Pont. At this address, Maurice had a radio shop, a small store on the ground floor of a stucco building with a living apartment upstairs. Maurice was awaiting the police in his living quarters, for he knew they must soon come to him. With him were his wife and Gerhardt Petiot, sixteen, the son of the doctor. Maurice bore a remarkable resemblance to the doctor, at least in profile. He too was dark, of rather spare build, and slightly taller than the average Frenchman. He differed from his brother however in that he was calm and deliberate in his gestures, lacking his brother's intense and excitable air. He did not constantly rub his hands together. He greeted the police without any uneasiness. They would like to have him get into the police car, they said, and guide them to 18 rue des Lombards. Maurice seemed surprised that they had that address and asked who had given it to them.

"We are asking the questions," said Massu, in the traditional police manner. But there was certainly no mystery about the address, when it had been posted in plain view at 21 rue Le Sueur.

Rue des Lombards proved to be a street as deep and as narrow as a gorge, with ancient brick walls and stone houses rising high on either side and almost shutting out the sun. Number 18 was an ancient château or fortress, with iron grills at every window and long vertical slits in the wall through which bowmen might aim their arrows, or empty vessels of molten lead on the heads of attackers. The high, forbidding walls of the building, the police discovered, enclosed a handsome house and a beautiful, terraced garden. There were no suspicious-looking suitcases, nor any trace of human blood. Underneath the main building, the police found a cellar, and below that a huge subcellar cut deep into bedrock and designed in the shape of a huge cross. This building, it was said, along with the adjoining building and everything behind the walls, once belonged to the huge Gothic cathedral which still towered over the town. As in many medieval towns, the church and center of resistance to raids and war was the well-centered and protected religious enclave. The subcellar was supposed to be part of an escape system to or from the cathedral but the police found no connection to the cathedral there now. All they did find was mold and deposits of calcium built up through centuries on the dark walls. In the regular cellar above, they found several bags of quicklime, from the same source as supplied the lime used at 21 rue Le Sueur. Now they felt they had at last picked up some sort of trail. The living quarters in the main building had the look of disuse—dust on everything, everything in place, except that there was a bed in the bedroom that had obviously just been slept in. Massu turned quickly to Maurice Petiot.

"Who slept here?" he demanded. "Your brother?"

Maurice turned white and for the first time seemed a little shaken. But he shook his head firmly.

"No. It was M. Neuhausen, a friend who lives at Courson-les-Carrières."

Massu immediately sent one of his inspectors to Courson-les-Carrières. Then he questioned Maurice impatiently. Where did he spend the night? Here at home? Massu hoped he was not lying.

"I am really distressed with you," he told Maurice. "I think you have lied to me and have been bluffing me right along. Hiding a criminal makes you liable for prosecution, too."

Massu ordered Maurice confined in the local lockup and then hastened to the railroad station to join the inspector who had already been assigned there. And there on the platform, petite, pretty, but large as life, stood Mme. Marcel Petiot herself, ready to take the next train, now less than a mile away. She was not so cool as Maurice. When the police identified themselves, she was overcome by fear and at the police station she fainted and had to be carried to the police car by two gendarmes. While the police removed her, Gerhardt stood there, watching it all, tears running down his face.

Maurice and Georgette Petiot rode back to Paris in the police car with Massu in utter silence. Georgette rested her head on her brother-in-law's shoulder and sobbed quietly. Massu urged his chauffeur to greater speed. He perhaps felt now he was on the verge of uncovering the doctor himself.

Word of the arrest had of course reached the Paris newspapers before the car returned and when they arrived at the Quai des Orfèvres there was a tremendous press of reporters and photographers, all intent on getting the first word and the first picture of the two prisoners. Georgette Petiot, when the cameras began to pop right in her face, reeled again and had to be half carried into the building. Commissioner Massu himself helped her up the stairs, while the magnesium lights flashed before them. She was on the verge of losing consciousness, her hair disarrayed, her lips white, but finally, in Massu's office, with the press locked outside, she recovered well enough to be questioned. Her answers seemed contradictory and evasive, yet there was no concrete evidence of her guilt. She was nevertheless to be held in jail for more than a year.

Why did she flee to Auxerre? To be with her son. Did she know of the house on rue Le Sueur? She knew there was such a place in the vicinity of L'Étoile. Her replies were given in a voice so low that the questioner could hardly hear her. Sweat formed on her forehead. She carried a small handkerchief clutched in her hand.

Did she approve of the purchase of the building on rue Le Sueur? No, it was too grand. But she did not mix into her husband's affairs. You were present when he received the phone call about the fire in the chimney? Mme. Petiot sank deeper into her chair and put her hand over her eyes. She began to sob.

"I do not know. . . . I do not know. . . ."

"But what did your husband tell you?"

"I heard the word 'police.' Marcel hung up, took his hat, and went out."

"He did not say where he was going?"

"No, he gave me no explanation at all."

Did the doctor often go out without telling her where? Sometimes. She never questioned him. She did not remember when he purchased his bicycle or the trailer—both at the same time, most likely. She may have known no details and never asked. But she knew her husband loved her and she loved him. He was sweet and kind and did much good. He treated the poor without taking a penny. . . .

She was talking clearly now, her face flushed and her glance earnest and intense. Now then, where had she spent the night after her husband left? She had sat up all night, in an armchair, in her apartment. (But witnesses saw her go out. . . .) Did she always sit up when her husband went out? No? Then why this time? Did she know he had decided to run away? No. No. She had not listened. It was just that word "police" that upset her. But why should it upset her, if she knew her husband was incapable of doing wrong? Ah, in these times, one never knows what may happen when a man has business with the police!

"Had you then thought of going to rue Le Sueur in the morning to find him?"

"No, I decided to go to Auxerre. I thought perhaps my husband had gone there. But when I went to the Lyon station, I learned there was no train until Monday. So I went back to rue Caumartin. But I did not go home."

"Why not?"

"Oh, a premonition of some sort . . ."

"Was it not perhaps the sight of two policemen at the door?"

"Perhaps . . . I do not know. . . ."

And afterward? Well, she went into a church, she prayed, then for part of the afternoon she wandered through St.-Lazare station. Not to escape recognition. No. She felt safer in a crowd. She had bought a paper and read her own name on the front page, or at least her husband's name. To her, it was the same thing.

But why not then go to the police? If you knew nothing, you risked nothing. No. She went to an apartment house her husband owned at 52 rue de Reuilly. She sat all night on the stairs there thinking he might come. She had no reason to think that the stories in the paper were true. No one saw her there. When she heard the door open, she would hide. Afterward, she had gone to a restaurant near the Lyon station and had not bought her ticket until it was almost time to board the train for Auxerre. This restaurant-hotel at 207 rue de Bercy was a familiar place to all the Petiots. Maurice stayed there a few days each week when collecting the rent from the tenants of Dr. Petiot's apartment buildings. Dr. and Mrs. Petiot stayed there often in connection with their frequent trips to Auxerre, Villeneuve, and Seignelay.

And if she had met the doctor there, would she have told him he was being sought by the police? Perhaps. She did not know. He was her husband, the father of her child. She certainly would have demanded some explanation of what had happened since he left rue Caumartin.

And where had she gone in Auxerre? Why, to her brother-in-law's on rue du Pont. Not rue des Lombards? At this question, Mme. Petiot was momentarily speechless. Apparently she had not realized the police knew of that place. Massu reminded her that the address had been given in a notice posted at 21 rue Le Sueur. Mme. Petiot stared at him for a moment, then slumped in a faint. Or did she pretend to faint, so as not to have to explain what she knew about the fortress on rue des Lombards? At any rate, when she was revived, there were no more questions. Massu told her she must accompany them now to her apartment on rue Caumartin. This meant running that gauntlet of reporters and photographers again, but the police, this time, managed to divert the newspaper people long enough to get Georgette Petiot into the car and on the way.

On rue Caumartin, however, the cameras lay in wait in larger force than ever. Even a motion-picture camera had been set up to take pictures of the arrested member of the Petiot family. And, of course, drawn by the photographers, there was a crowd of curious citizens outside the door. But this time the petite Georgette, who had been too weak to walk when first she faced these people, turned into a tigress. While they were unlocking the door of her apartment, she turned angrily to face the crowd. "Assassins!" she screamed. "You know I went to Auxerre only by my own free will, to comfort my son! You are all cowards!"

Safe in the apartment, Mme. Petiot tried to describe the sort of life she and her family had led: ". . . like *bons bourgeois* going to the theater or the movies. Nothing wrong with that, as far as I know." (Of course, this was wishful thinking, for Mme. Petiot was no Catholic bourgeois, born July 15, 1904, the illegitimate child of a maid, Georgette Villard, and a wagon-lit porter, Georges Lestor Lablais, who later made a success as a butcher and restaurant owner, no doubt with the help of Petiot's plunder.) The mother and father married November 24, 1906, twenty-eight months after the birth of the future Mme. Petiot. Dr. Petiot also was no *bon Catholic bourgeois* but an atheist and Socialist elected to public office on an anti-bourgeois ticket. He had joined the French Communist party as a student and knew both Maurice Thorez and Nguyen Sat Thank (Ho Chi Minh), leaders of the original French Communist organization in Paris.

But in 1920 did the doctor have so much free time? Well, he obviously could not always stay for an entire show and might have to leave early. He went to visit the sick, for a certainty.

But the antiques and paintings and rugs that he carried home in his trailer, did they not surprise her? Did she not ask questions? Of course. He attended many auctions and bought them there. And the erotic pictures? He was simply a collector. Mme. Petiot had begun to weaken again and seemed close to fainting. Massu then eased up on the questioning and had her taken to the Salle Cusco, a part of l'Hôtel-Dieu of the Paris Hospital,† where sick prisoners and witnesses were often held. But she was not yet charged with any crime.

Massu felt she had not been truthful. How could she not know the schedule of trains to Auxerre, when she traveled there so often? There were only two trains a week. She must have known when they ran. And what would prompt her to hide, when she

---

† Built in part by the fortune of Mme. Maupin, the lesbian opera singer and deadly duelist who fascinated Petiot in his readings as a student. Books on the career of this deadly character were found in Dr. Petiot's library.

knew only that her husband had gone to investigate a fire? And what about the witnesses who placed her outside of her apartment when she said she was waiting there for the doctor's return?

A really vital clue was turned up by Inspector Poirier—a long-distance call made by Dr. Petiot on the evening the charnel house had been discovered—indeed, at 8:20 P.M. when the police were still descending on 21 rue Le Sueur. Petiot had gone into the Bezayrie bar, owned by patients of his, and made a call to his brother in Auxerre. "Burn the papers!" he had said, according to one witness. It seemed almost certain to the police that Maurice Petiot at least had guilty knowledge of the crimes his brother had committed. Maurice lied to them freely when they questioned him, and when caught in his lies he grew surly and would not talk. Perhaps Dr. Marcel Petiot, like Landru, had kept a record of his victims.

Then, of course, there were the suitcases. It turned out there were indeed at least forty-nine of them stored with the mysterious Mr. Neuhausen, a storekeeper at Courson-les-Carrières—the man who was supposed to have filled that bed at 18 rue des Lombards. The police quickly placed official seals on the bags, although, of course, they might have been opened countless times between the time they were seized and the time they had been removed from rue Le Sueur. And at the home of Mr. Neuhausen's in-laws, Mr. and Mrs. Mourier at St. Sauveur, also in Yonne, the police gathered up some odds and ends of clothing definitely identified as having come from the baggage taken from rue Le Sueur. This lot contained thirteen women's dresses, twenty-four ladies' panties, sixteen girdles, three blouses, eight bras, fourteen ladies' nightgowns, and other peculiarly feminine accouterments. But the other suitcases held nearly every personal article for men, women, and one child.

There were five ladies' fur coats, twenty-one ladies' cloth overcoats, seventeen men's overcoats, nine pairs of shoes, thirty-six handbags, four raincoats, thirty-four complete suits, thirteen boxes of Kotex, three mink stoles, forty-two sweaters, ninety-six collars, six hair nets, eighty-two pairs of gloves, 521 handkerchiefs, eleven pairs of eyeglasses, eighty-eight pairs of men's socks, 112 ladies' dresses and suits, fifty-two ladies' nightgowns, sixty-four pairs of pajamas for adults, children's pajamas, cigarette cases, lipsticks, combs, brushes, towels, sheets, compacts, even nail files! Obviously, nothing escaped the doctor, who apparently treasured any article he had not paid for, no matter how valueless. There were over 3,000 articles in this cache alone.

It began to appear now that acquisitions were one of the keys to the mystery. For this was obviously a business the doctor was operating—perhaps not to exterminate traitors and the enemies of France but merely to store up wealth and security for the doctor and his family. It became apparent early in the investigation that the doctor was being paid by these people to spirit them out of France, and that he had urged each client to bring with him all his or her money, jewelry, and articles of value—indeed, anything negotiable—but a minimum of clothing and toilet articles. Later, Petiot even had asked that their furniture be committed to his care, once he had successfully gotten them out of Occupied France.

Like a true Frenchman, the doctor was keeping the business right in his own grasp, or that of his immediate family, to whom alone he seemed to be devoted. It seemed that he was operating a murder factory for high profits, not for patriotic or political purposes but entirely for the Petiot estate. There was no question that the fifty-one real estate holdings—from the Paris apartment houses at 21 rue Le Sueur and 52 rue Reuilly to the beautiful country house at Villeneuve to the castle at 18 rue des Lombards of Auxerre to the cafés, hotels, farms, vineyards, and housing complexes at Seignelay owned by the Petiot estate—were not all purchased from Dr. Petiot's practice or even from the profits of his father-in-law. How much of his father-in-law's millions in real estate and other holdings were purchased with the doctor's earnings no one will ever know.

There were others in the business, but as far as police could determine, they were innocent hired hands, or "commission" agents or "finders" who had no knowledge at all of the true function of the business. These were the "scouts," or salesmen, who brought in to Petiot all sorts and conditions of men and women who needed help in getting out of France. Jews, of course, were among the most natural prospects. But there were also criminals of one type or another for whom the Paris atmosphere even under German Occupation had become unhealthful and there were among these Germans and collaborators.

But if Petiot constantly rubbing his hands together was the perfect type to play the lead in a Mad Doctor mystery, his two chief scouts would have been better cast as a comedy vaudeville team. One of them, Edmond Pintard, known as Francinet, was a comically lean Ichabod Crane type, with a prominent Adam's apple, a tuft of hair that kept dropping over his eyes, and a nose like the beak of a stork. He was a motion-picture make-up man, although the thought of a man so disreputable-looking, with soiled linen, unclean fingernails, and fingertips stained brown from cigarette butts applying make-up to the delicate faces of movie stars was in itself almost farcical.‡

Francinet's partner, the man who operated the clearing house, the first stop on the underground railway, was the skinny man's exact opposite. He was short and round-faced, like a man on a cereal box, with the permanently ingratiating expression of a hairdresser—which he was—and with hair probably tinted and tightly waved. One could easily imagine this pair, Francinet and Raoul Fourrier, bouncing out on the stage to do a comic soft-shoe dance together and slapping at each other to emphasize the punch lines of the gags. But there was nothing in the least comic about them. They were seriously engaged in recruiting, for handsome commissions, customers for the "escape to nowhere" that Dr. Petiot was operating at 21 rue Le Sueur. But Francinet, who was fifty-six years old, had indeed once been a singer in cafés, while Fourrier, age sixty-one, but still pink-cheeked and brown-haired, had been a friend of Francinet's for many years. Many years later they were both convincing in their assurances that they had accepted commissions but positively believed they were aiding persons in getting out of Occupied France.

Fourrier operated a hairdressing parlor and beauty shop one flight up at 25 rue des Mathurins. It was a rather barren place during the Occupation, its six small booths seldom filled and the furnishings sparse and out of date. There was nothing about it, however, to suggest its connection with a mass-murder plot. Nor is there any reason to believe that Fourrier ever considered he was doing more than picking up a fast franc or so through directing people to a man who could help them escape the Gestapo. The

‡ An interview with this gentleman was accomplished by the author only after a three-day and -night stakeout on his furnished room in a cheap Paris boardinghouse.

going price set by Petiot was 25,000 francs ($700), but Francinet was not above doubling this fee when he thought the traffic would stand it. Once or twice, however, in the presence of the client, the police learned, the good doctor put on a show of righteous indignation on finding that his "fee" had been quoted double. He was working, he assured the client, out of patriotism and sought only to defray his own basic expenses.

It was Fourrier, apparently, who had first learned that Petiot was operating an escape route and he recruited his friend Francinet. Francinet would then scout up the clients and refer them to Fourrier. It was at Fourrier's shop that the prospective voyagers would first present themselves to be turned over to the doctor. After that, there was usually a subway ride to L'Étoile station, a short walk to rue Le Sueur, and nothing more. The journey began and ended there. All good-byes were to be said before the clients approached rue Le Sueur, so that address was never given out to intermediaries. And those whom the doctor led there never walked out alive.

Arrests followed quickly after Massu's return to Paris with Maurice Petiot and Dr. Marcel Petiot's wife. The teams of Massu, now efficiently and quickly deployed, followed all the leads supplied by both the French and German police records. The following were jailed: Mr. and Mrs. Albert Neuhausen, in possession of the 21 rue Le Sueur suitcases, Léone Arnout, Mr. Lablais' maid, housekeeper, companion, and courier for Dr. Petiot, Edmond Pintard, alias Francinet, Roland Porchon, Raoul Fourrier, and René Nezondet. The last four were charged with being scouts or salesmen for Petiot's travel agency, although Nezondet was later cleared of any scouting activity.

This, then, was *l'affaire Petiot*,* the Petiot case in its essence, as it was originally presented to the people of Paris—a story of such

* The name of one of the early books on the subject, published in 1957, by two newspaper reporters. It was withdrawn from sale and all copies disappeared and no information on it could be obtained from the publisher. Reports were that the publishers were threatened with a libel suit unless they withdrew the book. Other reports were that the French Government, which had by then sequestered all records, had convinced the publisher to withdraw the book from further publication and sale. Still another report was that the French Communist Party had something to do with the disappearance of the book by various pressures. All copies released and for sale were all bought up! Here again book stores reported all copies picked up by an unidentified but attractive woman.

scalding horror that it washed the war off the front pages and very nearly out of the minds of many who read about it. And a story, too, so freighted with political portent that, when the doctor was finally brought to trial, the government impounded the trial record for fifty years and suppressed a book written by Petiot, and one written by one of the witnesses in the case. Many other books about it, in French and English and German, for many years after were mysteriously taken out of circulation in one way or another, some of them by threats of libel suits, some at the secret request of the French Government, and some, it was said, bought up by an unidentified attractive woman who resembled no one known to have been implicated in the case.

But the police knew, or should have known, that there had been many previous "Petiot cases," or to put it more accurately, the Petiot case itself had begun many years before when a very little boy with luminous dark eyes was turned out of his warm crib by his father and mother and sent to live with an aunt until he was all grown up.

CHAPTER II

Flashback:
child, young man, World War I soldier,
disability-discharged combat psycho with pension
wins an M.D. degree
1897–1922

Marcel Petiot never remembered any childhood with his real parents. He was born at Auxerre, Yonne, on January 17, 1897, a Capricorn. He was very young when his parents, Maurice Félix Petiot and Marthe Bourdon Petiot, sent him to live with his old-maid aunt, Mme. Gaston, and her servant maid, called "l'Henriette," in Auxerre, an ancient city on the river Yonne. His father and mother were both low-level postal clerks whose civil service government employment kept them moving about. His father served as a telegraphic operator of the Post Office Department (the telephone, telegraph, and mail services were all government-operated in France), and his mother was a mail-sorting clerk. Little Marcel, they said, would be better off in a permanent home rather than shifting from place to place and from school to school. But when Marcel grew old enough to think about it, he was convinced they had merely dumped him on his old aunt because they had never wanted him at all. In fact, in the notes he penned while in prison many years later, he stated that he believed he had been conceived by accident, perhaps before wedlock, by the blowout of a rubber condom. He even added, with his usual historical bent and wide reading, that this was not a French invention, as many persons believed, but the invention of a Colonel Condom of England's Charles II's guard regiment.

The little boy had a reasonably comfortable life with the two old ladies in a small brick house behind a high wall on a narrow cobbled street, with a yard where Marcel often played alone behind a locked gate. His very earliest memory of the place, at age seven, concerned this yard and its locked iron gate.

As he grew older, he had pets that fascinated him, but his interest was largely in their life and death. He learned early to impale living insects on pins and he found a peculiar satisfaction in tying the legs of beetles or other flying insects so he could watch them as they struggled to exhaustion. Without food and freedom, he discovered, they would soon die and he would watch, entranced, as death slowly overcame them. He found baby birds in a nest one time and kept them in a cage until they were large enough to fly. He was fond of pins and needles and sticking them into insects, moths, and butterflies. Then he decided to put out the eyes of his birds by sticking a needle into their eyes. He then watched in deep amusement as they blundered helplessly about, trying to find their perch. He quickly tired of feeding them by hand, however, and let them die of hunger and thirst, studying them curiously as they grew weaker.

By the time he was about nine years old, he had extended his "experiments" to cats and dogs. When he dropped a puppy and a kitten bodily into a boiling kettle to watch them die, he was caught by Henriette and thoroughly spanked by his aunt. Perhaps it would have been better if he had not been born. That, Marcel was later convinced, must have been what his parents thought.

He knew who his parents were, of course, and even visited them once in Villevalier, but only as a guest from Auxerre. There he heard people tell how important a man his father, who had been elected mayor, was. Hearing that, Marcel recalled, gave him no feeling of pride at all, merely a surge of jealousy and a determination that one day he, Marcel, would be even more important.

Marcel had an overwhelming curiosity and the ability to win advancement too, for he was a difficult but excellent student with an unusually retentive memory. By the time he entered school, he could already read and write as well as children five years older than himself. His studies were almost too easy for him and he had time to cultivate the many strange urges that began to bubble inside him. He captured stray dogs and cats and found opportunities—in secret now, as he had no desire for another spanking—to cut them apart and see how they were made. A few of his play-mates, surprising him in this activity, were horrified and avoided his company. But Marcel had no time for them anyway.

Marcel's home and the yard in which he played were in the shadow of the old Gothic St. Étienne Cathedral. It was here that his parents and his aunt made their first efforts to introduce him to the church and to the Catholic religion, into which he had been born. But he seemed more interested in the town, which had been a thriving commune with a large wine trade in Chablis as far back as 200 B.C., although at that time it was called Au-tesiodorum. Marcel showed great interest in the fact that Auxerre was hundreds of years old when Christ was born. In his prison notes Petiot complains that, from his childhood in Auxerre under the shadow of two churches, St. Étienne and St. Pierre, and the old abbey, St. Germain, and all through his later life, he seemed unable to get away from the Catholic Church, although he claimed never to have believed in God ever since he could re-member. However, in the end he confided in his pre-execution notes that he was no longer so sure, as a doctor and scientist, that there was no supreme being and no hereafter.

When Marcel was fourteen, and briefly visiting his mother and father one day, he heard his mother tell his father about some par-ticularly extraordinary erotic and sexual letters that were wrongly addressed and had been opened. Marcel was immediately seized with an almost uncontrollable curiosity to look into the dark se-crets of adult life in this way. He made himself a small fish-pole device, with a stick, a string, and a gummed weight, that could be poked into any mailbox in town to fish envelopes out of it. Then he set about to raid letter boxes all over Auxerre.

Of course, the good citizens of the town began to notice that mail was missing and a watch was set on mailboxes. Marcel was caught. Yet the result—the punishment—stuck in Marcel's mind as one of the pleasantest moments of his youth. There was the ominous appearance of the gendarmes at his aunt's door, driving Marcel's heart into his throat. But the boy drew the deepest satis-faction—a thrill not unmixed with fear—over the portentous visit of his father, who was to assess the punishment and provide the reprimand. This was the first time in his whole life that Marcel's father had come to visit him. And it was the first time his father had ever scolded him in person. The strange satisfaction this event provided stayed with Petiot all his life.

The only specific punishment, beyond the scolding that Marcel received for his mail thefts, was expulsion from school, but he had long since lost interest in school and in his schoolmates, almost all of whom regarded him now as a strange one indeed, and a fellow to be avoided. Marcel found far more enjoyment in studying by himself, hidden away in his own room where he could read whenever he pleased. He had a strong desire to succeed, to be rich and powerful, to be *important*, to be one that people of all conditions would treat with respect. So he stuck to his studies and passed his *bachot* (examination for credits to enter high school) with unusually high grades. At once he began to work on his aunt to use her influence with his parents to send him away to high school. He had begun to feel now the first leanings toward a desire to study medicine, not simply because of the chance it would give him to delve deep into the secrets of life and death but because Marcel had already observed the standing a medical doctor possessed, even in a town as small as Auxerre.

Without much real conviction that he would amount to more than a reckless young man, the parents agreed and let him go to the Lycée Boulevard Pereire in Paris, and later to a school in Dijon. Although he was advanced in many ways, better read than his contemporaries, and informed in matters deemed better left to his elders, Marcel had only just overcome a habit that would have disgraced him away from home. Until he was thirteen, he had hardly more control of his bladder and bowels than a baby and he had consistently messed his pants. This was one more peculiarity of his that encouraged his schoolmates to stay clear of him.

Like any boy of fifteen, Marcel, when he went to school in Paris and Dijon, developed a devouring interest in sex. While he read much about abnormal practices, he never exhibited any homosexual tendencies, even those that might have been considered normal in an adolescent. He indulged in masturbation, according to his own account, to an average degree, but he was eager to sample the joys of sexual intercourse. He made an effort to undress and make love to a little girl in the neighborhood but found himself unable to perform and the girl not knowledgeable enough to help him.

Marcel continued his reading, not just his studies but also his researches into the lives of great men, particularly those who had led abnormal lives. Like the usual sexually precocious youth, he took a sniggering delight in reminding his schoolmates that this or that great historical figure had been a sex diviate of some sort. Both Caesar and Alexander the Great, he liked to inform his companions, had been homosexuals.

Gradually, his driving and morbid curiosity—about life, about death, and especially about sex—began to win him away from ordinary pursuits. He neglected his schoolbooks to read books of abnormal sex behavior, the stories of the great legendary lovers Don Juan and Casanova, who were both bisexual. He avidly read the whole twelve volumes of Casanova and even found books on two other famous deviates: Mlle. Maupin and the Chevalier d'Éon, the first a lesbian who became one of the deadliest duelists in France and had killed many of the greatest swordsmen in Europe in single combat; the other an alleged transvestite (whose name the medical profession adopted, erroneously, eonism for transvestism) who was actually a man who posed as a woman in order to act as a spy for France and was reported to have seduced both the Empress of Russia and the Queen of England, wife of George III. The fact that both Maupin and d'Éon were deadly with hand weapons, she with a sword and he with both sword and pistol, seemed to increase their fascination for Petiot. Mlle. Maupin, the lesbian, was also bisexual. She became the mistress of the Elector of Bavaria, then the companion of the wealthiest woman in Spain, and acquired a fortune, turned to chastity and charity, and founded and built Paris' largest hospital. The chevalier wound up his career as the most famous fencing master in the world in skirts and in London. (Old books on d'Éon, Maupin, Casanova, and Don Juan were later found in Petiot's library.)

While still at Auxerre, Marcel had consumed at least a book a night and had come to treasure the silences and solitude of the midnight hours. After he changed to a school in Dijon, he had his first experience in sex and erotica as well—with a prostitute who demonstrated her skill at exciting him almost beyond endurance with absinthe and by introducing him to fellatio and cunnilingus.

Yet he found, both that time and in every later experience with all-out abandon in sex, that he never quite attained full satisfaction except for a short time.

In his late teens, he formed a brief liaison with a cabaret cancan girl named Denise. He remembered her always for the extreme excitement she derived from sex—to the point of screaming—and because she had beautiful breasts that stood out in the most extraordinary manner. She loved to have them kissed and sucked and during sexual intercourse she rubbed them with her hands in a circular motion. He became addicted to her and she was tireless. His whole career might have followed a different path had not Denise simply disappeared one day, to drop out of his life forever. Petiot later wrote in his notes: "This was the first and only mysterious disappearance of man, woman, or child in my life that was not later blamed on me." With Denise gone, Marcel was able to devote himself with new avidity to his premedical studies. Driven by an urge that seemed to grow stronger as he neared maturity, he buried himself every night, in his tight and airless attic room, in his schoolbooks. He knew that his father expected nothing from him—or, rather, expected that he would be useless all his life, given to mischief, and "dirty pictures," and to torturing small animals. Marcel was determined he would rub his father's nose in the fact that the son he had disowned was a superior person.

Then came 1914 and, at age seventeen, Marcel's efforts and plans received a setback as tens of millions of men all over Europe were mobilized for World War I. Marcel felt the same urge of patriotism that all good Frenchmen felt and thrilled, as his neighbors did, to the sight of soldiers marching to do battle and the sound of the glorious and heart-lifting strains of *"La Marseillaise."*

He would be called, he knew, when he became nineteen. Perhaps by volunteering a little ahead of time he might be enrolled in the medical corps and thus advance his training. His instructors advised him that it would be best not to interrupt his premed schooling, so he decided to complete his basic work as rapidly as he could and thus be ready to enter medical school when he came out of service. He had developed good study habits now and he allowed nothing to lure him away from his books, day or night. As a result, he was able to obtain his *Bachot d'Enseignement Secondaire* on July 10, 1915, when he was only eighteen years of age. He was now qualified to enter medical school. He passed his examinations with a special commendation, but his greatest glory was a letter from his father, acknowledging his membership in the family and urging him to come "home" and be one of them.

Marcel's reaction to this was a feeling of triumph. He had proved his father wrong and made him admit it! He had no desire at all to rejoin a family he had never belonged to. He did go back home to receive the traditional welcome of the prodigal son and he did savor the fatted calf for an evening, along with his father and brother Maurice (his mother was now dead). But after dinner, he bade them both an offhand farewell and went to join the army—never to return home again. The fact that his brother was named Maurice, after his father, born when Marcel was ten, and now pawned off on any aunt, further convinced him he was not wanted, even if legitimate.

Petiot always took pride in the fact that he had not waited to be ordered to arms. "My official enlistment number at Auxerre," he noted for any who might question the fact, "was 1097" (verified by French Army records).

The hatred of the French for the Germans, the hope of revenge for France's unexpected defeat in 1870, the dream of regaining Alsace-Lorraine, the appeal of France's great military traditions and glory all contributed to a solid dedication to winning this war "to end all wars." Petiot, years later, claimed that what he had heard was right—that it was the British who really caused World War I because of their centuries-old policy of causing divisions and wars in Europe to join the winning side, that it was a British-German rivalry for sea power and world trade that caused World War II, and that it was the British who helped arm Nazi Germany and refused to stop Hitler in the Rhineland. Petiot, while in jail in 1946, stated, "I am certain World War III will be caused by the British arming or selling food to the weaker side so it will think it is the stronger, although there will soon be an end to the British Empire . . . nothing but a little island will be left!"

In truth, Petiot, even as a young man, had no stomach at all for war. He did not submit easily to army discipline, was often on the punishment list, and was given to stealing valuables that others might leave unguarded. He felt the need, however, to justify himself by explaining, in later years, that his comrades had been stupid to leave money unwatched. He, one supposes, was teaching them not to be so stupid.

Although young, Petiot had requested duty with a medical detachment. He was inducted into the army on January 11, 1916, and after training sent into combat with the 89th Regiment of Infantry on November 16, 1916. He saw six months of the dreariest and bloodiest of combat duty, and discovered, as did millions of other men, that trench warfare held little glory, no romance, and hardly any drama. Despite bone weariness, he found it almost impossible to sleep. During a night bombardment, he would hug himself tight with terror and wonder if he would live until morning. Then, when dawn came, he would wonder if he would live till dark—or come out alive from the attack that was scheduled for dawn. The cold sweat of fear continually soaked his underclothes, as the chill mud-water seeped through his shoes.

The 89th Infantry was based at Sens, and there, notwithstanding Petiot's anti-Catholic feelings, once again he wound up in the shadow of a cathedral so beautiful and imposing he was forced to admire it, visit it often, and even succumb to its serenity and beauty and sit and even kneel in a pew. If he had believed in God, he would have prayed. The Sens Cathedral is the greatest example of thirteenth-century Gothic architecture and one of the greatest monuments in France. William of Sens, its architect, built the Canterbury Cathedral, although no Britisher will admit it.

His first major battle merely multiplied his fears. It was early morning as Marcel's regiment, marching since early dawn, left the road in route order, column of fours. Now it deployed into "squad columns"—little single files of eight men parallel to each other—across fields of uncut, yet packed down, hay and pasture land. On orders from the officers, his group began in columns to run forward, then deploy into a skirmish line toward an enemy they had not seen but whom they must skewer on their bayonets lest he strike them first. A bursting artillery shell hung human entrails, like some horrid holiday decoration, on the limbs of the barren trees. And somewhere songbirds began to sing! A word or two to the man at one's side, to help draw some courage. Then, without notice, the man is gone—just a body on the ground, or worse.

Petiot remembered war this way because, of course, his heart was not in it, but the battle in which he was wounded was the most horrifying of all. This was the action of the Chemin des Dames, so named because it was along a road built for the daughters of Louis XV, where Napoleon had won a great victory a century before. The Germans, in taking the Chemin des Dames roadway and ridge, which ran parallel to, and four miles north of, the Aisne River, had won the commanding heights in a strategic area, where they had clogged every glen with barbed wire and turned limestone caves into bristling fortresses. This was the key to the Aisne Valley. The Allied forces, could they cross the Aisne and break through here, might roll up the whole line and return the war to one of movement. The war, at this time, was near a stalemate and some French troops, long held out of action yet unable to go home, had mutinied. The attack on Chemin des Dames was, then, crucial for the sake of morale and for strategic reasons as well. Therefore, the fighting was especially bitter. Petiot's regiment, sent to seize the village of Craonne, one terminal of the German defenses, took their objective after a fierce battle and held on to it in the face of almost daily counterattacks. Holed up with his comrades in a limestone trench, sleepless, starving, choked with fear and thirst, Petiot saw the waves of Germans who charged again and again, and he died each time a barrage was laid down on the French position to prepare for each attack, the shells exploding with a terrifying ferocity. There was nearly two weeks of this, and each day young Marcel was convinced he would never see another.

A few Germans occasionally did get up to the limestone trenches and strong points of the French and, on May 20, some few grenades were lobbed into the French positions. On this day a grenade exploded, ostensibly in the trench where Petiot was standing, and drove a piece of steel deep into his left foot. It was a strange wound, for a grenade exploding in a narrow trench would naturally throw its fragments upward. How then could it strike his foot? One of Petiot's companions ("jealous of my going to medical school," Petiot maintained) spread the story that Petiot had wounded himself to escape from battle by pushing a French grenade into a drain pipe and placing his foot partly in front of it, and there were many who believed it. But Petiot, always strangely eager, despite an antisocial nature, to justify him-

self in the eyes of his fellow men, angrily insisted the story was a
lie.

At the field hospital, after Petiot's wound was dressed and after
he was given a powerful sedative, his stretcher was deposited in a
nearby cemetery. When he awoke, he was directly under a white
marble cross. Later, at the medical transfer point, he spent the
night in a Catholic church, or what was left of it. Nevertheless,
Petiot later commented, he remained a resolute atheist.

Petiot's foot healed quickly, leaving only a three-inch scar on
his foot, but fear had almost driven the ability to sleep out of his
body. He suffered continual headaches, could develop no appetite
for food, and began to lose weight steadily. Years later, as he
made notes in jail for his autobiography, Petiot remarked that he
had decided at this time to *pretend* to be mentally ill. But the
headaches were very real, as were the fear and the sleeplessness,
and there was certainly enough in his strange nature and background to make any doctor question his mental stability. He was
often trembling. He jumped at sudden sounds and his nervous
habit of rubbing his hands briskly together had become noticeably
exaggerated. He fainted often, had frequent dizzy spells, and occasional lapses of memory. Malingerer or not (and he admitted he
could not always tell the real symptoms from the imagined ones),
Petiot was committed to a series of mental hospitals—Sens, Navarre-Évreux, Orléans, Ivry, Fleury-les-Aubrais, Bagnères, Pithi-
viers de Crevant, Rennes. It is officially recorded in army files,
however, that sometime during his sojourn in the series of mental
hospitals, he formally requested that he be sent back to join his
unit at the front.

Whether or not one chooses to believe that Petiot was really
faking his mental state or following a well-thought-out, conscious
or subconscious, schedule of symptoms and misleading doctor
after doctor, it is a fact that while he was confined in these hospitals he had an excellent chance to further his medical studies. The
libraries were open to him for the attendants were happy to have
him off their hands, and he improved his lengthy leisure by reading whatever he could find that would add to his knowledge of
mental illness and its symptoms. He also dug deep into the books
on crime and criminal psychology.

It was at this time that Petiot first read the stories of Jack the

Ripper and his French counterpart, Vascher, *"l'Éventreur"*—the "Eviscerator"—a pathetic and horrible story of an unbalanced wretch who killed eleven sheepherders—four boys, six girls, and an old woman, disemboweling them all, then subjecting them all to sexual attack. Joseph Vascher, born in 1869, an army sergeant and an outstanding soldier, had attempted suicide while in the army and was confined for a while in the St. Robert asylum. After he had been discharged as "cured," he attacked his victims, suffocating each one, or strangling them or cutting their throats, then ripping open the abdomen. He stole nothing, had never known the victims, and clearly had nothing to gain from his acts, and had no understanding of what was driving him. Yet the French courts sentenced him to the guillotine. Apparently, Petiot later noted, the courts decided either that a quick and painless end was better than the lingering death of a madman or that society had the right to rid itself of such a creature.

Jack the Ripper was of great interest to Petiot because although, like Vascher, a sadistic killer, he was very definitely a medical doctor. Vascher assassinated and eviscerated only innocent farm people with a dull butcher's knife in the country (France). Jack the Ripper murdered and mutilated only prostitutes with a very sharp surgical knife in a big city (London). Vascher was caught and executed while Jack the Ripper was never even positively identified. However, Scotland Yard and its chief, Sir Basil Thomson, were positive he was one of two mentally disturbed doctors. The body of the most likely of these two, who disappeared after the sixth and last Ripper victim, was found floating in the Thames in 1888. Several books on Jack the Ripper were found in Petiot's library at Villeneuve.

It is a question if Petiot received, or required, any "inspiration" from this reading. Later on, he made a careful study of the Landru case that filled the newspapers in 1921 and apparently learned from that case to avoid some of the mistakes that led to Landru's conviction. This case appealed to Petiot, and a well-worn book on "Bluebeard," Henri Désiré Landru, the Sire of Gambais, was found in Petiot's private library at Villeneuve (*L'Affaire Landru— Les Grands Reportages,* Michel, 1924). He referred to Landru as the murderer who had been responsible for more books, movies, plays, jokes, and stories about marriages and the disappearances of wives than anyone in the history of crime. Landru had to be admired, thought Petiot—he "married" and killed many women for money to support his real wife, child, and a young mistress, all of whom loved him dearly. Landru's many disguises and aliases also impressed Petiot, as did the fact that, unknown to most people, Landru, prior to World War I, had a police record of five convictions and sixteen years of prison sentences. Yet there was never any direct proof of the murders and, just before his execution, Landru swore he was innocent. Only the cinders of some human bones and a notebook cost Landru his head.

What Petiot's study of abnormal behavior did do, he insisted, was to help him pose as being mentally unbalanced. Yet he did require a discharge from the mental hospital if he was to resume his studies and his supposed pretense carried him far past the end of the war. He argued later that he continued malingering only to establish his right to a pension; it is true that his acquisitiveness was becoming more and more exaggerated as he grew older.

Before finally winning a discharge from the army, Petiot was officially transferred first to the Romainville Military Police (August 28, 1918) and then to the 91st Infantry on September 15, 1918. At Sens, on July 4, 1919, a medical board discharged him as 40 per cent disabled. In April 1920, he reported back to the asylum at Navarre-Évreux. An army retirement board, sitting to determine his pension (July 7, 1920), obtained the following data to establish his mental condition before entry into military service. From grandmother Petiot: "My grandson was a very strange child. From an early age he was extremely intelligent but told exaggerated stories about himself and his importance. However, the strangest thing about him was that he did not want to sleep at night . . . he seemed fired up by darkness. He wanted to play or work or go for a walk at night . . . the later the better. He also had difficulties controlling his bowels and kidneys until the age of thirteen." (French army records.)

In September 1920, he returned to the mental hospital at Orléans. This time, on September 16, 1921, he was found 100 per cent disabled because of deep depression and suicidal tendencies (faked, he later insisted), requiring permanent and close observation, and he was retired on that basis by Dr. Reynau.

But Petiot reasoned that a 100 per cent disability rating would be a handicap to his medical career; he therefore tried, in March 1922, for a different finding. He insisted that he had learned, in his studies in abnormal behavior, to fake the kind of wounds on his own tongue that would come from biting it in an epileptic seizure. Whether a man could do that willfully, or whether a man who did do it willfully was wholly sane, remains in question. The fact is that he managed to appear before the board in such a state and this time, on March 31, 1922, a Dr. Valensi rated him but 50 per cent disabled as an epileptic with "fits of depression" but no suicidal impulses. This was further confirmed with respect to establishing his permanent disability retirement pension. On July 18, 1923, another examining board at Dijon confirmed this rating, with Dr. Violet of the board diagnosing his ailment this time as "dementia praecox."

Petiot took a secret and justified delight during this period in the fact that, while his mental instability was thus being certified and he was in and out of mental institutions being examined as a serious mental case, he was completing his medical studies with honors on a G.I. bill of rights. He was graduated from the University of Paris on December 15, 1921, with the degree of Doctor of Medicine. For his doctorate, he submitted as his final thesis a paper entitled "Contributions to the Study of Acute Progressive Paralysis" (Landru's disease). His thesis earned a grade of "superior" from a Sorbonne professor who is said to have described his own grading system in this manner:

"Normally, 'superior' is the mark I would give to God; 'excellent' is the mark I would give myself; and I would leave 'good' or less for the remainder of my students."

Petiot's mark in surgery, it should be noted, was only "average." Yet when the same professor who gave him that mark was called as an expert at Petiot's trial, he was obliged to acknowledge that he would have had to raise that grade considerably on the evidence gathered by the police. Even with the shadow of the guillotine falling across his shoulders, Petiot took a profound pleasure in that admission.

After graduation with honors before January 1, 1922, Petiot was assigned as an intern to one of the very hospitals where he had been confined. Here he won a "superior" mark for his special rapport with the unbalanced patients and his understanding of schiz-

ophrenia (dementia praecox), as well as a citation from the senior
psychiatrist Dr. Daday, yet none of the doctors or inmates recognized him.

According to French Army records (reproduced in a forty-eight-
page report with some fifty additional pages of testimony on the
Petiot case by the deputy inspector general of the Paris police for
the inspector general in April 1944 and acquired by U.S. Army secret agents in the Paris police), Petiot very definitely showed every
sign and symptom of being mentally deranged if not insane. His
wound, allegedly received in combat, was listed in army records as
a scar seven centimeters long on the dorsal face of his left foot.
On March 4, 1919, he was hospitalized for mental attacks and
guilty of several thefts resulting in fifteen days in jail. He then,
without explanation or any reason, fired a revolver in the direction
of one of his superiors in a seemingly insane moment. He then
went into a number of mental attacks allegedly with suicidal tendencies. On April 25, 1919, the chief surgeon at the mental hospital
of Rennes diagnosed Petiot as definitely mentally unbalanced
with acute melancholy and discouragement, with fixations of persecution and suicide. On April 18, 1920, the director of the insane
asylum of Navarre, where Petiot was a voluntary patient, reported
that Petiot had left after a few days to rejoin his family. On September 16, 1920, Petiot was officially retired by a medical board of
experts as 100 per cent disabled with the special benefit of Article
X, namely, incapable of any mental work with the necessity of *not
only hospitalization but constant surveillance in a mental institution*. Article X also provided for the special benefits of the major
medical cases such as total blindness: *having an attendant or
guard in any displacement outside of mental institutions*.

Later, on March 31, 1922, and again on July 18, 1923, at the initiative of Petiot himself, his disability retirement was reduced to
50 per cent. His symptoms were described as mental unbalance
with the overall diagnosis of dementia praecox. The frequency of
various diagnoses and retirements in the French Army at that
time called for disability examinations and degree ratings several
times over a period of four years before the resulting disability
pension became final and for life. (Petiot continued to draw his
pension paid him by the French Government as 50 per cent
"mentally disabled" until the French Government executed him

as the "sane" murderer of twenty-six persons.) Why this extraordinary record did not prevent Petiot from practicing medicine and why it was not used in any effort to defend him in his final trial as a lunatic not responsible for murdering twenty-six or twenty-seven or sixty-three or 150 persons is one of the many mysteries—if not the major mystery—of the Petiot case.

In any event, at the beginning of 1923, Marcel Petiot was an M.D. graduate with honors, qualified and eligible to practice medicine and with only a 50 per cent World War I disability retirement pension after a number of examinations over a period of four years.

CHAPTER III

Doctor and mayor of Villeneuve-sur-Yonne
1923–33

When he was ready to go into practice, Petiot, with his small pension, sought a place where competition would be less keen than in Paris and where living was less costly. He had no initial capital to purchase some retiring, dead, or departing doctor's practice and office, so he determined to look around for a nice, friendly, and beautiful town, somewhere between Auxerre, where brother Maurice lived, and Paris, but preferably closer to Auxerre. Villeneuve-sur-Yonne, a picturesque and historic town on the placid river Yonne, the capital of his native canton of Yonne, seemed made to order. Villeneuve was an old fortress village and royal residence, built in 1163, with drawbridge and Gothic watchtowers at either end, north and south, and a collection of centuries-old dwellings, all surrounded by a high wall with a moat which was once kept full of water by a connection with the mirror-surfaced Yonne River. The original village, without the fortress and royal residence, was reported to have been founded before the Romans and before Christ.

The main street, rue Carnot, runs north and south through the village, a cobbled street where, in the twenties, rumbling drays drawn by slow and heavy-footed horses outnumbered the popping automobiles of the day and where through traffic was very thin indeed. At almost the center of the old town, on the rue Carnot, stands a twelfth-century church, the church of Notre Dame, established in 1163 by Pope Alexander as the church of the King of France. At each end of rue Carnot are two matching entrances through Gothic fortified towers, the larger towers being over the roadway at each entrance, with two smaller towers on each side. Both of these now boarded-over entrances were formerly served by drawbridges. Nearby is the famous House of Seven Heads, named for the seven marble heads aligned under the front windows of the second floor.

A relatively modern bridge (1733) with fourteen arches crosses the wide Yonne into Villeneuve from the suburb, or *faubourg,* now called St. Laurent. On its way across the river, the high-crowned bridge sets its feet on a lovely green island where luxuriously thick willow trees weep into the water and form an almost impenetrable screen of leaves and branches. This was named the Isle of Love, or *l'Ile d'Amour.* The river Yonne at this point runs green, a clear mirror of the green willow leaves and branches in it and above it.

The young Dr. Petiot first rented a small villa of three rooms, a kitchen, and a garden. It was, as were many homes of Dr. Petiot, in the shadow of a church, Notre Dame. An uncle, a professor at Auxerre, found him an old woman, Violette, to keep his house and the doctor was ready to begin. At the very start, he revealed that he was "not like others" for, in contemptuous disregard of the stand the Medical Association had taken against any form of advertising, he ordered cards printed and circulated announcing his presence and his qualifications:

> Dr. Marcel Petiot of the Faculty of Medicine, Paris, former intern at hospitals and asylums, treats patients with the most modern methods but without exploiting them. As a result, the sick that have any sense have confidence in him. Villeneuve-sur-Yonne, Telephone 24.

There were already two doctors in Villeneuve and they must have felt entirely relaxed about the competition an upstart like this might provide. After all, this was a typical small town where strangers were not welcome. As a young bachelor, Petiot was soon well known in the town but had few close friends. One, René Nezondet, born in Migennes, Yonne, June 28, 1895, later became a clerk at the Villeneuve City Hall under Petiot when he became mayor. Fate would eventually place him in the same prison with Petiot. The two met originally when Nezondet was clerk to the

justice of the peace in charge of auctions in tax foreclosures and
Petiot began buying antiques and selling them as a hobby. Nezondet remembered the young doctor as a man who looked warily at
everyone he met.

He was also, said Nezondet, a man who seemed determined to
work his will on the whole inanimate world. He would drive his
battered yellow automobile about with a ferocity that seemed to
doom it to next week's junkyard. If the car stalled, the doctor
himself acted as his own mechanic. In his good suit—his only suit!
—he would crawl under the car and fish among the gears, joints,
and tie rod to find the trouble, then mend it himself, or patch it
up to get it going, ending up with grease on his hands and all over
his clothing.

This, said Nezondet, was just one more aspect of Petiot's really
astonishing stinginess. If Petiot had had to wear spectacles, Nezondet insisted, he would have taken care to look over the tops of
them so as not to wear out the lenses. When a lunch tab was to
be paid, Petiot never had anything in his pockets to pay for his
share. He wore his clothes until they were soiled and worn past recovery. Yet he always exhibited a special taste for fine cravats and
could, on formal occasions, turn himself out as if he had stepped
from a Paris show window. Just one more contradiction in the
make-up of this strange, strange man.

As a physician, however, Petiot was a spectacular success. To
begin with, he had only the patients who had been treated without result by the other two doctors in town, or the hypo-
chondriacs for whom the older doctors had no time. But Petiot
welcomed all the ill, even if their ills were largely imaginary, and
he treated them with a show of true concern, with kindness and
with authority. When the old people unable to afford treatment
insisted he take something, he invited them to dinner and
suggested that, to repay him, they might simply spread the word
about his abilities.

The situation favored him in many ways, although one might
think that such a staid little village, so full of farmers, vineyard
workers, and small *bons bourgeois*, would distrust a young man
whose behavior was so unorthodox. But the truth was that the
two doctors already established there had not kept pace with the
advances in medicine and were still prescribing the same old reme-

dies in the same old way and accepting many of the complaints of their patients as chronic. They were satisfied with their station in life, did not need to increase their practice, and had little forbearance for men and women who just wanted comforting. Petiot, despite his suspicious and even contemptuous attitude toward his fellow men, managed to cultivate a truly attractive bedside manner. He was drawn by nature to the disaffected, the rebellious, and the exploited. He was an atheist, so that he was almost automatically opposed to the bourgeois establishment. He had been a Socialist, then a Communist, as a medical student in Paris, and had met both Maurice Thorez and Ho Chi Minh. Both of these men left the Socialist Party to organize the French Communist Party in 1920. Ho Chi Minh's Paris background was as a skillful Latin Quarter painter of fake Chinese antiques when Petiot knew him. (Thorez was later to enter politics and help Petiot be elected mayor of Villeneuve on a Communist, Socialist, anti-bourgeois ticket.) Petiot's Marxist thinking put him in tune with the working-class politics of the day and he carefully cultivated the more radical workers in Villeneuve. He became known, to his own deep satisfaction, as the "worker's doctor"—not a stuffy, condescending professional, but a man of the people, offhand, gregarious, cigarette dangling from one corner of his mouth, ready to talk politics or crack jokes or offer irreverent comments on any subject to mechanic, housewife, waiter, laborer, or keeper of a small shop. He had a way, too, of anticipating what his patients were about to tell him, as if he could diagnose an illness by looking deep into a person's eyes with that smoldering look of his.

"I know exactly what you mean," he would say. "Do not tire yourself. I know just what your trouble is. . . ." Then he would outline their symptoms with such accuracy that they would look at him open-mouthed, with a sort of superstitious awe.

He did use strong drugs, in many cases, however, to the dismay of the local pharmacist, Paul Mayaud. "Horse cures!" Mayaud called the Petiot prescriptions and occasionally he would try to persuade Petiot to cut down on the strength of the dose. Patients, too, particularly those for whom he had prescribed laxatives, asked for mercy. Petiot treated all such requests with scorn. Everyone knew, he insisted, that pharmacists, and particularly Paul Mayaud, cheated on their prescriptions to increase their profits so that one had to order extra strength to get the dosage required. Mayaud, who was also mayor of Villeneuve, once dared to refuse to fill a prescription Petiot had ordered for the child of a stonemason—a child who had been treated unsuccessfully for a year. When Petiot was told of the refusal, he stormed into the pharmacist's shop and informed Mayaud that, mayor or not, he had no right to countermand the orders of a licensed physician.

Well, if the child is incurable, Petiot insisted, it is just as well if he dies from the medicine and takes a burden off his mother's back. But if he is curable, then this dose will cure him. Petiot had his way, the child took the medicine, and, by Petiot's later account, the child was cured.

Spectacular cures of this sort eventually made Petiot one of the most popular men in town, yet he remained a creature full of contradictions and given to behavior so erratic as to cause alarm sometimes to those who knew him best. He made a practice of seeking out companionship of a sort, not for friendship—which he did not seem to need—but to widen his circle of acquaintances, to make himself known throughout the valley and, one supposes, thus to increase his clientele. His interests and efforts were obviously that of an opportunist. It was as if he needed to know all that could be learned about anybody in order to further his sardonic and critical appraisal of man and all of man's institutions.

Sometimes he was far from silent in company and earned a reputation as a teller of tales, but of tales so exaggerated sometimes as to require an act of will to believe them, for he told stories not to entertain but to underline some point he was making or to prove the truth of some premise he was trying to defend. If, as sometimes happened, Petiot would himself become lost in the labyrinth of his own explanation, he would take refuge in sudden demoniacal laughter—a laugh so scary in nature that it would frighten even those who knew him best. He would give himself over to it, and the wild, cruel tone sounded like what might have been the cry of a werewolf in a primeval forest and would continue until Petiot was shaken and spent. Then, when it stopped with a horrible choking gurgle, Petiot would sometimes, much to his dismay, burst into tears.

This habit of weeping disturbed Petiot a good deal for he could not pretend it was a sham and he could not explain it to himself.

One spell of crying that especially disturbed him seized him after he had been visited by the local priest.

When the priest was gone, Petiot suddenly burst out crying and could not stop. Why? Why? Did he really believe in God? All his life he had been bemused at the manner in which his life had been entangled with churches—in Auxerre the great cathedral had overshadowed the town. In Villeneuve the ancient church of Notre Dame was his close neighbor. Before he went into combat he had visited the Sens Cathedral and had almost prayed there. When he was wounded in the First World War, he had been treated at a forward field hospital in a cemetery under a cross, then spent the night in a Catholic church. In Paris his office eventually would be near a church also. And, at the very hour of his death, the Church would come offering her sacraments—and he would accept them because, by then, his intelligence told him nothing is indestructible or disappears . . . absolutely nothing . . . even one's flesh and bones, so our soul and our self must go somewhere.

But at this particular point in his career, Petiot was not long troubled by conscience or by doubts concerning a hereafter. He was intent only on making his way in the world. He sought out methods of fattening his income—one way was accepting extra bits of goods from the trades people he treated, another way was raising his fees to the rich. He was ambitious for a better house, for more leisure, for a chance to buy the books he still could gulp down at a sitting, but now the books he sought were no longer medical textbooks only. He had long collected books on sex deviates; now he sought books on abnormal psychology, on crime, on police work, on forensic chemistry, even popular detective stories. He would often put in many hours reading, long after the world had gone to bed.

Petiot was pleased, as a Frenchman, to read the term "perfect crime" did not come from Edgar Allan Poe or Scotland Yard or Sherlock Holmes, but from the first crime detection organization in the world, the Institut Médico-Légal of Paris. The entire system of fingerprint identification came from there, the discovery of Alphonse Bertillon in 1886. Dr. Paul, the coroner of Paris, whom he was to meet under both pleasant and not so pleasant circumstances, was considered the greatest medical crime expert in the world. It was his identification of human bone cinders that was the crux of the Landru trial. Then, of course, there was Dr. Edmund Locard of Lyon and his book on police techniques and criminology. Petiot was particularly interested in the cunning of doctor-murderers. In addition to Jack the Ripper in England, there were doctors Lamson, Palmer, Pritchard, and Neil Cream. The last, an American, who killed a man in 1881, was convicted in Chicago and given life, but served only ten years at Joliet when his sentence was commuted by the governor of Illinois. Cream then moved to London, where he murdered four women with strychnine and was then executed. Petiot's nocturnal and vicarious excursions in crime seemed to satisfy some urge for more demanding and exciting action than reading after dark. (Many books and clippings on the criminal cases, as well as the deviates, were found in Petiot's possessions.)

The change that came over Petiot after the sun went down was one of his notable peculiarities. If ever there was a living example of a Dr. Jekyll-Mr. Hyde transformation, it could have been Marcel Petiot almost any evening. Only he needed no mysterious draught to change him. In the dark he seemed to be born anew. At night, Petiot's wit, always quick and penetrating, would leap to life, like a turned-on welding gun. His imagination boiled. His energy, with no need to conserve any for defense against the unknown assailant, became inexhaustible. He would go night after night without sleep and seem to grow stronger all the while. A few people even pretended to believe that Petiot could see in the dark—that he would, without a second's hesitation, pick up a pin off the floor in total darkness when ordinary men could hardly make out the floor.

It may have been this general feeling that Petiot was "not made like others" that permitted him to get away with his many petty thefts—of loose cash on a bedside table, of a few francs from an unwatched wallet or pocketbook (not all the money, just part of it), or of jewelry belonging to a patient who had died. Petiot pretended to himself that he stole because he needed more and more money. But, just as his friend Nezondet explained, he had always jokingly admitted or claimed he was a kleptomaniac, given to picking up any sort of trinket that attracted him, even goods on a shop counter. Hardly anyone in Villeneuve who ever invited the

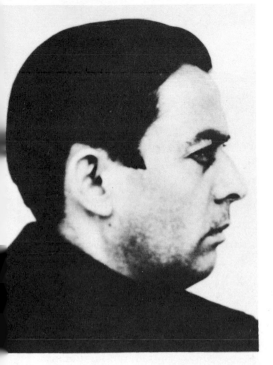

George Masuy, chief of the German Supply Service "Otto," who doubled as chief of a ruthless counterintelligence setup of the Abwehr at 101 avenue Henri Martin. One of the master spies of World War II. He had a definite but unknown connection with Petiot.

Maurice Petiot, brother of Dr. Petiot, manager of Dr. Petiot's real estate empire and operator of a radio and electrical shop in Auxerre.

*Henri Lafont, alias Chamberlain—
head of French Gestapo of the rue
Lauriston Gestapo.*

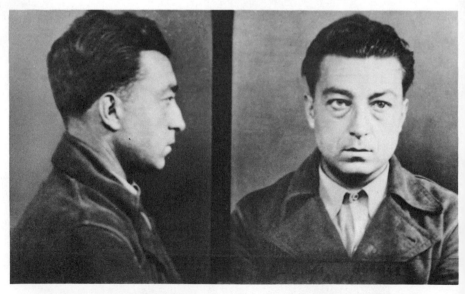

Lafont's nephew Paul Clavie, also of the French Gestapo rue Lauriston.

Roland Porchon, collaborator who
went from rags to riches during the
Occupation and was a Petiot scout.

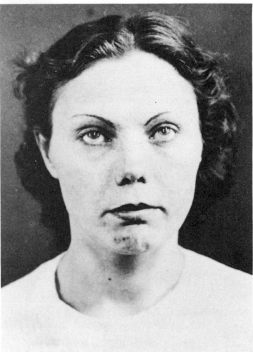

Jeanne Gaul, drug addict implicated
with Petiot and girl friend of one
of Petiot's victims.

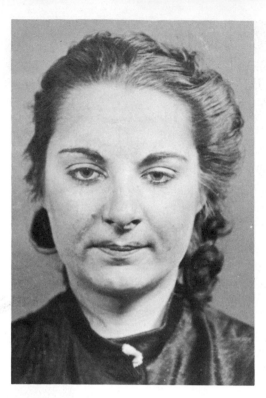

Raymonde Baudet, drug addict implicated with Petiot whose mother was one of Petiot's victims.

Joseph Piereschi, alias Dionisi "Ze," gangster with five convictions, collaborator with Lafont, another victim of Dr. Petiot. German Occupation Authorities.

Jo Reocreux, "Jo the Boxer," gangster with seven convictions, member of the French Gestapo, victim of Dr. Petiot. German Occupation Authorities.

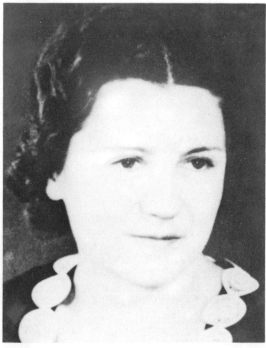

Gisele Rossny, night-club singer, mistress of "Adrien the Basque," and victim of Dr. Petiot. German Occupation Authorities.

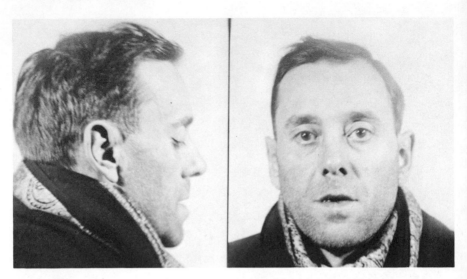

Adrien Estebeteguy, the Basque gangster with eight convictions, member of the French Gestapo and victim of Petiot. German Occupation Authorities.

Emil, brother of Adrien, Estebeteguy. He claimed his brother, victim of Dr. Petiot, was really executed by order of Lafont. Arrested as a collaborator at the liberation, Emil was released or cleared by amnesty. German Occupation Authorities.

Joachim Guschinow, furrier of 69 rue Caumartin, a wealthy victim of Dr. Petiot.

Jean Marc van Bever, a victim of Dr. Petiot to eliminate him as a witness in a dope case against the doctor.

Dr. Paul Braunberger, another victim of Dr. Petiot.

Kurt Kneller, who with his wife and young son, René, were liquidated at 21 rue Le Sueur en route to Argentina.

doctor to dinner did not find something missing after Petiot had left—and perhaps saw it later either on Petiot's person or in his home, unashamedly displayed as his own.

But three of Petiot's most spectacular thefts had no flavor of kleptomania about them, although they demonstrated a paranoiac superiority complex devoid of any fear of discovery or punishment. As a matter of fact, they were not so much thefts as acts of defiance, meant to put some of his traducers and detractors in their place. Eventually, he would be found guilty of one of the thefts, although he never granted that the matter was anything more than a frame-up devised by his enemies. All of them took place after Petiot had won a position of honor and power in the community.

Most spectacular, and most farcical, was his theft of the great Cross of Calvary from the local cemetery at the north end of town. This cross stood seven feet high and weighed over five hundred pounds. Petiot had long termed it a nuisance, inasmuch as it stood right at the entrance to the cemetery and forced hearses to back and twist and turn to make their way past it. He had often argued for its removal. Then he began to warn that "someday" it would be removed. When his warnings brought no results, he grew more specific. He was a great student of the literature of crime, of Sherlock Holmes, Arsène Lupin, and all the great detectives and crooks of fiction and he probably was borrowing an inspiration from them when he notified the gendarmerie of Villeneuve that on such and such a night, at midnight, the Cross of Cavalry would disappear. When the chosen midnight came and the cross did indeed vanish, the outraged gendarmes, who had brushed aside all the warnings, now descended in open outrage on Petiot. He received them with patience and sarcasm.

"I do not believe I have the cross on me," he told them. And they tore up the countryside, and even sent divers into the green depths of the Yonne—to no avail. Petiot knew well enough what had become of the cross. At midnight he had persuaded a farmer friend to bring his tractor to the cemetery—which was nearly opposite the headquarters of the Villeneuve police—to drag the cross up the road and dump it in the river a good distance away. It was an instance of Petiot's luck that a shower of rain fell in the early morning, just enough to wipe away all traces made by the tractor and the cross.

More personal, and rather more outrageous, was his theft of gasoline from the railroad station. Petiot committed this petty crime out of anger, just as in another case—that of the stolen electricity. This again was an act of irritation against a foe of long standing. Petiot had often accused the electric company of profiteering and he had been angered when they attached to his garage a transformer he felt no need for. So, in his anger, he decided to do something about it. Acting with customary disregard for the consequences, Petiot one night attached wires to the electric cable to by-pass the meter and for some time used the current without charge. Inevitably, the failure of his meter to register any current whatsoever led to the discovery of the by-pass wires, and this led to another criminal charge against Petiot. This further seemed to prove a lack of logical thinking but long before this matter clouded his days, Petiot's life in Villeneuve had taken some even more ominous turns.

The chief companion of his bachelor days, René Nezondet, had begun to believe that the young doctor, consumed by his drive to advance himself, had found a way to excise love utterly from his daily life. Then Petiot was invited to dinner, along with several others, at the home of a gentlewoman in the suburbs. It was a home to which Petiot would ordinarily not be invited except by grace of his position as a professional man. Petiot relished a good dinner, even though, when he was busy, he would wolf down his food as if it had no meaning to him. But a free dinner, lavishly served, that was something else!

This night, however, he had no memory at all of what he ate. His somber eyes were fixed all evening on the girl who served the meal, the maid Louisette. René Nezondet, who saw her soon afterward, described her in a book he wrote about Petiot (the book was promptly suppressed): "She was beautiful. That says it all! The freshness of her! The dazzling whiteness of her teeth!"

But Nezondet was not there that night to observe the electric attraction Louisette exerted on Petiot and the fascination Petiot seemed to have for her. She fussed over him, kept his wineglass always filled to the brim, brought him fresh bread before he had half finished what lay before him. Petiot could not keep from following her everywhere with his eyes. There was a childlike quality about her that stirred him deeply—her full mouth, the tender innocent eyes, the unlined freshness of her cheeks. Desire surged up in Petiot so that he hardly knew what he was eating. He seemed sunk in deep thought, but his thoughts were of how he could arrange to meet Louisette alone and win her into his bed.

The very next day the young doctor set out to discover all he could about Louisette's comings and goings. Through offhand inquiries among his patients and the village shopkeepers, he found that she was not really so innocent as she seemed, that she had been married and divorced, that she was twenty-four years old and that her name was Louise Delaveau. His passion now was so inflamed that he gave all his spare time to planning a rendezvous. He had found that Louisette stopped frequently at the shop of old André in the rue Carnot, that she attended mass at Notre Dame every Sunday, and, best of all, that she stopped sometimes at the bar of one Frascot for beer or coffee.

Frascot, who suffered from rheumatoid arthritis and had a bad postnasal drip, had several times been treated by Petiot. He was quick to agree to deliver a letter to the girl when he saw her next. In the letter, Petiot told the girl almost bluntly how he felt and he invited her, if she returned his feelings, to telephone him at his office. By this time Petiot had moved into a far more splendid house at 56 rue Carnot (where the town's leading physician, Dr. Le Maître, now lives) almost opposite the house of the Seven Heads, and had become an impressive and sophisticated figure. His house was a magnificent one, four stories high, with a beautiful garden and property that extended through from one street to another. His office, facing the rue Carnot, had wide windows that admitted the morning sun and signaled Petiot's own success. Of course, it was in the shadow of the Notre Dame church and, of course, the whole town knew he was still unmarried. The girl telephoned him promptly and agreed to meet him at Frascot's the very next evening at 10 P.M.

Petiot was almost ashamed of his own excitement as he prepared for the rendezvous. He was trembling, he said, "like a high school boy." He had denied himself almost all sex experiences for weeks and his anticipation grew so strong that he could hardly keep his mind on his patients. He was aware, too, deep inside himself, of a sort of whispering resentment against the girl, even as he desired her.

He had concealed himself at a screened table in Frascot's bar well before 10 P.M., but Louisette did not appear until twenty minutes past. Petiot could not repress a slight feeling of scorn for this obvious feminine ploy, even while his desire for her was shortening his breath. When she appeared, following shyly as the old man led her to Petiot's table, she was far more beautiful than Petiot remembered. He hardly dared fix his eyes on her, so overwhelming was his urge to take her in his arms. But he maintained his reserve, talked to her casually and politely, shared drinks with her, and then proposed, in the most offhand way imaginable, that he walk her home. As they started out, he suggested, with almost painful casualness, that they stop and look at his house on the way to the place where she worked. She agreed and Petiot actually began to tremble with desire.

At his place, he had to try for several seconds to control the tremor of his hands before he could get the key into the keyhole. The thought of having her alone, of laying his hands on her, of tenderly removing her clothes . . .

The girl proved as eager as he was and responded at once to his almost abrupt caresses. Within moments, he had taken her to bed and begun a liaison that was to set a new and tragic pattern for his life. He saw Louise (he could not call her Louisette, he said) three times a week after that and they went to bed together systematically, without regard for whatever else the world might be offering. It was like a drug addiction to Petiot—periods of growing, almost aching desire, followed by unworldly transports of ecstasy, sweeter than he had ever dreamed of. Petiot later admitted, or bragged, that he often made love to her several times during the night and again in the morning and actually had two or three orgasms a night. "When she had her menstrual periods, she sexually played with me in every conceivable way and would finally make me climax in fellatio. In return between her menstrual periods and in turn to thrill her more I made her come in cunnilingus!"

But there were difficulties in their relationship, and even they eventually had to make note of them—the awkwardness of inventing false errands to bring them together, the consciousness that the villagers had begun to notice and to talk about them.

Finally, Petiot proposed that Louise move in with him as his housekeeper, for now he had none, his old Violette having found the larger house and the stairs too much for her aging bones. There was never any talk or any thought of marriage on Petiot's part. He merely could not live without Louise in his bed. This was in 1924, by which time Petiot's practice had broadened to encompass as much as he could handle, which brought him an income that, had he been less parsimonious, would have enabled him to live as well as almost any man in the valley. There was one aspect of his practice that brought him inordinate fees and which eventually served to stir a quarrel with Louise—that was his performing abortions throughout the neighborhood. Petiot himself had no compunction at all about offering this service. He felt it was an act of kindness, rather than a crime, and the fat fees provided him a deep satisfaction. He maintained that the population explosion would prove the world's greatest problem, that birth control was sound and would prove, in the future, absolutely necessary, and that even the Church would have to withdraw from its position. Petiot claimed that where adults, whether married or not, did not want to bring a child into the world, it was cruel and unreasonable to force it to be born.

But Louise, who was a devout Catholic, was scandalized to learn of this sub rosa aspect of her lover's profession. She became uneasy, too, at their own use of contraceptives, which made their sinning, she felt, doubly sinful. These irritations served to ignite a number of petty quarrels between them and to add to the basic resentment Petiot must long have harbored that any human being could exert such a hold on him.

Louise was by nature open-handed, and she had no sympathy with her lover's stinginess or his habit of filling the house with "bargains"—trash he had picked up for a few sous at some of the country auctions. She also fretted over his persistent petty thefts when they went shopping, or his deliberately giving the wrong change to a patient who was paying a fee. She tried to make him dress more neatly and keep from spilling gravy and juice on his clothing, and she lost her temper sometimes when he would not give her money enough to manage the household and would try to avoid paying her her housekeeper's salary. Petiot, for his part, found her cooking less expert than that of his loyal old Violette and frequently said so. He complained when he found she was sending money to her family or salting it away somewhere out of his reach. He later admitted that no man likes to feel that he is exclusively possessed by one woman.

No longer did they hasten into bed with each other. Petty estrangements might last for days and Petiot began to look elsewhere for sexual satisfaction. Louise correctly guessed that it was Germaine, one of his patients. Then Louise became pregnant—on purpose, Petiot insisted, to force him into marriage. He urged an abortion but she would not agree. Then, as she temporized and resisted, she made the mistake of threatening to expose his secret life—his abortions, his thefts, his occasional ignoring of regulations governing the sale of narcotics and such matters. Once she took this tack, Petiot began to think of ridding himself of her. He first tried to reason with her, offering her money to go to Paris or Auxerre and begin a new life, but she grew sullen and began to quarrel with him openly, even in public. After that, he began to plan how to kill her without being discovered. After all, there was no Scotland Yard or Institut Médico-Légal to contend with, only the local gendarmerie.

His devoted interest in crime stories of all sorts had given Petiot an intimate acquaintance with the case of Dr. Harvey Crippen, that poor affection-starved physician whose life both in bed and out of it had become a private hell through his marriage to Kunigunde Mackamotzki, alias Cora Turner, a music-hall girl of no talent and a nymphomaniac. A frail, little man, past his middle years, Dr. Crippen was in love with his secretary, Ethel LeNeve, with whom he found all the sex satisfaction he needed. His wife, meanwhile, besides nearly bankrupting him and flaunting her extramarital affairs, pressed him to gratify her own sexual desire— and this was beyond him. He sought, therefore, to dampen his wife's desires through the use of hyoscine, which, he had learned from his own experiences in lunatic asylums in the United States and England, was often given to nymphomaniacs as a sex depressant. Unhappily, poor Harvey Crippen had forgotten the proper dosage since for many years he had been in the drug field rather than in the practice of medicine and he gave Mrs. Crippen five full grains in a cup of coffee—enough to discourage all her desires forever. Panic-stricken, the doctor had then decapitated and eviscerated the body, cut it into pieces, burned parts of it, and buried the rest in quicklime under the cellar of his home and disposed of the head. He explained then that his wife had gone away to California. (Dr. Crippen, although an American born in Michigan, had long made his home in England.)

Dr. Crippen then married his secretary and moved her into his house. The doctor, however, made the mistake of trying to turn some of his wife's jewelry into cash. And his new wife wore some of the jewelry in public where friends of the previous Mrs. Crippen recognized it and grew suspicious. Dr. Crippen still staved off investigation for a time by "confessing" to Scotland Yard that his former wife had really run off with another man and he had lied to avoid a scandal. But they, he and his new wife, decided to take off secretly for Canada. They were discovered, and, suspicious of this panic-like flight, the police were on the trail once more. This time, the police dug into the floor of the cellar of the old home and recovered a pajama top and a piece of flesh that had not been consumed—a section of abdomen that carried an appendectomy scar. Despite all his care, that scar, recognized by the surgeon who performed the operation, made the body identifiable and brought about the doctor's conviction and execution. (James Hilton wrote a fictionalized version of this case entitled *We Are Not Alone* that had great success as both a book and movie.) From this it may be assumed that Petiot learned two things—to take extreme care that no scars or other identifying marks be left on a body, and to remember that if a woman goes away to stay, she is expected to take her jewelry and that any jewelry may well tell tales.

Louisette had no jewelry to worry about. She had, as a matter of fact, nothing about her that would be identifiable except her lovely face and Petiot already knew what to do about that from his study of the Landru case, particularly the testimony of Dr. Paul, who had conducted the gruesome experiment with the burning of human heads. "It takes about one hour and ten minutes," Dr. Paul had said, "to burn to ashes the largest and toughest head in the world." And yet, Dr. Petiot noted, a police expert had been able to produce a small box of ashes taken from the garden of Landru's house and Dr. Paul had been able to testify that the charred ashes represented the residue of at least three human skulls. For a certainty, one must be careful indeed.

With this resolve taken, Petiot became patient and sympathetic toward Louise. Anyone who had seen them together at this point might have remarked on his solicitude, and his gentle efforts to woo her into better temper. But Petiot did not long postpone taking action. There came a night very soon when, for some minor complaint or other, he was able to "prescribe" for Louise a drug to be given by hypodermic. Petiot had already learned that poison was not necessary, that an air bubble injected into a vein would stop a human heart as if an embolism had struck it—leaving no trace beyond the tiny puncture in the arm. He gave Louise the injection and, within hours, she lay dead in his arms.

He felt no immediate remorse at all. He had spent much time in planning the disposal of the body and he had to move swiftly. He took her body to the bathroom, undressed it, laid it in the tub, and then carefully eviscerated it. Getting rid of the organs and intestines he knew would slow the development of offensive odors. The blood was washed quickly away in the tub before it could clot. The internal organs and contents of the rib cage Petiot carried to the kitchen stove (this was in the 1920s when most kitchen stoves still burned wood and coal) and burned them to ashes. He removed the head and put it in a canvas bag, which he tucked away temporarily in the cellar.

In preparing for this deed, Petiot had learned that Louise's fingerprints were not on file anywhere so there was no need to remove her hands or scrape off the ends of her thumbs and fingers. He had long before possessed himself of a large wicker trunk and in this he packed the headless body. He tied rope around the trunk to hold the lid securely, then, about 3 A.M., when only a doctor on an emergency call could be expected to be driving about the countryside, he took the trunk to his car and carried it sixty-two miles away to the outskirts of Dijon. In a field on an abandoned farm, in the pitch black, he unloaded the trunk and left it. Louise's clothing and her few personal belongings he had already committed to the stove.

The very next night, after he had completed all his calls, he methodically burned the head in the stove, using gasoline to speed the work. It did take over an hour to reduce it all to ashes. Petiot was determined, however, that there would be no little box full of residue to be identified. As soon as the ash or cinders were cool enough to handle, he shoveled them carefully into a small pot which he carried in his car to the cemetery just outside the south gate (Porte Joigny) of the town. Patiently, a handful at a time, he scattered the ashes on the ground and in the grass around the tombstones, to be rained and trodden on and lost.

Once Louisette was disposed of, Petiot was assailed by grief— very real grief that brought tears. When he met his friend Nezondet in the street a few days afterward, he did not have to make any pretense of his sorrow as he took hold of René's hands and exclaimed, "She is gone!" The moisture in his eyes was real. Nezondet, however, was astonished for, apparently, all the doctor meant was that Louise had abandoned him. Petiot told the village that there had been a disagreement and the girl had moved away. The local police questioned him in a perfunctory manner, but there was no one to pursue any inquiries.

The 1926 files on the disappearance of Louisette Delaveau at Villeneuve and the finding of a headless corpse in a wicker trunk in the records of the Dijon police disappeared before the end of the war. Petiot, as medical examiner and mayor of Villeneuve, could have filched his town's records, but only the German Occupational authorities or its agencies such as the Paris Abwehr could have removed the Dijon records. The one man who seemed to have had a faint suspicion of what had become of the girl was old Frascot in whose bistro she and Petiot had their first rendezvous. Or possibly the sly digs and sarcastic comments he made were just a form of crude country humor.

For a long time, the anti-bourgeois, the Socialists, the Communists, and the unions had talked to Petiot about becoming a candidate for office on their ticket, so, with more time on his hands, he decided to go into politics. He liked to pretend that his concern for the lot of the working people of the village and the down-on-their-luck was pure cynicism, just a means of winning public office, but as his understanding of schizophrenia, which earned him such high grades during his internship, seemed to spring from his having shared that lot, so he must have had some natural sympathy for the dispossessed and the poor. Whatever the reason, he seemed to speak their language naturally as he joined the discus-

sions at Frascot's tavern or at the markets. He quickly picked up
the catch phrases of communism and helped articulate the desires
of all who looked for a better lot in life.

His practice took him right into the homes of the people whose
votes he needed. He could see with his own eyes what they lacked
and could hear their complaints. He assured them all that were he
elected, the rich would have to let go of some of their wealth to
provide help to the old and the sick, to build better schools, play-
grounds, and, above all, a modern sewer system so that the village
would not have to consume its own filth. The incidence of typhoid in the village was a scandal and, of course, it was the laborers and the poor who suffered most. Of course what made his
tirades effective was that they were true.

To a few intimates, mainly his brother and René Nezondet, Petiot admitted that he did not believe in any political party or any
government or any religion of man or any institution of man. "It
is dog eat dog, and to hell with the hindmost. The Communist
Party appeals to me for it is a new party based on the have-nots
who believe they should have and is therefore overwhelming in
desire and numbers, although just as unsound as any other form
of dictatorship. It won't actually work, for it removes incentive
and allegedly divides everything equally, no matter what share
each person may deserve. It was the first form of government in
the days of the caveman and again in the early communes of
farmers, only there, if a farmer did not work properly, he would be
thrown out of this early form of co-operative agriculture. When
drones who will not work are given money for nothing, they will
soon want more and threaten to bite the hand that feeds them.
The only form of support is, in a way, sometimes part of the
Communist system, namely, it will distribute or contribute work,
and jobs, never doles. What chance would I have to be elected
anything except by joining the Communist Party or being supported by the Communists.

"To prove my point," Petiot added, "socialism and communism
both lead to dictatorship. Let's take Mussolini, Hitler, and Stalin.
All three were originally Socialists, leftists, and extreme liberals
who used this to obtain power. Once power was attained, absolute
dictatorship followed. The only trouble with capitalism and democracy is that it has left too few too long in command, and, also,

softness has crept in. You don't see college students or demonstrators rioting for any principles, only against everything. I might as well use this to attain power myself by promising the people what they think they haven't got and can get."

Dr. Petiot's "program" had a strong and immediate appeal in the village. This was a time when many of the small towns in France were ripe for Socialist or even Communist slogans, for the rich and powerful had become set in their ways and the country was outgrowing many of its old-fashioned systems. Not only was medicine in the countryside often behind the times, but homes lacked the twentieth-century comforts and schools were bursting their seams. Therefore, the radical talk that Dr. Petiot used so glibly and naturally fell on eager and sympathetic ears.

In 1927 Petiot was elected to the *Conseil Municipal* on his very first try and he was then appointed deputy mayor. The mayor at this time was still Paul Mayaud, the pharmacist who had once refused to fill one of Petiot's prescriptions. In the campaign, Petiot had amazed his followers by his ability to do without sleep. He could work a full day in his office or calling on his patients, then, without a minute's sleep, take to the campaign trail, talking to small groups, meeting with his supporters, calling on voters in their homes. For several days on end he did not sleep at all. A few of his patients—naturally some of the wealthiest—turned against Petiot at this time because of his espousal of the radical cause, but the plain people of the village began to worship him. He was such a fighter! He would stay up all night to defeat the bourgeois and the big landholders and their hired hands. What a love for the people he must have! And he never charged a poor man a dime for his services! (It is true that Petiot, at this point in his career, seldom sent a bill to any of the needy villagers he treated. He did, however, once he was in office, put their names on the welfare rolls and billed the government for his services to them and, in many cases, collected from them also in services, groceries, meat, fruit, etc.)

Soon after Petiot took office, Paul Mayaud died and Petiot found himself mayor. He was also chosen medical examiner, or coroner, of the village so that he found himself in a position to "investigate" any mysterious deaths and to certify as to cause of death. Petiot gloried in his power. He was a strong mayor and used his office not only to advance his own fortunes but also to push through changes he felt the town required. (The removal of the cemetery cross was one of these.)

One of the first steps Petiot took after he got elected was to get married. He chose a girl not in a burst of passion this time, but in a level-headed and deliberate manner. She was a beautiful girl, petite, well-formed, and seven years younger than Petiot. He loved her, without question, but he also looked into her background and found at least that she was ostensibly the daughter of a substantial businessman from Seignelay, a town in the Yonne valley, fifteen miles southwest of Villeneuve.

The girl was Georgette Lablais and her father was Nestor Lablais, a butcher and the keeper of a prosperous hotel and tavern. Georgette was his only child. (Petiot never knew he married the illegitimate daughter of a former pullman porter and a young domestic worker, the girl whom Lablais later married.) The prospective father-in-law thought well of his son-in-law to be. He was already a success in a fine profession and seemed to have a gift for politics. Why, the man might even become a member of the Chamber of Deputies! Like Dr. Clemenceau, who once practiced medicine in New York City, he might become Premier of France. He lived in a splendid house, was mayor of his town, and was noted for his thrift.

With the added responsibility of a wife, Petiot immediately applied for a larger pension as a wounded veteran of World War I, since the 50 per cent disability pay he received was for his head. Although his foot did not bother him much, he felt he should be compensated for this wound also. Much to his disappointment, his claim was disallowed, although his finances and those of his family never sagged.

Georgette shared Petiot's regard for money and was every bit as stingy and acquisitive as he was so there would be no falling out on that score. She was well schooled in the French virtues and was not likely to pry into her husband's affairs so long as he kept the purse well filled. They were a perfect match—as their devotion to each other throughout all Petiot's troubles would demonstrate. They were married, as all proper French country couples should be, at a high mass in the Catholic Church, with all the men in cutaway and top hat and the bride in veil and flowing gown. Once more Dr. Petiot was an unwilling subject of the Catholic Church and had to bow and kneel to God. The marriage took place on June 4, 1927. In April 1928, a son was born. While Petiot had often invited his younger brother to visit him, and had developed a real devotion to him, there had never been anything in his life like this. A son! His son, Gerhardt, would want for nothing all his life, Petiot vowed. He would attend the finest schools! He would become a famous doctor. Petiot never flagged in his devotion to his son nor was the boy ever tainted in any way by Petiot's own deviations. He was brought up by parents who loved him in a family that, as far as the boy could see, led a normal, staid, and honorable life. Strangely enough, supported by his father, he became a Catholic. Perhaps Dr. Petiot was especially concerned for his son when he did not have him live with his father and mother in Paris during the Occupation. It was no wonder that the boy stood weeping openly to see his mother, that day in Auxerre, carried off by the police.

The police in Villeneuve, however, were loyal to their mayor— all, that is, but one, who seemed almost too smart and too intuitive to be a small-town gendarme. That was Brigadier Gouraud, who became a particular enemy of Petiot. The man, said Petiot, had the nose of a bloodhound and he felt certain he could read in Gouraud's eyes a deep suspicion of his, Petiot's, motives. But for a time at least, Petiot was free of public suspicion. He found he enjoyed political power and that he had a gift for public speaking, particularly for the sort of extemporaneous comment that could swing a whole audience to his side. His father-in-law was enraptured by Petiot's success in politics. The old man had bought a restaurant near the Chamber of Deputies where he knew he could sow seeds that would sprout into a strong influence for his son-in-law in the right places. He even persuaded one deputy to mention Petiot in a speech as "the Clemenceau of Villeneuve."

Petiot could see himself as Clemenceau—the "Tiger" doctor-turned-statesman. He found a deep satisfaction in winning a crowd to his side, in bathing in the applause. At one political meeting his enemies talked too much of his "crimes"—not just his theft of electricity and gasoline and his enrolling his patients for welfare payments, but his charging his own tires to the town and in other ways fattening his own purse at the public's expense. Petiot's wife preserved the clipping that told what happened after that:

"When Dr. Petiot's turn to speak arrived, he rose and slowly advanced toward the podium amid a profound silence. He turned and, with his right hand over his heart, said in majestic but sincere tones: 'Citizens of Villeneuve-sur-Yonne, I admit to having committed a crime . . . a very great crime! That of having loved too well the people!' A moment passes, then a wave of applause breaks the silence and the assembly rises, cheering. Dr. Petiot . . . is swept into office by a landslide."

This was about the level of his electioneering but, in that less sophisticated day, on that day, in this tight little hamlet, it served as well as any utterance by Demosthenes. Petiot *had* helped the people. He had almost wiped out typhoid fever with his modern sewer system, on which, it must be granted, he managed to collect a pocketful of graft. Whether he got any public money for his work or not, he had attended the poor when they were sick and had even cured them. Had he himself been a less tortured being, he could have gone on to greater heights in politics and have lived in legend in Villeneuve as long as the town stood there.

But Petiot would continue to steal while his wife took back the ashtrays and silver pieces he "borrowed" from the homes of friends.

Once, to be exact on October 28, 1923, in the fever of enjoying his own speeches—a disease familiar to politicians, Petiot had laughed at his "disability" and had "confided" to a crowd of his constituents that he had just pretended to be crazy to assure himself of a pension. One of his enemies (of which he now had a number), a certain M. Candy, saw to it that this remark was duly reported to the Minister of War. If anything, the authorities decided, the remark just seemed to prove the board's findings. Petiot had other enemies—in fact, a whole collection of them, as political feelings became polarized. There was, besides Brigadier Gouraud, a M. Guttin (a Fascist type, said Petiot) who was among the first to discover that when Petiot treated the poor for nothing, he was really listing their names on a medical aid program and collecting government cash for work he pretended was charity. Guttin, a wealthy industrialist, tried to block Petiot's advancement and expose his collection of graft. But neither he, nor anyone else in Villeneuve, except possibly old Frascot and Brigadier Gouraud, owned an inkling of how black was Petiot's real guilt.

Petiot's thefts became bolder as his position became more secure. In 1929, while visiting in his capacity as medical examiner the residence of a man who had just died, Petiot, left alone with the body, looked into the drawers of the desk and bureau in the room and found some truly valuable jewels as well as cash. Suspicion brushed him this time for he was one of the few who had been in the house before the valuables disappeared. But there was no accusation because no one had proof even of the existence of the jewels and cash that were taken. A quiet investigation led quickly to nowhere. Petiot, in his own good time, broke the jewels out of their mountings, threw the mountings in the Yonne, and "invested" his return, as he had begun to do with most of his savings now, with his father-in-law, who used them to buy real estate or to finance his various businesses. Petiot, therefore, grew no richer as far as the village knew. And no one questioned his prosperous father-in-law's acquisition of new real estate and new activities.

Having free access to the records in the city hall, Petiot lifted out some of the deeds to choice pieces of real estate in the town. The clerk who had charge of the records was suspected, but nothing was proven. Petiot, in confessing his tampering with deeds years later in his autobiographical notes, said he burned the papers. But there was one curious transfer of real estate that, so far, has never been properly explained. The house that Petiot lived in at 56 rue Carnot had been that of Brigadier General Pierre Charles Robillard. The general, retired from the regular army, had willed the property to the town of Villeneuve with the proviso that the usufruct should accrue, during her lifetime, to his widow, a lady with the grand name of Mathilde Françoise Marguerite Gabrielle Lucie Lechene, who died in 1922, about a year after Petiot had come to Villeneuve. In a lawsuit, settled in 1923, Petiot secured title to the house on payment of a token sum. It is not clear as all the records were strangely destroyed while Petiot was mayor. How this was accomplished, no one knows. Had the old lady been his patient and had he signed her death certificate? (M. Guttin, years later, claimed that Mme. Robillard was Petiot's first murder victim.) Was the theft of property records from the town hall intended to cover up some hocus-pocus connected with this transfer? These questions were never answered and now can never be answered. The house, title to which had been renounced by Petiot's widow, perhaps to avoid any legal seizure by a criminal court, was sold for 800,000 francs in 1951 by Gerhardt Petiot of Rio de Janiero.

Petiot's domestic life, after the birth of his son, became tranquil, even dull. Georgette was an even-tempered girl, a good cook, and a thrifty housekeeper. For a time she had been an exciting bed partner for Petiot too. But eventually—he being always charged with energy at night and his wife often worn out with the care of the child and the big house—their sex life dwindled to occasional routine encounters. Petiot's eye, therefore, began to wander.

This time, having learned from Louisette the dangers of sudden infatuation, he chose his mistress with as much calculation as he had chosen his wife, although meeting her was pure accident. She was the manager of a dairy co-operative in the Faubourg St. Nicolas, just north of the Sens gate to Villeneuve. And, by a strange coincidence, Petiot met her through old Frascot. The old man had asked the doctor to lunch with him and look at his constantly ailing throat (his uvula was too long, Petiot said, and he was too old to be operated on). When Petiot arrived, he found an attractive woman in her forties already there. This was Mme. Debauve. Of course Petiot had known of her existence, but she had been just a businesswoman to him. Now, for the first time, he noticed that she had a very attractive figure—even voluptuous—with large firm breasts and a narrow waist. The three of them lunched together and Petiot was delighted with the lady's wit. He himself had a quick enough tongue, but she was a match for him, and they laughed frequently together. Mme. Debauve quite obviously was attracted to the doctor, who was probably the best-read man in the town and whose strange fascination was then, when he was in his thirties, at its height. She earnestly invited him to visit her at the dairy. "But come in the evening," she urged him, "after eight o'clock, for until then I am busy."

The advantages of this arrangement were immediately obvious to Petiot. No one could question his making calls at any hour, day or night. And here was no twentyish troll looking for a man she could marry or a rich sponsor whose bank account she could drain. This was a woman of substance and brains, not one who was going to turn up pregnant, nor a child who would have to be taught how to behave in bed. Within a week, Petiot, having made an evening call in a nearby village, stopped in at the dairy and found a sincere welcome. Mme. Debauve talked to him like a crony and turned the subject quickly to sex. She told him that the local priest had warned her once about thinking too much of the joys of bed.

"Be careful, my pretty," the priest had warned her. "Remember a fire burns fastest in an old chimney!"

Petiot undertook to set the fire going and he found the lady a delightful sex partner, one who knew how to add to the excitement of their encounter by delays and teasings and interruptions. From that time on, the doctor's car was often seen in the dairy dooryard of an evening. Not that there were many nearby to notice and the mayor was discreet. But whenever he found himself within decent distance of Mme. Debauve's after eight o'clock, he would make a visit—to take a drink or even stay for dinner—but always to go to bed. She was at an age when she was grateful for the attentions of a vigorous young man and she treated the doctor with unfailing graciousness. He came to look forward to these evenings more than he did to the return to his own fireside. He did not, however, really neglect Georgette, and his wife never had occasion to reproach him. He was, it is true, often late for dinner, and sometimes had to take his dinner on the road. But this is exactly what one had to look for when one married a doctor.

The only mild irritant in Petiot's blissful arrangement with the dairy lady was that old Frascot knew all about it. For some reason or other, Frascot often bicycled out to the farm of an evening and twice he came when Petiot and Mme. Debauve were together, obviously enjoying each other's company. Petiot and the lady agreed, however, that Frascot was not a gossip. The keeper of a bistro could not afford to be. Still, Petiot did not like people to own any sort of ascendancy over him.

The weight of his office and the expense of campaigning for re-election began to tell on Petiot after a time, particularly as his opposition, led chiefly by Guttin, had become virulent. Guttin had actually caught Petiot red-handed in funneling public moneys into his own pocket, in making deals with contractors and suppliers that would fatten Petiot's purse, and in charging all sorts of personal expenses, even automobile tires, to the town. Moved by righteous indignation, Guttin had dedicated himself to bringing Petiot down. Petiot's health began to yield to the strain. He was more excitable and nervous than usual—and he had never been a phlegmatic man. He rubbed his hands together, in his characteristic gesture, a hundred times a day and often found himself trembling for no reason. Although his income, whether it was from legal or illegal sources, remained good, he painfully begrudged the cash he must lay out to win re-election. Money was constantly on his mind so when Mme. Debauve, during one of his visits, spoke for the first time of money, Petiot's heartbeat began to accelerate.

The good lady had never been one to let talk of business interfere with their dalliance. But this night she apparently had an unusually large sum of money on hand and it made her uneasy. When Mme. Debauve began to speak of the extra cash she had had to lock into her strongbox, Petiot wanted to know how much it was.

"Two hundred and eighty thousand francs," she told him. A quarter of a million francs! Petiot had never dreamed that money in this amount passed through her hands. Why this was more than he had ever seen in one lump before. (It was worth at that time about $15,000.) But wasn't it dangerous to keep such a sum in this isolated place with no one to hear her if she were attacked by robbers? The lady laughed easily. Why, that was nothing. Counting her own money and the money already on hand that belonged to the co-op, she probably had that much money again locked in the safe.

Petiot, already on the way to getting undressed, lost interest in sex. His heart seemed to hammer to get out of his chest.

"Look," he said excitedly, "why don't we stage a fake robbery? Let me tie you up and take all the co-op money. Hide your own money somewhere else. Then when the milkers and helpers come in the morning, they will find you and you can tell the gendarmes that strangers held you up and made you open the safe, took the money, bound you, and took off in a car."

Mme. Debauve laughed again, perhaps laying some of this scheme to the action of the brandy they had drunk. When Petiot persisted, she simply brushed him off. It would be a foolish stunt. Too obvious. It had been done so many times. And besides, she would certainly deserve half of the proceeds. She went about the job of putting the cash away and Petiot stood by her. When he saw the fat bundle of bills already in the strongbox—over half a million francs altogether—he began to tremble. She started to close the strongbox but he quickly pushed her aside, instinctively reaching for the money. This was evidently a matter that the lady wanted no nonsense about. Petiot's sudden nudge made her drop the money and she lost her temper.

Quick as a flash, she reached over and seized a hammer that happened to be at hand and tried to strike him with it. He took the hammer away from her and automatically beat back at her. In whatever manner it happened, he suddenly found himself pounding the hammer into her skull. She fell heavily to the floor, limp as a feed sack. He bent down and struck her several times more, viciously, until all movement ceased. A strange noise rose from her throat, half groan, half gurgle. Then there was no breathing.

Petiot made note of the fact that there was surprisingly little blood, but there was no question that her skull had been fractured in several places. He checked her pulse and found no beat. Then he methodically lifted all the money out of the strongbox, retrieved what she had dropped on the floor, and put all of it on a nearby table. He was uplifted now, almost outside himself, and his brain worked quickly and coolly. The whole scene seemed to be taking place at a distance, while he stood by somewhere, delightedly watching. He took some of the money off the table, returned it to the strongbox, and closed it. He had divided the money so that there was still a hundred thousand francs left. Now the colors in the room began to run together until the scene became all gray. He seemed to be walking on air. He grew dizzy and thought he would fall. Was he going to have an epileptic fit—a real one this time?

But no. He steadied himself and gradually the room returned to normal. There was much to think about. Fortunately for him, no blood had splattered on either his hands or clothes. But there was the hammer to be got rid of. And of course the money. Mme.

Debauve had a small briefcase in which she carried the money to
the bank and Petiot used that to pack it in. There was a newspaper on the table—just right to wrap up the hammer. He took
these two articles to the car. Then he came back and wiped the
strongbox free of fingerprints, leaving it locked. He returned the
key to its proper place in a drawer, and wiped all the furniture
nearby . . . still, there were bound to be traces. The body itself,
for one thing.

Landru's solution had always been fire. Petiot appraised the pos-
sibilities. There was a good wind blowing—it was March—and the
farm was isolated. A fire would get a good start before even the
rural fire department could gather itself together and get out
there. However, he must make sure the blaze looked natural. It
would not do to use too much gasoline. He started the blaze
slowly and stayed long enough to make sure it had a good hold.
Then he drove away, without a glance backward.

At home he burned the newspaper and the briefcase in his own
furnace. He counted the cash. It came to 412,000 francs exactly.
He locked this away in his own attic strongbox. He had thrown
the hammer away after wiping it free of fingerprints.

He had trouble getting to sleep for he was still in a high state of
excitement and the cognac seemed to keep his heart pounding for
hours. So, in the morning, he lay in bed late. He had not even
finished dressing when the telephone rang. It was city hall.

"Did the mayor know that the co-op dairy had burned to the
ground in the night?"

"That Mme. Debauve could not be found . . . ?"

"Was the mayor going first to the scene of the fire, or would he
come to Town Hall to sign some papers . . . ?"

"Did the mayor know . . . ?"

"Yes, yes. He had much to do this morning," Petiot answered.
"A dozen calls on his line. He could not say just when . . ."

Petiot, over coffee and a croissant, fretted over the possibility
that he had been seen at the dairy last night. Well, he had not
been there even as long as usual. There had been no lovemaking.
There had been a professional call first—then only a comparatively
short stay at the dairy before coming home. It would not be difficult to account for the time. He decided it would be best to find
out first just how much the police and firemen had learned. He

was, after all, the medical examiner, and it would be his duty to sign the death certificate. He got into his car and drove straight to the dairy.

The main house had been almost destroyed, but not completely. A farmer, seeing the red glow in the sky, had telephoned the fire department. The body of Mme. Debauve had not, after all, been consumed by the flames. The firemen and policemen had first assumed she had been overcome by smoke and had perished in the fire, but Brigadier Gouraud, with his bloodhound nose, was on the job. He beckoned the mayor over to view the skull of the badly burned body. There were marks on it, the brigadier pointed out, that clearly indicated the woman had been beaten with a blunt weapon, probably a hammer, and her skull fractured. Petiot, exhibiting surprise, agreed that the woman had probably been murdered. Then a chill touched his heart when he saw Frascot there, with his damned bicycle. Frascot found an opportunity to draw Petiot aside and tell him he knew Petiot had been visiting Mme. Debauve the night before. There was even a hint of threat in his sly remarks.

Eventually, Petiot signed a death certificate, after conducting an inquiry. Frascot testified at the hearing that he had seen Petiot near the dairy on the evening of March 11, the date of the fire. Yes, the mayor admitted, he had indeed called on the lady to treat her for a minor ailment and he was probably the last person to see her alive. The police testified that Mme. Debauve had apparently been murdered by repeated blows on the head and that the criminal had apparently set the fire to cover up his deed, but there was money in the safe. . . .

Nothing came of it all, finally, and Petiot was able to breathe more easily, except that he now kept a wary eye on old Frascot. He also resolved never again to act on impulse, but to work out any further liquidations in detail so as to leave nothing that might incriminate him. The killing of Louisette, he told himself, had been perfectly planned and executed.

Now he settled back into his old routine—the workers' doctor, the people's mayor, the champion of the exploited and the poor. He spent his free evenings with his books or playing chess and checkers with the villagers. He actually became checker champion of Villeneuve. However, he arranged through his political connec-

tions to have Brigadier Gouraud transferred as otherwise this policeman made him nervous. As mayor, however, he congratulated
Gouraud on his work and wished him well.

One day his father-in-law, M. Lablais, butcher and restaurant
owner, invited him to attend a dinner of the famous Societé la
Bidoche, where he met the famous Dr. Paul, with neither knowing they would meet again. It was during this dinner that Petiot's
father-in-law sold him on the idea of even further investments in
real estate through him. In France, he pointed out, practically
every real estate transaction is partly over the table for tax and
front purposes and partly under the table with no taxes, cuts, or
takes. Petiot promised to increase his investments through his
father-in-law, especially as he had little to lose, since Lablais' sole
child and heir was Petiot's wife. In addition, the suggestion gave
him an idea—to invest some of his clandestine gains in his father-
in-law's name might be a very safe haven to hide major increases
in his estate . . . and to prevent any possible confiscation based
even on criminal charges.

Shortly after the Bidoche dinner, Dr. Petiot ran into Frascot
again. Frascot seemed to run into the doctor more frequently than
ever. Invariably, there was some cryptic remark with a vague
threat hidden somewhere. And now word began to get back to Petiot that Frascot was talking rather freely in public places, that he
had more than once suggested that were he to tell all he knew
about the Debauve matter . . . well . . . one might see the mayor
arrested. It was to his enemies an excellent beginning of an attempt to unseat the people's champion. Obviously Frascot must
have cast his lot with Guttin . . . that Fascist! They would undoubtedly try to use these foul accusations to defeat Petiot in the
1931 elections.

Petiot was not sure about Frascot. The old man had always
been a friend and a patient. It did not seem likely that he had
joined with Guttin. Perhaps the old man, in need of money, was
laying the groundwork for a bit of blackmail. He might even have
seen the doctor setting the fire. . . . Whatever the truth, Petiot
told himself, he clearly could not allow the old man to live.

Petiot this time took care to make his opening move in front of
witnesses so there would be solid confirmation. He waited until he
next met Frascot in a public place. A week later the two met on

rue Carnot in front of the Hôtel du Dauphin. Petiot took the old man by the arm.

"Come in, my friend. Let's have a drink together."

They went to the hotel bar where everyone knew them both and they joined a whole circle of acquaintances.

"How goes it with your rheumatism?" Petiot asked.

Old Frascot made a face. "Not good at all."

"Ah, well. We cannot have this. There is a new treatment I don't believe you have tried. A new injection treatment. Immediate relief! It will not cure the rheumatism, but it will do away with all pain. A brand-new formula. I never tried it on you?"

"No," said Frascot, all unsuspecting. "This I have never had."

"Well, then," said Petiot, "we must fix you up at once. Finish your drink and come down to the office."

At the office, Petiot went through all the standard routine. He had old Frascot remove his coat and roll up his shirt sleeve. He brought out the hypodermic, after going through the motions of filling it with the "new" medicine. He found the vein. He dabbed alcohol on a spot on the skin. Then he carefully injected the fatal air bubble, knowing that within three hours the old man would fall dead. As it worked out, Frascot had time to get back to his own place on the rue du Pont before the embolus struck his heart and he went into violent convulsions before it stopped beating. He was found dead on the floor.

This time there was not even a hint of suspicion, for the death seemed neither untimely nor violent. Petiot examined the body and solemnly set down the cause of death as "by accident . . . from heart shock or some unknown side effect resulting from a hypodermic injection." And the old man went to his grave without a voice being raised against his murderer.

Even the elimination of Frascot could not ensure Petiot's reelection. The opposition was determined and ruthless. The prefect of police, probably paid by the owners of the large properties in Villeneuve who were now united against Petiot, set the gendarmes to work tearing down all the posters that called for Petiot's election. But the good doctor was not to be outdone. His turn came when a public debate was to be staged between the mayor and the opposition candidate. Petiot, with uncharacteristic generosity, allowed the opponent to speak last. The poor man did not have Pe-

tiot's command of the language or his quickness of wit and he had
to read his speech from the papers he carried.

Petiot talked with his customary nervous vigor, recounting all
his accomplishments, his generosity in treating the poor, his devotion to the workers, his opposition to the bourgeoisie, his insistence that the great wealth of the town should be shared more
equitably. He received a thunderous reception. Then he left the
platform to his enemies, but he did not take a seat in the audience. Instead he went downstairs to the electric control panel and
calmly inserted a copper rod that blew out all the fuses and put
the entire building in darkness. The speaker was suddenly speechless, for he could not read his words. The audience sat stunned
and embarrassed. The janitor scurried about looking for fuses, for
candles, anything. A candle was lit at the podium. The speaker
bent close over his papers, adjusting his eyeglasses. He could
hardly read a word. The candle was brought closer. Slowly and
haltingly, like a first grader at his primer, the man began to deci-
pher his speech but, in the darkness, his audience was quietly tip-
toeing away. That "debate" seemed to settle matters together
with some help from Thorez in Paris, who got all the local Communists to support Petiot. Petiot was returned to office with a
huge plurality.

M. Guttin was a very discouraged and violent man when he
found out Dr. Petiot had once more defeated all his plans to
block the latter's re-election, and that as mayor, Petiot had successfully obtained the transfer of Gouraud from the gendarmerie
at Villeneuve as persona non grata to the mayor and the town.
Several other friends of Guttin felt Dr. Petiot's reprisal moves.
Later, both in Villeneuve and in Paris, Petiot, remembering his
power struggle, frequently told a funny but true story about a
nearby commune he frequently visited.

"There the local baker ran for mayor on the Communist ticket
with his speeches and his platform in complete support of the
Marxist state with no private business. After being overwhelm-
ingly elected, one of his opponents, a major property owner, visited the new mayor at his bakery to congratulate him. While
there, he said, 'Well, Étienne, now that you are such an avid
Marxist and you were elected on a Communist ticket, I understand you are going to distribute free bread, croissants, and

brioches to the poor every morning in the proper tradition.' 'Oh, no,' quickly snapped the baker-mayor. 'I only became a Communist to get elected mayor—but, as a baker, I am a capitalist!' "

It was during Dr. Petiot's second elected term that the case of the stolen gasoline developed. As doctor, medical examiner, and mayor of the town and as a member of the Department Council, Dr. Petiot surely needed gasoline. The cheapest method of supply was to order tanks or containers sent by rail and truck, but the stationmaster was an enemy of Petiot's. So he delayed and delayed while six containers intended for Dr. Petiot waited at the station. Finally, Dr. Petiot borrowed a truck, went to the station at night, loaded the containers on the truck, and took them to his garage. The next day the stationmaster was wild and came to collect for the gasoline with the bills and invoices. Dr. Petiot refused to pay him since he had no receipts for delivery. The stationmaster then went to the police with alleged witnesses and charged Dr. Petiot with stealing the gasoline from the station, claiming also that the six containers were for someone else. While Petiot as mayor could not be arrested, charges were pressed. A lawyer for Petiot, together with the prosecutor, produced a Paris psychiatrist, Dr. Heuyer, who testified that Dr. Petiot was not mentally responsible for his action and the case was dismissed. Of course, Petiot did not fail to laugh at his opponents. Dr. Heuyer, fourteen years later, was to testify that Petiot was sane at a trial where he was accused of twenty-seven murders.

But before long, Dr. Petiot's enemies had more solid charges to lay against him. Petiot's incurable greed had led him to accept kickbacks over the years from contractors and suppliers. The arrangements became so routine that a knowledge of them became widespread and the police began an investigation. In 1933, Petiot had to use his official muscle as chief magistrate of the town to shut off the inquiry.

Then came the business of the stolen electricity—a "frame-up" Petiot called it, but the facts could not be denied. The assistant chief of police was assigned to investigate the matter and he quizzed Petiot for an hour. The doctor explained glibly and sincerely that the "crime" was an invention of his enemies. Said the assistant chief afterward:

"At the end of one hour I was convinced of his complete innocence. Two days later, I had absolute proof of his guilt."

Now, for the first time in his career, a criminal charge stuck to Petiot. He was tried at Joigny in early 1934, found guilty, and sentenced to fifteen days in prison, with a 200-franc fine. On appeal, the prison term was lifted and the fine reduced by half, but the guilty finding stood. Petiot later voiced regret that he ran such a risk for such a petty advantage—really just getting even with the electric company. The money he saved could have been counted in a few francs.

With Petiot's conviction, some of his popular support began to melt. Heretofore, one had always been able to persuade one's self that all these whisperings and accusations were the work of the bourgeoisie and their mouthpieces—lies and frame-ups and canards. The "dump Petiot" movement grew stronger each week. Signs appeared that read "Drain Petiot out in his graft-built sewers." There were demands that he resign from the Department Council or face legal ouster. Finally, on the basis of his conviction, his mayor's warrant was revoked. He was removed from the Department Council by M. Bienvenue-Martin. So ended the career of the first Socialist mayor of Villeneuve, who was also supported by the Communists.

Petiot affected to take it all with resignation and contempt. He noted with satisfaction that his enemies were unable to vote a candidate into his job and had to resort to appointing an administrative commission to replace him. But there is no question that this defeat must have rankled him. Petiot then resolved to move on to Paris, where his really unusual skills would find a wider field and where his already substantial fortune and that of his father-in-law might multiply. This move, however, had been carefully prepared. A large truck at the entrance of 56 rue Carnot and a small truck and Dr. Petiot's car on rue du Grand Four at the garage and rear entrance of 56 rue Carnot signaled the departure of the Petiot family.

There was real mourning in Villeneuve, for there were many in the town who felt they owed their lives to the doctor. There were sturdy schoolchildren whom he had brought into the world. There were needy old people whose pains he had relieved and whose lives he had made easier. There was cleanliness in the town, where once there had been filth and an obsolete sewerage system. And there were political supporters who would remember him always as a valiant fighter for the underdog; a resourceful, witty, and indefatigable campaigner; and a man who knew how to play wonder tricks on his enemies. None could ever believe that he was a mass murderer for his own gain. All, without exception, agreed that he must have been a misguided patriot, believing he was killing for his country and perhaps for its cure—a Communist France.

As one old woman and former patient put it, "He just went plain crazy from the war and France's shame with as many traitors as patriots and with the Communists changing sides, first with the Nazis, then, when the Nazis appeared to have lost the war, against them." Little did she know that all kinds of evidence indicated that Petiot's own diagnosis of himself as a "genius paranoiac" and his disability retirement pension as a victim of dementia praecox proved that he was indeed insane! Little did the old woman also know that while "genius" was a guardian spirit and a household god in the Roman religion, "genius" corresponded to the Greek demon whom Socrates obeyed implicitly, and further that a paranoiac usually has superior intelligence.

CHAPTER IV

Prewar Paris
1933–36

In his notes with respect to his move to Paris, Petiot called attention to the fact that "in 1933 when I started planning my move, Adolf Schickelgruber, better known as Hitler, was named Chancellor of the German Republic by President von Hindenburg, and that in 1934, when I moved to Paris, von Hindenburg died and Hitler became the Fuehrer or dictator of Germany and began mass liquidations and the moves that led to World War II on September 1, 1939; and that in 1933 Joseph Dzhugashvili, better known as and renamed Stalin ('made of steel'), came into absolute power in Russia with mass murders and his famous purge trials; and that Benito Mussolini, by 1934, had gained absolute control of fascist Italy and prepared to attack Ethiopia." In other words, the period 1933–34 was a turning point, according to Petiot, in world history and "also in the lives of Hitler, Stalin, Mussolini, and Petiot—all four paranoiacs." He even added that "Stalin had five arrests and one bank robbery to prove his instability."

However, Petiot did not move to Paris without careful preparation. As soon as the "dump Petiot as mayor" drive in Villeneuve had grown to dangerous proportions, Petiot had begun frequent trips to Paris. This time he was looking for a successful doctor who was ready to retire or move and sell his practice and give up his home and office. He interviewed many, but it took him a long time to find the deal that suited him. Some doctors were in rundown neighborhoods or lived in seedy or cramped apartments. Some simply wanted too much money or hoped to collect a continuing percentage from their former practice. Petiot wanted none of that. He hoped to settle his family into comfortable, if not fashionable, quarters and he wanted no silent partners to skim the cream off his income. He particularly wanted to give nothing away with respect to his expansion of any normal practice to occasional abortions, traffic in narcotics, and macabre cures.

Finally, Petiot found a "Dr. Charles Valéry," a neighborhood doctor whose combination home and office were in the Ninth Arrondissement, called "Opéra," a lively, busy, interesting area that encompassed hotels, restaurants, shops, night clubs, theaters, the largest department stores, banks, bars, and the better brothels. This was both the theatrical and tourist section of Paris. The office and apartment at 66 rue Caumartin was less than six blocks from the grand boulevards and the largest department stores— Galeries Lafayette and Le Printemps—and close to the Casino de Paris, the rue Pigalle, and the Folies-Bergère. Here tourists came from all over the world, but most especially from North and Latin America. Most of the Paris prostitutes operated on these streets. Throughout the area were any number of *maisons de rendezous*, where couples could get a room and a bed with no intention of sleeping and no need to register. And, of course, there were the *maisons de tolérance*, where feminine charms were for sale most of the day and all night.

These "hotels" ran the gamut from a flophouse room, furnished only with a bed, to plush suites with the finest antique furniture, thick and expensive rugs and draperies and modern bathrooms, complete with bidets. In this district not so long before had been the most famous house of assignation in the world, The House of All Nations. Here one could order a girl and a room with decor to match from any nation in the world. Even Sahara belly dancers were available who made love on a bed of loose sand. Here also was a special bed long on exhibit once used by the King of England, grandfather of the late Duke of Windsor, who turned in his crown. "Grandpa," although King of England, liked to visit Paris incognito, but because of his very large stomach had to be helped with a specially constructed bed to enjoy sexual engagements. In this tourist neighborhood when Dr. Petiot moved to it, and to this day, are located many theaters, night clubs, restaurants, and the headquarters of American Express, Cook's Tours, Drake, and other travel agencies from all over the world. It was also the neighborhood of secret intelligence and espionage activities and spies of all nations circulated here as businessmen, tourists, travel agents, or merely—and mostly—as rich playboys. It was indeed a neighborhood that needed a doctor or two—day and night.

Hardly a spot on earth could have been found to contrast more sharply with the *bon bourgeois* provincial atmosphere of Villeneuve-sur-Yonne. The Paris Opéra area is, without doubt, the most sophisticated enclave on earth, where a doctor with ambition and not too aggressive a conscience might find a half dozen new ways to gather in pockets full of francs. Dr. Valéry—or was it Dr. Garnier? (there is some confusion on this in the Paris records)—had made no special effort to build his practice but had merely accepted what came his way.

Ten years later, Petiot took on the identity of a Henri Valéry, born February 20, 1895, at Elbeuf Seine Maritime. He possessed a complete set of authentic identification papers to which he had added or superimposed his picture and fingerprints. As Henri Valéry, he joined the F.F.I. (French Forces of the Interior) after the liberation and became a captain in charge of hunting down collaborators, but with no known connection to any Dr. Charles Valéry. When asked by the police how he obtained the identification papers, he laughed and stated, "Perhaps Valéry may show up someday," but no Valéry ever did. Even in his notes and in his confidential admissions for the author, Petiot would not divulge any information beyond claiming that both Dr. Charles Valéry and Henri Valéry were once living persons. Further than that he again became mysterious, adding, "Perhaps I liquidated them both!" A further investigation revealed that while it was Dr. Garnier whose home and office and clients Petiot took over, a Dr. Valéry from outside Paris often assisted Dr. Garnier. Dr. Charles Valéry was reported by a former neighbor, years later, as having escaped from Occupied Paris to Buenos Aires in early 1942.

The apartment at 66 rue Caumartin was a snug one. It was not, of course, comparable to the beautiful house on rue Carnot in Villeneuve, but it was comfortable and well suited to the Petiots, who had no money to lavish on luxuries but wanted to save money. Office and apartment were on the second-floor front, at the top of a steep narrow staircase that led from a small hallway to the left of the main entrance. The rent was 12,300 francs a year (about $700), plus service costs. Directly across the street—in keeping with the predestination that seemed to follow him—Petiot found the Roman Catholic church of St. Louis d'Antin, built by Brongniart in 1780 as a novitiate.

Petiot's luck held out, for he had no trouble getting his license to practice medicine in Paris with the recording of his medical diploma by the Paris police on July 2, 1934, although in Paris an appeal against his criminal conviction for stealing electricity in Villeneuve in 1933 was turned down. The appeal court upheld the conviction on July 26, 1934. This was Petiot's first actual police conviction.

Petiot found many acquaintances, and acquaintances of acquaintances, already in Paris, and he did not hesitate to cultivate them in order to widen his practice. His old companion Nezondet had a friend named Betrand Millier who managed the Bazar d'Amsterdam—a department store not far from Petiot's office. Petiot saw to it that Millier sent all his employees to 66 rue Caumartin when they were ill. There was a cousin of his wife, Andrée Lablais, who worked as a secretary at N.V. Philips, the Dutch R.C.A., at avenue Montaigne, and a Mr. Girouy, who had been a notary at Villeneuve, who had an insurance office at 11 rue St. Martin, and the Raymond Vallées, cousins of his wife. Mr. Vallée, in the insurance business, was able to help Petiot, not only in finding new patients, but in insuring his properties and fattening his bank account. Petiot, however, was not satisfied with this sort of word-of-mouth promotion. Without any qualms, he again put out an advertising circular that sent chills down the spine of the staid members of the Order of Doctors (the equivalent of the American Medical Association). Petiot made claims so wild that, by themselves, they might have cast further doubt on his sanity. He could, he said, eliminate all the pain of childbirth, sciatica, rheumatism, neuralgia, neuritis, ulcers, and cancer! There was hardly any disease pulmonary, gastric, cardiac, or venereal that he did not claim to be able to alleviate or cure. As for his fees, they would, he said, always match the income of the patient, even the poorest. As for veterans of the World War, he, being a veteran himself, would treat them without charge! The circular wound up with Petiot's address and lucky-sounding telephone number, Pigalle 77-11.

The circulation of this incredible flyer inspired prompt protests. Dr. Raymond Tournay of 63 boulevard des Invalides brought charges of charlatanry against Petiot before the Order of Doctors, and he was supported by a Dr. Millet. But nothing, Petiot gleefully announced, ever came of this. Publicity, he said, could have dangerous repercussions for all doctors. So the matter was allowed to expire in silence, especially as, shortly after, France was torn asunder with the Stavisky scandal. This indicated the deterioration of the Republic and presaged the fall of France with its dishonest defense contracts and political appointments made through influence and especially bribery. On August 1, 1934, Stavisky killed himself at Chamonix, or, as the underworld and police both whispered, was killed by the police, or by a government assassin, so he could not involve top French government officials.

It was not long before Petiot was involved in a more serious incident than that of violating the ethics of the medical association in advertising.

The Petiots, when first they came to Paris, had hired a dressmaker, in keeping perhaps with their new station in life. But, in typical Petiot fashion, they had managed to secure one at far less than the going rate. Mme. Petiot had found a girl of twenty-six, both destitute and depressed, and had given her dressmaking work to do at bargain prices. Grateful enough at first, the girl, Raymonde Hauss, had finally decided she must have better wages. She went to Petiot to ask for more money, and he found some way, known only to himself, of appeasing her. When, soon afterward, she developed trouble with an impacted wisdom tooth and sought Petiot's help, he gave her some optalidon and urged her to go to a hospital or a dental surgeon. When she failed to do either, Petiot, according to his own telling of the story, "felt sorry for her," gave her a shot of morphine, and cut the gum to relieve the pressure. He placed her in the spare bedroom of his apartment to sleep off the effects of the drug. That night her mother came to take Raymonde home in a taxi. She found the girl in a deep coma. Petiot gave the mother two Coramine pills and told the mother to take the girl home and give her coffee. Soon afterward, he was summoned to the girl's home. He found her dead, with the mother and some neighbors gathered around in frightened silence. Petiot heard one sharp whisper from a neighbor he could not identify: "No wonder she's dead, with all the pills that quack gave her!" Had she then taken the entire bottle of optalidon pills? Petiot could not sign a death certificate. He was no longer in Villeneuve. Instead, he gave the mother a written statement of facts. Later, he telephoned Dr. Paul of the Institut Médico-Légal, whom he had met at the "green meat" dinner with his father-in-law. He did not reveal to Paul what medication he had given. This, Petiot asserted in his notes, was "to see if the coroner's office really made a thorough autopsy." Apparently, Petiot noted, no autopsy was made, for the death certificate (police file D 190-012) contained the phrase "result of autopsy unknown." A valuable bit of information, Petiot told himself. The police do not *always* perform autopsies, even in cases of mysterious death.

After the discovery of rue Le Sueur, many references by the press and the police suggested that perhaps Petiot had murdered the girl. Some stories even recounted that Raymonde's skirt and underwear had been torn in a sadistic attempt to molest her sexually. The police themselves claimed that he had taken her home and they hinted at rape. The girl, they pointed out, never gained consciousness all the time Petiot was alone with her.

In 1934, Petiot became involved in an abortion matter. Insufficient evidence resulted in his acquittal and, at his request, destruction of all the papers. Dr. Piedelievre of the Institut Médico-Légal was the medical expert in the interrogation, but this matter was unrecorded and never mentioned in the trial, although featured in a magazine article in 1966. Dr. Petiot remained steadfast in his belief in birth control and abortions when desired by both parents. He was an admirer of the American Margaret Sanger. "I feel certain," stated Petiot, "that the Catholic Church and all civilized countries will someday legalize birth control and abortions, as have all Communist nations."

According to Petiot's opinions and oft-repeated statements, another stupid and uncivilized reaction of an underdeveloped civilization was trying to prevent the cure of drug addicts. How can an M.D. refuse to give dope to an addict to prevent the addict's torture or complete breakdown? Petiot contended that giving a prescription to a dope addict for a reasonable price of 100 francs might prevent that addict from murdering someone to get 500 to

1,000 francs to purchase dope from pushers. He affirmed the fact that the most successful way to cure dope addicts was not to stop their supply, but to reduce it gradually.

Here again, there is the strange contradiction. Petiot liked to pretend that he was motivated only by his desire for gain. Yet he sold narcotics to men and women who came to him at decidedly reasonable rates—about one tenth of what they would have paid in the undercover market. Dr. Petiot's prescription for a shot cost only one or two hundred francs ($10.00 to $15.00) . . . hardly worth the risk, and there is good reason to believe that he tried, many times, to help addicts break the habit—doing so at some risk to himself. Twice Petiot's good heart got him into serious difficulties. The sympathy for the misfit and the misbegotten persisted, despite Petiot's pretense of contempt for all lesser creatures.

There were literally thousands of dope addicts, and still are, among the whores and strippers of Montmartre and the Opéra districts, and many more among the homosexuals and procurers in the night clubs and theaters. There was a never-ending parade of girls at Petiot's door. There was Antonia Bella, once a chambermaid whose first lover gave her the habit. To satiate her desire for dope, she became a thief and a prostitute. Then came Madeleine St.-Yves and Henriette Francard and France Tonnelier, from far-away Buenos Aires, all prostitutes who, without dope, might well murder for want of it.

He made the acquaintance, naturally, of these and others of the town's most renowned prostitutes, many of whom were hopelessly addicted to heroin—or *confiture* (jam) as all narcotics were generally labeled by the adepts. He took part of his fees certainly in professional services, for he was able to recount in lurid detail some of the special skills the girls possessed. He maintained that a girl who is just experiencing the stimulating effects of a narcotic was at the height of her sexual enthusiasm; too, while one who is drowsy from the aftereffects or crazed for a shot of the drug was of no use in bed at all.

Petiot continued to steal. All this kleptomania was a pretense, he insisted. His family and friends did observe that after moving to Paris he no longer picked up trinkets or worthless articles at dinners or parties, but only things of value with little risk. When he attended auctions at the Salle des Ventes, he frequently saw opportunities to steal knickknacks and, occasionally, when he was loading some of his purchases on a truck, he would manage to slide an extra piece of furniture into the lot and make off with it. Also, in Paris, he seemed to develop a defense mechanism and seemed to want to justify any thievery he was ready to admit. He liked to dwell on the fact that the people who sold their belongings at auction were getting money for things that would ordinarily go to the junk pile and what few things were stolen from them just cut into their indecent profits.

There was a petty theft, however, that had a really shattering effect on Petiot's career, no matter how he tried to rationalize and belittle it. As a matter of fact, it eventually cost him his head. This occurred at a time when Petiot was deeply immersed in his "inventions"—one a perpetual-motion machine, the classic crackpot preoccupation, and the other a fecal pump, to cure constipation by means of a swirling circulation of water in the colon. In working out the details of this second invention, Petiot needed any book on the general subject. He finally found one in the Librairie Gilbert, a bookstore near the School of Medicine. It was, he said, a shabby, worn, dirty volume priced at 25 francs ($1.75). Petiot had no change, he said, and did not want to join the long line at the cashier's, so he slipped the book in his pocket and started out the door. A sales clerk had seen him, however, and immediately plunged toward Petiot to seize him and keep him from going out. Petiot, still an agile fellow at the age of thirty-nine, dodged to one side, neatly kicked the man's feet from under him, and shoved him headlong. Petiot made off. But it was no good. He had been recognized and was soon summoned to appear at the St. Michel police station.

The result was a psychiatric examination for Petiot by a Dr. Ceillier, who reported on July 22, 1936, that after an examination at St. Antoine Hospital, he had found Petiot deeply disturbed. Petiot had wept convulsively at the examination, had not even bothered to wipe the tears from his face, and could not speak connectedly except when trying to describe his inventions. The inventions themselves, the psychiatrist said, were only delusions.

Petiot, of course, looked back on this as a complete and successful pretense. He knew from his studies, he said, how to act so as to appear disturbed, and his threats of suicide and his hysterical laughter were all carefully put on. Whether that is strictly so must remain a mystery, for there were some doctors who believed that Petiot was malingering and many more who believed he was unbalanced.

For the moment, however, the charges were suspended, and he was ordered committed to an asylum or sanitorium for mental cases in accordance with the psychiatrist's recommendation. At his court hearing, Petiot had suggested that he understood his own problems and preferred to go into a private clinic. When the psychiatric report was accepted, therefore, Petiot was allowed to enter the clinic of Dr. Delmas, at 23 rue de la Mairie, Ivry, to remain until cured. Georgette Petiot appeared to make all arrangements and to give the appearance of having selected the hospital, but she was directed in every detail by her husband. Then, after Petiot had been confined for a month, he and his wife began to compliment Dr. Delmas on his treatments, and the doctor, exceptionally well paid and glowing with the Petiot flattery, recommended he be released.

During this enforced vacation or interruption in his busy schedule, Petiot did a lot of reading and studying. He became particularly interested in the studies of Cesare Lombroso, the great Italian criminologist who was a professor of psychiatry and who studied in Vienna with all the other greats. Lombroso found all criminals had physical, nervous, or mental anomalies, i.e., irregularities, due to atavism or degeneration, but that genius is also a morbid degenerative condition presenting similarities to insanity and is far from alien to crime. Petiot in his prison notes sarcastically wrote that whether Lombroso would have considered him insane or merely a genius paranoiac he entered the Delmas clinic at Ivry on August 1, 1936, at the strong suggestion of the Paris police. While at Dr. Delmas' clinic on rue de la Mairie (renamed rue Joseph Stalin after the Liberation but, after the purge of Stalinism, rue Lenin), Petiot was again in the shadow of a Catholic church, the imposing St. Pierre-St. Paul and not far from the Ivry Cemetery, where, ten years later, he would be laid to rest.

The police medical inspector, Dr. Rogues de Tursac, then examined Petiot, found him relaxed, friendly, intelligent, and well disposed, and supported Dr. Delmas' recommendation. All seemed well, but there came a hitch. The police record listing Petiot as insane seemed contradicted by the latest police record confirming Petiot as a licensed practicing physician. Then there was an arrest for traffic in narcotics—without conviction—and his involvement in the mysterious death of Raymonde Hauss. Then probably his conviction for stealing electricity had also come up. It was decided that Petiot must undergo a more thorough examination before a team of experts. To Petiot, this new group was a bunch of fakers. He was enraged that they were to examine him. Why, one of them, according to Petiot, Dr. Genil Perrin, was himself crazy! Another, Dr. Laignel Lavastine, was a notorious "couch-man" with the ladies! And a third, Dr. R. Claude—a nonentity!

Petiot tried every device to avoid being examined by this crew, but no amount of affidavits and the testimony before court officials of his wife, brother, friends, and neighbors were of any avail. On October 23, 1936, the hearing was held. Petiot was in an evil mood indeed, unable any longer to play either the work-worn, jittery professional or the calm, reasonable, thoroughly "cured" ex-patient. His blood pressure was high and his temper was higher. As a result, the report, delayed to December 19, 1936, gave a picture of Petiot that would eventually be used to later condemn him to the guillotine.

All his past history and records, the report said, serve to expose the true image of Dr. Petiot as a man without scruples and with no sense of moral values. . . . Dr. Petiot, after a short rest at the Ivry asylum, was still the same basic man he was before, and, we add, the same man he always will be.

As a precaution for society and public order, we desire to call particular attention to this specific situation. We wish to state that in any further crimes or irregularities by Dr. Petiot, this case and his internment for mental disturbance should not apply or be a precedent. Petiot's legal and penal responsibility must be decided without reference to this medical case or to his past psychiatric history.

. . . he does not have any psychopathic trouble to justify any further internment. He can therefore be released.

Based on this report, he was released on February 20, 1937, in the *custody of his wife, who was definitely and specifically briefed that she was positively responsible for his future conduct.* So Pe-

tiot was free but stealing a book for his invention to cure chronic
constipation had cost him so much money that Petiot for the first
time sold, instead of acquiring, a property. In order to meet the
expenses of his legal battles and his stay at Dr. Delmas' clinic, he
sold 58 rue Carnot in Villeneuve, the building next to the Petiot
mansion at 56 rue Carnot, to Mr. Arsène Blanchet, the town
baker. But he had spent his last penny of credit on the insanity account and, when circumstances put him in desperate need of another such plea, there was no play-acting and no sly pretense that
could wipe out the damning phrases of this report.

Petiot, however, gloried at the moment in the fact that his return to freedom found his practice bigger than ever. His reputation had not suffered one iota—or perhaps he had even gone up a
notch or two in the estimation of his underworld clientele. He
had found a good source of chloralhydrate crystal morphine,
known to the nonmedical as heroin, and he put in a large supply,
although he still sold it at far less than the pushers. Still, as one
authority would eventually comment, if there are customers
enough in a day (or a night), the total receipts could amount to a
very respectable income. The 504 vials found at his office after the
fire at 21 rue Le Sueur were worth over $30,000.

It was known, too, that Petiot performed abortions—not indis-
criminately, but for those he thought needed and deserved them.
He never had considered an abortion a criminal deed and argued
that a more rational age would probably see all births planned
and programmed, possibly even by artificial insemination with sexual intercourse reserved for enjoyment. Naturally, too, with the
clientele he had chosen, he had an extensive practice in the treatment of venereal disease. He was fearful of infection, however,
and tried to keep this part of his practice clear of his respectable
patients.

Also, quite naturally, he made the acquaintance of the Police
Brigade Mondaine, the Vice Squad, charged with morals, prostitution, procurers, dope addiction, traffic in dope, licentious or improper books or publications, which had its informers all through
the neighborhood. He was, rather early in his Paris days, picked
up for traffic in dope in connection with heroin prescriptions and
the sale of narcotics he had somehow secured from Germany, but
the charges fell through for lack of evidence (police file D

322-519). Then Petiot considered making a deal with the *Brigade Mondaine*, to inform on the many addicts who came to him for help. This also fitted in with his intelligence and gossip gathering that, as an informer, he supplied or sold to an active espionage market. However, after sampling the "information" he fed them and finding it full of false names and nonexistent personalities, the police decided they would prefer to have Petiot back on the other side of the fence.

During 1937, Petiot not only had a rather unsuccessful relationship with the Vice Squad, but also met two persons prominently involved with the Paris police and who later became established Nazi collaborators. Both had been his patients. One, Pierre Bonny from Bordeaux, was a highly publicized inspector of police who had been labeled by Monsieur Cheron, Minister of Justice, as the "number one policeman of France." This was the result of Bonny's finding of the check stubs that broke the Stavisky scandal. Later, Bonny had been in one jam after another and had been thrown out of the police department for blackmail and shakedowns. He later became a private detective. He was to become famous during the Occupation as a high-level German supporter and as deputy chief of the French Gestapo, who almost certainly worked with Petiot. Bonny was a small, thin man with a rather handsome face who looked like a concert violinist. Petiot had treated him for anemia, a nervous stomach, and possible stomach ulcers. He was dark, wore horn-rimmed glasses, and had a small mustache. He was a bitterly cynical, unhappy man, but known as a cunning and ruthless policeman who did not hesitate to frame or entrap suspects.

The other person Petiot met through his Opéra practice was a lovely lady with a lurid reputation. Her real name was Madeleine Coraboeuf, although she was known as Magda Fontanges (named after the passionate seventeen-year-old mistress of Louis XIV). Her father was a famous artist. She had married young, but her husband died shortly after, leaving her a widow at nineteen with an almost insatiable appetite for sex. She dreamed of a theatrical and movie career, but her progress was too slow. She became a French republican Pompadour and mistress of the key statesmen of the French Government, notably Désiré Terry and Paul Boncour. The latter, when he was Foreign Minister of France, wrote

Magda a love letter in which he wrote: "To kiss your breasts I would ignore Czechoslovakia" (re the Nazi takeover). Mr. Terry, who owned a paper, made her a correspondent and sent her to Rome. In Rome, Magda had a press interview with Mussolini and quickly became his mistress and even overcame his interest in Ethiopia, but the police were well informed and caused her deportation. Petiot attended her shortly thereafter and found her in a highly nervous state and was convinced she would become a mental case, based on his particular and unusual understanding of mental problems. Later, Magda, still raging from her expulsion from Italy and believing the French Ambassador to Rome, de Chambrun, was responsible, waited for him as he arrived on a train at Gard du Nord and shot him with a revolver. She only wounded him but was arrested for attempted murder. She was defended by a young lawyer whom Petiot had heard about in the underworld, Maître René Floriot. She was sentenced to a year in prison but the sentence was revoked and she walked out of court after receiving a million dollars' worth of publicity. Floriot's performance was so great that Petiot made the resolve that no one but Floriot would ever handle any matter for him. Magda went on her mad way as correspondent to Madrid, where she had an interview with Franco. The very next morning, Franco had an expulsion notice at her hotel. In World War II, she became a German secret agent, 800G4, and again was to interest Petiot and to be defended by Floriot.

As an expert on split personalities and death drives and paranoia, Petiot knew, and told all his friends and his patients, that Hitler was a paranoiac who would force a war on Europe, if not the world, and that Stalin was another paranoiac. He denounced France and England as decadent when they refused to fight for the Ruhr and for Austria and tried to avoid war by appeasement. As a result, in addition to all the properties he acquired directly or through old man Lablais, destined for Georgette and his son Gerhardt, he worked toward the acquisition of money, particularly in gold napoleons and jewelry, for he knew the French Army was in poor shape, that France would be overrun, and that property could then be acquired cheaply.

Petiot also reminded his friends and patients in long tirades that the French colonial empire would disappear and that he believed what his friends Thorez and Ho Chi Minh had publicly announced in the late 1920s, namely, that if France turned Communist, Europe would follow, and if French Indochina fell to communism, Asia would follow. This, affirmed Petiot, would mean Africa and Latin America would be easy Communist takeovers, completely sealing the fate of the United States. To further prove that Stalin was a paranoiac and a murderer and that the tenets of communism were simply raw opportunism, he referred to the speeches and articles in France of General Alexander Barmine of the Russian Army Intelligence and diplomatic services, who defected in Paris in 1937 and denounced Stalin and his Moscow purges by which Stalin murdered all his former close associates and friends. The detailed documented exposé by Barmine was printed in all the French newspapers on December 5, 1937. Many attempts at Barmine's life followed. Barmine later escaped to America and worked for the OSS but was a marked man. Pro-Soviet and pro-Communist influences in Washington forced his dismissal from top-secret work involving his command of the Russian language and his knowledge of Soviet cryptographic systems. He was sent as an aged recruit to some encampment where he could not work on U.S.S.R. intelligence. However, later he was used and became a very useful member of the Voice of America until the strain of being constantly marked as a dangerous anti-Communist with full knowledge of Soviet objectives undermined his health.

Hitler, to be later joined by Stalin, invaded Poland on September 1, 1939, and World War II started. Petiot was very positive that neither France nor England could save Europe, but he believed as far back as 1939 that the United States would again come in to win the war. He kept insisting to his friends and patients that "if the Americans are smart, they will continue to defend themselves in other countries far from home and never trust the Communists. As for me, it would seem that becoming a Communist would be my best bet. The Allies with the Americans will win this war but the U.S.S.R. and communism will take over Europe by 1980 and most of Asia and Africa by 1990."

The coming of World War II, which he had long foreseen, did not frighten Petiot, nor did the collapse of France, when the Germans rolled up the Maginot line in May 1940, surprise him. Petiot believed France and the Third Republic were soft and rotten

from dishonest politics, selfish and weak bureaucrats, and a decadent people. But he was not one of those who sought passage to
the south when the Somme line broke on June 6 and turned the
panzers loose on Paris, which fell on June 14 without a shot being
fired. While thousands of men and women, by auto, train, boat,
bicycle, barge, bus, truck, and horse-drawn carts and wagons, deserted their homes to seek refuge in Spain or along the Mediterranean, Petiot stood fast. He had promptly offered his services to
the authorities—not to work at the front but to become official
medical examiner for his own (ninth) arrondissement. In the beginning, he acted as assistant to a Dr. Houdard, who was the official medical examiner, but before the war was many months old,
Petiot had become the medical examiner in fact. He saw in this
job excellent opportunities to pick up valuables in the homes of
those for whom he would have to sign death certificates. After all,
as Judge Berry later described it, "Petiot became the eyes of the
police and the courts."

There were other opportunities that beckoned him. As he had
expected, the market in real estate collapsed with the coming of
the Germans. Then people who owned fine buildings throughout
the city hastened to turn their holdings into cash that they might
carry away with them. And Petiot now made a more earnest effort
to find, not only income-producing properties, but that fine building he had dreamed of, where his antique treasures could be suitably stored, displayed, and later sold, and where he might build a
clientele of the well-to-do, or even a clinic or private hospital.

In July 1941 he discovered the house in the rue Le Sueur, in the
finest residential district in Paris, very near the Bois de Boulogne.
It was everything he desired. It had housed nobility and was actually owned by a princess. It was imposing from the outside, four
and a half stories high, with twelve large front windows, while inside the rooms were of magnificent proportions. On the main
floor, besides parlor, dining room, and toilets, there was a room
ideally placed and shaped for an office. There were two entrances,
one that gave on to the stairways that led into the building and
directly into the court, and another that dropped down under the
front wall of the building and led into the courtyard. Here were
splendor, quiet, and even isolation. Yet the Arc de Triomphe,

which dominates Paris, was just over there and the Métro stop
Étoile was a step away.

It is doubtful that Petiot immediately envisioned the purpose
to which he might put the house besides using it as a storeroom
for his antique business and as a clinic after the war. But it might
have occurred to him that the sewerage system had a special advantage. The big kitchen in the basement had an exceptionally
large drain that led directly into one of the famous *égouts*—the
legendary Paris sewers, fourteen feet wide and seven feet to the
bottom, measured from the catwalks that ran along either side,
with an arched ceiling eleven feet above the catwalk. The Pereire
sewer, into which the sewers of the rue Le Sueur emptied, led to
the Clichy treatment plant where the sewerage was neutralized before flowing into the Seine.

An emergency drainage sewer for rain and surface water also
passed directly under the building and flowed directly into the
Seine not far away. While this may be unnecessary detail, to a
doctor with a forensic medicine and criminology background this
meant the easy disposal of intestines and organs within the rib
cage which would handicap, if not completely eliminate, the discovery of poisons as a cause of death in an autopsy and completely eliminate the smell of corpses.

Petiot bought this imposing house or "hotel" as it is called in
France for 400,000 francs ($80,000) from the Princess Colorado
de Mansfeld in August 1941. She had lived in it with a full complement of servants from 1924 to 1930 but for eleven years had
rented it to the stage star Cécile Sorel who had used it largely as a
storage house for some of her precious belongings. When Petiot
took it over it was already musty, cobwebbed, deserted, and full of
abandoned antiques, but it could not have suited him better.
Rue Le Sueur ran from avenue Foch to the avenue de la Grande
Armée. Today, completely renovated, it is worth about $2 million.

Petiot did not make much noise about his purchase of the
building and the title was in the name of his son, Gerhardt Petiot,
then age thirteen. His wife knew about it and disapproved of
using hard cash to buy things that might fall down or burn up.
Besides, she thought it altogether too splendid. But Petiot, view-
ing the stables and the deep pit nearby, the two basements and

the splendid kitchen and the almost secret courtyard and inner rooms, began to have visions of what it might be good for. Whether the possession of the house prompted the plan for establishing the liquidation business, or whether the purchase was part of the plan, one cannot be sure. It seems from what Petiot said later that the ideas blossomed together, one fitting neatly into the other. It is not even certain that the little triangular room with its reassuring false door was a creation of Petiot's or if the door had been put there years before to connect with a neighboring building and then blocked off when it became useless. But it is certain that Petiot, very soon after taking over the house, began to rebuild it somewhat to make it more secure. He had one of the courtyard walls raised to make it impossible to look into the court from the outside, and he worked to make the little triangular room tighter and more soundproof. He told the workmen that it would be his X-ray room. He did not explain to anyone the purpose of the Lumvisor viewer that he put into the wall so he could see into the room from the stable, but it was naturally assumed that it was to observe his patients without their knowing it. By the time the work was that far advanced, he had perhaps already decided how he would use these premises to enrich himself. In any case, even before his official takeover on August 11, 1941, Petiot began moving in his vast store of furniture, antiques, rugs, paintings, bric-a-brac, old books from Auxerre, Villeneuve, Seignelay, and 66 rue Caumartin.

Liquidation of men and women for all sorts of reasons was becoming commonplace in Paris now. And the German authorities themselves had already begun the systematic looting of the goods and bank accounts of any who might be deemed enemies of the Reich. They had turned out of the jails some of the country's most notorious thieves and strong-arm men and, at the beginning, had meant to employ them to smell out their hidden victims. But the tough characters of Paris had long ago learned that one's first loyalty must be to one's self, and often they used their new connections and opportunities as a means of lining their own pockets. While the Gestapo paid a commission on every piece of gold, jewel, or money find of the French criminals working for them, the Germans soon found themselves short-changed with many a murder of a Jew or a resistant spelling spoils for the killers only.

Early in the game, and before he had perfected his plans, Petiot not only renewed his acquaintance with Pierre Bonny, who had become deputy chief to Lafont of the French Gestapo of rue Lauriston—the organized and liberated criminals of France busy murdering and pillaging for the Third Reich and for themselves, but also renewed an old friendship with Paul Clavie, nephew of Lafont and a Paris underworld character, also with the French Gestapo. His contact with these people was confidential and clandestine, for they wanted informers and plants and most Frenchmen would not want to publicize any connection with them. In addition, possibly, unknown to the French Gestapo, unless they received a share of his spoils, which is likely, Dr. Petiot expected to use them to finger some of his victims.

Petiot also came to know another infamous character of the Paris Occupation—Christian Masuy, whose real name was Georges Henri Delfanne. Masuy was a muscular, brown-haired man, weighing close to two hundred pounds, with the look of a lion. He had blue-gray eyes. But there was an air of the hyena about him, too, something sidelong and sneaky, that made men suspect he could not be trusted. He was a Belgian by birth, a German by choice, and a Nazi by predilection. His mother had married an Adolphe Delfanne, who legally adopted him, although his father was unknown, even to his mother. In 1939 he had been rejected by the Belgian Army because of a heart ailment, and he had gone for some reason of his own into Germany, where he was soon arrested on suspicion of being a spy for the Belgians. He quickly convinced his captors he was no such thing and he became a secret agent instead for the Germans—which may have been his aim all along. He seemed to have a love and a genius for undercover work and may well have been one of World War II's most cunning intelligence operators. Before the Germans swept into France, Masuy had been arrested by the Belgians. He was a prize possession because he could recite almost from memory priceless details of French and Belgian fortifications and military logistical secrets. He was an accomplished linguist, speaking French, Flemish, German, Spanish, and English. The Allies clung to him even as they pulled back before the rapid German advance, and when the Nazis marched into Paris, Masuy was still locked up in a prison somewhere. But he had made a good friend in Germany who prized his skills. That was Otto Brandl of the Service Otto, the official "purchasing agency" of the Nazis, charged by Marshal Hermann Goering with sniffing out strategic materials and supplies and gathering them in, by hook or by crook—and sometimes even by honest purchase—for the service of the German armies in occupied countries. Brandl ordered Masuy dug out of whatever cell the French had hidden him in. He was tucked away in the South of France, and SS Haupsturmführer Herbert Senner put on the needed pressure to have him released, whereupon Brandl set him to work in Paris for the Service of Supply. In this job, Masuy often worked with underworld go-betweens who would simply steal the precious goods that were needed and then sell them to the German Army. Petiot suspected, with good reason, that Masuy cut himself in on these deals, too, and was quietly building himself a fortune. In fact, he met Masuy through a friend, Adolf Braun, who worked for Brandl.

Masuy's real penchant was for espionage and counterespionage, especially the latter . . . running down spies and resistants and sweating their secrets out of them. He must have fascinated and even frightened Petiot as Petiot himself sometimes fascinated and frightened the people who knew him best. Like Petiot, Masuy seemed wary of everyone he met. Whereas Petiot had schooled himself to be pleasant and charming, Masuy made no effort to hide the ruthlessness behind his neatly tailored and well-barbered front. Petiot "did business" with Masuy, several times removed, through Adolf Braun. Petiot was able to locate and secure 2,000 bottles of fine cognac for Braun for German officers' messes. Later, Masuy supplied Petiot with heroin to sell in quantity but at reduced prices at regular intervals, although no positive proof can support this.

Spymaster Masuy was to meet and use Petiot at a later date. Even with the Nazi's cunning, perhaps Petiot was to get more than he gave. It was some years before they got together again. Masuy became head of a special counterintelligence branch of the German Abwehr (military intelligence) at 101 avenue Henri Martin. Petiot, on the other hand, had already acquired a taste for intelligence and espionage or as a one-man listening post for highly valuable strategic information. He also found that under the stress of the Occupation, prostitution and narcotics and underground conflict made a doctor's business—and that of the official medical examiner of the Opéra district—very profitable.

Needless to say, Masuy and his Abwehr group, the Abwehr headquarters at the Hôtel Lutetia, the Lafont, Bonny, Clavie French Gestapo, the regular German Gestapo, the German Army, and the Paris police under German authority did not get along with each other, nor did the various underground resistant movements of the French, namely, the Free French (directed from England), British intelligence, the local French resistance groups, and the Communist underground and Soviet intelligence apparatus. As we shall see, he successfully played them all against each other with the possible exception of the latecomers, the U.S. Army's secret agents, who had the advantage of having evaluated the doctor's original duplications from some very valuable sources.

As a licensed doctor, Petiot would often give prescriptions for narcotics to a client under several different names, each time exacting a promise that the client would, if caught, testify that the doctor had written the prescriptions innocently, not recognizing that it was the same person coming back under another name. The *Brigade Mondaine*, however, or their stool pigeons, were not to be taken in this way. Twice in 1942 they charged Petiot with illegal traffic in narcotics (Germaine Debrienne and Mme. Cadinot), and, although they were never able to get him into jail, they did succeed in hampering his operations somewhat and making him more wary. It was at this point that he tried offering his services as a police informer, only to wind up being charged with giving false information to the police. He was able to talk his way out of this charge but he never convinced the *Brigade Mondaine* of his innocence. His secret intelligence operations were far more successful, although often referred to by evaluators as a "paper mill." He could always avoid secret intelligence contacts by the threat of exposure.

Petiot had bought with his ever-increasing profits several apartment houses that were fully rented. He put his brother Maurice in charge of them to collect the rents and manage the properties. Two buildings at 52 and 54 rue de Reuilly, with twenty-one occupied apartments, and many properties in Auxerre and Villeneuve and Seignelay, were paying off. But even this additional income was not what he had in mind.

Neither was he interested in the money he made on dope prescriptions, abortions, and his medical practice. He had visions of sudden great wealth, of fat bank accounts, hundreds of thousands of francs, double handfuls of precious jewels. Apparently the solid reality of wealth and the power that went with it were what he dreamed of . . . not niggling bits of profits or gradually increasing annual income cut into by taxes. He envied Masuy for both his power and his access to stores of hidden wealth as one of the master espionage executives of World War II . . . his wealth believed to be safely hidden in Spain and Switzerland was estimated to be well over $15 million!

He would find a way to acquire a fortune, even if he had to imitate the French Gestapo while restricting his efforts to collaborators or persons marked for certain death and pillage.

More important, he would find a way to get vital military and political information to sell as well as to help France and her Allies—and especially the Americans—win the war.

He would outdo both Lafont and his French Gestapo and also Masuy and his Abwehr and he would do it alone, with no one to share in his profits, thought Petiot.

Petiot knew that he had an extraordinary antenna for highly classified information, the kind that frequently leaked out at a bar or on a pillow or in a torture chamber. He had already obtained superior and strategic information from repatriated prisoners sent back home to France from Germany to die . . . or from escaped refugees from Poland and Russia, especially when compensated with gold napoleons (each worth $20 plus), the common currency in espionage.

CHAPTER V

Espionage production
1936–44

Petiot, with his inquiring mind, a regimen of very little sleep, an unquenchable interest in criminology and insanity and unlimited reading of crime, detective, and spy stories (real and fictional), had become interested in espionage. He also realized, as few do, that useful intelligence is often the result of talk, gossip, observations, and in the exchange of information. He often referred to his army experience at Chemin des Dames in World War I when the Germans had been forewarned of a French attack simply by a captured French courier carrying the uncoded French plans. He frequently claimed that World War I had actually been started by Great Britain in her historic pattern of splitting Europe by wars and always being on the winning side. He claimed that Britain's Secret Service was the greatest in the world from Napoleon to Hitler and kept Britain's enemies off balance but that the British were badly outwitted in World War II by the Soviet Union's clandestine service of information, aided by Communists even within the British Secret Service. He often explained how in the old days "every British valet, chauffeur, reporter, and businessman anywhere in the world was also a British secret agent." Petiot also claimed how the British Empire would soon be reduced to a backward and weak island, shorn of its colonial empire and even of Ireland and that even South Africa and Canada would be partitioned or troubled by racial or language differences stirred up by the Communists. As always, he was true to his philosophy of undermining, detracting, and criticizing even his own idols.

Long before Petiot's move to Paris, political, racial, and religious refugees from Europe and Asia, and more specifically from Germany, Russia, Poland, and China, had somehow escaped to Paris, the "city of light," and for centuries a haven as well as a world capital of pleasure. All these refugees had an ax to grind, namely, reporting any and all information against the Nazi or Communist (Bolshevik) enemy that had made them refugees. The greatest single intelligence contribution in World War II was "Enigma." This was a machine of the Nazis which ciphered the top-secret communications of Hitler and the German General Staff. This machine, which deciphered as well as ciphered, was rebuilt from memory for the British by a Polish escapee who had originally worked as slave labor in the German machine shop that developed the machine. Its produce was referred to as "Ultra." Only once did it fail, then in not signaling the Ardennes offensive, which, strangely enough, was signaled by Petiot, as well as by Marshal Goering's "surrender-to-the-West-only" offer.

From some of the early refugees and displaced persons—sick or dying—that Petiot treated in the Paris underworld and from those in show business, he had collected, firsthand, intelligence information to which he often referred . . . in most cases, stories of a type usually collected only by spies, newspaper reporters, or paid informers and, in most cases, rarely known to the public and sometimes of great importance. He soon became an informer—a role he practiced extensively as the opportunities increased with the world conflict. The war, as in so many of his activities, was an excellent help. His initial story of importance usually was one obtained from some Dutch contacts, as he frequently treated personnel of the Paris office of N.V. Philips, the European RCA, as well as many Dutch motion-picture executives and personnel, many of whom were frequent commuters to Paris and all of whom were, of course, anti-Nazi, although many faked at being collaborators to be more useful in ultimately defeating them. One story he told was of how the Dutch military attaché in Berlin, in December 1939, in some unknown manner (but claimed to be the result of some anti-Nazi German intelligence leak), reported the general plan for the attack on Holland, Belgium, and France with details —and that the attacks were to be expected soon, but with no exact date. All the countries involved, and British intelligence, were duly notified, but nothing was done about it as the report was not believed. Later it was even credited to Admiral Canaris, who was trying to save Germany from Hitler's suicide course.

An unusual story that Petiot seemed very proud of involved a rich young Panama playboy named Carlos. Petiot never gave his full name or perhaps he had forgotten it. An early patient of Petiot's in Paris as a result of a fight over a girl in a night club, Carlos described to Petiot a spy story from Panama. It appeared that the United States had recognized the Soviet Union in November 1933 although Russian secret agents had been caught subverting a U.S. Army corporal who reportedly came up with the plan of the U.S. Panama Canal Zone defenses. The corporal was tried on August 30, 1933, at Fort Sherman Canal Zone and found guilty. However, on review, he was retried and found not guilty in May 1934, and although the story was censored in Panama, Petiot's Panamian knew about it and pointed it out to show that Russia was not only Communistic but also imperialistic with very ambitious world plans. It was checked out and duly told to responsible parties in Paris before 1934 and at least once before 1942.

Unknown to Dr. Petiot, but as a follow-up to later prove the story, the same former U.S. Army corporal was involved in 1945 as a civilian employee of a U.S. government agency in another attempt to pass on to Soviet agents Panama Canal defense plans to identified Soviet agents but because of the unusual fairness of American law was not again tried for espionage. The FBI, however, identified the members of the Soviet spy ring, which included a medical doctor in New York City. This was all included in an FBI report to the White House on December 4, 1945, which also described how the secret of the proximity fuse was stolen by this same Soviet spy ring. Later all of this information from the FBI report was published in the New York *Journal American* on November 13, 1953 (leaked by direction of J. Edgar Hoover). The story, or its first part, was told to Petiot and told by him in 1934 and thereafter and relayed to the U.S. secret intelligence cutouts in 1942 to prove his capabilities. This is all part of the promised disclosures exacted from the author by J. Edgar Hoover and General Walter Bedell Smith referred to in the Preface.

Another story told by Petiot was that of two British secret

agents—a Major Stevens and a Captain Best—who had negotiated with members of a group involved in an alleged complex German military plot to get rid of Hitler and how they were egged on (perhaps to mousetrap an early British attack on Nazi Germany) and how they were trapped by the German SS in Venlo, a small town near the German border, but in Holland. They were captured and kidnaped into Germany but in the gun battle that ensued a Dutch Army lieutenant, Klop, was killed. This was in January 1940. It should have definitely signaled to the world the coming conflict but did not, although it encouraged Petiot to seek out the clandestine agents of all sides for payoffs, whether for exchange of information or, even better, for money. Petiot's only failure as a paid informer was reporting to the Paris police on narcotic traffic, but that was because he had a conflict of interest in this field.

Even more significant and illustrative that espionage and intelligence often collected by mere individuals and informers or gossips but relayed through secret observers or agents or cutouts to protect the actual agents is often ignored by bad evaluation is illustrated by another Petiot story. This story was obtained from his German Abwehr contacts or perhaps from some wounded Belgium officer or refugee he treated or perhaps from some officer's talk on the pillow with some luscious French but overly curious dancer as Petiot's clients picked up information at bars, on pillows, from homosexuals, from dope addicts, and from just travelers. The story begins when two German Wehrmacht officers, bearing the detailed plans and the date of the coming German attack on Holland, Belgium, and France, missed their train after a party they had been at in Munster. A German Air Force officer at the party offered to fly them to Cologne, their destination, and they, of course, accepted. However, bad weather forced the plane down near Malines, Belgium. When the officers tried to destroy their papers by burning them, the Belgium police seized the papers and arrested the two men. Notwithstanding the fact that the plan gave the details of the forthcoming attack and the date, May 9, 1940, it was ignored by the authorities and it is doubtful if the material seized was properly distributed. Hitler and the German General Staff, although very annoyed by the carelessness of the officers involved, decided the plan would be considered a hoax and they were right. The captured plan not only showed how the key to the attack was to outflank the French Maginot line where it joined the Belgium defenses, but more important and solid intelligence was how the plan involved the capture of the key fortress of Eben Emael at this point by the world's first parachute drop in force. Again, no attention was paid to this pivotal and detailed intelligence report.

Another ridiculous error in the evaluation of intelligence was secured in some manner by Dr. Petiot, it is believed from a patient who was a French civilian employee of the U.S. Embassy in Paris. The story was that Colonel Mott, a pre-World War II U.S. military attaché in Paris, received a report in 1937 from a French-American businessman (a former U.S. regular Army intelligence officer) that the Stavisky affair and contacts and contracts of his in French industry, politics, and the Armed Forces led the American businessman to be certain that the logistics and supplies, as well as the command of the French Army, were so badly deteriorated by graft and inefficiency that an all-out attack by the German Army, with its new panzer divisions, could crush France in three weeks. This was at a time when the world—and especially England and the United States—believed the French Army second to none and well able to defeat Germany by itself. The report was considered so wild that it was not even relayed to Washington or given to the French or the British. In fact, Colonel Mott threw the report into the nearest wastepaper basket as mere gossip and ordered the signature of the informer in the military attaché's book of visiting U.S. military personnel eradicated. This was, according to Petiot, another instance where correct intelligence was poorly evaluated and not believed. As was usual, as a paranoiac, Petiot criticized and undermined everything. Yet U.S. intelligence, the OSS, and, much later, the CIA all erred on evaluation based on source instead of on box score of source irrespective of source's station in life. Box score of past information which later proved correct.

One more intelligence produce of great importance that could have saved thousands of lives and which Petiot rarely spoke about but which when repeated was checked out in 1948 to 1952 and several persons confirmed the fact that they had been told the story in 1940 before its climax occurred. Many details of how acquired, when and how and to whom relayed, and why no attention was paid to the advance warning, are all unknown. But that Petiot had advance knowledge and tried to alert the parties involved without avail has been supported by many witnesses with no possible reason for not telling the truth.

It is the story of how the NKVD and/or the Russians and the French Communists and some violent de Gaulle supporters or the ever-present violent anti-Vichy Frenchmen on many occasions and in several ways floated, repeated, and affirmed the report that Vichy and the French Vichy Government and the French Navy were negotiating a deal with the Nazis for more food, medicine, and easier terms for Vichy in return for the turnover of the French fleet or part of it to the Nazis. The objective of course was to sour the relationship between the French and the English and to help de Gaulle's cause and that of the French Communists and of course to weaken the naval power of both France and Britain to the future advantage of the U.S.S.R. Had Petiot been listened to, it would appear that a horrible incident would not have occurred for on July 3, 1940, a British fleet attacked the French fleet anchored just west of Oran at Mers-el-Kabir. The French Navy, as later established, had no intent or orders or even the slightest idea to surrender or turn themselves over to the Germans. The casualties were very heavy, with 1,000 French and 2,000 British dead. On July 5 the British fleet returned to attack one of the French ships that was severely damaged from the July 3 action. Petiot claimed, and witnesses supported his claim, that he had warned any number of persons of the plot to bring about a fight between the French and the British, and later records of the German Abwehr and of the Gehlen organization indicated that they had intercepted and decoded Soviet messages definitely exposing the Russian efforts to cause the British to attack the French fleet in fear of its being turned over to the Germans. So, once again, unknown to the world, Petiot proved as effective and cunning an informer as in his role as a master murderer.

The extermination plans of Hitler and the violent hatred of the Russian Bolshevik against the former upper classes excited Petiot and may well have contributed to his mania of sympathy for the many sick and dying escapees from Nazi Germany and Communist Russia. He repeatedly labeled Hitler, Stalin, and Mussolini as genius paranoiacs and very similar to himself. Already officially diagnosed as suffering from dementia praecox, he realized, from his medical knowledge, that he was prone to self-glorification, hence he classified himself along with Hitler, Mussolini, and Stalin as being above the average man and possessed of genius. This may well have also contributed to his final monomania or drive for killing whether inspired or justified by patriotic or by selfish reasons but always acceptable in light of the murderous period he was living in. There is no doubt that Petiot finally and definitely assured himself that he was liquidating an enemy or traitor of France or giving a sudden painless death to persons definitely marked for the slow and cruel death of German concentration camps and also preventing the properties and fortunes of these victims from being acquired by the Nazis.

One of the most extraordinary stories he was ever told and that he tried very hard to relay to persons he thought were important observers or cutouts or actual agents for some underground organization or some intelligence setup was one so violent that it must have further reduced his evaluation of human life and must have also led him to seek further extraordinary stories that no one would believe but that, in his estimation, with his unerring cunning, he believed in. Yet in this case it had come from someone who had been there or had obtained firsthand information from someone who had been there. The story was told by a dying Pole who could have had no possible reason for fabricating the facts or even exaggerating them in a dying statement.

This Pole was an escapee from Poland when it was overrun by the Nazis and Communists together when they divided Poland—the real immediate cause of World War II. This man claimed to have been a witness or had direct contact with a witness who had seen or had firsthand contact with the story, which seemed unbelievable. The story as told to Dr. Petiot and repeated by him involved the massacre of 18,000 Polish Army officers, including a Major General Smorawinski, by the Russian Army or the Russian NKVD. The mass massacre was in the Katyn Forest, an enclave of the NKVD that no ordinary Russian had access to. The Polish officers who had been assembled there from many prison camps, both German and Russian, were reportedly about to be released in order to return to their homes but instead were all shot by a single revolver bullet in the back of the head after being tied securely, so arranged that their bodies fell conveniently into a deep trench of great length, which, when filled with others, was covered over, and trees were planted over the entire mass grave of many trenches. The order for this massacre was by Beria by order of Stalin, who had stated publicly that Poland would never again be a nation. Although this event definitely happened in the spring of 1940, the exact date the information was supplied to Dr. Petiot by his source is unknown as well as the exact date of the massacre. Although not defined by Petiot, it is believed to have been in 1941 and Petiot undoubtedly told the story many times until in early 1942 he finally told it to someone related to U.S. Secret Intelligence or to some underground or information-gathering service that had contact with a source available to the U.S. Secret Intelligence Branch.

The only other detail supplied Dr. Petiot and duly relayed was that among the victims were many military doctors and priests. Since Petiot's murders may well have started, and in fact did start in early 1942, this story proving the cheapness of life at this time where both the Germans and the Russians were actually murdering millions of persons may well have been very well received by Petiot and repeated to many persons all in justification of, in his own mind, his own murderous activities and plans. In any case, as soon as the report was received in Washington, it went to the Evaluation Unit of the War Department General Staff Intelligence. The director of this organization was Colonel Alfred McCormack, a top New York lawyer without a birth certificate and with an adopted name who received his commission as a full colonel on the War Department General Staff Intelligence without any prior military or intelligence schooling or past military service, though supported by a very high-level political sponsor. An order came down from the Evaluation Unit that the report be immediately eliminated and that the report received by Evaluation had been eliminated as enemy or German propaganda injurious to our ally, the Soviet Union, and from an unknown "paper mill" or gossip relayer. The Secret Intelligence Branch was directly ordered not to distribute or disclose this report to anyone in Washington. This, incidentally, followed a pattern from early 1942 to late 1946, namely, to eliminate and discourage all information on or against the U.S.S.R. or Communist activities anywhere in the world, so much so that a detailed project (1641) was prepared in 1946 with detailed data and a detailed list of eliminated reports eliminated for various reasons but later proven correct, and with specific proof of Washington's subversion!

And now here we must stop a minute from the story of Petiot's espionage production to indicate both the unusual character of this particular Petiot report and what happened to verify it and why the report, record, and credit for it was never known, although its accuracy was proven many years later.

An international group of neutral scientists and doctors and observers were invited, assembled, and taken by the German Army to the Katyn Forest in April 1943. The International Red Cross had first asked to sponsor this study but the Russians vetoed this. Some 15,000 Polish Army officers, including Major General Smorawinski, had disappeared and all efforts of the Polish Government-in-exile to find or obtain some clues as to their whereabouts were of no avail. A major part of the Polish officer corps was missing but the Russians by diplomatic means and by Moscow radio claimed that they had been liberated by the Russians but done away with—executed by the Germans—an explanation accepted and in fact violently defended and supported by both Elmer Davis and the OWI in the United States and by Ambassador Harriman in Moscow.

To the international group assembled by the Germans for a study of the Katyn Forest massacre were added two U.S. Army officers who were German prisoners of war. This, however, was kept secret. The group, including the two U.S. Army officers, collected irrefutable proof that the Katyn massacre was committed by the Russian Army or the NKVD and Colonel Van Vliet of the U.S. Army collected not only notes but pictures and photographs proving the existence of the massacre and the identity of the murderers. In addition, some 800 to 900 identifications of the victims were completed. It was then, and only then, that a more detailed number was arrived at, namely, 15,000 in lieu of 18,000 as reported by Petiot, although no positive evidence was ever available on the exact number of victims killed and buried in the Katyn Forest or killed in their forced assembly and transportation to this liquidation site. A total may be closer to 18,000 than to 15,000. Actually the Katyn investigation was abruptly terminated by a strange and sudden attack by the Russian Army, which soon took over the Katyn Forest in September 1943 for no particular military or strategic reason. Later it became evident that the Russian attack was to prevent any research or search for further bodies of the missing 15,000 or more Polish officers. No further progress was made in this matter until May of 1945 when Colonel Van Vliet was liberated as a German prisoner of war, one of the U.S. officers the Germans had flown to the site of the massacre. As soon as released, Colonel Van Vliet reported his findings, with notes and photographs, to General J. Lawton Collins, who had Colonel Van Vliet immediately flown to Washington "with all haste."

In May 1945, Colonel Van Vliet reported by prearrangement to General Clayton Bissell, Chief of Army Intelligence, and to Colonel Alfred McCormack, still Director of Evaluation of the Intelligence Division, WDGS. Behind closed doors, General Bissell had Colonel Van Vliet dictate a detailed report supported by detailed notes and photographs but, after the report had been typed, General Bissell collected all of the copies and all of the photographs and notes of General Van Vliet and directed him not to discuss or disclose the matter to anyone under threat of being court-martialed. His excuse or strange reason for this strange instruction was because of "political implications." This seemed to indicate that there was an iron curtain in Washington, D.C. Neither the OWI nor the War Department nor the State Department ever released anything against the propaganda of Moscow that still maintained and broadcast that the Nazi Germans were responsible for the murder of the 15,000 Polish Army officers at Katyn. The Katyn massacre was one of the original incidents or charges for which the Nazi leaders—not the Russians—were going to be tried at Nuremberg.

However, the United States could not be fooled so easily and finally, in September 1950, a special investigative committee was organized in the Congress but they were unable to get or find the original Van Vliet report and photos given to General Bissell. All they could do was to get Colonel Van Vliet to dictate another report from memory. A year later, in September 1951, the House of Representatives formed a committee to investigate the Katyn massacre. Lieutenant Colonel R. S. Stewart, the other U.S. prisoner of war with Colonel Van Vliet at the Katyn Forest, testified and supported Van Vliet's testimony fully. This final investigative body found no possible conclusion to deny the Russian guilt but could not find the original report and photographs turned over to General Bissell, and of course there was no trace or knowledge of the much earlier Petiot report from the Secret Intelligence Branch based on its Paris informer. General Bissell, under oath at the congressional committee, claimed he delivered the report and photos to the State Department but the State Department claimed they had no record of ever having received this material. In any case, the material was never found. Ambassador Arthur Bliss Lane, in his article about the Katyn massacre in the *American Legion Magazine* of February 1952, stated: "Of course many Americans believe our present history might have been changed had the facts of Katyn been exposed to the U.S. before the Teheran sellout to Stalin, before Yalta and Potsdam and our other Washington blunders. Who at the very top level of the U.S. government ordered the hiding of all U.S. intelligence reports unfavorable to the USSR and to only accept Soviet and Communist lies and propaganda?"

Naturally as the Secret Intelligence Branch of the War Department General Staff, G2, under covers of several kinds, was still operating in 1952, the Petiot report could never be brought up or referred to without dangerous disclosures, but the original report had been eliminated in 1942 by the Evaluation Branch of the WDGS-G2 in the War Department's Pentagon incinerator where classified papers were destroyed. But now we must return to Dr. Petiot in Paris. Both before and after the fall of Paris, Petiot frequently volunteered or was called on to treat refugees, displaced persons, and, later, the forced laborers sent out of Germany to be treated or to die, namely, when they were not worth the food they consumed as workers. Among these were many Poles and White Russians who preferred to be sent to France rather than back to their own countries under Communist control. These people were a great source of intelligence information, which Petiot collected and distributed not only to the French underground but wherever he could see some advantage to himself. He even relayed some of the reports to the Abwehr and to the Gestapo, in many instances twisting and slanting the information. He did this, he claimed, for the good of France. However, he never gave any indication whether he was for a de Gaulle France, a Giraud France, or a Communist France, especially before Germany attacked Russia. One thing, however, was that after the United States entered the war, and even before, he made every effort to locate anyone possibly connected to U.S. intelligence to make sure he relayed any and all intelligence which he believed to be of value to the United States. In fact, he frequently claimed that even before the fall of France and before the United States became involved in the war that he called on the U.S. Embassy and passed—or tried to pass—along information to members of the embassy. He did later become an informer of two insulated sources of the U.S. Army Secret Intelligence Branch who then through cutouts relayed Petiot's information—whether mere gossip or valuable intelligence. He had already figured out that a certain Paris police headquarters official with a strange German Abwehr contact and with certain business executive friends from Holland, Switzerland, Sweden, and Spain were somehow connected with U.S. intelligence. To prove their business or to help it, money, jewels, or favors or other information were exchanged after originally only information had been exchanged. Petiot was smart enough to know and to realize that such organizations as IT&T, with its worldwide affiliates and personnel, would work for one side or another, or both sides in a world conflict. He knew, for instance, from a very sick IT&T traveling executive that in 1939 and 1940 and thereafter IT&T could and did use both the diplomatic pouch of the Germans and the British for some of their top-secret business, commercial or industrial information, and that Sosthenes Behn, top executive of IT&T, was often referred to by his own employees as "the spy master."

The U.S. Secret Intelligence Branch, or as referred to in France and by Petiot as the "Cinquième Bureau," was organized just before the U.S. became involved in the war or a short time thereafter, but certainly long before the OSS. In fact, it began operating officially and actively under covers toward the end of 1941 and certainly by early January 1942. Petiot being Petiot, he never lost an opportunity to ask for recompense in addition to any exchange of information, namely, cash for expenses, often doubling or crisscrossing his interests and often in such confusion that he himself could not always tell whose interests he was advancing except his own. He also frequented the many travel agencies in the Opéra Arrondissement.

However, there is no question that in his saner and more logical moments, his loyalty and adherence were definitely anti-German and anti-Nazi and anti-Vichy France, and his special enthusiastic friendship was first to the United States and then to France, but certainly as time went on and after the Germans attacked Russia, with a Socialist and, later, a very definite Communist preference. With the early influence, power, and violent control of the Communists and the Soviet Union, Petiot, who respected power and began to believe that a Communist France might be in the making, began to favor communism. He unquestionably hated the Germans but definitely played with them, being careful to play the French Gestapo and Bonny against the special German Abwehr Branch, headed by Masuy. (Although clandestine and impossible to definitely prove, he maintained a secret relationship with both. Positive evidence, however, tied him up to two fairly long personal interviews with Masuy and frequent but more secret meetings with Bonny, and, more difficult to understand, Petiot always came away from these interviews in one piece.) It could only be Masuy who arranged his release from his Gestapo imprisonment or approved it. And, as duly proven and covered by testimony before preliminary police hearings and at his trial, he did help British pilots and air personnel downed over Europe to escape via Spain, Portugal, or by fishing boats to England, especially in the early part of the war, although he disliked the British. This later became more difficult as German security drew tighter and tighter.

It must be remembered that the Abwehr headquarters in Paris, at the Hôtel Lutetia, was accessible to Masuy, who headed another branch of the German Abwehr. Masuy was therefore also related to the Abwehr intelligence unit which concentrated on U.S.S.R. intelligence and Communist activities. This organization, headed by General Reinhard Gehlen, was so outstanding that the U.S. took it over after the war together with General Gehlen, a very loyal Nazi General Staff officer. Allen Dulles and the CIA spent millions of dollars supporting it because of its outstanding penetration and infiltration into the U.S.S.R. and the worldwide Communist activities and organizations. Therefore when Dr. Petiot came up with outstanding information on U.S.S.R. activities and on the secret agents of the Russians, it was not merely the delusion of an insane murderer but leaks and information which came indirectly from the most advanced and the only intelligence and espionage service deep into Russian and Communist activities—certainly the earliest! Once again the oft-proven principle in the espionage and secret intelligence field is never to evaluate information received based upon the source alone that often is a relay.

Secret high-level Soviet plans for the distant future indicated not only the complete takeover of Eastern and Central Europe but of Southeast Asia, Africa, and Latin America, and particularly the undermining of their most serious opponent—the U.S.A. Definite plans were discussed for the activation of a Communist takeover of Cuba and its use as a submarine base, a base for rockets, and later for Russian planes or for a Cuban air force trained and equipped by Russia. Also, an important objective was the Panama Canal . . . so important for the defense of the two flanks of the U.S.A. Here, as for Cuba, plans involved a Communist takeover of Panama and proper pressures to have the U.S. give up its "imperialistic colonial ownership" of the Canal Zone. The Soviet Navy actually began mapping a Cuban submarine base and also another in the Pacific along Panama's Pacific coastline. According to Soviet plans known to the German Abwehr in World War II, Russians actually believed that by 1980 a Cuban submarine base and a Cuban air base would exist in a Communist Cuba and that the Panama Canal would no longer belong to or be controlled by the U.S.A. This of course further supported the Soviet espionage activities in and about Panama long before World War II, also covered by Petiot in his reporting.

To further indicate how well informed Petiot was on all espionage coverage in Paris, we find in most books on Petiot mention of his famous conversation with an official of the German Gestapo after his imprisonment and torture by the Germans, when told he was to be released. Dr. Yodkum, one of the Gestapo chiefs in Paris, asked Petiot for 100,000 francs as a token payment for his release; Petiot replied that he had cancer of the stomach and was a dead duck anyway and didn't give a damn if he was released or not! This conversation, as Petiot knew, was witnessed by Yod-kum's secretary who was, as he also knew, a British secret agent. Of course, he did call his brother later and his brother did put up a token payment of 100,000 francs, which resulted in Petiot's release, although there is no question that the Gestapo was evidently ordered to release him by Masuy of the German Abwehr, who outranked and outpowered the French Gestapo. In court, at Petiot's trial, incidentally, several persons testified that Petiot had secured false identification papers for Jews and for persons of the Resistance who had to escape from the Germans. He also had furnished false identification papers and aided in the escape of several British Air Force officers trying to complete their escape from the Germans and get back to England. Some of these undoubtedly came from his co-operation either with Masuy or with Bonny.

In the meantime, more and more very sick slave labor and civilian refugees, many fatally ill, found their way to Paris and, naturally, to a doctor. As a self-styled intelligence terminal, Dr. Petiot reveled in getting information of all kinds and using it to his best advantage. By that time, he had well-established, definite contacts with the French Gestapo through Pierre Bonny and the Abwehr through Masuy and with various French underground personnel and contacts he believed were agents, informers, or cutouts of British and U.S. intelligence. Some of these were in the Paris police and were actually true insulated intelligence agents. Unknown to Dr. Petiot, one of his contacts was evidently a never identified U.S. secret agent in the Abwehr with Masuy in Paris. Most of Petiot's information was paid for originally by other information or favors but later by remunerations in cash, jewels, or perhaps even drugs. While never proven, the large stock of narcotics found in Petiot's house came from Merck and probably from Masuy, whose secondary chore was that of digging up and maintaining supplies of all kinds for the Germans.

In 1940 and 1941, Dr. Petiot reported on a German operation called "Boomerang" and "Vengeance" and a strange new weapon that, according to his sometimes dying patients, was being developed in the Nazi weapons laboratory in Berlin, later transferred to a factory near or on the Peene River. The weapon was believed to possibly mean winning the war without troops or casualties and to be aimed particularly at England. It was not to be confused with another secret weapon associated with the Kaiser Wilhelm Institute that other former prison laborers spoke about; this secret weapon was some kind of a superbomb in some way connected with a heavy-water plant in Norway. Later the new patients further located the Vengeance project at Peenemünde, a small island at the mouth of the Peene River in Prussia.

In May 1942, Dr. Petiot, by then a well-established U.S. Secret Intelligence insulated source (PC-P-9), reported that the Peenemünde plants were, in fact, turning out a "flying missile" of fourteen tons, forty-six feet long, and sixty-six inches in diameter. This was later confirmed by U.S. Secret Intelligence sources in Norway with pictures taken of Peenemünde from Norwegian fishing boats. This was, incidentally, long before Allen Dulles in Switzerland and the OSS later claimed reporting on the V-1 and V-2 and, finally, the finding and shipment of one of the missiles accidentally directed or accidentally landing in Sweden to London. Dr. Petiot was delighted to learn that top U.S. Secret Intelligence from Norway, via the U.S. diplomatic pouch from Stockholm, was given to British couriers and secretly opened by the British Secret Intelligence, then supplied to the U.S. as information secured by British intelligence. The U.S. S.I. Agency had even been criticized for the resulting duplication, although it was actually their original collection. However, tipped off through Petiot, the U.S. Army Intelligence organization in Washington requested that the FBI laboratory be given U.S. diplomatic pouches delivered from Sweden to the State Department via British couriers (Stockholm to London) and found that the seals had been broken, the pouch then opened, then resealed by the British. From then on, of course, pouches from Sweden, and in fact from anywhere, were carried by American couriers only. Possibly beginning with Petiot's original report on this subject, Peenemünde was frequently attacked by Allied bombings, starting with an all-out bombing on August 10, 1943. Of course, the world knows of the all-out use of the V-1 and V-2 rockets in attacks on England.

In early 1942, PC-P-9 reported information secured from the Abwehr headquarters at the Hôtel Lutetia that a certain high-level Abwehr agent had been sent to the United States via Spain and via Trinidad, code name "Crow," real name Alfred Meiler,

Arthur Krohler, or Arthur Koehler. The report further described it as part of a Dutch Abwehr operation involving many persons in the motion-picture industry in Holland and in Paris and the Abwehr headquarters at the Hôtel Lutetia. Henrique Kusters, a Dutch motion-picture executive, traveling between Holland and Paris, was involved. The major objective of Crow's mission was to find out U.S. progress in developing an atom bomb. The report also mentioned another Dutch motion-picture Abwehr agent scheduled to visit the U.S. Unfortunately, this report was only distributed to the War Department in the U.S. as no regular liaison had that early been established between the Secret Intelligence Branch with the FBI, although it is probable that the State Department received a copy and informed the FBI.

Again in 1944, this time as renamed source D-P-6, Dr. Petiot reported that Crow was still in the U.S. and that the other Abwehr agent, Joseph Letsch, was to leave from Spain for the U.S. soon. Dr. Petiot's report also contained the fact that the Abwehr in Paris suspected that Crow was now controlled and therefore worthless. Due to close liaison with the FBI that had been established long before 1944, the report was immediately forwarded to the FBI and M. Ladd, the FBI deputy chief who was the liaison to the War Department's S.I. Branch. He stated that, yes, Crow was definitely a controlled agent of the FBI, perhaps based on the 1942 report that evidently the War Department S.I. had a high-level source in the German Abwehr and could it ascertain if Crow was useless or not and to do anything possible to try to convince the Abwehr that he was not controlled or under observation. Actually, Ladd claimed that Crow was active and operating with a clandestine radio from the Hotel Astor on Times Square in New York City. Ladd stated that the entire FBI coverage of the Abwehr agents was being undermined and ruined by the efforts of the OSS and its amateur interference. He also explained that Crow's FBI name was Arthur van Loop. Incidentally, other Abwehr personnel in the U.S., Spain, Paris, and Portugal, known as Van Gelder and A. Holmes, were contained in Dr. Petiot's reports to the U.S. Secret Intelligence Agency and in their resulting reports to the War and State departments and the FBI. Actual help was requested by the FBI in convincing the Paris Abwehr that their agents were not controlled.

It was later brought out that Crow (van Loop) and the other controlled agents had been fed some correct information but basically were fed wrong information, especially for the Kaiser Wilhelm Institute. In fact, in the latter case, they were fed information that would delay the final answers to practical aspects of the gaseous defusion separation (process) of uranium isotopes and other problems in the development of the atom bomb. So a strange informer may well deserve some credit for the final defeat of the Nazis.

Dr. Petiot's Abwehr sources also often relayed Abwehr gossip, especially that of the Paris headquarters where they noted the early all-out personal fight between Colonel Waag, the early Paris Abwehr boss and the nephew of Mme. Canaris, and Captain Gruner, with the latter finally being relieved and sent to the Russian front. There were also stories about the division of opinion on a young Yugoslav playboy who seemingly was trusted by both the German Abwehr and British intelligence, particularly that branch referred to as "Doublecross." This young man was known as a double agent and used by both sides in a typical doublecross operation. He was constantly in trouble with spending too much money and having too many girl friends. The British or the Germans or both tried to get rid of him by sending him to the U.S. but he outwitted everyone by collecting large sums of money before he left from both the British and Germans. Later, claiming loyalty only to the British, he offered his services to the U.S. for a price and when refused later claimed in a book published in the U.S. that he had warned J. Edgar Hoover of the possibility of an attack on Pearl Harbor in August 1941. This proved amusing for Winston Churchill had written a letter of warning "from a former naval person" to President Roosevelt in November 1940 based on the same detailed facts which were involved in the alleged Hoover warning by the double agent playboy and involving the destruction of an Italian fleet by a British air attack at Taranto in November 1940. So therefore the information would hardly have been disclosed by British intelligence through a double agent for relay to the FBI and outside of normal official channels and also duplicating the warning from Churchill to President Roosevelt (as duly recorded in Churchill's memoirs). The FBI, to further prove the true facts, publicly denied the claim of ever having been alerted or of any Hoover confrontation with the playboy double agent involved. The FBI reaction in the press resulted from both a book and magazine article by the easy-spending but hungry-for-further-income, self-styled hero informer turned writer.

Then there were stories about Colonel Herman Giskes and his transfer to Paris from Holland where he was responsible for the famous Dutch traitor and Abwehr secret agent "King Kong" (Christian Lindemann), six feet tall and weighing 262 pounds.

Among the information obtained by PC-P-9 and D-P-6, both actually Dr. Petiot with a changed cutout or contact, was that covering the Abwehr's information on U.S. intelligence and the OSS operations and personnel. The Abwehr considered Allen Dulles, OSS chief in Switzerland and later head of the OSS and its after war survival as the CIA, a dupe. The Abwehr laughed at the great number of Communist Rote Kappele members and Russian agents that Dulles worked with, such as Noel Field, Dr. Wilhelm Hoettl, Kurt Ponger, and others. Last but not least was the story from the Abwehr in Paris that some of Dulles' crypto systems had been compromised, leading to the capture and execution of some OSS agents. It is interesting to note that Dulles placed a lot of trust in Otto John, a well-known homosexual who was classified as a poor security risk with contacts with the Rote Kapelle that had been reported on through Petiot in early 1942 from the Paris Abwehr. Dulles, much later and long after the period covered by this book, helped John obtain the job of director of the West German police and intelligence and invited him for a tour of the U.S. and its defense and industrial plants, etc. This was much opposed by the FBI and many security agencies in the U.S. based on the reports obtained from Petiot and many other sources. Immediately after Dulles' special VIP treatment and the visit of Otto John to the U.S. sponsored by Dulles, John defected to East Germany and the U.S.S.R.

Probably the two most important intelligence items practically scavengered by source PC-P-9 (Petiot) was one that involved an incident in World War II that is generally unknown and one still unknown. They are:

1. That on Christmas Eve of 1943, three British officers, a Colonel Petersen, a Major de Chartellani, and a Captain Metzeanu, were dropped by parachute into Rumania and requested

and obtained an interview with Marshal Antonescu. That at this interview the British officers produced a secret official German proposal to the Russian Government for a separate peace in which, together with other conditions, Germany guaranteed Russia all of Rumanian territory to the Seret River. Of course this proposal, whether true or not, should have been made only by the British after due notification to its allies. It is doubtful, however, if this was done, for the reaction to this report in Washington was very unusual and it was immediately ordered highly classified with very limited distribution. The officers, however, were unusually well chosen as Colonel Petersen had been an executive of the Ploesti Oil Company, Major de Chartellani was a director of the Unire Rumanian Oil Company, and Captain Metzeanu was a British subject, but a naturalized, native-born Rumanian. All three had lived and been in business in Rumania (in Bucharest) and all three spoke fluent Rumanian and had many business and social friends in Rumania. Knowledge of this proposal caused a very pronounced anti-German feeling in Rumania and increased the great fear of a Russian takeover.

2. That Colonel Robert Solborg, U.S. military attaché at Lisbon and once an OSS executive especially sponsored by Allen Dulles, was both a British and a Soviet secret agent. Although duly reported, it was never believed, though Solborg quite willingly admitted that (a) he was a White Russian-Pole who had been an officer in the Imperial Russian Army and (b) that he had once served a civilian agency of Russia but when faced with the Communists had "defected to the U.S. and become a U.S. citizen" and (c) that he had indeed served as a British secret agent in Europe before the war. However, in retrospect, many facts seem to support, if not prove, this extraordinary claim, picked up by Dr. Petiot from the German Abwehr in Paris. In the negotiations on preparations for the U.S. invasion of North Africa and the all-out conflict of various French groups who at the time refused to cooperate, Colonel Solborg disobeyed explicit instructions from Washington and from General Donovan, director of the OSS for whom he was working, and double-crossed a definite plan, seriously sabotaging U.S. efforts, for which he was promptly fired from the OSS by Donovan. However, he was neither tried nor removed from military service. In an effort to make peace and ap-

pease Donovan, he flew to the U.S. to see him, but was refused an interview. He then, in some unusual manner, obtained or retained the assignment of military attaché in Lisbon, proving his high-level support in Washington. As attaché in Lisbon he very definitely sabotaged any and every U.S. Secret Intelligence plan or organization seeking penetration into Axis Europe, especially Eastern and Central Europe.

On finding out about a top-secret operation involving an arrangement by which Admiral Horthy and the Hungarian Government would secretly serve U.S. intelligence, as arranged on a White House level, Colonel Solborg tried to first penetrate, then sabotage, this operation which, of course, certainly could not have been looked on with any favor by the U.S.S.R. It involved possible sabotage or all-out military action by Hungary to join the Western Allies to save themselves from Russian domination. This effort, Colonel Solborg's final plot to sabotage the operation and frame G2's Secret Intelligence Branch's Lisbon representative, enabled documentary proof to be collected to indicate false official statements by Solborg attributed to the Hungarian ambassador in Lisbon (an affidavit from the ambassador secured by the Secret Intelligence Branch proved Solborg a liar and saboteur and breaches of security on Solborg's part). His immediate superiors in the War Department requested his removal. But for some unknown reason, nothing was ever done to end his career as an officer in the U.S. Army or even to relieve him, at that time, from his job as military attaché to Lisbon. Strange and unknown parties in Washington supported him.

What surprised the Abwehr in Paris was that Solborg had not been identified as a Russian agent by the Western Allies, especially the U.S., in the face of his record alone. In 1942 and early 1943, with the ostensible support of the British and certain U.S. sources but with no authority of any top echelon, he organized what was actually a leftist, if not Communist, planned revolution to unseat Franco. This, notwithstanding the fact that Franco was known to have every intention of remaining neutral, which was to the best interests of the Western Allies. Any revolution such as Colonel Solborg planned in Spain would have been of possible advantage only to Russia as it would definitely have slowed up the Western Allies and their plans to liberate Europe and Germany.

It also would help the Communists obtain control of Spain and Portugal ahead of schedule. Fortunately, the Allied top authorities found out about it through the Abwehr to Spanish intelligence to the British and just in time prevented it by ordering all plans suspended and canceling the supply of arms and other materiel which had been promised. This earned merely a reprimand for Solborg.

However, there is no question that certain pro-Russian and pro-Communist influences in Washington worked effectively to prevent Solborg's recall, if not a court-martial, for whatever interests he served. It must be remembered that Washington influenced many things in favor of the Soviet Union, even to sending U.S. money plates, paper, and inks by which the U.S.S.R. produced some $20 million currency and first introduced in the U.S., through Dexter White and Alger Hiss, the idea of giving back the Panama Canal to Panama, who never, of course, had any claim to it and were paid many times for its ownership in perpetuity by the U.S.

Later, the accidental death of aviator Antoine de Saint-Exupéry and the attempt to murder General Giraud by a Moslem assassin were believed by many high-level French in the intelligence services to be the work of de Gaulle to assure his winning his fight for the future control of France. After the liberation of Paris, it will be recalled that de Gaulle turned to the Communists for final support for his leadership, returning Maurice Thorez from Russia and pardoning him as a wartime deserter and making him his deputy. This no doubt convinced Petiot in his future as a Communist. After General Giraud had recovered from his wounds in an assassination attempt, he was retired and relieved of command and was allowed to return to France only months after the liberation of Paris, in late 1944. He died in 1949.

However, probably the most dramatic secret intelligence acquisition of all, although not exclusive, highlights the intelligence potential of Dr. Petiot as a relay service and insulated informer. It was confirmed by a more reliable and more highly evaluated source but practically at the same time, namely through Marshal Goering and his art agent. It presaged the Ardennes offensive, usually referred to as "the Bulge." This was the last great offensive of Nazi Germany and Hitler to turn the tide of World War II or

perhaps only to lead to what Hitler believed possible—a negotiated peace with the West only. Sometime in the early part of August 1944, through Petiot, a report was duly relayed that Hitler
and Nazi Germany were planning an all-out offensive to reverse
the tide of the war by a master counteroffensive of major importance that might be successful or at least lead to separate peace
terms between Germany and the West. The attack was further
described as to be accomplished by parachute drops, all-out armor
and tank attacks, and all kinds of sabotage and behind-the-lines
activity. It was planned for the early winter when the ground
would be firm for tanks and other vehicles and the weather clear
for the air force and before the heavy snows. Specifically, it was
set for the middle of December and so was its location specified—
the Ardennes. This was duly relayed by Dr. Petiot from a Dutch
motion-picture executive who was a great art collector and who, in
turn, had as a source none other than the art agent of Marshal
Goering. The plan time and location were both confirmed by another more highly evaluated source: Goering's art agent himself.
An alleged proposal by Marshal Goering was made through this
agent—that Goering offered to bring about the surrender of Germany to the West if he and his wife were given immunity. He
proposed to fly (piloting the plane himself) with his wife to Sweden and then be transported to Rome, where, under the auspices
of the Catholic Church and the Vatican, he could broadcast to
Germany, which, combined with his prearranged plan and preparation in Germany, would bring about a surrender to the Western powers. Otherwise, an all-out offensive would be launched in
the middle of December in the Ardennes that might well reverse
the military situation but, in any event, would cost the Western
Allies tens of thousands of casualties. The all-out rocket attacks
on England would also increase. This report, supported by another, was the subject of discussion between the Allied powers.
Evidently the decision was to ignore it. Both reports, one through
Dr. Petiot and the other an unofficial but formal proposal from
Goering, were turned in by the S.I. Branch of the War Department Intelligence Branch and duly relayed to the State Depart-
ment, but no official answer of any kind was forthcoming for
Goering, not even a negative one.

However, as far as it is known, no warning or alert based on the report was ever relayed to General Eisenhower's headquarters, which expected no attack on December 16, 1944, as indicated by his intelligence summary of that day. Great efforts in the War Department General Staff G2 were made to relay the report on the Ardennes offensive, duplicated by two different sources but, at the insistence of Colonel Alfred McCormack and the well-known, and to some the infamous, Evaluation Branch of G2 in Washington and certain high-level supporters of this organization, no alert or report on this was sent.* This evaluation organization was famous for eliminating all reports on U.S.S.R. or Communist plans for the takeover of the Balkans and Eastern and Central Europe. Based on special private and New York police investigations, two highly suspicious but highly influential members (a couple) of Colonel McCormack's G2 Evaluation Unit in Washington were found to be major participants in the elimination of all reports on Soviet and Communist activities. One was partly educated in the Soviet Union and the other was born and raised in the Soviet Union and bore a false name, and both had been identified by their neighbors before entering the service as Communists.

* A much later conversation between the author, to explain his all-out efforts to have the information relayed to General Eisenhower's headquarters, and General Walter Bedell Smith, the Chief of Staff for General Eisenhower at the time, resulted in his being told categorically by General Smith that even if he had been able to get the report sent, no one in General Eisenhower's headquarters would have paid any attention to it. The reason no report could ever convince the commanding general of the Allied Armies staff that an Ardennes attack was imminent was because the Germans very cunningly and purposely had prisoners taken of specially briefed German soldiers by U.S. patrols and especially arranged for alleged deserters to establish the fact that the line at the Ardennes was maintained by third-class divisions of old men and young boys and further weakened by broken-up and low-morale units from the Eastern front with no sign of any first-class combat troops. Of course this was all prearranged and convinced the intelligence officers of U.S. front line units that any attack on this front was completely unlikely at the time. However, General Smith did comment that perhaps sinister and subversive influences could have prevented the distribution of this information from Washington. He sincerely believed that there were Communist and Soviet infiltrations in Washington eager to see a slowing-up progress of the Allied Armies in Western Europe. Later, the same biased evaluations and other discoveries involving the security of certain evaluators in the G2 Evaluation organization caused its breakup and reorganization. This also later forced the resignation of Colonel McCormack as the new intelligence director of the State Department, a new assignment his high-level, pro-Soviet supporters had obtained for him at the end of the war but they could not prevent his demise after the facts came out on his G2 evaluations.

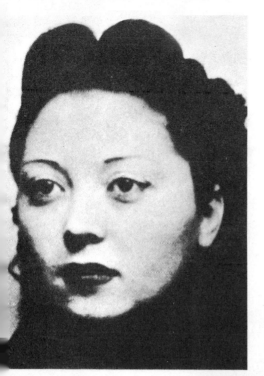

Petiot victim Paulette Grippay, "La Chinoise," prostitute girl friend of Gestapo gangster. Traced by the dressmaker tag on a dress.

...e. Kahan immediately after her ...est as a Petiot scout and accomplice. She was later released for want of evidence.

Maurice Wolff of Antwerp, Belgium, one of the Jewish refugee victims of Dr. Eugene.

Lina Bruan Wolff of Breslan, Germany, one of the Jewish refugee victims of Dr. Eugene.

Theatrical picture of Gine Volna, night-club singer, model at Patou in Paris, former secretary, educated by the nuns at St. Christian at Metz, but victim of Petiot as Gisele Rossny.

Madeleine Coraboeuf, alias Magda Fontanges, during the short period when she was a mistress of Mussolini. Patient and friend of Dr. Petiot. Later German secret agent. German Occupation Authorities.

François Albertini, "the Corsican," one of the gangster victims of Dr. Petiot. Albertini had been arrested often and was a master pimp, but had no convictions. German Occupation Authorities.

Judge Marcel Leser. Gift of Judge Leser for my book.

Dr. Paul, City of Paris coroner, testifying on the gruesome details of the dissected and dismembered cadavers found at 21 rue Le Sueur and at some three other sites in Paris. Gift of Dr. Paul.

A tous Services   PRÉFECTURE de POLICE - POLICE NATIONALE -
GENDARMERIE NATIONALE.

— : — : — : — : —

Il y a lieu de rechercher activement :

P E T I O T, Marcel, André, Henri, Félix, né le 17 janvier
1897 à Auxerre (Yonne), de Félix et de BOURDON, Marthe, Docteur en
médecine, ayant demeuré 66 rue Caumartin à Paris, auteur présumé
de plusieurs assassinats à Paris .

PETIOT est susceptible de circuler sur une bicyclette d'
homme, de couleur verte, immatriculée : 3866 RD 7 .

Il peut être accompagné de sa femme, née LABLAIS, Georgette,
Valentine, 40 ans environ, - de taille petite, teint pâle, visage
mince .
PETIOT, Marcel, doit être considéré comme dangereux .

SIGNALEMENT : 1 m 80 environ, assez forte corpulence,
cheveux châtain foncé, rejetés en arrière, légère calvitie frontale,
moustache rasée, mâchoire forte, menton légèrement proéminent,
vêtu d'un pardessus ample .

Au cas de découverte, maintenir le nommé PETIOT, ainsi que
sa femme et aviser sans délai la PRÉFECTURE de POLICE, Direction
de la POLICE JUDICIAIRE - Turbigo 92.00, automatique 357 .

Paris, le 13 mars 1944.

LE DIRECTEUR GÉNÉRAL de la POLICE JUDICIAIRE ,

T A N G U Y .

Wanted poster for Dr. Petiot and his wife.

Clichés Nº {
869 619
R. nº 43.047 } ED. Nom : *Petiot*

Ecroué
le _____
Nº _____

Prénoms : *Marcel André Henri Félix* profession : *Docteur en médecine*
Né le *17 Janvier 1897* à *Auxerre* , dépt *Yonne*
Fil de *feu Félix* et de *feue Bourdon Marthe*
Papiers d'identité : *S.P.*
Dressé à **Paris** le **2.11.1944** par M. *Isabel*
Inculpation : *Sur Note I.J. Centre) Identification,*
VRF CE JOUR *Salin*

22.11.44. IDF *Guillaud*
s/ demande M. Gollety
change serré —
à 1 H sans barbe)

PHOTO·CE·JOUR

Aur. g.	Ann. g.	Méd. g.	Ind. g.	Pouce g.
1	1	1	1	4

Police identification card of Dr. Petiot (November 2, 1944) with finger-prints after his final arrest with note that Juge d'Instruction Gollety, District Attorney, had ordered him to shave for another picture on November 22.

Picture of Dr. Petiot as arrested on November 2, 1944, under his identity of Captain Valéry, although he had been forced to change from his F.F.I. uniform to civilian clothes.

Petiot's espionage activities and his secret relations with the French Gestapo and the Abwehr changed as the war progressed and the U.S. Army advanced toward Paris. Many persons closest to the Petiot case, particularly the French police, have frequently claimed that Dr. Petiot was too careful to have been responsible for the fire, the smoke, and the rotting cadavers found in the charnel house. They believed that Petiot, encouraged by the success of the U.S. Army and of the U.S.S.R., began to renege on whatever arrangements he had with the French Gestapo or, more likely, with Masuy and his Abwehr outfit, or with both on splitting his spoils or on certain exchange of information. As a result, his former partners decided to frame him to expose what he really was— and what they finally had discovered him to be—a murdering, insane but cunning, paranoiac thief without any real patriotic motivation. By that time, with the U.S.S.R. and the Communists in the ascendancy, the power-hungry Petiot became an enthusiastic Communist. As he put it, only as a Communist could he have an unlimited future! Hence his joining the Communist Party and his becoming a Communist card carrier before his final arrest.

Of course after the liberation of Paris, Petiot as Petiot had disappeared and Petiot as Captain Valéry alias Dr. Wetterwald as we shall see was an officer of what was both an intelligence and security organization as well as part of the French military forces. So while Petiot's secret intelligence and informer activities stopped, his plan for an escape under his two successful and new identities was naturally to apply for a position in the secret intelligence field: to the DGER for an assignment as Dr. Wetterwald in French Indochina, an area that had always interested him (he once stole a book on Malaysia as noted in his Paris police record). He would try to sell himself to Colonel Passy on the basis of knowing Ho Chi Minh.

Could this be connected with the DGER orders to proceed to Saigon reportedly found on Petiot when he was arrested by Captain Simonin (DGER) alias Inspector Soutif of the Quimper police, an alleged violent collaborator or a double agent but who disappeared together with Petiot's DGER orders (seen by only one other person)? Could this be the reason why neither Dewavrin alias Colonel Passy nor Captain Simonin alias Soutif nor Claire Davinroy, whom Petiot named as having been assigned to be his cutout for resistance intelligence purposes, showed up at the Petiot trial although they all three had been summoned to do so?†

However, according to at least one witness, Petiot's arrest may have been forty-eight hours before Dr. Wetterwald's alias Captain Valéry's departure for Saigon so the "letter to the editor" turned over to the editor by Petiot's counsel and which fingered Petiot under his new and successful aliases and identities was absolutely pivotal.

Any recognition or even temporary assignment or any admission of co-operation with Petiot or Petiot's espionage activities for France by the DGER, even if an error of judgment, would have proved highly embarrassing to the French Government but would definitely have established Petiot as an official resistant of a sort. It could be a coincidence but three persons, all related to both Petiot and the DGER, for some reason did not show at Petiot's trial, notwithstanding the complaint, on both sides, when they did not appear. This is one more of the many mysteries of the Petiot case.

The unusual Washington "shockers" only prove that in the secret intelligence field there is nothing unusual about highly unworthy and undependable persons turning in highly important and correct intelligence such as that produced for the Germans by Cicero, a Yugoslavian valet to the British ambassador in Ankara whom the Germans paid off in counterfeit money. He passed on correct information on the Ploesti air raids and on the Normandy landings that were ignored. Another example is the British ignoring correct information passed on to them by the pimp of Mussolini's whore who relayed Mussolini's pillow conversations based on his early meetings with Hitler when told his Axis partner's plans. That is why sophisticated evaluation should be based on box score —proved value of past production judged with the passage of

† Although Judge Leser, the prosecuting attorney, Dupin, newspapers, and court records agree on this point, Mr. Dewavrin alias Colonel Passy when interviewed by the author denied he had been summoned to the Petiot trial. He stated he knew nothing about Petiot or about Captain Simonin alias Inspector Soutif and had nothing to do with the Petiot case. As is well known, Passy was relieved from his intelligence assignment at a later date and charged with financial irregularities, but later the charges were withdrawn and dropped and Colonel Passy was cleared of any and all charges.

time, which is far more important than the position or standing of the source. Yet the CIA consistently evaluated its intelligence by the nature of the supplier and insisted on violating security by carding all of its sources with all possible data on them. More sophisticated operations are based on one or more code names with true identities, sometimes screened by several and separate centrals. Next, of course even more important, is that the evaluators be open-minded and without preconceived ideas, theories, or slants, much less political or ideological concepts.

A survey of the evaluation of the S.I. Branch of U.S. Army Intelligence in World War II and thereafter by two well-known, recognized, and impartial experts resulted in the claim by both that there was definite bias in all evaluation where the Soviet Union or the Communists were involved.

To return to Petiot before his execution. He knew not only about the Nazi liquidations being responsible for over several millions of persons in prison camps alone but that of the Communist mass executions in liberated France against more anti-Communists than German collaborators. He also of course enjoyed repeating the story of the Katyn massacre but for the first time criticized the United States and enjoyed pulling down the two great Americans he had previously put on pedestals. "Operation Keel Haul" was not missed by the jailed former intelligence informer who had access to newspapers as well as to prison talk and gossip. Petiot did not miss the fact that by the orders of generals Marshall and Eisenhower, the U.S. Army turned over two million White Russians and anti-Communists of Central and Eastern Europe, both prisoners and displaced persons, to the U.S.S.R. by force and irrespective of their desires. As a result, the men who were returned to the Russians were tortured and killed and the women raped and killed. Petiot—once more in his paranoiac critical element—remarked that the Germans and the Russians and the French Communists and the Americans were all guilty of inhuman conduct far greater than his perfectly explainable killings of only the enemies of France in some way and of persons marked for worse deaths than he gave them. He further added that only Americans did not have the stomach to do the killings themselves but turned over only live bodies.

Apologists for the U.S. Army's Operation Keel Haul claim that the matter was based on an agreement at Yalta signed on behalf of the U.S. by General John R. Dean on February 11, 1945, which provided for exchange of prisoners and liberated civilians "regardless of their desires" but to be returned to "their country of origin." (Later defined as of September 1, 1939.) Secretary of State Stettinus and his assistant, Alger Hiss, entered into this agreement despite the all-out opposition of Ambassador Joseph Grew, then Acting Secretary of State. The herding and forced loading into box cars by the U.S. Army of human beings to certain torture, rape, and death was so revolting to the U.S. Army and the War Department that it was designated as "Operation Keel Haul"— the most cruel naval form of punishment, usually ending in death.

According to the Geneva Convention any decision in this field was "not to look behind the uniform." Colonel Harold E. Potter, U.S. Army official historian, stated that even the Yalta Agreement could not justify forced repatriation. It did not contain any reference to the "use of force." Strangely enough, few if any Americans today know about Operation Keel Haul and even fewer know that the U.S. Army was ordered to conduct forceable repatriation before Yalta and its agreement or that General Eisenhower is reported to have used force to repatriate even the Russians, Poles, and Hungarians who were in military action with the Allied Armies against the Germans, to whom the Yalta Agreement would not apply.

One severe critic of this U.S. action claimed that "There have been few crimes in history more brutal and more extensive than this forced repatriation of anti-Communists to a revengeful Stalin to which General Eisenhower committed the honor of the U.S."‡

However, when a man like Dr. Petiot justifies his killings with

---

‡ This little-known fact is the subject of a book by Count Tolstoy published by Scribner entitled *The Secret Betrayal* 1944–47. General Walter B. Smith, Eisenhower's chief of staff, stated to the author long after the war that Keel Haul, according to Eisenhower, was the result of very definite and specific orders to him from the White House. Could this have been another ploy of Dexter White (Soviet agent in the White House) or a strange conviction of a mortally sick President? The press and history seem to blame Marshall and Eisenhower for Keel Haul as a military order.

the mass, cruel, and insane killings by all sides both in World
War II and thereafter, one has no difficulty in understanding why
Petiot had a sardonic smile on his lips as his head fell from the
lunette of the guillotine!

CHAPTER VI

Initial Paris liquidations and
the beginnings of a plan
1941–43

In his intelligence activities, Petiot was often faced with information about Jews and other "enemies of the Reich" who were trying to keep their fortunes from the Nazis. In any event, Petiot himself began, in late 1941, to dwell on the fact that there were Jews among his own acquaintances who would pay large sums to escape from Occupied France—and who might have fortunes hidden away in bank notes and jewelry and furs.

Petiot was well aware of the skulduggery that went on as underworld characters, assigned to help ferret out the Jews who owned secret stores of gold (declared forfeit to the Reich under the gold program), crossed up their Nazi employers and kept the gold for themselves. The Communists were also busy. He knew, as everyone did, that in this greedy scramble, Germans, collaborators, Jews, and resistants were being exterminated without compunction by all sides. It began to seem almost his duty to himself and his family to take advantage of the times, to liquidate Germans and collaborators on one side and Jews and resistants on the other, but only those latter individuals who were against the "Boche," who were positively doomed anyway. Why it would be an act of charity to painlessly and quickly end the life of a Jew or a refugee from Poland or Holland or Germany but definitely marked for arrest and deportation to the German concentration camps. More important, why should the money and belongings of these unfortunates fall into the hands of their Nazi murderers?

He had, for instance, a client and neighbor, Joachim Guschinow, a Polish Jew, who had operated a prosperous fur business right across the street at 69 rue Caumartin, with a partner named Jean Gouedo. Guschinow most certainly was marked for early arrest by the Germans. He had already been forbidden by the German Occupation authorities to engage in business and had had to leave his affairs in the hands of his partner. Here was a fellow who would surely like to get clear of France before the Gestapo reached out and grabbed him. Guschinow, an incurable ladies' man, was being treated every day by Petiot for gonorrhea (according to Petiot) so they had come to know each other intimately. Petiot, in his notes, claims that rue Lauriston and its French Gestapo had Guschinow on their gold program. Bonny may have tipped him off, and possibly he might have owed Bonny a cut of the Guschinow spoils. In July, Petiot let drop the information that he knew of an escape route via Occupied France and Spain to Argentina. Guschinow did not react at once but when Petiot told him that the French Gestapo were about to arrest him, he begged Petiot to make the arrangements. Argentina seemed the perfect refuge to Guschinow. He had good friends there and should be able to set himself up in business quickly, provided there was some way to get at least part of his Paris stock of furs to Buenos Aires. Petiot assured him that he could arrange this very easily.

"I know someone very important at the Argentine Embassy," he said with such quiet authority that Guschinow never doubted him. But of course there was much planning to do. There was the matter of his wife. Would she be financially secure? Petiot needed to know all the details of his finances. Guschinow, with the taste of freedom in his mouth, hastened to reassure Petiot. There would be plenty of money. His wife, Renée (LaGendre), was a Catholic and had nothing to fear from the Nazis. She would keep a large part of their money, while Guschinow himself would sew 500,000 francs into his clothes. Another 700,000 in francs could be hidden in the handle and in the false bottom of a suitcase. Then he would leave in Petiot's care a million francs' worth of furs, to be forwarded to Buenos Aires with the help of Petiot's friends in the Argentine Embassy at Vichy.

This was the sort of thing Petiot had been waiting for. His little execution chamber—that deaf room at number 21—had already seen one young man die in convulsions, a young man who was never identified and for whose death Petiot was never tried. His body was found stuffed in a trunk floating in the Seine. But Guschinow, without question, would be the fattest fowl yet to come to the slaughter. In one evening—more than two million francs! (This was equal at the time to about $40,000 in U.S. dollars.)

Petiot noted with satisfaction that Mme. Guschinow was not the type to fret about her husband's absence. The shrewd doctor even caught a hint, or merely imagined, that perhaps the two each had a side interest and would be relieved to be rid of each other. Mme. Guschinow had decided that when her husband left, she would go to stay with friends in the country, but Petiot firmly reminded her that she must not try to communicate with her husband except through Petiot. Well and good. That avenue was closed up for a good time.

Now for Guschinow. On Christmas Day, 1941, Petiot invited Guschinow for a drink and they went over the details of the escape. Petiot, at this interview, made a mistake which he never repeated. He gave Guschinow the address—21 rue Le Sueur—making the man promise never to divulge this location to anyone. But, of course, Guschinow told his wife. He also had advised his partner of his impending departure and had also told him about the money and jewels, but did not mention the furs he had given Petiot. In fact, he had asked Petiot to keep this secret. The plan was for Guschinow to come to the address, all alone, on January 2, at 9 P.M., with pictures for his passport, with all identification removed from his person and his clothing, with his suitcase packed for his trip and all the valuables carefully hidden.

Guschinow took the Métro with his wife and got off at L'Étoile. Undoubtedly, there had been some eagerness on his part to leave his wife behind, but now, with the moment at hand, he found it was not so simple to say good-bye. Instead of parting at the Arc de Triomphe as they had intended, they walked along in the dark like lovers, unwilling to leave each other just yet. They came out from under the shadow of the great arch and strolled the wide avenue to the rue Pergolese, within two blocks of rue Le Sueur. How the doctor would have writhed to know how close he was coming to betrayal! But finally, the two kissed each other fondly and held on to each other for a moment. Until we meet in Argentina then! And keep safe!

At number 21, where all was dark because of the blackout, Petiot had disconnected the *sonnerie*—the bell system that unlatched the door as the bell rang inside. Guschinow rang the bell but the doctor had to come himself to open the door quietly and usher him wordlessly into the black interior. He led him to his neat office, where he had everything in seeming readiness. Guschinow sat in one of the deep armchairs while Petiot fussed with some papers on his desk and drew out a blank passport. He took the passport pictures from Guschinow and made a show of fixing them into the book. He questioned the other man closely: were the valuables all properly hidden? Was he sure he carried nothing to contradict this phony identity they were going to give him?

And now, there were some medical problems. He could not get into Argentina until he had been vaccinated for smallpox and inoculated against typhoid. The serum and the documents were all here and it could be managed in a few minutes. If he would just take off his coat and roll up his sleeve? Guschinow hastened to do as he was told. Methodically, Petiot prepared the fatal shot —a large bubble of air to be driven into the bloodstream to cause an embolism of the heart. Guschinow held out his arm and watched the needle slide in. There, it was done with. Now, if he would just come into the next room and rest for a moment, he would be ready for the vaccination. There might be some slight soreness, perhaps some stiffness. . . .

Guschinow grabbed up his coat, the coat that held the bank notes in the lining, and put it on, then took the suitcase—the suitcase with the jewels—into the triangular room with him. He could see there was a wide exit on the other side. And a little cot.

Now if he would just lie there. Petiot would complete the paper work and then there would be just the one more. . . . Petiot drew back and closed the door very gently, then silently slid the bolt. In due course, he would go to the stable to watch Guschinow in his death struggle. When Guschinow began to choke and gasp for life, it was plain from his expression that he suddenly knew what had been done to him. Some type of poison? He cried out, but was hardly able to rise. He called to Petiot. If he would save him . . . they could divide the wealth! There was much, much more!

Oh, my God! There was much more! They could divide it all! Help me! Please!

But his cries would never have carried beyond the walls, and he showed no fight like Petiot's first and younger victim. In twenty minutes, he was dead. Petiot could see that the man was still. Petiot hurried to the door, slid the bolt, and immediately checked the man's chest with his stethoscope. The doctor took the coat off Guschinow's body. He rubbed his hands briskly together, as he always did, in moments of excitement. He carefully slit open the lining. No need to ruin a good jacket. The money was all there. Petiot relished the feel of it, even the smell of it. A half a million francs!

He had all night to work on the body, with no danger at all of interruption. He removed all the clothing with care, folded it neatly, and put it carefully away, to pack it into a suitcase for later shipping to a safe hiding place. He dragged the squat fleshy body to the kitchen and heaved it onto the table between the sinks. It was a tedious job to eviscerate it, to sever the head, to remove the hands. Once or twice, Petiot had to rest, sheathing the scalpel deep in the right thigh of the body, as all medical students are taught to do. Every last bit of entrails he flushed down the wide drain, where they would not cause comment even if someone found them along the line. Human entrails—and especially fetuses —were nearly as common as cigar butts in the Paris sewers in these days.

The take in cash and jewels was just what had been promised— 512,512 francs and 60 centimes in cash; at least 700,000 francs in jewels. And here in one pocket was Petiot's own receipt for a million francs in furs. Well, that could be got rid of.

After a suitable delay, Petiot sent Mrs. Guschinow "news" of her husband's safe arrival in Casablanca, via Marseille. After another suitable interval, he had better news for Mrs. Guschinow. Her husband, without meeting any difficulties, had reached Buenos Aires and already entered a very successful business. There was even a letter from the Alvear-Palace Hotel urging Petiot to persuade both Mrs. Guschinow and the partner to follow.

The flaw in Petiot's scheme—the failure to provide written evidence that the victim had truly escaped and still lived—was one that he must immediately remedy. Future victims would be persuaded somehow to write personal letters testifying to their escape and urging trust in Petiot. Of course, if need be, Petiot might be able to forge some, but there was that strange drug made from cactus—peyote, or *peyotl*—that was supposed to weaken the will. He had studied the German scientists who claimed the Aztecs gave this to the sacrificial subjects in their sun-god ceremony and actually could get the victims to tear out their own organs. Not only would peyote enable him to get his victims to write letters, but would silence them during their incarceration and their death struggle.

Guschinow's body, when eviscerated and dissected, was taken away to the Seine late at night in the trunk of the bicycle trailer with the tarpaulin cover on, just as if it were another consignment of pictures or lamps such as Petiot often bought and sold. The Nazi curfew and the blackout removed any risks. Police later concluded that the earlier victim, found floating in the wicker trunk in the Seine, must have been Petiot's first victim, for Dr. Paul recognized the dissection as the work of Petiot. This body, found in May 1942, in the river near St. Louen, was indeed the first client of 21 rue Le Sueur, Petiot admitted, if he can be believed. But the body was not identified, nor would Petiot name the man. He was not charged with this killing. The head, with scalp and facial features removed, undoubtedly found its way into the Seine as well.

Years later, Dr. Paul commented on the cunning and medical skills of Dr. Petiot, for whom he had a strong admiration. Dr. Paul could never find the cause of death of any Petiot victim, nor could he ever identify any Petiot cadaver or debris. According to Petiot, Dr. Paul alone concluded that his first victim of 21 rue Le Sueur was that found in a roped trunk in the Seine on May 7, 1942—a male, thirty years old, who had been eviscerated and was headless, with both feet and hands cut off. He recognized Petiot's expert surgical dissection. Dr. Paul begged him, as one scientist to another, to disclose the identity of this victim and to explain how he killed his victims. Unknown to Dr. Paul, even when he died some years ago, Dr. Petiot in his notes states he almost talked because of his affection and respect for Paul. It was only to Paul that Petiot confidentially admitted that he may have liquidated some 150 persons but frankly had lost count of the number of his victims.

Petiot's extreme care and planning that went into the disposal of the bodies of his victims—the removal of all identifying marks, even fingerprints, the lifting of the face off the skull, the separate disposal of the head as well as the preparation of cover stories of all sorts to persuade the friends and relatives that the victims still lived—all seem to argue against Petiot's having been so careless as to allow that foul black smoke to pour out of his chimney for days on end, announcing to the whole neighborhood that something outlandish was taking place at 21 rue Le Sueur. It seems probable that this disaster was the deliberate effort to betray the existence of the charnel house—perhaps by one of the many parties or sides he played against each other for his own advantage. The French Gestapo on rue Lauriston—which later pretended to know nothing about number 21, although there is every reason to suspect they did know about it—could have been responsible. Petiot eliminated several of their principals and at least two former friends that Lafont and Bonny, those notorious traitors who presided over the rue Lauriston group, wanted rubbed out. At least one important witness testified at the Petiot trial that his brother had been liquidated by Petiot acting for rue Lauriston.

Or could the burning of the bodies have been an act of panic by someone less calculating and confident than Petiot? It was clear enough that the existence and even the purpose of 21 rue Le Sueur was known to at least one or two others. Even though Petiot's brother Maurice was never brought to trial for complicity, he had to own some guilty knowledge. Maurice helped secure the lime that was used in the pit at number 21. Maurice held the keys to the place while Petiot was in jail. Maurice transported the fifty or more suitcases from rue Le Sueur to Auxerre. Maurice was privy to the sudden growth of his brother's wealth, for he helped manage the buildings Petiot had bought and he himself was set up in the radio business in Auxerre by means of his brother's money.

Several police principals in the Petiot case, after many years of review and thought, believe that Masuy probably ordered the sabotage of 21 rue Le Sueur. There is evidence that Petiot, for a price, may have disposed of some of the bodies of prominent resistants tortured to death by the Abwehr. Also, Masuy may have been the guardian angel of 21 rue Le Sueur for a cut in Dr. Petiot's profits. In either case, with the Germans on the run, Petiot may have tried to switch sides, and no one could double-cross Masuy. One certain fact is that two secret meetings between Masuy and Petiot did take place while Petiot was held prisoner by the rue des Saussaies' German Gestapo and released shortly after the last meeting. Petiot's release by the Gestapo and his protection during the Occupation must have come from Masuy or Lafont or both. The unexplained destruction of some of Petiot's old records seems to point to Masuy, as it is doubtful if Lafont would have ever had the authority to eliminate records.

René Nezondet, the old-time friend of Petiot who eventually became a jail mate at Fresnes prison, testified that Maurice had confessed to him that he had found "sixty" bodies at number 21 in December 1943, had been horrified by the realization of what was going on, and had declared his brother a dangerous madman. But Nezondet was given to outright invention of fanciful tales about the doctor who had been his friend and his enemy in bygone days.

In order to properly trace the circumstances that spelled out the deaths of three persons for which Petiot was later charged, it is necessary to go back to the early days of the Occupation.

A month's search at that time could probably not have turned up in Occupied Paris two more forlorn waifs than Jean van Bever and Jeanne Gaul. Van Bever, a coal peddler in his forties, could have been cast for an escapee from a concentration camp, or even the assistant to a mad doctor. He had deep-set burning eyes, a haunted face, and long dark hair. He carried himself in a permanent slouch. His clothes hung on him as if they had been selected from rag heaps. He was furtive, hungry, lean, altogether without spirit, and almost without friends.

Van Bever had been born into a well-to-do family at Marly-le-Roi (Seine et Oise). His father, Adolphe van Bever, was a man of great note in the literary world, author of a number of erudite books and editor of a famed anthology of French poets. His mother, the former Marguerite de la Quintinie, a society belle, was the niece of the great French artist La Quintinie. But Jean Pierre Marc Ernest van Bever was a nobody.

His family had sent young Jean to an exclusive prep school—Louis-le-Grand Lycée. Jean had earned an A.B. and had gone on, under pressure from his parents, to study for his master's, but his ambition petered out before ever that goal was reached. He was called up for army service in 1939 but was soon discharged for physical disability. He then idled from one small job to another, showing aptitude for none. By 1941 he had been married, had a little girl, had been divorced, and was out of work. His wife and daughter went to live with his wife's parents and Jean put them out of his life.

At his father's death, Jean inherited half a million francs and a house. He sank the money in celebration and in a small printing shop, which perished very quickly of neglect, taking the last of Jean's inheritance with it. By 1942, Jean had been reduced to selling odd lots of coal to government buildings and installations in the Twentieth Arrondissement. He lived in a small furnished room in a "hotel"—actually a cheap boardinghouse—at 56 rue Piat. Defeated, lonely, constantly hard-up, and haunted by a feeling of inferiority that made it impossible for him to win friends, Jean found solace in the company of women. Hardly a night passed when he did not bring a Paris streetwalker into his narrow bed. But it was companionship he sought more than sex, and this seemed the only way he could buy it. Then he met Jeanne Gaul.

Jeanne was a whore, and far from a pretty one. Like van Bever, she was an outcast, an unlicensed prostitute, addicted to morphine, who spent her days haunted by loneliness, by her gnawing need for the drug, and fear of arrest. She had never been a pretty girl, but years before she had known a tomboy atractiveness that, with a better break in life, might have earned her a happy future. She had a pert, rosy-cheeked, even saucy face, with turned-up nose, large, slightly bulging eyes, and pigtails. She had been born in Bar-le-Duc in 1907 and had grown up during the First World War, when food was scanty, and her family, being poorer than many, had suffered from want. But young Jeanne developed a generously curved body all the same, and by the time she was sixteen, she had begun experimenting with sex. By the time she was seventeen, she was pregnant and could not say for certain which of her many boy friends was responsible. Her family would have none of her then. So young Jeanne was bundled off one night to a *sage-femme*, a midwife who performed an abortion, and Jeanne went then to Fontainebleau, to work as a chambermaid in a private family.

Jeanne, however, yearned for more excitement than the life of a small-town domestic could offer, so she soon found a job in Paris, with the Viscountess of Ginestat. While Jeanne, with her pudgy little face and her frog-like eyes, looked the part of a housemaid, she was still the frisky tomboy who had had more boy friends than she could count. At age thirty, in 1937 or thereabouts, she met a dashing Dutchman who won her heart, and she went off with him. This fellow, who had a years-long police record under the name of Van Wyseburgh, earned his living by selling narcotics and added extra spending money by booking prostitutes. He introduced poor Jeanne to both his professions—helping her become addicted to dope and then peddling her body all over Paris and collecting her fees.

As a prostitute, Jeanne, for a time, was a great success. She had both a strong appetite and aptitude for sex and was able to transport her customers by means of sexual techniques that left them exhausted while her sturdy little body stood always ready for even more turbulent exercises. But her need for narcotics grew ever stronger and she had to work harder and harder to find the funds that would keep her habit fed. After Nantes, she "worked" for a time in a *maison de tolerance* in Clamecy, then in Nievre, and (of all places) in Auxerre. Within a short time, she became the private property of still another pimp, this time a tougher and more dangerous character named Henri Baldenweck, but known to his associates as "Henry the Jailbird." Baldenweck made a living from Jeanne for a time but found it impossible to cope with her addiction, which had become insatiable. He abandoned her in Paris, and Jeanne, without a "manager" or a house to work from, had to operate without a license, haunting the cheap bars and dodging the gendarmes. In a bar near La Madeleine, one night in 1941, her glance fell on a figure as woebegone as herself. But this was no pimp, procurer, dope pusher, or addict. This was Jean van Bever, forty-one years old at the time and looking fifty. Jeanne herself was thirty-four. Could it be called love at first sight? Or was it just the sudden deep sympathy of one unwanted soul for another? They talked. Jeanne went home with her new boy friend and shared his bed and meager supper. By November, Jean had persuaded Jeanne to give up streetwalking and live with him. She promised to try to cure herself of her addiction and Jean became a new man. Stimulated by his new responsibility, he decided to go into business with a young Italian, Ugo Papini, who lived at the same "hotel."

Together, van Bever and Papini organized an odd-lot delivery service of charcoal for small office buildings and apartment buildings that did not want to purchase fuel in quantities large enough for truck delivery. From this enterprise, van Bever, with his college degree and his literary background and his command of several languages, began at last to earn a decent living. It was no trouble for Jeanne to give up prostitution and to perform her sexual circus for the sole benefit of her lover. Van Bever was delighted. But her addiction did not yield to their attempts to cure it. Poor Jeanne's thighs wore a dozen sores from constant hypodermic injections. And sometimes Jeanne's recollections of her ardent nights in the whorehouses depressed and irritated van Bever.

Her reminiscences did not sit well with van Bever and finally they made Jeanne less attractive to him. Eventually, when his Jeanne was lying at home in a drugged stupor, van Bever would be out carrying on with another prostitute—France Mignot. France was far more attractive in face and figure than Jeanne had been. But she was cruel, ruthless, without an ounce of decency or kindness. Her own parents had made her a prostitute.

Soon after van Bever met France, she decided he was well-to-do, and she played up to him strongly, even inviting him down to visit her family at Troyes. The visit, however, was a trap. As van Bever was undressing to go to bed with the daughter of the house, the bedroom door burst open and in rushed mother and brothers. They hurled themselves upon him, threw him down, beat and kicked him, stole his wallet and his suitcase, and threw him out of the house. He was so badly injured that he had to go to a nearby hospital for treatment. Poor van Bever could never understand this reception.

"I don't know what they were after," he told his partner Papini. "But whatever the reason, I have reported the incident to the police and I must go back to Troyes on March twenty-fourth to testify at the Tribunal Correctionnel. In fact, I intend to sue for damages."

Before any such suit was filed, however, the Vice Squad, in the persons of detectives Dupont and Gauthier, raided the room where van Bever and Jeanne Gaul lived and discovered many empty vials that had contained heroin, all traceable to prescriptions given by five different doctors, including seven from Dr. Petiot. In twenty-two days, the bottles indicated, Petiot had given out five prescriptions in Jeanne's name and two in the name of van Bever. Each prescription represented a visit to Dr. Petiot's office at a fee of 200 francs (the equivalent of $10 to $12 in purchasing value) per visit. Van Bever insisted to the police that he was not an addict.

"Dr. Petiot knows I am not an addict," he told them. "He used my name just so he could give Jeanne some extra prescriptions to satisfy her demands and to help her overcome her habit."

As a result of this raid, the two lovers were brought to court, and Petiot was summoned to confront them. Petiot was righteously indignant.

"This man van Bever certainly *is* an addict," he declared. "And so is his mistress, as you can very well see. I gave them prescriptions, it is true, but I consider it better to give an addict a small amount of the drug he craves than to allow him to go out and steal, or even kill to get it. Besides, it is the normal practice, the only known cure, to supply an addict with his needs and then cut down gradually on his dosage.

"Besides," the doctor added casually, "they will have to admit I charged only two hundred francs a visit for my treatment and prescriptions. Certainly you are not going to accuse me of being an illegal dispenser of dope, a criminal, if I try to aid these unfortunate victims of the dope habit through compassion. Cures can sometimes be effected. Is it not worth trying? Am I at fault if I try to help them?"

In the Gaul–van Bever case, the police may have felt that they finally had Dr. Petiot in a corner. It seemed a certainty that van Bever would testify against the doctor and it was likely that Jeanne Gaul would too. A conviction of violation of the dope traffic laws could mean the lifting of Petiot's license—a death sentence to his career.

The outlook for Petiot was grim, indeed. Van Bever had hired the old family lawyer, Maître Menard, and had challenged the judge to inquire of many friends to learn if there was any truth in this charge of drug addiction. Van Bever's partner, Ugo Papini, was ready to testify that van Bever was not an addict and others with whom he had done business would offer the same testimony. Petiot secured the man who had won his admiration in defending Magda Fontanges and was well known in the underworld as "the Great Mouthpiece," Maître René Floriot. There did seem definite evidence that Petiot's motives had been humane, even though his act was illegal. There was the matter of the small fees—ten to twenty dollars, or less, a visit in U.S. money of the time—and there was positive agreement that he had refused van Bever a third prescription. Would a doctor in Petiot's position—a former mayor, a medical examiner, owner of substantial properties, an obviously wealthy and successful professional man—would he risk it all for a mere 100 francs?

On March 15, 1942, van Bever was conditionally released. He was to return on May 26 to testify before the Tribunal Correctionnel in the case against Dr. Petiot. On Saturday, March 21, van Bever told his partner Papini of a strange rendezvous that he had with a man he did not know. He was to meet the man in the rooming-house bar at 8:30. Van Bever had been ten minutes late and the man had not waited. He would try again Sunday. It was very mysterious. Papini had no idea what it was all about. Perhaps something to do with Jeanne Gaul, who was being held in jail pending trial.

On Sunday morning about 9 A.M., Papini and van Bever met on the narrow circular staircase of their rooming house at 56 rue Piat. They both went into the bar. There they found a man in his forties, husky, dark, clean-shaven, wearing a Basque beret. The man approached van Bever and spoke to him in a voice so low that neither Papini nor the bartender could hear what he said. After a short exchange, van Bever turned to his partner and said:

"Ugo, I must go with this gentleman. He is the man I missed yesterday. He is the husband of one of Gaul's old friends and is going to deliver a letter to me from Jeanne. I'll see you at your parents' this afternoon."

Papini was surprised at this sudden decision, but he had an appointment of his own and had to go at once. He followed van Bever and the swarthy man out the door. He watched the two of them walk down rue Piat toward the spot where tourists are often taken to get a breath-taking view of Paris and where there is a winding wooden stairway that leads to the rue des Couronnes, some five stories below. But they did not descend the stairs. Instead, they turned down a side street to the left and were immediately out of sight. Van Bever was never seen again.

Finally, Papini, deeply concerned for his friend and for their business, went to see van Bever's attorney, Maître Menard. The lawyer urged Ugo to report the disappearance to the *procureur de la République*—the attorney general—for immediate investigation by the police. On March 26, Papini wrote the attorney general a letter in which he not only reported the strange disappearance but also suggested that the family of France Mignot, who had beaten and robbed van Bever, might have abducted him to prevent his appearing against them on March 24, when the suit was scheduled to be heard.

On the very day Papini mailed this letter, a young man appeared at the office-home of Maître Françoise Pavie, the young woman lawyer who had been assigned by the head of the lawyers' guild to defend Jeanne Gaul. He left two envelopes with Miss Pavie's mother, then hurried away. One letter was addressed to the lawyer, the other to Jeanne Gaul. Both were signed by van Bever. Miss Pavie knew van Bever, for he had visited her earlier, after a telephone call, to assure her he would pay her a fee for defending Jeanne. He had planned to visit her again, after Miss Pavie had talked with Jeanne in jail. When Miss Pavie visited Jeanne at the Prison de la Roquette, the latter had received a warm and encouraging letter from van Bever stating he would call on Miss Pavie. But van Bever never did come again, and Miss Pavie had just that morning received a *pneumatique* from Jeanne Gaul, explaining that she had heard from Papini of van Bever's disappearance. Now she looked at these letters with some astonishment. The one addressed to the lawyer read:

Maître:
I am sending you a letter to please relay to Miss Jeanne Gaul. You will present my apologies to my lawyer and tell him I no longer need his services. Kindly accept my respectful salutations.
    Jean Marc van Bever

Miss Pavie promptly called Maître Menard, who was, even if no longer van Bever's lawyer, an old friend of the van Bever family. Together, they opened the letter addressed to Jeanne Gaul. It carried no date. It read:

My Love:
It is no longer necessary to tell any stories. You know I am an addict to the tune of one to four shots a day. You know that Dr. Petiot examined me in the next room. The proof is that he saw the scabs of my hypos. If I made false statements, it was to get temporary freedom to make a new life for myself somewhere else. We will meet on your release to try to make a new life together, far from all filth.
I kiss you very warmly.
                    Jean Marc van Bever

It was clear to both lawyers that this letter was better designed to exculpate Dr. Petiot than to serve in any way the cause of the Mignot family at Troyes. Had Petiot himself dictated it, it could not have been more happily worded for him.

The trials of Petiot, van Bever, and Jeanne Gaul were held in the Tenth Police Court on May 12, 1942. All the principals were represented by eminent counsel but without van Bever the case against Petiot, defended by Floriot, and the druggist, Boudier, defended by Maître Lefont, was seriously weakened. There was always the possibility that van Bever *had* been an addict and had indeed secured the prescriptions for himself. And the case was weakened even further by the absence of the court expert on narcotics, Dr. Desaille. The German Occupation authorities had, strangely enough, officially forbidden him to attend the trial. Of course this could mean that either Bonny or Masuy was protecting Petiot . . . probably the latter. The hearing was thereupon canceled and Judge Olmi was heard to remark on several occasions that Petiot had "strong support" and it was useless to move against him. The judge's remarks were made with the innuendo that Petiot's backing was unhealthy. "Does Petiot then have German friends?" men and women around the court asked each other.

A week later another hearing was held and this time brought to a conclusion. On May 26 the court announced its findings and imposed sentences: Jeanne Gaul, guilty—six months' imprisonment and a fine of 2,400 francs; van Bever, guilty (the verdict based on Petiot's assertions)—one year's imprisonment and 2,400 francs; Dr. Petiot, guilty—one year's imprisonment and a fine of 10,000 francs, with the prison sentence suspended. The druggist was absolved. An appeal filed later by Maître Floriot won a reduction in the fine to 2,400 francs but more important was that Petiot did not lose his medical license. It was this that van Bever had threatened, and it would have doomed Petiot.

The case was far from over. Van Bever was still to be found. With the war beginning to turn in favor of the Allies, the American victories of the Coral Sea and Midway, Doolittle's raid on Tokyo, and with talk of an invasion of Europe, hardly anyone in Paris was too deeply concerned over the disappearance of an obscure coal dealer. But the police continued to study the case, and the friends of van Bever and Gaul pressed for solutions. Those letters signed by van Bever—were they real or were they fake? There were several clues to indicate they had not been written by the missing man. Why, for instance, would he sign his full name to a love letter—unless to establish his identity firmly so that the letter would serve Petiot. Eventually, it would come out that Petiot was a devoted student of graphology. He was also an accomplished artist. His doodlings and drawings in court and in jail proved that. At this juncture, the authorities could not agree on whether these letters were real or mere imitations of the script of the missing man. Later, handwriting experts were to testify that they were authentic but written under some influence and seemingly dictated or, perhaps, even copied.

There was one policeman, however, who remained convinced that Petiot had engineered van Bever's disappearance—and who was to become even more convinced when a strangely parallel case soon developed. That was Police Inspector Gignoux, who made up his mind right then that Dr. Petiot had gotten rid of van Bever.

On May 28, 1942, Jeanne Gaul was released from prison, having served a week longer than three months. She promptly returned to prostitution and the use of narcotics. Without van Bever, her life held no more meaning. Strangely enough, she also returned to Dr. Petiot. Why? Was she merely seeking the only source she knew who might provide her with drugs? Or was she planning some complicated vengeance on the man she was sure had killed her lover? (Earlier, she had told Inspector Gignoux: "The disappearance of Jean astounds me. He certainly would not commit suicide. . . . I think he may well have been the victim of Dr. Petiot, for Jean's testimony would have convicted the doctor." Or did she perhaps hope that by renewing her relationship with Petiot, she might actually find van Bever? No one will ever know. Jeanne Gaul died, at the age of thirty-five, in the Emergency Hospital of Cité University as a result of an infection while undergoing treatment for dope addiction. A doctor at the hospital confirmed that she had died of tetanus (lockjaw), the result of an injection by an unclean hypodermic needle given some time before she entered the hospital.

Dr. Petiot, when informed of Jeanne's death, remarked that fate and "The Conquest of Chance" (this was the title of a book he was planning) had worked matters out in a fairly satisfactory manner. Van Bever and Gaul had double-crossed him after he had repeatedly helped them and now, apparently, both had received their just desserts.

But Petiot, in the intervening months, had been involving himself deeply in other matters and had earned the devoted attention of the police. Even before van Bever disappeared, Petiot had been arrested for providing multiple prescriptions to a Mme. Cadinot and had again made his offer to co-operate with the Vice Squad by providing them with a list of addicts. A druggist on the rue des Écoles soon afterward reported that a Petiot prescription had been tampered with, and the police, armed with a search warrant and accompanied by Judge Olmi, raided Petiot's apartment. Here they found an enormous supply of heroin, which they confiscated, along with a list of ninety-five addicts. Petiot readily admitted he had been "treating" all these people in an effort to help them.

The prescription in question (the one that had been tampered with) had been made out to one Raymonde Khait, who, as Raymonde Baudet, was well known to the police as a drug addict. Apparently Petiot, after refusing her an additional prescription for heroin (he had already given her four), gave her, instead, a prescription for Soneryl, a harmless sedative. One of Raymonde's boy friends (she had numbers of them), a man named Daniel Desroulet, had persuaded Raymonde to remove the word "Soneryl" with ink eradicator and substitute the words "14 vials of Heroin." The crude forgery was discovered at once and the police were notified. Raymonde Baudet was thereupon taken promptly to La Roquette prison and Dr. Petiot was charged with still another violation of the dope-traffic laws.

Petiot was justifiably enraged. Could he be blamed because some brainless ass had tried to alter a harmless prescription? He had merely been trying to help the girl—for his usual small fee— and this was his reward!

But Raymonde Baudet got Petiot into an even tighter fix by reporting to the police that her mother was also an addict and that the earlier prescriptions had been for both her mother and herself. This was a reasonably convincing story and might well have worked had she not told her half brother, Fernand Lavie, an administrative clerk with the police department, that Petiot had prompted this tale. To understand all that followed, it is necessary to examine the structure of the Khait family.

There was first of all Mme. Khait herself, who had been successively Mme. Lavie, Mme. Baudet, and finally Mme. Khait. Now in her mid-fifties, Mme. Khait was a neat, stout lady who kept a clean house and gave little thought to her appearance or her clothes as long as her husband was well cared for and her home and her clothes were spotless. Her husband, a busy tailor, was Jewish and so living under a constant strain in German-Occupied Paris. He was a quiet man of considerable courage who refused to skulk or to keep his peace when he thought he had been wronged. Her stepson, Fernand Lavie, held a good steady clerical job with the police and was never in trouble. But her favorite child, Raymonde, daughter by her second husband, was a cause for constant worry. Raymonde, now in her twenty-eighth year, had never married although she had never been without a boy friend, often having three or four at a time. She was a long-time addict who had been arrested on that count three times and twice convicted.

There seems no question whatsoever that Dr. Petiot was seriously trying to help Raymonde—first by giving her heroin prescriptions, then by refusing her any further dope but trying to get her off heroin and onto a harmless sedative. Mme. Khait was, perhaps, aware of this and she must have known, too, that Raymonde was completely under the influence of this dark-visaged, nervous doctor with the hypnotic eyes. It was not too strange, then, for the mother herself to pay heed to whatever the doctor suggested might help her troubled daughter, and even what might help him.

When the police came with Judge Olmi to raid his apartment and offices, Dr. Petiot had been outwardly calm—indignant, but self-assured. Yes, of course he admitted to possessing some heroin. As for the list of addicts, he was concerned with curing them. Judge Olmi, while the police officers poked through the files and cabinets, idly pulled open the drawer of a desk. It was crammed with jewelry.

"What's all this?" he demanded.

Petiot answered without a tremor:

"You know this district—theaters, night clubs, whorehouses. Often my clients have no money. I am not always inclined to take my fee in trade, so I sometimes accept their jewels in payment. Why, I have some old-time theater stars who have nothing left of their riches except the jewels they were given and they use them to pay me for treatments. Besides, I am something of an antiquarian myself. You can see my receipts if you wish. I often buy jewelry at the auctions at the Salle des Ventes."

This glib and convincing reply seemed to satisfy Judge Olmi.

But once the police had gone, Petiot moved like a demon. Fernand Lavie told what happened next at the Khait home:

"Around twelve-thirty in the afternoon, the bell rang and I let a man in. He said he was Dr. Petiot. He told my mother that he had given a prescription in my mother's name to Raymonde, her daughter, that Raymonde, being an addict, had been arrested and was in danger of a long prison term for falsifying one of the doctor's prescriptions. To save Raymonde, he said, my mother would have to testify that she herself, my mother that is, was frequently sick and a user of narcotics and that the prescriptions her daughter brought to the druggist were given her by Dr. Petiot in the treatment of her mother's addiction as well. As all the heroin prescriptions were in the name of Khait, this story could stand up.

"My mother at first refused to agree to this plan but the doctor was very persuasive in convincing her that this was the only solution to my sister's very difficult position. It was the only way, he said, to save Raymonde from certain charges and a long prison term. My mother finally agreed."

Then, said Lavie, as the family was about to sit down to lunch, the doctor "practically pounced" on Mme. Khait. He wanted to give her, right then, "a few blank hypodermics of distilled water."

"The marks of a few shots on your thigh," said Petiot, "will support your story and remove any doubt by the police. Let us go to your bedroom."

Mme. Khait agreed and she and the doctor went into the bedroom together. After the doctor had gone, Lavie reproved his mother for agreeing to give false testimony and for allowing the doctor to put marks on her thigh to sustain the perjury.

"Oh, well," said Mme. Khait. "I have already done so much for Raymonde, I might as well do this for her, too."

Under her son's persuasion, however, she went to see her own physician, Dr. Trocme, a typical Parisian neighborhood doctor, tall, spare, square-shouldered, with a small mustache and glasses, a gentle, considerate man past middle years, so deeply involved in his studies and practice that he was sometimes absent-minded. He lived and kept his office at 13 rue La Grange, an old-fashioned walk-up apartment only a few blocks from the Khait home. Despite the cynicism natural to members of his profession, he was shocked past belief that a licensed doctor could stoop to such action. He looked up Dr. Marcel Petiot in the doctors' directory to assure himself he was indeed licensed.

Dr. Trocme urged Mme. Khait to abandon her plan to use these scars to support any false testimony. Instead, he urged her to take her story to the police. Mr. Khait was also furious and insisted that his wife go to the police. But before she followed this advice, she warned Raymonde that she was not going to pretend to have been using narcotics. Raymonde, still under Petiot's spell, phoned him of her mother's change of heart and he hastened to the Khait apartment, his eyes afire with rage.

"You should never have told Raymonde of those blank shots, or anyone else either!" Petiot told the mother, darkly. "There is real trouble ahead for you if you do not stick to your story of being an addict." Apparently satisfied that his threats would suffice, the doctor left. He seemed to have decided, afterward, however, that this was a threat to his career as serious as that

posed by Jean Marc van Bever, for on March 25, 1942, just three
days after van Bever had walked into oblivion, Mme. Khait, at 7
P.M., hurried out of her apartment and never came back. She told
her husband she had an appointment with Petiot and then with
Raymonde's lawyer, Maître Veron, whose fee Petiot had agreed to
pay. She left the household laundry boiling in a large kettle on the
lighted stove. Her identification papers, her food ration tickets,
her pocketbook were all left behind. When she had not returned
by a decent hour, her husband suspected Petiot had somehow had
a hand in her disappearance. Had he persuaded her to go into hiding? Had he . . . It was undoubtedly a matter for the police, but
Khait, a Jew, and realizing the police were under German and
even Gestapo control, hesitated to turn to them.

The next morning, he found two letters that had been slipped
under the door of their apartment. They seemed to be in the
handwriting of Mme. Khait. One was addressed to her son Fernand, the other to her husband. Khait opened his and noted immediately that it was dated March 21. But today was March 26,
and she had gone away last night! He read the letter:

> I am escaping to the free zone of France. Do not worry about
> me. In the best interest of my daughter, I must do this, for the
> police must believe that I am a drug addict. My absence will save
> me from difficult testimony and any cross-examination and diffi-
> culties. I am actually a user of narcotics, unknown to you, in order
> to relieve pains I have in my heart.
> I will be in the free zone where, using the same methods, you
> can rejoin me. Then later Raymonde will also join us. Please, for
> your sake as well as mine, do not report my absence to the police.
>   Marthe

The letter to Fernand, giving much the same information, was
signed "Mama." It, too, was dated March 21.

They must have been delivered by Mme. Khait, it seemed, for
the dog had not barked, as he surely would have at a strange step.
Also only someone intimately acquainted with the house could
have found the apartment without ringing the bell and rousing
the concierge.

Khait immediately sought Dr. Petiot at his office at 66 rue
Caumartin, convinced that the doctor was behind all this. Petiot,

with cold self-assurance, denied any knowledge of the letters or of Mme. Khait's whereabouts.

"I did not receive any visit from your wife on March 25 and I have not seen her since," he declared. "I don't know where she is. I do know she wanted to get away from Paris and I did recommend someone for her to see." Petiot scribbled for a while on a postcard and gave it to Khait. "Take this card and mail it," he said.

It was an "interzone" postcard addressed to a M. Gaston, at Plagne via Loupiac Cantal. The message read: "Have you seen the party whom I sent to you?"

Khait was puzzled. It is true his wife had wanted to visit her family in the free zone. It might be that the "party" mentioned on the card was his wife. The doctor was so calm and reasonable. And the letters. They *must* have been delivered by Marthe herself. When one escapes, one does not spread the news about beforehand. It is better that it look as if one has just stepped out on an errand. Mollified, Khait went home. Nothing was said to the police and he tried hard to believe that his wife was safe.

He was not the only one to get letters from Mme. Khait. At half past ten on the morning of March 26, a woman came to the home of Raymonde's lawyer, Pierre Veron, and handed an envelope to the maid. The maid was certain that the envelope was delivered by Mme. Khait herself, whom the maid had seen several times in the lawyer's office. (Later, the maid told police it was an unknown lady whom she had mistaken for Mme. Khait.) In the envelope were two letters and 300 francs. Both letters were dated March 21. They gave the same information contained in the letter to Khait—that Mme. Khait was in the free zone, that she wanted to avoid being a witness at her daughter's hearing, and that she was an addict, exactly as Dr. Petiot had said. The 300 francs was Mme. Khait's contribution to Maître Veron's fee for the defense of her daughter.

There was no one to make note of this fact at the time, but there were striking parallels between the van Bever letters and those purporting to be from Mme. Khait: all bore the same date, all were in strikingly similar handwriting. Yet there were a number of persons who were convinced that they were in the handwriting of two different persons. Even the handwriting experts could reach no consensus. Some said they were all forgeries by the same hand. Some said they were written by the people themselves but written under great stress—as under the threat of torture or death or under the influence of some drug and dictated to by some other party. (Edouard de Rougement, one of France's greatest handwriting experts, endorsed the latter view.)

Petiot at this time, spring 1942, was deeply involved with the police. He had been charged with giving them false information—after offering to act as informer—and his case came up in May. He was set free, with an apology from the court. At about this time, while he was passing through the halls of the Palace of Justice, he met Khait, who was distressed at not having heard any further from his wife.

"Your wife did not go to Plagne at all," Petiot told him. "I have heard from my connection there. I do not know where she is." Nevertheless Petiot affirmed his promise to pay the legal expense of Raymonde's defense.

The disappearance of Mme. Khait was finally reported to the Paris police on May 7, 1942, six weeks after she walked out of her apartment. This event, coming so soon after the disappearance of van Bever, prompted Inspector Gignoux to double his efforts to build a case against Petiot. The police were thoroughly convinced by this time that there was more than coincidence in the fact that key witnesses in two unrelated cases against Petiot should both disappear at the same time. Also, six letters (two to Maître Veron, two to Maître Pavie, and two to the Khaits), all clearing Petiot, were all dated on the same day and on an incorrect date. However, Petiot seemed untroubled. When questioned, he was always confident, sometimes calm, soft-spoken, sometimes blazingly angry and sarcastic. He was never at a loss for an answer. He could be overbearing to those who seemed the least in awe of him, or persuasive and pleasantly assured to men in authority. His reactions were instantaneous.

Maître Veron, the attorney for Raymonde Baudet and the supposed "friend" of Petiot, faced him often in various hearings and confrontations that followed and found that Petiot was a man who "gave you goose pimples." By this time, Petiot, driven by his gathering ambitions, harried by enemies, was worn-looking, drawn in the face, with a pasty complexion. But his eyes still burned with an inner fire and he was as cunning and quick as ever.

The central figure of the Khait case, however, was still Raymonde Baudet and she seemed to take pains that she should not be thrust into the background. She relished the notoriety that made people point her out, sometimes in night clubs where she awaited a pickup. She regaled reporters and police with stories that became increasingly fanciful until the press and the police began openly to doubt her. She did, however, win front-page attention for herself when she told Inspector Gignoux (specially assigned to both the van Bever and Khait disappearances) that Petiot had offered her a bribe of 100,000 francs if she would withdraw the complaint against him for the "sequestration"—i.e., kidnaping—of her mother. No witness was ever found to support this offer, nor any corroborating evidence whatever. Her brother, Fernand Lavie, who was one of the complainants, had never heard of the offer and doubted that it was really made. He recalled, however, that just before one of the hearings to be held in Judge Olmi's chambers, Petiot had indicated that he would like to talk to him alone. But the constant flow of witnesses and court officers made it impossible for them to find any privacy and he never learned what Petiot planned to say. Lavie admitted that perhaps Petiot wanted to make a similar proposal to him but that he didn't have to, for Judge Olmi seemed afraid of Petiot and had told him after the hearing that Petiot was stronger than he and that any action by the court might prevent a later prosecution when there was sufficient evidence.

To all accusations, including that of attempted bribery, Petiot was openly contemptuous. His supreme self-confidence made observers wonder, as they had before, what secret influence the doctor might own that made him so sure of himself. One time, in a hearing before Judge Olmi, Fernand Lavie was astonished at the timidity with which the judge treated Petiot. Petiot actually refused to reply for the record and insisted he be heard by Judge Olmi in private. The judge hastily closed the court, asked all others to leave the room, and heard Petiot without witnesses. Then he reopened the court and read the statements reportedly made by Petiot, but so rapidly that Lavie, at least, could not follow them.

However, Khait, husband of the missing woman, was not to be silenced. Unrecorded in any printed court record or unheard of in any police interrogation, the courageous Mr. Khait did have his day in court. At one of the hearings, he stood up suddenly and, pointing at Petiot, exclaimed:

"Miserable! It is you who assassinated my wife!"

Petiot hardly glanced at the man. With a sneer and a shrug of his shoulders, he gestured toward Khait.

"That man is mad," he said. "He should be locked up."

A new search warrant issued by Judge Olmi in furtherance of this investigation yielded nothing except a vigorous complaint from Petiot at this invasion of his privacy and the disturbance of his son and ailing wife. But the hearings went on and Petiot continued to object. Finally, one of Judge Olmi's assistants smilingly reassured him:

"Please, Dr. Petiot. We are not accusing you of anything. This is all mere formality. We really don't suspect you of burning van Bever and Marthe Khait in the furnace of your central heating."

Did Petiot's nerves perhaps tingle a little at this startling remark? If they did, he gave no sign. (On the other hand, it was perhaps only the Gestapo or the Abwehr who used the furnaces of 21 rue Le Sueur.) He was always cool, always self-assured, and often righteously indignant, and he always seemed to have a secret weapon up his sleeve. Only Mr. Khait kept after him. A few weeks after Khait had accused Petiot in open court, there was an early morning knock at the door of the Khait apartment. Few people were even up or about in the neighborhood. However, word got out. It was the German Gestapo. They had not come to ask questions. They had come for Mr. Khait. They took him with them and he never returned and was never heard of again. Later, a Gestapo double agent averred that Khait had been fingered by the French Gestapo, rue Lauriston, who had acted on a tip from a doctor informer in the Opéra Arrondissement!

Inspector Gignoux' investigations brought no results, although Gignoux and his associates remained convinced that Petiot had done away with the missing witnesses. But Petiot would admit nothing except that he had tried to help Mme. Khait get away.

"I agreed to take care of her daughter's legal expenses," he said. "Maître Veron asked for 1,000-franc fee. I therefore planned to

give Mme. Khait 500 francs. Finally, I gave her 1,500, partly to
keep my promise and partly to cover her extra expenses because
she desired to leave Paris. I gave her the addresses of two friends—
one at Plagne in Cantal and one in Lyon—my friend Nezondet."

Inspector Gignoux and his men checked everywhere, at Plagne,
at Lyon, throughout the free zone, and found no trace of either
Marthe Khait or Jean van Bever. Ultimately, Gignoux reported to
both Judge Olmi and the district attorney:

"The conclusion which is now almost certain in each of the two
cases is sequestration [kidnaping] or assassination."

As for Raymonde Baudet, she soon dropped completely out of
sight, although there is a record of her having been arrested in
1943 and sentenced to four months in prison as a drug addict.
After that, there is no trace.

All during these hearings and confrontations, Petiot continued
his varied activities, not merely his professional duties but his antique dealings, his pushing of narcotics and narcotic prescriptions,
and his active efforts to recruit "customers" for his "escape" route
. . . not to mention his intelligence and gossip gathering. And he
found time to live the life of a seemingly busy Paris physician
with few leisure hours. Sometimes he did give an evening to
bridge at the home of some friend or relative. Late at night he
still devoted to reading. He was not really a social being but when
it served his purpose, he could bandy small talk, deal charmingly
with his companions, make little jokes, and submerge his very real
contempt for most other humans and all of man's institutions.

On a rainy Paris evening in April, Dr. Petiot and his wife, Georgette, attended a small bridge party at the home of Raymond
Vallée, the insurance agent who was married to Mme. Petiot's favorite cousin, Paulette. The Vallées lived not far from the Petiots
in the Opéra Arrondissement at 20 rue Concordet. Vallée handled all the insurance business for the various Petiot properties,
having secured the business through his wife's influence. Actually
he did not know Dr. Petiot at all well and confessed to feeling a
little afraid of him but had arranged this party to bring Petiot together with his own family doctor, a staid gentleman, almost seventy, who wore old-fashioned clothes, including a wing collar and
wide cravat and an old-fashioned Napoleon III beard, neatly

trimmed to just the width of his mouth and coming to a blunt point about two inches below his chin with a heavy-drooping mustache. Vallée was interested to see how this conservative old professional, Dr. Braunberger, slow-talking, deliberate in all his gestures and prosperously dressed, would hit it off with the volatile, progressive, and somewhat sloppily turned-out Petiot. After arranging the party, he expressed some misgivings to Paulette, his wife:

"I don't know if they'll get along. You know Braunberger is getting a bit senile, keeps repeating himself and forgetting things and plays a filthy game of bridge. Petiot is just the opposite, a sharp player who will raise hell if someone pulls a dumb play."

His misgivings were in vain, for the two doctors, after several friendly rubbers of bridge in which another neighboring couple joined, fell into an amiable and animated discussion of the treatment of cancer. Mme. Braunberger, a wispy old lady with a deeply lined face, took no part in the discussion nor did the others, but after the Petiots had gone, Vallée asked the older doctor what he had thought of his colleague.

"A very interesting man," said Dr. Braunberger. "And I will tell you what I think—the man is either a genius or a madman!"

Dr. Braunberger was not the only person to appraise Petiot in this manner, although no one had put it so succinctly before. Years later, just before his trial, Petiot was to make a sarcastic comment on this view: "If he, Petiot, had been declared sane by so many psychiatrists . . . well, then . . . according to Lombroso, he could well be a 'genius paranoiac'!"

No one at the small party dreamed of what was to come of this meeting. Perhaps there had been some thought that all might become closer friends. The Braunbergers lived a short walk from the Vallée apartment while the Petiots lived about the same distance in the other direction. Vallée did not know if they ever met again, but they certainly never came together again at his home. Petiot's private dealings with Braunberger were some weeks in the future. For some weeks, Petiot was absorbed by his troubles with Judge Olmi and Inspector Gignoux. And when they had almost cleared up, a face from the past suddenly appeared at his door. A pretty face, but not really a welcome one.

The face belonged to Denise Hotin, a young lady of twenty-

seven, and by a twist of fate, another witness who, if she had been
so minded, could have put Petiot in danger of losing his license.
She was no addict, nor a prostitute. She was a charming girl with
a seductive figure, a former model and saleslady at Lancel, famous
couturier and perfume shop, who had married into a well-to-do
family. But she represented to Petiot a serious mistake in judgment and he had hoped he would never be reminded of her. To
have her appear at his door on June 3, 1942, just when the van
Bever and Khait cases were cooling down, made it look as if fate
had determined to keep raining blows on his head until he gave
in.

Petiot showed none of his inner dismay to his visitor. She was
friendly, cheerful, and ingratiating. She had come to Petiot as to
an old friend, seeking a favor; but Petiot recalled vividly the first
time they had met, in 1941, and the disaster that almost followed.

Denise Bartholomeus, a thoroughly sophisticated Parisian girl,
had married, in June 1941, Jean Hotin, the son of the mayor of La
Neuville-Garnier (Seine-et-Oise). Her new father-in-law, besides
being mayor, was a wealthy farmer, and her husband, Jean, was a
dutiful and apparently beloved son. There seemed no reason why
they should want for anything, but the elder Hotin was as tight-
fisted as only a French peasant knows how to be. He believed that
the women of his household should work in the fields, keep house,
raise children, and comport themselves modestly. Denise had not
quit her modeling and sales job to become cook, housemaid, and
farmhand to an old man and his son. She had believed herself
pregnant when she got married and now she felt trapped. She realized, too, that the townspeople, with the mayor's family in the
public eye, could reckon back nine months as well as any gossips
in France and would realize that the child was perhaps abnormally "premature." She determined, therefore, to seek an abortion.

She had come to Paris then, not seeking Petiot—for in 1941 she
had never heard of him—but looking rather for a midwife some
friends had recommended, a lady who practiced her profession in
the St. Lazare section of Paris. The sage-femme would have none
of the case. The midwife she went to had an ad in a Paris paper.
Yet she offered, strangely enough, to make an appointment with a
doctor of her acquaintance who would perform the operation for

a 5,000-franc fee. This was a great deal more money than Denise
had brought with her but she had the woman make an appointment with the doctor all the same at the home of an old friend,
Mme. Mallard, who lived at 6 rue des Dames.

The doctor she met at Mme. Mallard's did not identify himself,
nor did anyone press him for his name. He was dark, nervous, intense, with eyes that seemed to look a person through. He made it
clear very quickly that he was no "abortionist" quack but a man
who deeply believed in the right of a mother to refuse to bring an
unwanted child into the world. He remained to be convinced that
this abortion was really needed. As he questioned Denise, his
burning eyes remained fixed on her face and he continually
rubbed his hands together.

Denise's youthful charm and sincerity—and the fact that the
money was readily available—had its effect on the doctor and he
agreed to perform the abortion. Denise then returned to the farm
to get the money. Her husband, Jean, had originally opposed the
idea but he could not resist his young wife's entreaties and his father did not want any possible gossip. In any case, Jean was not at
all sold on this too-pretty, too-sophisticated city girl who did not
want to work in the fields, so Denise was soon back in Paris with
the 5,000 francs.

The operation was performed at Mme. Mallard's apartment at 6
rue des Dames. Dr. Petiot, one can assume, was no more painstaking in disinfecting his instruments or scrubbing up for the operation than he had ever been. As a result, Denise developed an
infection that soon put her in danger of her life.

Petiot knew, even better than his patient, what disaster now
threatened. Should Denise die and he be exposed, as he was sure
to be, as an abortionist, he would lose his license at once, to say
nothing of the jail term that might be awarded him. So he frantically sought to stem the progress of the infection. It was a fearsome struggle that reached its climax one terrible night when he
was summoned by a frantic girl, Mme. Mouron, daughter of
Mme. Mallard, with the word that Denise was dying. Petiot's
prompt response was all that saved her. But in the course of the
struggle his identity had to be revealed to all involved, particularly
because it was necessary for him to urgently get his prescriptions

filled. This seemed a minor disadvantage compared to the catas-
trophe that might have occurred.

With Petiot luck and one whole night and almost two days of
constant attention, Denise returned relieved and well to the farm
at La Neuville-Garnier with her father-in-law's reputation saved
and her husband never realizing how near he had come to losing
her. That should have been the end of the affair for Petiot, who
felt well rid of the girl. What a risk to take for a 5,000-franc fee!

And now here she was again, on top of the van Bever and
Mme. Khait disappearances, with all her damaging knowledge of
Petiot's deeds, with his home address, and with the ability, should
she be strongly tempted, to blackmail him out of his fortune. Not
that she seemed the least inclined to threaten him. But the request she was making of him carried more than a hint of danger.

She explained her problem to him as to an old friend, or to a
family doctor. It was, in essence, in-law trouble prompted by the
sort of small-town gossip doctors certainly must be familiar with.
Somehow the word had gotten around that her trip to Paris had
been for the purpose of seeking an abortion. What seemed to
trouble her father-in-law most was that if the story were true, it
meant that the potential heir to his extensive properties and to his
honored name had been scraped out of her womb with no more
ceremony than if he had been a calf of a mixed breeding. The old
mayor, who had the young man completely under his thumb, had
gotten the husband stirred up too so that he was demanding proof
—in the form of a doctor's certificate or some equally incontrovertible document. Her father-in-law had even hinted possible investigation by police. (Was this the father-in-law talking, Petiot
must have wondered, or was his charming visitor choosing this
way of warning him of what *she* might do if he refused?)

There were just too many witnesses—not just Denise and the
midwife, but Mme. Mallard and her daughter. They all knew his
identity and were privy to his crime. He must find a way immediately of scotching this threat. But none of this inner turmoil
revealed itself in his manner. Petiot made up his mind in a flash.
Why, of course he would help her. It would be simplicity itself. A
simple statement to the effect that he had treated her for a respi-
ratory ailment, or something equally innocuous. But he must ask
her to come to his other office. Come in the evening. Just ring the

bell and wait for him to open the door. There was no concierge. The address? 21 rue Le Sueur!

Denise Hotin was delighted. Suddenly her worries had been lifted off her shoulders and she could look forward to peace with her husband and father-in-law. Until tonight then! She smiled and bade *au revoir* to the good doctor. Then she hurried to the apartment of Mme. Mallard to thank her once more for her kindness and to bid a final good-bye. She was to see Dr. Petiot tonight and then she would be off to La Neuville-Garnier on the night train. But Denise did not take that night train. She did not return to La Neuville-Garnier that night or any night. No one who knew her, unless it was Dr. Petiot, ever set eyes on her again.

Soon afterward, her husband received a letter, posted in Paris, in which Denise said that she had decided to go to the free zone for a while. The handwriting seemed strange—as if written in a hurry or under a strain, but, fortunately for Petiot, there were no immediate inquiries. To have three potential witnesses disappear within a few weeks' time—that would have been too much for even the slowest-witted detective. The Hotin family, however, were neither surprised nor disturbed that Denise failed to return promptly. It was well known that she had no taste for existence in that penny-pinching household and certainly no intention of working in the fields. Small-town life and farm life, they had never been for her, and with her father-in-law's dislike for her, well, it was no wonder she had chosen to run away.

It was not until the middle of the following winter that her husband, finally beginning to fret at her long silence, came to Paris to try to pick up the trail of Denise. He first visited Mme. Mouron, who directed him to Dr. Petiot. Jean Hotin went then to 66 rue Caumartin, where he found the doctor's sign. He noted that he was not in time for the listed consultation hours. He hesitated. He was still a shy country boy, and he had no stomach for bursting in on an important doctor without an appointment at the wrong hour. So he did not even go up the stairs to learn if the doctor was in. Instead, he went back home to his father and gave up the search.

Years would go by before anyone would attempt to connect the disappearance of Denise Hotin to Dr. Petiot. Even eighteen months later, in 1944, when the fire at 21 rue Le Sueur revealed the possible liquidation of hundreds of persons connected to Dr. Petiot, the Hotins did nothing. On April 17, 1945, Jean won a divorce in the local court, aided by his father, claiming his wife had abandoned him. However, the parents of Denise did not forget her, and later Denise's name was added to the list of probable Petiot victims . . . but years later.

Meanwhile, Dr. Petiot was finally out from under the threat of exposure and could begin to give some untrammeled thought to the further building up of his estate. It was his deepest intent to create in his lifetime a body of wealth so substantial that neither his wife, whom he loved, nor his son, whom he adored, should ever know want. His brother and his family had to be taken care of. The interest that accrued from investments with the Crédit Lyonnais seemed too picayune for him. As his father-in-law had often told him, real estate was the thing. Even with wartime inflation, real estate in Occupied and defeated France was depressed and there were still properties to be had that would give steady income and security and growth and provide a hedge against further devaluation of the franc. Of course, to obtain the best of these properties, one had to be ready to deal both over the table and under the table, to recognize that the official price was but a fraction of the true purchase price.

So Petiot, officially paying 175,000 francs on the table and another 400,000 francs under the table (according to his notes), purchased, in the name of his son, two apartment buildings on the rue de Reuilly. One was three stories high and the other four. Together, there were twenty-one apartments, all rented under long leases to responsible and prompt-paying tenants. In every respect, the buildings were prime investments: their condition was excellent, maintenance costs were small, and the neighborhood was one of the best. The management of these buildings, like that of other properties he had bought, was given into the hands of brother Maurice, who could be counted on to provide honest and faithful stewardship. Petiot took a deep satisfaction in the conclusion of this deal, yet his acquisitive nature drove him to seek out still more opportunities to salt away small bits of wealth and to turn extra profits.

He continued to make frequent visits to the Salle des Ventes to buy antiques, rugs, furniture, paintings, old books, and jewelry, not for investment merely, but partly as a means of making further profits and partly as a cover for his gradual acquisition, through his "business" at 21 rue Le Sueur, of the property and jewels of his "clients."

He had completed his "apprenticeship" in murder now, having done away with three, possibly four, people in Villeneuve and three people in Paris, all out of necessity rather than for profit. Then (according to his notes) there was Guschinow and two others in connection with his planned "escape" operation. He had made a few clumsy mistakes that were wholly out of character—phrasing the letters in such similar fashion, dating them carelessly all on the same date. He had also learned about an important supplement or complement to his operations in his will-weakening or hallucinatory drug—peyote. Now he would take time to work out his plans in detail and with deliberation. And, of course, he would have the advantage of wartime Paris, where disappearances, even violent deaths, nameless bodies, and screams in the night were growing almost commonplace.

CHAPTER VII

Dr. Eugène's escape agency
1941–43

While Dr. Petiot was busy perfecting his plans in a very restricted
and limited area in Paris in the summer of 1942, he noted that
"four hundred million people in Europe lay under the yoke of
Nazi Germany, from the Arctic to the Mediterranean, from the
English Channel to the Black Sea, and almost to the Caspian.
Hitler's panzer armies had reached the Volga and were nearing
the Nile. In the East, his new ally, Japan, had engulfed the col-
onies of older empires. From the Pyrenees to the Steppes there
was no other sovereign state but Switzerland and that only to provide a base for espionage and a safe haven for those who hedged
their bets." According to Petiot in his remarks, Hitler, Stalin,
Franco, Mussolini, de Gaulle, and Pétain all had money in numbered accounts in Switzerland. (Could this mean that there is still
a numbered account in Switzerland, probably with a Geneva
bank, belonging to Dr. Petiot or perhaps willed or transferred to
Mrs. Petiot or Gerhardt Petiot or to Petiot's attorney?)

In Paris, in recounting it afterward, Mme. Braunberger and the
Vallées could recall only one small hint that the two doctors, Dr.
Petiot and Dr. Braunberger, who met at the Vallée apartment that
wet April night, would ever meet again. There had been a discussion at the bridge table of Dr. Braunberger's impending troubles
with the new Nazi racial laws and the ever-increasing power of the
Third Reich. Jews were being snatched from their homes, even off
the streets, almost every day to be carried off to labor camps. And
now there was talk that doctors were much in need there. Dr.
Braunberger was Jewish although his wife was not. It seemed alto-

gether too likely that one of these days the Nazis would get around to him—perhaps when his doctor's license would be canceled. If they did, could he hope to hide or escape somewhere?

Very quickly and without any special emphasis, Dr. Petiot had told the doctor:

"Well, whenever you want to escape, let me know very discreetly. Confidentially, I know a way it can be done. There is a method of getting into the free zone and even to Africa and South America."

Nothing else was said on the subject at that time. Dr. Braunberger in the following weeks never mentioned to his wife his having any dealings at all with Petiot. But he and his wife were both troubled as the tension increased in Paris. The fact that Dr. Braunberger had built a distinguished career since 1902 and had served as a captain in the Medical Corps in World War I—these were of no account in the face of the fact that he was a Jew. Before summer began, he learned that his license to practice would be revoked on June 22. Then, approximately six weeks after the bridge party, at half past eight on the morning of June 20, Dr. Braunberger received a telephone call. A man's urgent voice asked him if he could call on a sick person on rue Duret.

"Yes, certainly," the doctor told his caller. "Give me the exact address."

"Meet me at the entrance to L'Étoile Métro station," said the voice. "I will take you there."

It was after ten-thirty before Dr. Braunberger was ready to leave. There was no special good-bye for his wife as he went out the door, nor any indication that this was more than just what it seemed—a routine sick call. It did seem a little strange that the man, apparently a stranger, should arrange to meet and conduct the doctor to the sickroom, but the citizens of Paris in those days were always taking small precautions. The doctor went calmly out of his apartment and was never seen again. His rendezvous was probably with Dr. Petiot although this was never supported by any evidence.

Mme. Braunberger was not left to wonder about her husband. That very day a *pneumatique* arrived at the apartment of Raymond Vallée. It was a special delivery letter with Dr. Braunberger's letterhead and unmistakably (according to Mme. Braun-

berger) in the doctor's script, even though it seemed cramped and
hurried:

> *I was almost arrested but managed to escape. Notify my wife
> that I will not return and have her pack two suitcases with our most
> valuable possessions to escape to the free zone and thence over-
> seas. I will advise her through you where she can join me. She must
> tell no one anything and she must advise my patients that I fell
> sick in a suburb of Paris and could not get back.*

Raymond Vallée was much surprised that a letter of this sort
should have been sent to him. He had never been a close friend of
the doctor's, only his insurance agent and the husband of Dr. Petiot's cousin. One of the reasons for the bridge party was to see if
he could develop a slightly closer relationship with both doctors.
When Vallée hurried with the letter to Mme. Braunberger, she,
too, was surprised that her husband should have entrusted a mission so delicate to a man he did not even like. He could have written to his brother, Dr. Marcel Braunberger.

The doctor's nurse and secretary, Miss Callede, also expressed
surprise that Vallée should have been selected as intermediary.
She was positive that Dr. Braunberger disliked him. Yet there he
was with this dangerous and confidential message. And there
seemed no reason to doubt the letter's authenticity. It had been
postmarked at the rue La Boetie branch post office, which is just a
half mile from 21 rue Le Sueur. Two days later, on June 22,
came a letter directly to Mme. Braunberger, this again in handwriting that could be identified as Dr. Braunberger's, yet so
cramped and shaky it seemed to have been written by a man of
eighty. It bore no date but was sent from the same La Boetie
postal zone, and opened in a manner strange indeed. "My dear
friend," it began. Never in their married life had Dr. Braunberger
used such a phrase in writing or talking to his wife. Then it went
on:

> *I was almost arrested. I was able to escape arrest and all that
> would have followed. We cannot see each other for the present be-
> cause that would be dangerous. You must be under surveillance,
> therefore be forewarned of anything and do not talk to anyone. I
> will get word to you as to what you should do. We must save what*

we can. Write letters to notify persons of our departure, but let
them be delivered after our departure. I kiss you.

On June 23, still another undated letter, postmarked at La Boetie, came addressed to Mme. Braunberger. This letter was written
on plain paper. Had the doctor so suddenly run out of stationery?
And how had it happened that he had taken personal stationery
with him on an emergency call in the first place? Once more the
handwriting was recognizably the doctor's own, yet so tortured
that he seemed ill or under some nearly intolerable strain or
influence.

My dearest:
    I do not write for fear my letters will be read. Be courageous. I
wrote to my friend Vallée what to do. Take directions. Prepare your
departure for next Saturday and do not tell anything to my brother
nor to anyone. Act for the best. See you soon. I embrace you very
dearly.
P.S. Destroy all my letters.

The next letter, which arrived on the following day, came to
Vallée. This letter was registered, written on plain paper, again
undated and postmarked at the branch office of rue Bayen. (Rue
Bayen is in the Seventeenth Arrondissement but is only six blocks
from 21 rue Le Sueur.) Once more the handwriting was strained
but recognizable:

Dear Friend:
    I know that your cousin, who is a doctor, has purchased a small
apartment house near the Av. du Bois [a very small street a few
hundred yards from 21 rue Le Sueur] *that he will live in only after*
the war. Would you please do me the favor of arranging everything
with him in order to move my household effects and all that is in
my apartment to his place. I am counting on your co-operation for
this should be done within the next forty-eight hours. Many thanks.

This letter astounded Vallée. He knew about 21 rue Le Sueur,
for he had written the insurance policy on it but he had never
talked to Dr. Braunberger about any of Petiot's properties, nor
had Mme. Braunberger ever heard of it. Vallée promptly telephoned Dr. Petiot and told him it seemed odd indeed that Braun-

berger should know about 21 rue Le Sueur or know that he, Vallée, knew about it, for only Petiot himself could have revealed that. As for moving household goods to that address, Vallée earnestly assured Petiot that he would have none of it, that he had read of Petiot's recent involvement in the narcotics cases in which witnesses had disappeared and Vallée could not afford to become involved. Nor did he want to know anything about any escape plans for Dr. Paul Braunberger or for his brother, Dr. Marcel Braunberger. Such knowledge could cause his arrest if ever any escape was discovered. Petiot apparently agreed to all this without protest and the household goods were not removed.

The next communication came by telephone to the Braunberger household. The maid answered the call. Without preliminaries, a male voice she did not recognize began to recite in a stilted way, as if reading from a paper:

"I am talking to give you news of the doctor. I guided him through to the free zone but he was a little out of his mind. In the Métro he began to act funny and at the border he nearly caused our arrest. Let Madame take care of herself as best she can. I will not guide her through. I have been too poorly paid."

The maid asked very quickly: "But how is the doctor and where did you leave him?"

"I left him headed in the direction of Spain and Portugal."

The maid, Rosalie Nonnemacher, a quick-witted person who was extremely loyal to the Braunberger family, promptly tried to encourage the man:

"Come here," she said, "and you will be paid."

"No," the voice replied. "I can't be bothered. Incidentally, I have a letter I was supposed to deliver, but I prefer to put it in the mail. And if the doctor's brother, Dr. Marcel, knows what is good for him, he'll get out of Occupied Paris too."

That was all that was said. The letter the man mentioned arrived the following day, July 1. Again, it was undated, on plain white paper, and this time the handwriting seemed even more distorted. This letter had been posted at a point much closer to the Braunberger apartment, the Quai de Valmy post office. It read:

My dearest:
Follow the person who will give you this letter and you will get

*instructions on how to rejoin me. I will be seeing you very soon. I
embrace you.*

But, of course, as it turned out, there was no one to follow, unless one wanted to follow the letter carrier. Besides, Mme. Braunberger was deeply uneasy about many small things. The handwriting, so cramped, so tortured and trembling, disturbed her.
And the phrasing of the letters did not seem right. Her husband
had never addressed her in any way other than "My Dearest
Maguy." Yet in the letters he had never used this form once, and
the signatures had been painfully formal, as if full identification
was all-important: they were all signed "Dr. Paul Braunberger."

Two days after the last letter was delivered, on July 3, a German soldier came to the apartment house where the Braunbergers
lived. He spoke authoritatively to the concierge:

"I am from the German police and I am looking for one of
your tenants. A man who was a medical captain in the First
World War and is now a civilian doctor."

The concierge solemnly shook her head. "I know of no such
person who lives here now."

This was a truthful reply, of course, for Dr. Braunberger was
gone. The German soldier did not pursue the inquiry further. But
his visit was reported to Mme. Braunberger. It may have
confirmed her decision to say nothing to the French police. After
a few more weeks, when the doctor had been gone for just a
month, Mme. Braunberger asked a friend, Mme. Simone Mon-
teaux, to come live with her. They lived quietly, afraid to speak of
the doctor's disappearance. Mme. Braunberger had determined to
make no effort to "escape" on her own.

Rosalie, the maid, kept urging Mme. Braunberger to report the
doctor's disappearance to the police. Finally, on September 12,
1942, convinced that no harm would now follow, Mme. Braunberger formally reported to the police of the St. Vincent de Paul
precinct that her husband had been missing since the twentieth of
June. Such a disappearance at that time, with so many being
snatched off the streets—and especially the disappearance of a Jew
—did not arouse the Paris police. They decided to do nothing.

What had really happened after the doctor walked out of his
apartment? Only the autobiographical notes written by Petiot in

his cell gave any inkling, but these notes were as enigmatic and complex as their author and were all destroyed. Petiot indicated no satisfaction in the death of Braunberger, although he seemed proud of the skill with which he carried it off. He indirectly admitted that he had selected Braunberger in order to test various methods he had hit upon to get letters written with less danger of detection. He would never again act so stupidly as he had in the past. As Braunberger was well on in years and already slightly senile, he seemed an ideal guinea pig. And his being a Jew made it less likely that his disappearance would start a stir.

Once Braunberger had reported to 21 rue Le Sueur, Petiot kept him hidden for many hours, administering peyote or some crude form of what is now called mescaline as a will-weakener to keep Braunberger in a docile state, and giving him food and water, while promising that both the doctor and his wife would soon be secure in a distant place where he could re-establish his practice. Petiot had Braunberger leave the dates off his letters. Petiot commented that he may have given Braunberger more letters to copy than he should have, for his handwriting grew more and more tortured. In the end, he injected Braunberger either under the excuse he was finally going to pass him through the borders of several countries or while Braunberger was so far gone under the influence of peyote that he did not resist. Then Petiot watched through the Lumvisor periscope as the old man went into his final convulsions and called weakly for help.

The return for this killing must have discouraged Petiot as too trifling to justify the risk: just a few small diamonds and less than 100,000 francs. Petiot had expected to receive all the jewelry and most of the cash the Braunbergers owned, for it had been agreed that the doctor would get his wife to join him or to follow him. Perhaps the failure of Vallée to co-operate foiled Petiot's plan to handle the Braunberger couple and all their worldly goods. Petiot was proud, however, of his cleverness in having the German soldier sent around to make sure the Braunberger household would not be too aggressive in investigating the doctor's disappearance.

On September 6, 1944, after the liberation and when the entire Petiot case was featured in the newspapers and after the discovery of the suitcases from 21 rue Le Sueur, Mrs. Braunberger sent a detailed report to the Paris police. She was requested to search the effects found in Petiot's various caches and found some clothes and articles of her husband's.

Petiot's chief scouts, the Mutt and Jeff combination of Edmond Pintard, known as Francinet, and Raoul Fourrier, had been active since early in 1942. Even during Petiot's deepest difficulties with the police on dope-traffic cases, these two gentry had been busily scouting out prospects for voyages to nowhere via 21 rue Le Sueur. Although they were clearly in the business for the commissions and the bits of the spoils it brought them, there was never any reason to believe that they knew the true destination of the people they brought to Petiot. There is no question that they accepted commissions and even articles of jewelry or clothes Petiot stated the travelers had left behind. They believed Petiot to be a sort of Scarlet Pimpernel helping resistants, refugees, and Jews escape from the Germans.

It also developed that these scouts secured new scouts for Petiot so that the doctor's recruiting system began to spread like a web. Petiot was now known in underground circles as "Dr. Eugène" and was reputed to be the head of a ring that specialized in spiriting fugitives out of Occupied France and eventually to South America. Just the whisperings about him gave substance to the fable that a large group was operating to provide safe escape routes out of Nazi-occupied France and encouraged prospects seeking escape to hunt for ways of making contact with this mysterious "Dr. Eugène." (The whispers naturally reached the Gestapo of rue des Saussaies, with devastating results that will be dealt with later.)

Francinet did much of his recruiting in the shabby bars he frequented. In one such place, in the Faubourg St. Martin, he met an old acquaintance named Henri Guitrand, known variously as "Henri the Marseillaise," and "Henri the Pimp." He was both of those things and had first known Francinet while haunting stage doors in search of girls whose flesh he might peddle. He had served several terms in jail. Now he had an eye out for any way to pick up some cash. Francinet, after a drink or two, suggested a new and most interesting way—finding passengers for Dr. Eugène's underground railway.

Three days later, Henri the Pimp ran into an underworld physician, Dr. Louis Théophile St. Pierre, who, despite many arrests for

assault, abortion, adultery, and larceny—and four convictions—
still was licensed to practice medicine. The doctor mentioned to
Henri that he knew of a rich Jewish family recently come to Paris
looking for a way to escape and with plenty of money to pay their
passage. Henri promptly arranged a meeting with Francinet, Dr.
St. Pierre, and the doctor's girl friend, Eriane Kahan. Eriane was
to make a lasting impression on "Dr. Eugène."

But for now she was to serve merely as the go-between among
Henri the Pimp, Dr. St. Pierre, Francinet, Fourrier, and the so-far
unidentified prospects for escape from the Nazis. She first met Petiot—as Dr. Eugène—at Fourrier's shop where she mentioned to
him that she understood his escape fee to be 50,000 to 75,000
francs per person. Petiot was enraged. Such a price, he felt, might
make prospects suspicious. He resented, too, the notion that the
go-between might be making more profit than he was.

No such thing, he told Mme. Kahan, with a show of righteous
anger. This was a patriotic operation and the fee was just to cover
actual costs. But Eriane, in a pleasant way, made it clear that she
was in this operation only for the money and would have to be
sure her own expenses, as well as her investment of time, were
well recompensed. There would be luncheons, dinners—Petiot, responding to her charm with charm of his own, quickly agreed. Of
course, she must not lose money on her efforts. Let us say that the
price will be from 25,000 to 50,000 francs, depending on Mme.
Kahan's own estimate of what the prospect could afford. As for
her commission, that would be 20 per cent of what the prospect
paid.

Petiot had no real illusions about Eriane. He knew from his
many connections that she was not only Dr. St. Pierre's mistress,
but also the girl friend of Luftwaffe Sergeant Welsing, an Aus-
trian-born clerk in the German Air Force Paris headquarters, and
he suspected she might even be a double espionage agent. Still, he
had no fear of dealing with her, nor with any of the other doubtful characters who began now to move into his orbit.

Eventually, Petiot learned all there was to know about Eriane
and what he learned intensified his interest in her. She was Jewish-
Rumanian born and had entered France in 1933. She was always
in funds which she said came from a small fortune of 350,000 prewar francs hidden away somewhere in Italy. She was also the re-

cipient of periodical largesse from a certain Dr. Hymans, a Dutch engineer who often visited Paris. Then there was Mr. Sassi, an Italian industrialist who bestowed frequent sums of cash on her when he came to Paris from Milan. These payments, Eraine maintained sturdily, were just remittances from her sister in Italy, presumably part of the small fortune Eriane had left behind. This diligent sister apparently also transmitted funds through another conduit, for once when a Mr. Cestini came to Paris from Italy, in September 1941, he had 250,000 francs for Eriane.

This group of two relay teams, consisting of Eriane, Henri the Pimp, Dr. St. Pierre, Francinet, and Fourrier, brought a breat deal of profit to Dr. Petiot for, directly and indirectly, they sent his way not only a number of wealthy Jews but also a collection of even wealthier criminals who, having double-crossed the rue Lauriston group, were in a burning hurry to get out of Paris. Yet not one of them ever dreamed that the customers he helped direct to "Dr. Eugène" were destined to end their journeys in the small triangular room at 21 rue Le Sueur. Indeed, Francinet long maintained that Dr. Petiot was a good man, a fine doctor, a loyal Frenchman, and the benefactor of many men and women who might have fallen victim to the Nazis, and he averred solemnly, even long after Petiot's conviction, that his friend the doctor had been the victim of a cruel and complex frame-up.

But before the clients began to flow in from these sources, Petiot lined up a promising customer through a German Swiss who owned a small plant on rue St. Lazare and others and who worked closely with the Germans. His main office was near Petiot's office at 66 rue Caumartin. The new prospect was Kurt Kneller, an electrical technician who had left Germany in 1933 to settle permanently in France. He had married, in France, another German refugee named Greta Lent and, in 1935, they had a son who was registered as a French citizen. Kneller himself had sought French citizenship too. In 1939 he volunteered for service with the French Foreign Legion and served until the fall of France. It was whispered among the neighbors in the Sixteenth, or Auteuil, Arrondissement, where the Knellers lived, that the family had a great many valuables stored away, along with a good deal of money they had taken with them from Germany.

Kneller could not seem to make up his mind about leaving

Paris. He wanted to go, for the lot of a Jew in Occupied France grew steadily less bearable. His small son, now seven, had been baptized a Catholic and would be raised in that faith, but the Knellers were faced with the constant threat of arrest and deportation to the death camps. Still . . . if one could hold on a little longer. . . .

Kneller had already become a patient of Petiot's through his employer, Ernest Jorin, who denied in later years that he had ever known Petiot personally or had anything to do with Kneller meeting Petiot but whose plant and office was around the corner from the doctor's office. In any case, there had been a meeting with the doctor at the apartment of Mme. Christine Roart, who lived in the same apartment house as the Knellers at 4 rue du General Balfournier. Here, Petiot explained, he could help them, whenever they wished, make their way to South America, where Mrs. Kneller had relatives. He made them a "special price" of 125,000 francs for the whole family and gave them a detailed rundown of how the escape would be accomplished: There would be forty-eight hours in a rest home where they would receive false papers, medical certificates, vaccinations, inoculations, etc. Then they would cross the line into the free zone and be escorted to Marseille and then to Africa, whence they would set sail to South America. They should plan to bring at least a million francs in cash and jewelry, which would have to be sewn into their clothes or concealed in their luggage. All present identification marks on clothing and luggage would have to be removed.

Mrs. Kneller was eager to leave, for the dread of arrest and the danger to her little son had made it almost impossible to sleep. But her husband, though a quiet man, was essentially a fighter. He loved France. He considered himself a Frenchman and it was not in his nature to turn and run. He seemed so mild, with his soft voice, his gently receding chin, his big black-rimmed glasses, and the hair that was farther and farther back on his forehead. But, at heart, he was still a member of the French Foreign Legion and the thought of deserting, perhaps forever, pained him deeply. Still, he thought seriously about this escape business. He even went, in the *vélo-taxi* Petiot provided, to have his passport picture taken by a photographer the doctor had recommended on Boulevard St. Martin. But he kept postponing the date of departure.

Then, while he and his wife were visiting a friend on Thursday, July 16, their neighbor, Mme. Roart, telephoned to say that the Gestapo had been at the Kneller apartment seeking Mrs. Kneller. The concierge had admitted them—they had looked around the Kneller apartment and had promised to return. A cold finger must then have touched Kurt Kneller's heart. There could be no returning to the apartment now, and they would have to summon Dr. Eugène. Mme. Roart carried some of their clothes over to them and agreed to keep the little boy until arrangements had been completed. Kurt Kneller asked her to pack their suitcases for the journey and said he would call for them.

The man who called for the suitcases next day was the dark, slightly shabby man with burning eyes whom Mme. Roart knew to be a doctor, although she had never heard his name. He carried away two large suitcases and five smaller bags. He told Mme. Roart and the concierge that he would come back for the furniture. When he returned, with a baggage cart and a man to help him, the concierge and Mme. Roart would not agree to let him have the furniture although they let him take the linen, silverware, and utensils.

"I must have the furniture," the swarthy man insisted. "Otherwise, I will not help the Knellers escape." He came into the apartment where the Kneller child was staying and picked the child up to talk to him. He tried to hold the child on his knee but the boy drew away. The man, by this time, was almost atremble with annoyance at not being able to pack the furniture right onto his cart. Eventually the furniture was given into his care although he had to come back for it at another time. The following day, Saturday, Mme. Roart took little René Kneller over to the Noé apartment at 19 rue Erlanger to join his parents. That evening Petiot appeared at the Noé home to take Kurt Kneller on the first steps of his "escape." The arrangement was that Kneller was to go first and that his wife and son would follow a day later, then all would meet at the "rest home" where they were to be hidden while their papers were being prepared and their inoculations and vaccinations taken care of. The fee had been paid in full to Petiot when he brought their baggage.

On leaving the Noé apartment with Kneller, Petiot was very disturbed and uneasy. He thought that he had been followed and that they were all in danger. He instructed Mme. Noé to follow the two of them as they walked to the Métro station and if she saw they were being followed to overtake them, as a warning, before they entered the station. Otherwise, she was merely to stay about 150 meters behind and go home after the two men had entered the Jasmin entrance to the Métro.

Dr. Eugène and Kneller proceeded to 21 rue Le Sueur. Exactly what passed between them there, no one will ever know. Kneller was probably killed almost at once. Evidently Petiot was afraid that even the peyote would not subdue the will or fight in this man or saw no reason for keeping him alive to write letters. Once having determined, through his viewer, that Kneller was dead, Petiot left the body in the triangular room and pedaled to rue Caumartin on his bicycle, eager to get home in time to take his wife and son to the cinema. Only when the show was over and Petiot had seen his wife and son safely home did he return to 21 rue Le Sueur where he removed Kneller's body from the triangular room to his dissecting parlor.

The next day, suave and ingratiating as only he could be when there was profit in sight, Petiot led Mme. Kneller and the little boy to the Métro and thence to number 21 where the boy would "meet his father." It is presumed, from what followed, that Petiot used the same methods on Mme. Kneller as on Dr. Braunberger. He may have left Mme. Kneller and René locked up at number 21, perhaps under sedation (from his vast store of narcotics) so there would be no cries to alarm the neighbors. It was Petiot's long habit to spend Sunday with his family and he seldom allowed anything to interfere with this plan. Sometimes they would go to visit his father-in-law at Seignelay or his brother Maurice at Auxerre and spend the day in the country, perhaps even visiting the various properties in which his father-in-law or brother had invested some of the Petiot funds.

It was, however, a difficult project in wartime, what with the curfew and travel restrictions, to go by train even to Auxerre. Petiot and his wife, Georgette, had made it a habit, therefore, before starting for Auxerre to spend the night at the hotel right next to the Lyon railroad station where they would take the train in the early morning. Petiot and his wife were known as steady patrons there, slept always in the same room, and sat always at the same table in the dining room. Henri Alicot, the owner of the hotel, became their good friend and never failed to make the Petiots welcome.

On this particular July Sunday, however, it is doubtful that Petiot left town, for he had unfinished business at rue Le Sueur that would require his early attention on Monday. His conscience troubled him not at all for now the act of killing a "client" had become a routine to him.

In his prison notes, written some four years later, Petiot is very explicit that he killed only criminals and collaborators, persons who had unfairly threatened his career and the security of his family after he had helped them, or Jews whom he would have gladly helped but who were on the point of arrest by the Gestapo for deportation to the concentration camps. Instead of this, he offered a quick and painless death, admitting that he took the spoils for his family that would normally have gone to the Third Reich. He claimed that he had ways and means to learn the names of those marked for arrest before the directives for their arrest were issued. As in the case of Mr. Khait, it seems that Petiot could also denounce someone to the Germans or finger someone for immediate arrest. He went on to explain that most of his victims were spared even much of the pain of the fatal convulsions because he doped them up with his own prescription of narcotics. These he gave them under some pretext or other before his injection of the air bubble; they were made so amenable to his will that he rarely had any trouble with them and could even get them to write letters dictated by him or copies from drafts he wrote and slipped under the door of the triangular room.

The strange part about Petiot's prison notes is that there is not a single case that fails to fit this pattern of excuse. Several travelers, after establishing that they were neither collaborators nor wanted by the Gestapo, were not taken to rue Le Sueur and, in every case, were given their money back. Every other victim was either a criminal or collaborator or someone Petiot had good and sufficient reason to believe was a collaborator, or Jews that could well have been marked for arrest. There were too many close and coincidental visits just before or just after the departure of Petiot's travelers by the Germans to doubt the last. There was even one case where a neighbor couple turned down his offer to help only to be later arrested, deported, and never heard from again.

The Knellers, of course, were never seen alive again. But there was one aspect of the Kneller killing that made it distinctive. In this instance, as in no other instance in the whole series of liquidations, the police came very close to finding an identifiable body. On August 8, 1942, nineteen days after Dr. Eugène had led Mme. Kneller and little René away from Mme. Noé's, parts of the body of a male child, about seven years old, were found in the Seine River near Asnieres. No identification could be made, but it was long afterward presumed (aided by the boy's ration card found on Petiot when he was arrested) that this could only have been what was left of the friendly little boy Petiot had held in his lap the month previous. Yet Petiot claimed at his trial and in his pretrial interrogations that the Kneller clothes, the Kneller child's pajamas and his identification card were all left behind by the Knellers under their new escape identities and that Petiot had turned them over to a *passeur*, or guide, who was to get them out of Occupied Paris one step ahead of the Gestapo. While admitting many killings, Petiot swore that he did not kill the Knellers. Yet he noted that he had collected some 950,000 francs as a profit after paying the guide. Not quite as much as Guschinow.

Soon after the disappearance of the Knellers, there was practically a flood of correspondence from them, letters and cards written either by Petiot or by Mme. Kneller after she had been drugged. Mme. Noé received a card. Many letters and cards came to Ernest Jorin (he had the jewelry). Mme. Roart received a letter posted in Paris and three postcards from Castres. The letters all told a tale similar to the one related in the Braunberger messages —that the husband had suddenly grown mentally unstable (this would explain why he wrote no letters—a significant fact indicating that he had to be killed without preliminaries or risk) and that the journey was beset by difficulties. One letter suggested they were "bothered" with the presence of the child, and one reported that Mr. Kneller might have to be confined! But every letter and every card ended with the same urgent warning: "Burn this!" And the cards and letters were all destroyed except the very last one received by M. Jorin. This one, postmarked from Castres and dated September 14, 1942, was strangely uninformative, even disconnected:

> Sir:
> We left very quickly because it was necessary. Now that my husband has become sick, I do not know what will become of us. Keep our things. My husband always speaks well of you. Good health.

The card was signed, as was all the Kneller correspondence, "Marguerite."

Much later, Jorin testified that he saw a very close resemblance between the tight and wretched scrawl in which this card and the others were written and the stingy scribbling used by Petiot on his prescriptions that he had seen reproduced in the newspapers. No one thought the writing looked like Mme. Kneller's. And Petiot still could not break loose from his own paranoia enough to change the pattern of his procedure—again, it was the "hard time crossing the border" and, again, it was the husband "starting to act funny." (Psychiatrists insist that paranoiacs are extremely repetitive and are "absolute slaves to a single pattern.")

The letters and cards this time, however, did have the desired effect. There was no fret over the Knellers' disappearance and no effort to follow their trail. As a matter of fact, the disappearances were never reported to the Paris police at all. Even when the charnel house had been discovered and Petiot's picture had appeared on the front pages, no one thought to suggest that the Knellers, too, might have been among his victims. It was not until August 13, 1944, two and a half months before Petiot was finally arrested, that any inquiry about the Knellers was made. At that time the French Justice Department received a letter from the Jewish Deportees Service of the American Joint Distribution Committee of New York, relaying a query by a Mr. Siegfried Lent of La Paz, Bolivia, as to the whereabouts of M. Kurt Kneller, his wife, Greta Lent Kneller, and their son René, last heard of at 46 rue de General Balfournier.

The letter from New York explained that the Kneller family had planned to escape Nazi persecution to South America and that an investigation indicated that a resident of the apartment house at number 46 had asserted they had left on the first stage of their escape with a certain Dr. Petiot. (Mme. Roart, by this time, had read the papers and learned the doctor's real name.)

Furthermore, the letter said, this Dr. Petiot had had the apartment stripped bare of all furniture and utensils—so completely that when the Germans came a few days later, they found nothing to loot. No need of wondering now what had become of the Knellers.

While relishing the fruits of this labor, Petiot was also handling two new bundles of clients recruited through his chain of scouts. The most innocent and helpless victims were sets of Jewish refugees who had escaped the Nazis in Poland, Austria, Holland and were still on the run. All of these were found by scout Eriane Kahan, a Jewish alien who desired also to get out of Europe. She was assisted by gossips and would-be good samaritans. The other more interesting and dangerous of the two groups was a hard-bitten set of "bad boys" and their girl friends who had fallen out of favor with rue Lauriston, the French Gestapo. Dr. St. Pierre and Mme. Kahan had nothing to do with them. It must be understood that while armies battled on the front line and war was at its height, an even more bitter struggle ebbed and flowed behind the lines in Axis Europe as Communist and democratic and local independent resistance groups sabotaged the Nazi forces and sometimes, in a contest for power, each other. Almost as bitter, but on the other side, was the rivalry among the Abwehr, the German military intelligence group; the Otto Service, which was concerned largely with looting the occupied countries and funneling vital materials into the German war machine; the SS; the Gestapo; and the French Gestapo of rue Lauriston. The latter force, under the leadership of Lafont, the typical gangster boss, and Bonny, once the top policeman of France who looked like a schoolteacher, was concerned mainly with the Third Reich's gold program. They found gold, jewelry, rare art work, property, anything valuable and preferably negotiable, then arrested the owners or killed them, if necessary. The spoils were divided—50 per cent to the German Government and 50 per cent to the French Gestapo, who divided it among the "finders." Of course, the finders were principally interested with advancing their own fortunes, and the personnel of the agency were a collection of hard-core criminals—thieves, pimps, gangsters, burglars, robbers, and murderers, many of them released from French jails to serve Lafont, Bonny, and their German superiors.

As was inevitable, this convocation of charmers held out a large percentage of their findings and finally fell to looting on their own account and murdering only for their private benefit. Too often their employers discovered that the ransacking of the home or shop of a wealthy Jewish family returned nothing to the rue Lauriston while fattening the purses of the hired hands. When called to account for this, some of the group turned upon their employers and added a few collaborators and even German bodies to their score. As a result, the names of a particular group that had double-crossed management stood high on the list of ladies and gentlemen with whom the French Gestapo would most like to spend an afternoon. Further, they were on the wanted list of the German authorities and the Paris police.

The top man at rue Lauriston, Henri Lafont, was actually Henri Chamberlain, born in Paris in 1902, an orphan at thirteen, and three times convicted of crimes before coming of age. He was a French Army deserter when World War II began but was arrested and assigned to a work camp at Sepay Loire. In 1940, when France fell, Lafont offered his services to a Gestapo official named Radeck and sold the Germans on letting him organize a group of criminals to be released from jail. His unit would find and steal from and, if necessary, murder Jews, resistants, and anyone not protected by the Third Reich, all profits to go to the Gestapo with a finder's commission for the unit. This, in essence, was the major task of the French Gestapo with headquarters at 93 rue Lauriston and 3 bis Place des États-Unis. Later, the organization hunted down resistants and maquis and organized a semimilitary Nazi militia with the help of an Arab, El Maadi. The Gestapo had chosen as Lafont's deputy the former number one policeman of France, Petiot's friend, ex-Inspector Bonny of the Opéra precinct. Lafont's number three man he appointed himself, Paul Clavie, his nephew, a young man with an extensive police record.

One of the leaders of this band of roughnecks who dared cross Lafont was named Adrien Estebeteguy, known as "Adrien the Basque." He had been particularly greedy in his endeavors with his employers and had been summarily fired, having learned how simple it was with Gestapo identification and German authority to lay hold of large quantities of loot. Adrien went into business for himself with a few associates, posing as Occupation police or as the Gestapo and committing wholesale extortions. Adrien was a tough-looking fellow, with a humorless face and eyes as cold as a loan shark's. He had a record that included eight convictions and uncounted charges of burglary, larceny, swindling, assaults with a knife, resisting arrest. He was in jail when the Germans overran France, but Lafont had obtained his release. Adrien had been a long-time friend of Lafont, whom he had known since he was using the name Chamberlain and had been acting as manager of the mess at, of all places, the Paris prefecture of police. However, friendship ceased when Adrien held out on his boss.

Allied with Adrien in his extortions and posing also as "*police allemande*," was a dandified young fellow named Joseph Reocrcux and known as "Jo Jo" or "Jo the Boxer." Jo had a police dossier even bulkier than Adrien's, with convictions for theft, for procuring, for burglary, for possession of an unlicensed gun, and with two warrants out for his immediate arrest. Jo, too, had labored for Lafont and had fallen out of grace at rue Lauriston. Now he deemed himself the leader of this little cell of gangsters. A dark-eyed, truculent-looking young man (he was thirty-four to Adrien's forty-five), Jo, with his full-lipped mouth, was even handsome, in a heavy-featured way, and he dressed in what would have been known in the United States as a zoot-suit fashion, affecting double-thick soles on his pointed shoes. In Paris, he could be recognized at a glance for what he was—a pimp.

Jo had two ladies under his "protection"—Claudia Chamoux, known as Lola, at twenty-five a veteran whore with a face as hard as a hangman's who had "labored" at Senlis, comforting members of the Wehrmacht at standard rates; and Annette Bassett, a pretty girl with a permanent squint, who had come to Paris from Lyon to be near her beloved Jo Jo. Annette was a young and relatively innocent prostitute who used the name Annette Petit but was fondly known as "*La Pute*," or "Little Bedbug," and was much sought after for her skills in bed. Both girls were kept busy in Paris and both faithfully turned over their earnings to their protector. Still another member of this unlovely set was Joseph Piereschi, known as "Dionisi" or "Zé" (pronounced Zhay), a well-known operator of whorehouses, four times convicted, and himself a former friend and assistant of the ineffable Lafont. With him was his mistress, Paulette Grippay, "*La Chinoise*," the Chinese woman. Then there was François Albertini, called "François the Corsican," another pimp who had worked for rue Lauriston and had also lost favor there. François had not a single conviction against him, yet he was an experienced criminal and a procurer of long standing. Another member of the group was Charlot Lombard, also with a well-filled police record and a penchant for women but who was not getting along with his wife. Lombard was a husky young man who frequently served as a bodyguard.

As it turned out, Jo the Boxer was the first of this group to make contact with Petiot, although he was not the first to leave. Painfully conscious of the earnestness with which both the Gestapo and the Paris police were seeking him, Jo let it be known to his friends that he would give much of what he owned to be safe in Buenos Aires. He mentioned this one night to Henri the Pimp at a bar, the Café Mollard, on rue l'Échiquier, and Henri passed the word to Francinet, the man who knew the "prominent physician" Dr. Eugène who could help people get safely out of France through a mysterious and efficient organization. Francinet arranged a meeting between Jo and the doctor at Fourrier's hairdressing parlor at 25 rue des Mathurins. Jo was not really much impressed with this "prominent physician" who looked as shabby as a peddler. After much discussion of price, methods, and dates, he told Fourrier and Francinet (after the doctor had gone): "Your doctor is a pain in the ass!"

It may have been this immediate impression that prompted Jo to suggest that one of the others go first on the underground railway. At any rate, it was decided that François the Corsican should take the initial plunge. There being no deep mutual confidence among these men, and there being a small fortune in gold and jewelry and other loot to be taken along, well over twenty million francs (almost $300,000), Jo finally decided that it would be best if one man's girl friend should accompany a different man, to keep everybody honest.

Thus it happened that Claudia Chamoux, although attached to Jo the Boxer, was selected to make the journey overseas with François the Corsican. It might be thought that Petiot would have hesitated to cope with an assortment of thugs as hard-bitten and desperate as Jo, Adrien, and the rest. But not at all. The only condition he insisted on for security reasons was that he could take them only two at a time. In many ways, they were more gullible than the other fugitives he was to deal with. They had all heard about the famous Dr. Eugène in their own circles, and they apparently never doubted his omnipotence—even though Jo was at first slightly leery of him. Besides, it was a matter of pride with some of these worthies not to haggle over price—and the price for them was 100,000 francs a head for the men and 50,000 francs for the women. If that was the fee, well and good. They were ready to lay it on the line. They may even have felt more secure to know that whatever may have been said about the doctor's personality, he was going to see that they traveled first-class.

The trip that Claudia Chamoux and François Albertini took together, however, was far shorter than they envisioned—shorter even than some of the others had known, for Petiot was not going to temporize with a crew as dangerous as this. No letter writing. The necessary letters he would write himself. Who would know the difference? In his notes years later, Petiot indicated that he had administered so much peyote or narcotics to his gangster travelers before they ever reached the triangular room that they did not even know for sure when he inoculated them.

It was important that the rest of the gang have news of these two for there was a great deal of loot still in the possession of those who were still to take the journey. Petiot therefore saw to it that Jo the Boxer received a message from the first pair of voyagers. In a sprawling childish hand, he wrote a note to Jo announcing that they were at the port of embarkation, all safe and sound. And he signed the note with François' name. Inasmuch as men in Jo's circle did not often write letters to each other, Jo had no way of identifying the handwriting. (Petiot admitted at his trial that he had personally written all the notes and letters of the so-called gangster group.) It certainly looked as if it was from François, so Jo was content. Now he knew a safe way to get out of the country when the heat grew too intense. He did, however, have a few more fish to fry before he and the others boarded the mysterious express to the Promised Land.

Paris at this time was full of fears. The course of the war had shifted so that the hope, even the probability, of an eventual Allied victory became more than a dream. Even through the curtain of lies and silence imposed by the Nazis, Parisians began to hear talk of a possible invasion of Europe. The Nazi advance in Russia had obviously come to a halt. On November 8, American and British forces had rolled onto the beaches of North Africa despite a show of resistance from the French. The United States and Britain landed 300,000 men. In retaliation, the Nazis had taken over all of unoccupied France and Italy and were feverishly rooting out all disaffection, even hints of resistance, and all the Jews they could discover.

New help from America and England had strengthened the forces of resistance inside France and the Germans had responded by brutally wiping out all those who were even suspected of traffic with the enemies of the Reich. Even the underground forces sometimes battled each other. For instance, all Communist groups were ordered at the beginning of the war to sabotage France. Then, on June 22, 1941, all Communist apparatuses received opposite directives when Nazi Germany and Communist Russia fell out. Then, in 1942, all Communist underground resistance was stopped until the Allies opened a front in Europe. Before the liberation, secret agents from Moscow, seeking future power, often denounced agents from London, who were then shot by the Gestapo.

In December 1942, when the Nazi terror in France was at its height, M. Émil Joulot, who owned a château and estate called Chabridou at Hautefort, Dordogne, was hiding a rich Jewish textile executive named Gilbert Saada of Nice. The two of them had settled into a feeling of temporary security when, on the morning of December 14, four desperate-looking men presented themselves at the château entrance and, with pistols drawn, forced their way inside.

"*Police allemande! Nous sommes le Gestapo!*" they announced. "You have been holding a Jew wanted by headquarters. He has been operating a clandestine radio from here. Where is he?"

At this point, Saada, no doubt afraid for what might be done to his host, walked out and said in a firm but strained voice: "I am Saada. You want me?"

The four men promptly seized both Joulot and Saada and locked them in a small room. Then they searched the place, breaking open drawers, a safe, and trunks. They found a large amount of U.S. money, 530 napoleons (worth $11,666), a great many French francs, jewelry, and other articles, including some fine shirts with the initials G.S. They packed everything into a pigskin bag they found there, then brought the prisoners out of the small room. They put handcuffs on Saada and led him out to a car that had been assigned to them by the Gestapo. But they were not Germans at all. They were Jo Jo the Boxer, Adrien the Basque, Charlot Lombard—a ready-for-anything young man who was serving as a sort of bodyguard to Adrien—and a fourth man who was not positively identified but who is believed to have been Abel Danos, a member of the French Gestapo who died in 1952 before a French firing squad. There is no question that this raid by the renegades of the French Gestapo was based on information secured from headquarters at rue Lauriston and that Chabridoux and its host and guest had been fingered by some local source and was at the top of the list for the gold program. There is no question that Dr. Petiot had access to these files also.

In the car, they told Saada they were taking him to Toulouse. As they drove along the dark road, they talked to their prisoner and soon made him understand that for a suitable "reward" they might be persuaded to arrange matters so he would not be shot or deported to a work camp in Germany. M. Saada thereupon invited his captors to dine with him at the Hôtel Regina. They drove up to the hotel, where M. Saada was evidently well known, removed his handcuffs, and went in together to enjoy a hearty dinner with fine wines. The discussion continued and finally the five agreed on a fee of 200,000 francs, which he would send from Chabridoux for his release. On his return to the château, he found, of course, that all his funds had been "confiscated." M. Joulot and he immediately decided that the *"police allemande"* had been fakes and they notified the real police who in turn informed the Gestapo. The police, aided by the Gestapo, brought photographs to Chabridoux, where Joulot and Saada quickly identified Jo the Boxer, Adrien, and Charlot. Lafont, hearing of the "raid," promptly put the men on his own wanted list. They had just deprived Saada—and perhaps indirectly the Third Reich —of about eight million francs.

Jo the Boxer knew just how he would spend part of his share—

by buying an escape to South America via Petiot's underground railroad. He was satisfied that François the Corsican and Jo Jo's girl friend were now happily in Buenos Aires and Jo Jo was impatient to join them. Besides, they all four began to feel the hot breath of Lafont and the French Gestapo on the backs of their necks.

Jo Jo sought out his previous connections with Dr. Eugène and had them signal the doctor that Jo and his entourage were ready. This time Jo wanted to take two girls with him, even though the doctor had laid down the rule of two persons at a time. But the doctor, for some reason, relented, so Jo, with Annette Petit, the Little Bedbug, and with a girl whose identity was never established, turned up one night at the terminal of Dr. Eugène's underground railway, 21 rue Le Sueur. They had not even the faintest suspicion that it was also the last stop. With a faith far more childlike than any of the previous victims had shown, Jo appeared at the doctor's door with almost three million francs in gold napoleons (the most common tender in payment of espionage agents in World War II), U.S. bank notes, and in French francs—painstakingly concealed about his person. Jo also wore a fine wristwatch of distinctive design, a beautiful finger ring, and a diamond and gold tie clasp. Annette brought all her beautiful jewels, including a ring with a large, flawless emerald surrounded by small diamonds. The other girl brought jewels too, although nothing was known of their value. Some who knew Jo and his friends intimately said afterward that the two girls had drawn all their savings so that they might "start a new life" in a new country and that the total they carried between them in cash and jewels must have been at least half a million francs. The net worth of these three customers of the Petiot plant perhaps came close to five million francs (about $300,000 U.S.). It was no wonder that Dr. Eugène was willing to stretch his "rules" in their favor.

The exact departure date of Jo the Boxer and his friends remains a partial mystery. There were even stories that Jo had not fallen victim to the doctor at all, had somehow recovered from the effects of the "inoculation," and was back at his old trade as late as 1944. (On May 5, 1944, a crew of fake policemen robbed a Mme. Nespola in Nice and she identified a "mug shot" of Jo Jo the Boxer as the leader of the group. She was even able to describe scars that did not show in the picture but which, it was known, Jo had collected since the picture was made.)

On the other hand, the operator of the Café Mollard near the St. Lazare railroad station, one Paul Jobert, who was well acquainted with Francinet and with Jo the Boxer, insisted that in August or September 1942 he had helped Jo load two suitcases into a vélo-taxi for the journey to meet "a doctor friend of Francinet" who was going to arrange his escape, and that Jo had told him then he had three million francs in cash, as well as some jewelry with him.

Still, Petiot readily and even proudly confessed that he "liquidated" Jo and his gang, who were "enemies of France." And Francinet, some time after December 1942, met Petiot and made note of the unusual wristwatch he was wearing, a watch whose duplicate he had previously seen.

"I see you are wearing Jo Jo's watch," said Francinet. Petiot displayed it without embarrassment.

"Oh, yes," he commented quickly. "Jo was so glad to get out of France that he gave me his watch as a token of appreciation."

So it seems relatively certain that Jo took the same path as all those who visited 21 rue Le Sueur before him and that he and the poor Little Bedbug and the girl who went with them all died in convulsions on the floor of the triangular room.

Eriane Kahan had had two live prospects for the Dr. Eugène escape route since September 1942 when she had been asked by her dentist at 21 rue Cambon, a Rumanian woman named Dr. Rachel Gingold Sobelman (later to become the innocent gossip to send many persons to Dr. Eugène via Kahan), to find an apartment for a refugee family who called themselves the Valberts. After she had helped install the Valberts in her own apartment house at 10 rue Pasquier, Eriane learned that the Valberts were really Maurice and Lina Wolff, he a Jew born in Belgium and she a German Jew, born Lina Braun in Breslau. They were accompanied by Wolff's mother, Rachel. Together they had fled from Germany into Italy and had but recently come to Paris. They were not at home here, spoke little French, and lived in terror of their lives. Eriane soon brought word to the Wolffs that there was a way of getting out. It was costly—75,000 francs a head—but the Wolffs had a fat purse and their situation was desperate. Every day they listened for the knock at the door that might announce the Gestapo.

It had been Eriane's idea at first that she might go along. But she had only 25,000 francs and did not feel she could afford the fee. After she had explained her lot to Dr. Eugène, he had urged her to remain and work with him.

"We do need an intelligent woman like you," he told her earnestly. "Particularly one who can speak several languages. Stay and work with us. I promise I will arrange your escape before it is too late."

He made an appointment then to go with Eriane to the Wolffs to explain the workings of the escape apparatus. The meeting took place in early December 1942. Dr. Eugène began his explanations with a severe warning:

"Any mistake will mean twelve bullets in my carcass. For you, perhaps worse—deportation to the German extermination camps."

The Wolffs were suitably taken with the solemnity of the discussion. They answered his questions eagerly and listened with grim attention as he set forth the "rules":

"Only two suitcases per person. At least two million francs in cash and jewels. No identification of any kind. Money and valuables all to be sewn into clothing or secreted in waterproof bags or packages."

One particularly important rule, said Dr. Eugène, was no letter writing after departure. The Wolffs had to explain to their friends (they had just a few in Paris) that there would be no correspondence once they had escaped.

There must be complete and absolute secrecy, the doctor urged. They would spend two or three days at a rest home or clinic where they would undergo examinations, get all the necessary inoculations and vaccinations, and receive false papers and certificates. He would come one day to pick up the suitcases, then a horse and a carriage would come to bring them to the first rendezvous. The rule, said Dr. Eugène, was usually only two at once. This time, because of the mother-in-law's age, he would stretch a point but it would be impossible to include their friend Eriane Kahan in the party. She would join them at a later date.

Within a few days, Dr. Eugène sent them word of the departure date and shortly after that he came himself with an old man and a baggage handcart to carry the suitcases away. It was after seven and already pitch dark—it being December—when an old-fashioned fiacre, a sort of closed hackney cab with the driver perched outside and drawn by an ancient horse, grated to a slow halt outside 10 rue Pasquier. The Wolffs, in accordance with the arrangement, had been waiting at the entrance since seven o'clock. The driver, swathed in a shabby greatcoat many sizes too large for him and wearing a beaten top hat, nodded a greeting and the three people mounted silently into the cab. The driver urged the old horse along and the carriage rolled wearily over the cobblestoned streets, the old-time iron-shod horse clip-clopping, the iron rims (all rubber had long since been confiscated for war use) grating noisily. It was like a scene from a Sherlock Holmes movie. At boulevard Malesherbes, the fiacre turned slowly to the right to Place St. Augustin, and the Wolffs were never seen by their neighbors again.

On they rode, in the blackout, through the empty streets. The horse, in a grudging trot, drew them into Place St. Augustin, then along rue Boetie to the Champs Élysées. The carriage followed Champs Élysées to L'Étoile, where the Arc de Triomphe loomed, and around L'Étoile to avenue Foch. The Wolffs knew all these avenues and they were watching tensely to learn what their destination might be. Now they turned off the avenue Foch into a little street the Wolffs did not recognize. It was a fine residential section, all silent now, and the clop of the horse's hoofs echoed off the walls of the fine old buildings that lined both sides of the street. The driver was slowing his horse. They drew up before an especially imposing "hotel" and the driver climbed painfully down from his perch. The Wolffs could see the number of the building clearly beside the entrance. Number 21. The coachman, with old-fashioned courtesy, helped them all to alight, then walked up to the door and rang the *sonnerie*. The Wolffs, meanwhile, saw the street sign, dimly lit by the shrouded lamp: rue Le Sueur. The door did not open immediately and they waited in silence, the only persons abroad on the short street. Finally, the small door swung open and a figure stood in the darkness inside. The coachman raised his tottering hat, bowed ceremoniously, then turned back to his carriage and drove slowly off. The sounds of the horse's hoofs came back along the silent little street long after the carriage had gone out of sight.

The person who had opened the door was the mysterious Dr. Eugène himself. He greeted them with quiet enthusiasm, shaking hands with each one in turn, smiling and nodding graciously.

"Greetings and salutations!" he said. "Welcome to your first port of call! Step right in."

The Wolffs followed the doctor out into the open courtyard and to the right into the neat office. The doctor graciously offered the two deep armchairs to the ladies and had M. Wolff sit in the wooden chair by the desk. There was much to be done, he told them, but first he wanted the ladies to take a mild sedative so he could administer the needed shots without any discomfort. To the wife and mother-in-law, who obediently accepted the medicine from his hand, he gave a dose strong enough to put them to sleep within a short time. Then he had them all bare their arms for the "inoculation" and each watched calmly as the doctor methodically injected death into their veins.

Now if Mr. Wolff would just follow me into the examining room where he would disrobe, and if the ladies would excuse us. . . . Eugène led Wolff down the short corridor into the bare triangular room. Once there, with Wolff beginning to unbutton his clothes, Eugène called to Mme. Wolff to follow. She came along, stepped through the door, and Eugène quickly closed it tight and bolted it behind her. It must have taken them a few seconds to realize that they were trapped.

Dr. Eugène, meanwhile, had returned to the old lady, who was already nodding from the sedative. Her death came with relative quickness as her old heart yielded quickly to the terrible pressure. Then she lay as if asleep, with only her contorted legs to indicate her death agony. Petiot wanted to allow plenty of time to be sure there was no life left in the younger people so he took up a mystery book he had been reading and settled quietly back to lose himself in the story.

An hour later, Petiot got up, went out through the courtyard and into the old stable. From here he could see into the triangular room through his Lumvisor viewer. The Wolffs lay quite still, one on the bed, one on the floor. There was not even any sign of breathing. With unhurried step, Petiot went back through his office and into the triangular room. He applied his stethoscope to one body after the other. There was not a murmur of life. It was only now that Petiot's own pulse began to race, for now he would learn exactly what his profit had been. He set out quickly to rip open the seams of the clothing to spill out the contents of the waterproof packages and search the travelers' baggage.

There were valuables of every sort: jewelry, negotiable securities, bank notes. Petiot methodically counted it over, relishing every item. Altogether he estimated it would come to 2,100,000 francs. This was a slight letdown for he had anticipated another Guschinow. Still it was a handsome piece of business. Ah, these Jews! he may have told himself, they are too smart. Undoubtedly they transferred some of their wealth to a bank in South America. With Jo Jo and his allies, he might do much better. Those gangsters had no one to trust and would have to pack all their loot on their persons. Petiot set out then on the tedious task of eviscerating and dismembering the bodies of his victims to get them ready to be carried off in his bicycle trailer, to be dumped somewhere into the dark Seine. No one would ever find the bodies to identify.

The only message that came through was carried, undoubtedly in all innocence, by Eriane Kahan to a couple named Gang, friends of both the Wolffs and of Eriane's dentist, Rachel Gingold. Indeed, it had been through the Gangs that the Wolffs had met first Rachel Gingold and then Eriane. The message was simply that the Wolffs were all well and safe at their planned destination. It had been relayed to Eriane by Dr. Eugène and she never questioned its authenticity. The Gangs, of course, were deeply relieved, but when Eriane added that the Wolffs had suggested that perhaps the Gangs themselves might be interested in using the escape route, some instinct must have warned them to beware. Or perhaps they did not feel so instantly threatened as the Wolffs. They decided to stay on in Paris. When the horrors of rue Le Sueur were revealed, they hastened to the police with the full story of how the Wolffs had delivered themselves into the hands of Petiot through the dentist, Dr. Gingold, and Eriane Kahan.

After the truth about the horrors of number 21 was revealed or at least indicated in the press many of those who had been active as scouts with the mythical "organization" were overcome with eagerness to clear themselves of guilt while others were careful to hide out. Yet there was never any real evidence that any of the scouts, not even the villainous Guintrand or the elusive Porchon, had the slightest knowledge of what really became of the men and women who chose this route to freedom. Some confusion enters the Petiot story at this point but a confusion that can fortunately be straightened out. The liquidations under the auspices and front of "Dr. Eugène's escape railroad" came so fast from the summer of 1942 to the spring of 1943 that it appears difficult to follow them. However, it is not so difficult because they all fall into but two groups. One quota consisted of the gangsters or renegades from the French Gestapo, together with their mistresses or girl friends, who Petiot in his trial admitted killing for patriotic reasons. The others were Jewish refugees, some of whom Petiot denied killing and some he admitted killing because he believed they were trying to trap him and were working against France but, later, he more than implied that he killed all of this group to save them from deportation and slow deaths in concentration camps. The fact that all members of both groups had important loot taken by Petiot was purely coincidental, if Petiot is to be believed.

No discussions or disclosures were ever even mentioned about the espionage or intelligence activities of Dr. Petiot or "Dr. Eugène." No one—neither his sources nor the recipients of his reports, much less any clandestine organizations—not even the French DGER—could ever admit or identify themselves as being related to a mass murderer. Even if Petiot was, as he claimed, the head of "Fly Tox," a Communist terrorist liquidation unit, he had to be disavowed. Politically, the Socialists and Communists who had elected him mayor of Villeneuve had to forget about him. This is why in all of the newspaper accounts, in all of the pretrial testimony, and in all of the many books on Petiot, rarely is there any mention of the important but unheralded role he played as a strange but effective informer and spy.

Even at this late date, over thirty years after his execution, this

fact will be denied, questioned, and even ridiculed, but is nevertheless one more successful activity of the legendary doctor: politician, mayor, writer, cartoonist, antique dealer and expert, devoted
family man, World War I veteran, and—World War II spy.

CHAPTER VIII

Dr. Eugène versus the German Gestapo
1942–44

All through the Occupation a German flag waved over the front entrance of what was once the French Ministry of the Interior where rue du Faubourg St. Honoré and rue Miromesnil meet, at Place Beauvau in Paris. Gray-uniformed, steel-helmeted German soldiers were on guard at the entrance. The scene was grim and sad with an occasional unhappy Frenchman or woman hurrying along rue du Faubourg St. Honoré. But down rue des Saussaies, to the right of the same entrance and also running into the same square, was an even grimmer sight. There were some German sentries, but over the door of the building, 11 rue des Saussaies, was a large white oval plaque with a black swastika. This was the general headquarters in Paris of the dread Gestapo. On the second floor there was a door bearing the sign "IV B" 131. This was the office of Dr. Yodkum, who headed one of the sections charged with collecting information on resistant and enemy intelligence agents. Right then Dr. Yodkum and his unit were hot on the trail of a clandestine apparatus helping Jews, resistants, enemies of the Third Reich, and allied pilots and prisoners to escape to England, North Africa, and South America.

The key figure in Yodkum's efforts was a rich young Jew with the name of Dreyfus.* A slender, rather studious-looking man born November 30, 1907, and without the appearance or the air

---

* The same name as the French Army captain falsely accused of selling secrets to the French 75-mm cannon to the Germans prior to World War I, unfairly broken and sent to Devil's Island because of Anti-Semitic influences but afterward completely cleared when the real culprit, Major Esterhazy, was found to be the guilty party.

of a hero, Yvan Dreyfus had been safe in the United States in 1939 when France went to war. The son of a wealthy Alsatian family, he was in the silk business in Lyon, had studied in the United States, and at the outbreak of the war had been for some time in the States on a business trip. He returned at once to France to join the French Army. He served as a noncommissioned officer in the artillery until he was demobilized shortly after the armistice.

At that time, many of Dreyfus' friends and business associates, particularly those in the United States, urged him to move quickly to America with his family. Being a Jew in Europe was to live in constant fear. But Dreyfus would not go.

"I am a Frenchman," he said. "My wife and children were born here and my parents come from Alsace. My home is here. My business is here. Now that France is in trouble, I cannot desert her."

The silk business had dwindled to nothing after the war started, so Dreyfus became the representative, in un-Occupied France, of a U.S. radio and radio parts manufacturer. This position gave him an opportunity to supply components for the clandestine radios operated by the resistance movement and replacement parts for the sets parachuted into France by the Allied intelligence services. When the clandestine radio caught word that a Free French Army was being organized in England, Yvan Dreyfus and four of his cousins decided to escape to England. They joined with a group of forty similarly minded patriots. Guided by a *passeur*, they made their way to a rendezvous, where they would follow a secure and tested route to safety. However, the route had been sealed by the Germans. An informer or an imprudent talker had compromised the operation. At Montpellier, the group walked into a German trap and were jailed. They were then transferred to an internment camp at Nîmes, and thence to the German concentration camp at Compiègne, Oise, which was the regular way station or transfer point for Jews and active resistants and any enemies of the Nazis on their way to the extermination camps and crematories of Dachau and Buchenwald.

When the Dreyfus family learned that Yvan was at Compiègne they cast about for some contact that would enable them to "reach" an important Nazi, one who could be persuaded, for a price, to save Yvan from death. Many top Nazis of that day were often far more concerned with the advancement of their personal fortunes than with ideological principles. So the Dreyfus family soon set out on a trail of bribery, ransom, "gratuity," and "commission" payments that led right to Dr. Yodkum, chief of the Paris Jewish Affairs Section of the Gestapo (Section IV B), rue des Saussaies, who was also charged with the discovery and elimination of all resistance activities and escape apparatuses.

Links in the chain of corruption and collusion were a series of French quisling types: a lawyer named Jean Aimé Guelin, once defense lawyer for Bonny in the Stavisky affair, and an associate named Marcel Duqueker; Paul Pehu, a former chief inspector of police in the town of La Rochelle, who worked for Guelin; and Marcel Chantin, a bank director during the Occupation who had a speaking acquaintance with Fourrier, the hairdresser. The devious route that led Yvan Dreyfus out of the camp at Compiègne into the hands of Dr. Petiot is complicated almost beyond understanding. But these were the chief movers in the scheme. There was one apparently minor link in the chain but one that, in the end, became a pivotal one. That was Charles Beretta, a mousy little character who was as ruthless as a rat. Beretta provided the Gestapo, for whom he worked, with a connection to Francinet, who, of course, was one step removed from Fourrier.

At just about the time that the Dreyfus family was seeking an avenue to purchase some influence, Dr. Yodkum found himself under pressure to investigate an organization that was delivering Jews, resistants, Allied airmen, prisoners who had escaped from German jails, and other "enemies of the Third Reich" from the hands of the Nazis. In the beginning, two sections of the Gestapo, IV B and IV E, had been delving into this matter, unknown to each other. Dr. Illera was chief of Section IV E and Charles Beretta the top undercover agent assigned to the case. Finally, it had been adjudged the sole responsibility of Section IV B and Dr. Yodkum, who, like so many others in the Petiot story, could have been chosen from a casting office for the part he played. He had a bull neck, ruddy face, and gray hair, with a brush haircut, pale eyes, and thick-lensed glasses.

The document that started Gestapo section chiefs Yodkum, Illera, Kleibauer, and Berger (all doctors) on Petiot's trail came to

Picture of Dr. Petiot on November 22 after he had been ordered to shave his beard for identification by witnesses. This picture never obtained by press and one of best studies of Petiot's face.

21 rue Le Sueur as now remodeled. From avenue Foch.

Dr. Petiot sleeps quietly during the prosecuting attorney's long summation, necessary because of the number of murders involved. It is not a pleasant presentation judging by the faces shown in this picture. V.P.I.

Lao-Dol chez Quéré
17 Av. A. Briand
Cachan (Seine)

Camphre   8 gr 18
méthyl-Pyrocatéchine   1 gr P 7   ch. P.
Camphre de Menthe   1 gr P 7   Remes
laudanum de Rousseau   4 gr 06   EC 126-52
Méthane richloré   8 gr 18
éther méthyl salicylique   8 gr
salicyl. d'amyle   2 gr 05
____ benzyle   4 gr
code Boulime   2 gr 2
1 K
poudre colloïdal   2 g 23
scurocaïne   2 g 23
N 100 gr p Embrocation
N isporé ____

Actual prescription by Dr. Petiot.

Gestapo headquarters early in May 1943. It was dated May 8, 1943, was unsigned, and read as follows:

Repeated but unconfirmed reports indicate the existence of an organization in Paris clandestinely passing persons equipped with false identification papers with alleged Argentine nationality across the Spanish frontier.

I assigned a reliable informer to gather information on the conditions or arrangements and price of what appeared to be an escape apparatus for the eventual destination of the Americas. Every three weeks a convoy or group leaves for Spain.

The prospective travelers must at the first meeting pay 50,000 francs and supply the organization with ten passport pictures and their names and home addresses.

The name and home address of each person is then checked. This check is effected by a uniformed Paris policeman. The prospective traveler is then notified three or four days ahead of time of the day of departure of his group and is further notified at the last minute of the exact place and time where he is to report. A member of the escape organization meets him there, then conducts him to a hotel or to a doctor's office. The cost of the lodging at the secret hiding place is 400 francs per day. From this time on, all escapees have no right to write or communicate with anyone outside or to see anyone. Several days later they are conducted to a railroad station by two or three different members of the organization. There, again at the last minute, they are supplied with false identification papers and passports, but not before another payment is made by them of 90,000 francs in cash.

All money and jewelry must be turned over to the organization, but are returned in Spain once the Franco-Spanish border has been passed. Each person can take as much money as he or she may desire.

The management of this underground railroad for the escape of persons from areas under German control must be assumed to be found or sought out among France's leaders or upper classes.

The report bore endorsements indicating that insofar as Section IV E was concerned, it had been referred to Dr. Buchold for immediate and vigorous investigation and report. Dr. Berger, deputy chief of the section, had also endorsed the paper.

At about the time he received this report, Yodkum also received news from Jean Guelin concerning a Jewish prisoner named Dreyfus. Guelin in that period was working under Yodkum as co-director of the Theater des Nouveautés on boulevard Poissonnière, a property formerly owned by a Jew named Benoît Deutsch. (Yodkum was acting administrator of Jewish properties in Paris.) Marcel Duqueker was co-director with Guelin and it had been Duqueker who had first been approached by the Dreyfus family in the person of Dreyfus' wife. Duqueker required a payment of 100,000 francs ($5,500) from the family for laying his hands on the Dreyfus file to learn how best to proceed. Mrs. Dreyfus paid the fee promptly. Duqueker then carried his problem to Guelin, and Guelin required an additional 700,000 francs ($36,000) as the price of opening negotiations with the German authorities. This sum, too, was paid without delay and without quibble.

Guelin then discussed the case with Yodkum and suggested that a small fortune might be had for arranging Dreyfus' release. But Yodkum, who by this time had some acquaintance with the Francinet-Fourrier–unidentified-doctor combine that operated out of 25 rue des Mathurins, and who knew of Guelin's casual connection with Fourrier, concocted an even more fruitful idea. He could arrange the release of Dreyfus and, as one of the conditions of his release, require him to act as a plant, or, as the French put it, a *mouton* (sheep), to uncover the escape apparatus of Dr. Eugène. In this way he could not only fatten all their purses but could also conclude a fine stroke of business for the Gestapo, and for the greater glory of the Third Reich. More important, he would run no personal risk since the liberation, perhaps only temporary, of one German prisoner would more than balance the discovery and elimination of a major underground railroad. He could even tax the Dreyfus family an additional sum to be paid into the official coffers of the Gestapo, so that there would be no noses put out of joint anywhere along the line.

Guelin and Yodkum estimated that the Dreyfus family could easily afford a total of three and a half million francs as ransom for Yvan. This was worth, at the official exchange rate, almost $250,000 in U.S. money. The money would be divided, Yodkum indicated, in three parts—a million francs to the Third Reich; a million francs to Yodkum (who took "the greatest risk"), and a million and a half to Guelin to be divided among all his subordi-

nates and associates, as well as to supply Dreyfus with the money
he needed to pay his fare to Dr. Eugène for a ride on the under
ground railroad (this to be recovered once the arrests had been
made).

There were certain precautions that had to be taken. Dreyfus
would be required to sign a paper pledging never to bear arms
against the Third Reich or in any way to serve her enemies. And
he must also agree, in writing, to act as the *mouton* to betray the
escape route. Additionally, Dreyfus would be without papers—until the underground had supplied him with his false ones—so he
would be pretty much at the mercy of the Gestapo should he try
to double-cross his "benefactors."

To secure Yvan Dreyfus' agreement to these terms was the next
step and a difficult one. It would be simple enough for Yodkum to
arrange the release. There was hardly any question that Mrs.
Dreyfus and the Dreyfus family would put up the money. But
who would sell the program to Yvan Dreyfus?

For that job, Guelin had just the man: Paul Pehu, the fifty-five-
year-old former chief inspector of police from La Rochelle, now a
Gestapo courier.

With the necessary papers in his possession and full details of
the plan, Pehu needed only some way of assuring Dreyfus that
this plan was indeed on the level and had his family's backing.
Dreyfus' wife, Paulette, a pretty and stout-hearted young lady,
would have to help in this task. She had come to Paris without
proper papers and at the risk of her life to try to save her husband
from deportation and probably certain death. She met Pehu with
Guelin and told them that Pehu could use a piece of information
known only within the Dreyfus family: that the Dreyfus daughter
as a baby had been known only to her father and mother as
"*Pomme*" (Apple). With that password then, Pehu was on his
way to Compiègne.

But young Dreyfus rebelled at the very thought of foreswearing
his right to bear arms for his country. As for acting as a stool
pigeon: the thought turned his stomach.

But Pehu reassured him. This was all a matter of form, to
mislead the Boche. Why fret about a scrap of paper? Yvan
Dreyfus was, of course, too hard-headed a man to consider that he
must be bound by an oath forced on him by the Nazis. If he won

his freedom, he would fight for France. As for acting as *mouton*, this presented a challenge. Perhaps it would offer him escape to England and also an opportunity to outwit the Gestapo. They could not keep a Gestapo man at his side as he traveled the escape route. The best they could do would be to put a tail on him. And there were ways of eluding such people and warning his compatriots. One thing was certain. If he did not agree to this plan, he would be on his way promptly to a death camp. If he did agree, or seem to agree, there would be time. . . . And who could tell what opportunity might not present itself?

Dreyfus signed the papers. Pehu was delighted.

"You can expect to be brought to Paris in a few days and released," he told young Dreyfus. Then he hastened back to Paris with the documents in his pocket.

Guelin and Duqueker then had a meeting with Mme. Dreyfus and showed her the agreements her husband had signed. She was horrified. Her husband committed to never bearing arms against the enemy? Her husband become informer for the Nazis? Never! But Duqueker and Guelin were quick to comfort her. As a matter of form. No more than that. Besides, they had the papers, not the Germans. The important thing, after all, is to get your husband out of the hands of the Nazis. After that . . . Mme. Dreyfus was persuaded, as her husband had been. Who could tell what might not be accomplished once Yvan were free?

But Guelin and Duqueker had a pressing matter to be settled. More money would be needed. A new German go-between had come into the affair. There would have to be 500,000 francs for him. And then there was Pehu to be taken care of. His time and expenses . . . say, another 200,000? Mme. Dreyfus balked. Still more money. This could go on endlessly. She started to argue the point, then decided not to. She paid them the money, but a few days later Duqueker came back, this time seeking an extra million. Horrified, Paulette refused. This began to sound like there would be no end to the payoff and the victim still not delivered. She flatly refused. She reminded them that, according to their agreement, the 2,700,000 francs would be paid them only on the release or delivery of her husband. Then, fearful of what might be done to her husband, she paid 400,000 francs, which were gratefully accepted by Guelin.

There followed, on May 18, 1943, a meeting in front of Fouquet's restaurant on the Champs Élysées. Guelin, Duqueker, and Mme. Dreyfus met on a bench under the chestnut trees. Good news, Guelin told her. Her husband was now at Gestapo headquarters on rue des Saussaies. She must come there now, bringing the rest of the three and a half million francs. This time Mme. Dreyfus was firm: she would positively not set foot inside Gestapo headquarters. Well then, Guelin pointed out, she would just have to trust them with the money, for until it was paid, her husband would not be released. Mme. Dreyfus turned over the rest of the ransom and wondered if she would ever see Yvan again.

Then that night Guelin brought him to her. Speechlessly, they embraced each other. Of course, there were dangers and threats still. He had no papers. His four cousins were still at Compiègne, hostages for his behavior, and his wife had no permit to be in Paris. So the sword hung over them all. But for tonight, these things did not matter.

Guelin now undertook to accomplish the planting of the *mouton* on Dr. Eugène. That meant he must bring Dreyfus into the escape route without stirring any suspicions. It was at this point that the banker Marcel Chantin entered the plot, for it was Chantin who had established the connection with Fourrier. Chantin was the forty-year-old director of the Regional Paris Bank. He could be found almost any night during the Occupation, in some bar or night club in the Ninth Arrondissement. In his nightly rounds Chantin had met Fourrier at the Café le Dauphin on rue des Mathurins. He also met Guelin, who, in true barroom style, had exaggerated his own position into that of "Paris police official." In furtherance of this role, Guelin had invited Chantin to report to him, Guelin, any activities he heard about that might require police attention. Eventually, in a talkative moment, Chantin had described to Guelin all he had heard (and perhaps some things he *thought* he had heard) about an underground escape route for resistants, Jews, and other fugitives. He even knew one of the principals, a certain hairdresser named Fourrier. Guelin, having already learned from Yodkum of the Gestapo interest in this particular operation, begged to be introduced to the hairdresser. Thus Guelin came to know Fourrier and, when the time came, was ready to bring Dreyfus in as a prospect for escape without any doubt as to the young man's status as a Jew and a fugitive.

Now it was time to take the next step and commit Dreyfus to the betrayal of this whole complex. Guelin told Dreyfus that he would be given his correct papers by the Gestapo only if he cooperated. Of course he would have false ones supplied by Dr. Eugène. The Gestapo would also advance him the money for the payment of the doctor's fee. A way out now began to reveal itself to Dreyfus. There would certainly be a moment when he could explain to Dr. Eugène or his agents the fix he was in and there would be a chance to evade the tails set on them and then to make his escape, with the aid of the organization.

But what if the Gestapo had foreseen this? They would have their agent right with him probably until the final rendezvous. Well, all the better. They might by then have begun to trust him a little. It would be impossible for them to have a Gestapo agent at his side when he made the plunge into the underground. They would be trying to follow him unobtrusively, and he felt confident he could elude the man who was following him.

He went calmly then with Guelin to the rendezvous at Fourrier's hairdressing parlor—a dreary place, up a dirty staircase, into a shabby room with small, curtained alcoves. Fourrier met them at the top of the stairs. Dreyfus, he indicated, must come alone into an alcove, while Guelin should stay where he was. But Guelin managed to get a clear enough view through the parted curtains to see a man of above average height, with a dark and interesting face and burning eyes. Dr. Eugène!

But that was as close as Guelin came to identifying the mysterious figure. He was dark. He was rather tall. And his eyes were his striking feature. But who he was and where he made his headquarters he would be unable to report.

Dreyfus received a full description of what would be required and what would be accomplished, and was asked to return for further meetings with Dr. Eugène. He was told to bring ten passport photos—five full face and five profile—and 200,000 francs and his baggage. Then he would be taken to a secret hideout to await the departure date. While hidden there he would get new identification papers, a passport, vaccination, inoculations, and necessary medical documents. Once he was accepted by Dr. Eugène, he was told, he would depart the following Sunday. On May 19, 1943, Guelin accompanied Dreyfus to Fourrier's for his final departure, having supplied him with 200,000 francs and a suitcase. Somehow Dreyfus found an opportunity to explain to Dr. Eugène about the Gestapo plan and the crafty doctor promptly came up with a scheme to lose the men who were tailing them. What happened from that time forth was told in a Gestapo report typed on the morning of May 21:

P.V. PARIS 21 MAY 1943

SUBJECT: Information on a clandestine organization and underground railroad delivering passports to Jews and other persons desiring to escape from both occupied France and Axis Europe.

This organization is directed by a Doctor of Medicine and a hairdresser named Fourrier, whose establishment is on the second floor of the building at 25 Rue des Mathurins, Paris. The Doctor has not yet been identified.

With the co-operation of Yvan Dreyfus and several informers I brought about a meeting between Dreyfus and Fourrier. Dreyfus asked to be directed to a means of escape. After many precautions and several interviews including several with the Doctor at the domicile of the hairdresser, Fourrier, Dreyfus was finally accepted yesterday. After having given them an amount of 200,000 francs loaned him by one of his friends, also ten photos for a passport, and identification papers he was taken by the Doctor from Fourrier's place on Rue des Mathurins to a secret hideout. Here he must wait for the time of departure and while doing so get new identification papers, a passport, and be vaccinated and inoculated, etc. His actual departure is fixed for next Sunday.

Notwithstanding careful and proper provisions for surveillance and the double tailing of both Dreyfus and the Doctor from the time each one was first picked up by our surveillance, the Doctor and Dreyfus after leaving Fourrier dropped our tails and were lost. We therefore have been unable to either identify the Doctor or find out the location of the site where the organization hides individuals for escape and where they are supplied with false papers, passports, and start their trip to Spain, North Africa, and the Americas.

But now that I am certain that Dreyfus has been supplied with a false passport and that he has been taken to the secret base of this escape apparatus, I set a trap for the Doctor who on Saturday at 10 A.M. will meet one of my operatives at Fourrier's, who will in turn beg the Doctor to accept him for escape.

It is at this instant when Fourrier or the Doctor accepts the fee for this escape that I have chosen to arrest both Fourrier and the Doctor. Once we have them it will be simple to take full possession of both the hairdresser's and the Doctor's establishments and make a thorough search at both places. We should have no trouble finding the necessary names, addresses, phone numbers, documents, and other data on the entire escape organization that has evidently been functioning for some eighteen months (November 1941) or more. [The German Gestapo strangely enough were closer to being correct than the French police. The French fixed the start of Petiot's escape apparatus with Guschinow, January 2, 1942.]

It will also be possible to recover the fees paid in on all this traffic. These must total many millions of francs.

Once this apparatus and its operations are terminated, the Doctor and the hairdresser should be incarcerated and compelled, and if necessary tortured, to divulge the exact location where the immediate group furnished with false passports are awaiting their departure on the next day, Sunday. Since the hideout is secret and neither the travelers waiting there nor the Doctor and the hairdresser we will have arrested can communicate with anyone—even by phone or messenger—this should succeed.

Based on the reports of my informers, the Doctor does not only handle Jews, but all persons presented to him who desire to escape, including, as confirmed by several sources, several or more persons suspected of terrorist activities, notably even deserters from our Army or [Gestapo] Services.

The final embarkations are on neutral ships from a Portuguese port. The escaping travelers are routed there by train via Irun. [A commune or town—14,000 population—in Guipúzcoa province of Spain, very near the French border and Biarritz.]

Based on a long and detailed investigation and my all-out efforts, it would appear to me that this apparatus is organized in a remarkably efficient manner with every possible precaution against any communication or relationship between its various and successive echelons of travelers.

It might have been most useful to set up surveillance all along the route of this underground railroad in order to study the methods by which the line of demarcation and the various frontiers were negotiated.

Undoubtedly the doctor had set a new rendezvous. Perhaps the Métro station at L'Étoile? He and Dreyfus would have the advan-

tage of knowing where they were headed and perhaps even of recognizing the various "tails." How Dreyfus must have thrilled
when he first found himself out from under the cold stare of the
Gestapo. The rest of it, no matter what the risks, would be relatively easy now. Sunday he would be off, wary this time of any betrayal and careful to stay out of traps. Then, within weeks, perhaps even days, he would be in England, with the Free French
Forces at last, and to hell with any pledge he may have given to
the Nazis. To move through Paris once more, hunted, it is true,
but free! He would not dare call his wife for they would expect
that. But soon he would be with his companions, and then a soldier again and not a fugitive.

It seemed to Dr. Yodkum that if he had the doctor arrested,
this action might send everyone scurrying for cover, with the travelers all dispatched ahead of schedule and the entire trail obliter-
ated. Besides, he had no desire to have his own ransom deal with
Dreyfus exposed. He had pocketed an unusual fee. The danger to
himself was not over by any means. The hairdresser therefore was
not immediately arrested and tortured to find out the identity of
the doctor. It seemed best to Yodkum simply to infiltrate the Dr.
Eugène organization with a new plant, who might catch up with
the Sunday group, and permit the recapture of Dreyfus and the
recovery of the marked money that had been advanced to him for
Dr. Eugène's fee.

As it happened, Section IV E of the Gestapo had already
groomed and briefed a *mouton* to make his way into the Dr.
Eugène apparatus. He was Charles Beretta, the ideal secret agent,
so unobtrusive, so devoid of distinguishing features that he would
fade into any background. Beretta had been a secret operative for
Section IV E for some time, using the code names VM or VMX.
Despite the fact that Beretta's own wife, a Jew, was arrested and
sent to a German prison camp at Drancy, Beretta worked loyally
for the Nazis. Now his job was to break open what seemed to be
the most flourishing escape apparatus in France—a job that had
proved too much for Dr. Yodkum and his prisoner Dreyfus.

This was an easy job for Beretta. He had already met Francinet
and had been introduced to and closely questioned by the famous
doctor. He had even supplied the Gestapo with the best description yet of Dr. Eugène: "Age around 35 to 38; thin build; height

5'11" with dark-brown hair and piercing black eyes. He was clean shaven, wore a navy-blue suit. The most striking characteristic was his habit of constantly rubbing his hands together."

Beretta had also learned that Francinet (Pintard) was a make-up man at a certain motion-picture studio and he was able to give the Gestapo Francinet's home address. Fourrier and his establishment were also well known to him.

Having been accepted by Dr. Eugène for escape, he had already turned in the required ten passport pictures, had been shown a blank Argentine passport, and had a list of names of his supposed fellow passengers on the underground trip. He had also been able to talk the doctor into cutting the fee from 100,000 francs to 60,000 and had paid a deposit of 15,000 in marked money. Now the Gestapo planned to have Beretta taken on Friday, May 21, or Saturday, May 22, to the secret hideout, where he would join the group scheduled to leave the next day, Sunday, May 23.

Section IV E had turned the whole business now over to Yodkum's section, which was to receive all prisoners, documents, money, and other evidence collected. Beretta was supplied with a wad of numbered bank notes, recorded with the Gestapo, in denominations of 1,000 and 5,000 francs. At the appointed time, on May 21, the emergency plan was activated. Beretta appeared at Fourrier's shop, ready for departure. The operation had been put under the direction of Dr. Berger of Section IV E. But what was this? No one was there to meet Beretta but Francinet and Fourrier! Had the wily doctor, already having dodged a tail and made off with Dreyfus, smelled a rat this time too? Alarmed, the Gestapo ordered the agents to move in, just as soon as the money had been passed and accepted by the agents of Dr. Eugène. They could not risk having Fourrier and Francinet vanish also.

As soon as Fourrier had accepted thirty bills of 1,000 francs and three bills of 5,000, all marked from Beretta, Gestapo agents quickly invaded the hairdressing parlor and hustled the Mutt and Jeff team, Francinet and Fourrier, into an official car. At rue des Saussaies, Francinet would admit only that he knew Fourrier and "sometimes" brought to the hairdressing parlor persons who desired to meet the wigmaker. Fourrier admitted that he worked for Dr. Eugene but he insisted he did not know his identity. The Gestapo promptly fed him a few wallops with fist and hose and his memory came back to him. "Dr. Eugène" was Dr. Marcel Petiot, 66 rue Caumartin. He owned one other property that Fourrier knew about—two apartment houses at 52 rue de Reuilly. As for a "clinic" or "rest home," he knew only that Petiot sent his patients to Maison de Santé at 17 rue Milan.

By six o'clock that night, May 21, 1943, the Gestapo had arrested Petiot. They found him at 66 rue Caumartin with his wife and his son, Gerhardt. Ordinarily, Gerhardt lived at Auxerre with Petiot's brother Maurice, the doctor apparently wanting to keep him clear of his dark doings. It was simply bad luck that Gerhardt had to be there when the Gestapo arrived. The Gestapo also gathered in Petiot's old friend from his bachelor days at Villeneuve, René Nezondet. Nezondet had come to the Petiot apartment bringing three theater tickets, for a performance that very night. Nezondet was taken in by the Gestapo on the suspicion of being a member of the Dr. Eugène escape organization.

Here is the Gestapo report on the arrests:

Paris
May 22, 1943

svop (sd) kde paris
14 E 2a 15016
Chief: Dr. Illera
Deputy and author of this report: Kelibauer

1. The subject of this report is an escape apparatus particularly for Jews. Important data, reports, and evidence are already with Section IV B who were also working on this case unknown to this Section IV E. Further investigation and action has been delegated exclusively to the former section and therefore the following files are permanently transferred to Section IV B.

2. At the same time the following prisoners are turned over:

> Fourrier, Raoul
> Pintard, Edmund Marcel
> Nezondet, René.

This report has its mysterious aspect: Petiot is not even mentioned as having been arrested, though he was the very target of the whole action, the elusive Dr. Eugène having slipped out of their grasp just a few hours earlier. Why this special handling? Had his friends at rue Lauriston put in a word for him? Or was it

the Henri Martin group? Petiot had a good friend named Braun
with the German Otto Agency and had gotten Nezondet a job
with Braun. Was it Braun who had sought a special deal for Petiot?

Whatever it was, the special handling was of brief duration. On
May 25, a report from Section IV B of the Gestapo dealt with Petiot, reporting that a thorough check of his property on rue de
Reuilly had been made without results. No hidden fugitives. No
underground railway station. Just two old buildings fully rented to
ordinary peaceful tenants. No likelihood whatever of using this as
a hideout.

As for the "rest home," the Maison de Santé turned out to be
just that, a private sanitarium housing only women and old people. Petiot had brought only one recent patient, a forty-four-year-
old woman named Henriette Carriere, a drug addict, who had
been arrested on May 9, 1943. But she was neither a Jew nor a resistant and she certainly was not Yvan Dreyfus in disguise. The
manager of the rest home owned another establishment in Breteuil
sur Noye, but that housed only ten older couples. The operation
was completely legitimate. There was not a trace of any group
awaiting transportation. (Rudolf Braun, Petiot's friend with the
German Supply Agency, did know about 21 rue Le Sueur but for
some reason this information had not yet reached the Gestapo. Or
was it known only to Masuy?)

As far as Dr. Yodkum knew, therefore, the clutch of fugitives
hidden away at the secret rendezvous had made their escape, Yvan
Dreyfus with them, taking his knowledge of the Yodkum-Guelin
scheme. Yodkum might have breathed more easily had he realized
that the brave young Dreyfus had already submitted quite peace-
fully to Petiot's "inoculation" and had died in convulsions, as so
many others had done, on the floor of the triangular room.

This time Dr. Petiot was caught and arrested so now Yodkum
had to hurry to extract from Petiot everything there was to discover about the escape apparatus. Perhaps it might still be possible to halt that underground railroad somewhere between Paris
and the border. Yodkum had made a specialty of persuading pris-.
oners to talk. The interrogation, or torture, room was on the
fourth floor of the Gestapo headquarters. Here Yodkum put Petiot through "la danse" several times—running lighted slivers

under his nails, drilling his teeth, and beating him. Petiot spent one whole night—nine hours—in the office of Dr. Yodkum and was beaten every hour. Yodkum finally extracted a story from Petiot, but it was not the whole story. Instead, it was a fanciful but fairly convincing tale of a man named Martinetti, who, according to Petiot, was the *real* head of the escape apparatus or the next link in it, while he, Petiot, was no more than a collector.

Here in full is the "confession" Petiot made to the Gestapo (secured from the Gestapo records):

I, Doctor Marcel Petiot, temporarily examined while incarcerated by the German military authorities, do hereby declare that:

About eighteen months ago I met a man who came to my office as a patient named Robert Martinetti. I do not record my clients in any of my books. During the course of his visits for my professional services he told me that he was a member of an organization devoted to getting people out of occupied France to South America. He requested me to supply him with the names of some of my patients who might be interested in becoming clients of his. Originally the price he asked for each traveler to be gotten out was 25,000 francs, but later he raised this figure to 50,000.

Several months later I told Mr. Fourrier, the hairdresser, whom I knew for some time, about the escape organization and adding that if he, Fourrier, knew anyone wanting to leave Paris clandestinely to bring them to me. Fourrier was also a regular patient of mine. Following this, Fourrier did return and told me he knew several people who desired to make illegal departures. Martinetti in the meantime kept visiting me for treatment. I therefore relayed my conversations with Fourrier. The departures began about six months ago. My role or participation was merely to take the travelers and also their baggage at Fourrier's and to take them to a rendezvous at a time and place given me by phone one or two days before—usually Place de la Concorde where they were turned over to this same Martinetti. Fourrier at the beginning would give me the 25,000 francs for each person brought me for Martinetti. I did not like the people recruited by Fourrier. I therefore became concerned and took it upon myself to check upon them and interview each and every one of them about the reasons for their trip. From then on I reserved the right to accept or turn down the candidates for escape. It was always Fourrier who collected the fees from the travelers. I never had anything to do with the fees except once when I did intervene in one single case to reduce the price asked by Fourrier.

With respect to my methods of communication and contact with Martinetti, requested by you, they were mostly by telephone when he would ask for news about new travelers or set the hour and day for the rendezvous. I never had any phone number to call him. He always called me. The hour for the meeting of the travelers was always the same—between eleven and twelve noon, usually at the street-level entrance of the subway station at the foot of the rue de Rivoli [Place de la Concorde]. Martinetti, incidentally, always watched for me and tailed me from Fourrier's place, rue Mathurins, where I picked up the travelers to see if the travelers and I were under surveillance. It was understood that if we were being tailed he would not meet us and after waiting until a few minutes past twelve, I would release the travelers for another try and an appointment for another time. When I said that the meetings were always at the same place and time I must qualify this. Actually, there were two meeting places in case repeated meetings had attracted attention or in case my approach was under surveillance.

If for any reason Martinetti did not show between eleven and twelve noon at Place de la Concorde and rue de Rivoli, then by prearrangement, unless changed by a phone call, the meeting hour for another try would be between 4 and 5 P.M. and the meeting place would be the street-level entrance to the St. Augustin subway station. Here also my approach with the travelers would be watched by Martinetti.

With respect to your questions on what I knew of the escape organization, I can only answer that I knew only Martinetti and what he told me about it. At first he told me that the clandestine apparatus was under the protection of high-ranking personalities and that a foreign embassy furnished the passports to the travelers for their escape. He mentioned the Argentine Embassy, adding that travelers had the further protection of allegedly being commercial attachés of the Embassy with semidiplomatic status. The departures according to Martinetti were from a seaport very close to the Franco-Spanish border and the ultimate destination of the voyages was Argentina.

With respect to the repeated questions you have asked me about the base or hideout from which the travelers here leave Paris and where they are lodged for a period prior to their departure, I can only answer that I was never told anything about the place. All I knew and all I was supposed to know was Martinetti and deliver-

ing the travelers to him. I never saw any of the persons turned over
to Martinetti again.

You claim that I once told a medical patient and travel client of
mine whose wife wanted to leave with him that she should come to
the place where the travelers waited for a number of days only at
the last minute because it had very poor accommodations with no
comforts or modern conveniences. I definitely affirm that it was
Martinetti who made this statement. I personally could not make it
as I never saw the hideout or place of assembly and departure. Furthermore, I haven't the slightest idea where it is located.

I might add in conclusion that I was never guided in this matter
for any personal gain or profit. I was involved only to be of service
to people and to help them. I acknowledge this typed testimony
which has been read to me in the French language as being a true
report of my statements.

Petiot signed this statement and swore to it, undoubtedly with
some inner smugness at having been able to cling to his secrets despite the torturing. Fourrier, also roughly questioned, made a
number of admissions to the Gestapo, including the fact that he
and Francinet had recruited five persons who were taken by Petiot
from rue Mathurins to some destination they knew not of. In addition to those five, said Fourrier, there were Beretta and Yvan
Dreyfus, making just seven in all that they knew anything about.
Whether or not Petiot took others besides these, Fourrier and
Francinet, despite the memory treatments afforded at rue des Saussaies, could not recall.

René Nezondet, fortified by his own innocence, stoutly argued
his case with the Gestapo. He told his story with firmness and dignity. He had known Dr. Petiot for twenty years, since they worked
together in Villeneuve, he as secretary to the justice of the peace
and Petiot as mayor, physician, and medical examiner. He knew
nothing about any escape apparatus or of any rest home where escapees awaited departure. His only reason for calling on Petiot
when he did was to bring Petiot three theater tickets for Petiot,
Mme. Petiot, and Gerhardt, for a performance that very evening.
And he had the tickets to prove it.

This was the sum of all the Gestapo garnered from their careful
and foolproof plan to expose Dr. Eugène's escape apparatus. By
now the birds—and even the *mouton*—had flown, or so it seemed

to Dr. Yodkum, for the Sunday "departure date" was long past. But then Yodkum might have pushed harder for details from Petiot if there had not been interference from other quarters. Once Petiot had been arrested, Mme. Petiot began at once to summon up whatever influence she owned to have her husband set free. These were brutal days in Paris, with even suspected resistants sometimes shot without any pretense of legal process. It was important therefore to move quickly to keep Petiot alive. He had apparently been caught red-handed, in the very act of helping a fugitive escape from the Germans. After the surrender of Italy to the Allies on September 8, 1943, the Germans were far more ruthless than ever before. No trials or legal procedure were necessary. Anyone caught or even suspected of resistance, espionage, or any activity against the occupational authorities was summarily shot or deported to Germany's increasing labor camps. And the reports read that Petiot had not only helped spirit Jews away, but even terrorists, enemy airmen, and German deserters. It would not have been in the least out of character, or even a departure from normal procedure, for the Gestapo to execute Petiot out of hand and not even notify his family of his fate. Everyone therefore who possessed the least acquaintance within the Occupation establishment was recruited by Mme. Petiot and Maurice Petiot to intervene on the doctor's behalf.

Some of these friends, it seems certain, asked for help from Pierre Bonny, of the rue Lauriston group. There is definite evidence that the Todt organization also telephoned rue des Saussaies for reports about Petiot. Yodkum complained about the number of calls he received before he had even completed his questioning. Masuy, of the avenue Henri Martin organization, was particularly important. He wanted to talk to Petiot himself.

But Petiot, along with the others picked up at the same time, was first transferred to Fresnes prison, where a great number of resistants were housed. Here he was accepted, by dint of the scars he carried from his stay on rue des Saussaies, as a hero of the Resistance. He quickly made friends among the prisoners and was able in this way to cultivate at least a superficial knowledge of the underground apparatus and its jargon. A cellmate was Lieutenant Richard L'Heritier, parachutist, who had earned a medal for bravery. L'Heritier, who was later sent to Auschwitz, but managed to survive, never abandoned his deep admiration for Petiot, or his conviction that Petiot had been framed and had killed none but traitors. He was to testify eventually at Petiot's trial.

René Nezondet did not stay long at Fresnes. On June 12 he was released after an informer who had been put into his cell reported that Nezondet was telling the simple truth when he said he knew nothing of any escape organization. Petiot himself was taken out of Fresnes prison three times, to travel under armed escort to Paris. The purpose and the result of two of these trips were never made clear. Georges Masuy wanted to talk to him. Apparently all they did was talk for Petiot, as far as could be learned, never saw the inside of Masuy's torture chamber but conferred with the lithe and fierce-looking Nazi at great length. The first Petiot-Masuy private interview was ninety minutes long. Masuy's longest interviews outside of his torture chambers usually lasted five minutes. These positive and official meetings prove conclusively a connection between Petiot and the German Abwehr authorities, i.e., Masuy.

Petiot's second visit to Paris was at the request of the Paris police, who wanted to try to wrap up the Khait–van Bever cases, in which Petiot was suspected of kidnaping or murdering key witnesses. The Gestapo consented to Petiot's attendance at the hearing on the condition that he not be questioned about the escape route or about his dealings with Beretta or Dreyfus. The brief hearing (2:30 to 6:30 P.M., on November 10, 1943) resulted in no definite conclusion, although some participants could not be restrained from wondering aloud at the strange parallels between the three cases or from asking themselves if perhaps Dreyfus had not "joined" Mme. Khait and Marc van Bever.

Petiot's third visit to Paris was again under armed escort to the office of Masuy at 101 avenue Henri Martin. Once more Petiot walked out without a scar and with no evidence that he had been put under any physical pressure. It was obvious—indeed it was practically certain—that some kind of deal was discussed and finally agreed to. But what was it? Did Petiot agree to spy on his fellow prisoners, to learn code names, secret meeting places, passwords, communication methods, ciphers? Or did Petiot and Masuy already have a possible double-cross espionage relationship? There is strong suspicion that some sort of arrangement was made or was already present between these two geniuses in crime. Petiot did return to Fresnes prison and continued to associate closely with other resistants there and insult his guards! But on January 13, 1944, Marcel Petiot was unconditionally, and inexplicably, turned loose by the Germans. Neither Yodkum's office nor that of Masuy bothered to notify the French police, who were under their jurisdiction, that Petiot had been released, else he might have been promptly picked up for further questioning or might at least have been put under tight surveillance. This sort of thing simply did not happen to a man who had been caught in the act of aiding enemies of the Reich. Yet it did happen to Petiot and more than one man in Paris must have wondered why.

It is true that Mme. Petiot and Maurice had enlisted the aid of every influential person they knew to save the doctor from a death camp. Yodkum frequently referred to some nine phone calls he had received, all of them requesting him to spring Petiot. Yodkum was hard pressed but hated to give up his foolproof plan to liquidate the escape apparatus. On the other hand he had made a lot of money on Dreyfus; still he did not believe the Martinetti story of Petiot. He summed it up effectively: *"C'est de la merde!"*

Even so, mere back-scratching would not have been sufficient to win freedom for a man as stained with guilt as Petiot seemed to be. Moreover, his conduct at Fresnes prison and at rue des Saussaies had been so anti-German and anti-Nazi that it had earned the abject admiration of his fellow prisoners, almost all resistants, and many a fierce beating from his guards. There simply had to be an arrangement of some sort and that may very well have included a confession of what had truly been going on at number 21.

Number 21 rue Le Sueur was not, after all, such a tight secret. Porchon seems to have known about it. (He was identified from a photograph as a possible visitor there during the time of Petiot's imprisonment.) Maurice had to know about it for he had the keys and he had been seen there more than once. On August 28, 1943, Maurice had brought 1,320 pounds of quicklime from Auxerre in a truck. Even Rudolf Braun and his family were said to have visited there.

But as soon as Petiot had been picked up by the Gestapo, there was a scurrying to cover up his tracks. Maurice Petiot came to

Paris from Auxerre and stayed, as all the Petiots did, at the Hôtel Alicot. It was he who, accompanied by two chauffeurs, Marcel Reine and Maurice Léon, brought the truck to rue Le Sueur on May 25 to carry away the suitcases about which the neighbors gave such varied accounts. Three witnesses at least were able to testify to the date, time, and details of this deed.

From the Muller Garage, next door to the Hôtel Alicot, the suitcases were taken to the Paris-Lyon railroad station the next morning, carried the short distance by Maurice Petiot and the hotel clerk, Charles Marot, using a four-wheeled railway platform cart. Maurice dispatched the cases in three separate shipments to Auxerre by train. (According to later and painstaking study, fifty-two pieces of luggage were shipped but only forty-five recovered.) In Auxerre, Jean Eustache, the chauffeur who had taken the shipment of quicklime to 21 rue Le Sueur, picked up the suitcases and delivered them to the combination store and home of Albert Neuhausen, who sold bicycles and radios. The Neuhausens were all prepared to store the luggage away, for they had been notified of the shipment by Léone Arnout, servant and "companion" of Mme. Petiot's father and courier for the Petiot family.

All the stories and "confessions" of the various people involved with Petiot at this period contain contradictions. They accuse each other in some instances and deny the accusations of others. But it is difficult to accept the fact that Maurice Petiot, for one, had no guilty knowledge of the doings at number 21. While his brother was at Fresnes prison, Maurice was seen several times, and by more than one witness, visiting number 21. Once, he came in company with the two chauffeurs. There is also the matter of the quicklime, which Maurice arranged to have delivered. Surely some suspicion of its purpose must have entered his mind.

On February 18, 1943, in a truck driven by Jean Eustache, Maurice sent 300 kilograms (660 pounds) of lime to his brother at 21 rue Le Sueur from a quarry at Oisy-sur-Armançon. Maurice was at the Hôtel Alicot and told the proprietor (who eventually told the Paris police) that he had come to supervise the delivery of some quicklime to his brother's place. But the truck carrying the lime broke down en route. The two men driving it, Jean Eustache and Robert Massonnière, had to abandon the vehicle at Ponthierry, where they placed it in a garage belonging to Paul Henri

Lafort. They said they would return, but they never appeared again. These men must have believed (until the news of the discoveries at 21 rue Le Sueur appeared in the papers) that they were transporting building material. But what did Maurice believe?

According to René Nezondet, he notified the Paris police when the Germans released Dr. Petiot on January 13, 1944, that Maurice Petiot had come to him, sometime in December 1943 during the time the doctor was in jail, and frantically sought Nezondet's aid in building a wall at 21 rue Le Sueur to conceal the bodies Maurice had found there. Maurice told Nezondet that his brother the doctor was certainly mad. He was almost hysterical when he described finding some sixty bodies, all black as if dead from some black plague, and a book or diary with the names of the victims, their vital statistics, and the dates of their execution. But Maurice denied ever telling such a tale to Nezondet. The Paris police, themselves trying to explain a reluctance to follow up on leads, later pointed out that Nezondet had never volunteered this story but that they had to chase after him and interrogate him and that it was only much later that he told it to avoid being charged as an accessory. Fortunately for Nezondet, several of his friends had heard the story told by Maurice and repeated to them by Nezondet before the discovery of 21 rue Le Sueur.

Roland Porchon, however, after the fire, did volunteer a story to the police concerning the murders at number 21. Nezondet's mistress, Mme. Lesage, in a separate statement, also affirmed that she had told the Paris police what she had heard about Petiot's execution chamber. The three of them—Nezondet, Porchon, and Mme. Lesage—named police officers Doulet, Bouygues, and Gignoux as the men they had made their statements to. Not so, said the police officers. It was true that because of Petiot's apparent patriotism, Nezondet and Mme. Lesage had decided not to tell the police about 21 rue Le Sueur until after the German Occupation, as the bodies might be those of Germans and collaborators. It was also true that Porchon had told them, in August 1943, about an unidentified doctor who murdered, in an unidentified cellar, travelers who had paid him from fifty to 100,000 francs to escape. Besides, Porchon admitted that he had brought two prospective clients to Petiot and evidence indicated at least two others, and he had never identified Petiot as the killer or number 21 as the charnel house. It was only after the discovery of 21 rue Le Sueur that Porchon linked his story to the police to Petiot.

It seemed generally understood that Petiot operated under some sort of protection from the Germans. Both Porchon and Nezondet testified that some police, whose names they could not give, had once said to them about Petiot:

"The Germans have let him knock off thirty or forty travelers and there is nothing we can do about it."

The Paris press, both before the liberation of Paris (August 24, 1944) and more especially after, severely criticized the police for its negligence in the Petiot case and especially after his release by the Germans from Fresnes prison on January 13, 1944. Criticism was so great that two famous white papers were prepared on Petiot, one in March 1944 and again after the liberation in September 1944. Both were prepared under the supervision of the inspector general of the Paris police and both involved dozens of witnesses. One was forty-six pages, the other eighty pages long, with appendices. (Both were clandestinely obtained in the preparation of this book, before the government closed every access to all Petiot records.) However, two facts must be borne in mind. The Paris police during the entire Occupation were controlled, intimidated, and at the mercy of the German authorities, the Abwehr and the Gestapo. Then after the liberation came there was an exaggerated purge; and then because de Gaulle was too busy or too hungry in his grasp for power, the Paris police were taken over by the Communists. The latter were not interested in law and order, only in division and chaos, the seizure of power and the liquidation of all anti-Communists. The confusion that resulted enabled a man like Petiot, who played all sides, to get away with murder.

The police might have had a case against Maurice Petiot, too, if they had so desired. Maurice was clearly a weaker character than the doctor, not nearly so bright, a much simpler person in every way. He was a kinder man, too, anything but egocentric, even modest and retiring, and he might very well have sincerely believed his brother was acting as a patriot. But Maurice did obviously profit by the operation, for he could never have bought all the properties he owned from the money he was making in the radio business. By the time the doctor was tried in 1946, Maurice was already dying of brain cancer and his imprisonment or trial would have served no useful purpose.

When Petiot came out of prison, he had a joyous reunion with his family at the Hôtel Alicot. Here he and Gerhardt, now sixteen, and his wife probably met in order to proceed together for a needed holiday. But before they ever left, Petiot had some serious business to discuss with Georgette:

"Collect all your jewelry—every piece—and turn it all over to me immediately. I think I am going to be arrested again and I don't want the police and the courts to get it."

Mme. Petiot obviously did just as she was told and the doctor successfully rid himself of all the valuables. Even though a number of witnesses had seen many pieces of valuable jewelry at the doctor's home, packed into drawers or in his office desk—some purchased at the Salles de Ventes or taken from female patients in lieu of fees—and perhaps some from Dr. Eugène's travelers—not a single piece was ever recovered, not even Jo Jo's prized wristwatch. What became of it all, together with a fortune in gold napoleons, cash of every type, and furs is a mystery that has long plagued investigators.

The most fantastic story told by any of those who eventually "confessed" to having some knowledge of what was brewing on rue Le Sueur was a tale spun by Porchon in 1944. He reported to police that René Nezondet had visited him at the end of 1943 to propose a deal on a radio station to be licensed by the Germans. Nezondet then told Porchon, who must have known it himself, that Petiot was in jail.

"Petiot is 'King of the Pirates,'" Nezondet told Porchon, according to the tale. "I would never have believed he could ever commit murder!"

It was Nezondet then, according to Porchon, who told of seeing sixteen (not sixty) cadavers in a cellar at a place he did not identify. All had been killed by Petiot after he had promised to help them escape. Nezondet affirmed, when questioned by Porchon, that he had seen the corpses himself.

"They were all black," Nezondet said, as Porchon recalled it. "They must have died of poison or some injection."

On March 17, 1944, the police brought Porchon and Nezondet face to face and Nezondet denied ever having told Porchon any such story. What he *had* done, he said, was relate what someone else (undoubtedly Maurice Petiot) had told him and it was a somewhat different story. Porchon did not recall it that way, and denied all knowledge of Petiot's ownership of the building on rue Le Sueur. Two days later Porchon told police that he remembered having told Chief Inspector Petit and Officer Bouygues of the Paris police that he had seen Petiot in a basement dressed as a workman plastering a wall. The next day he recanted this story. But he continued to maintain that Nezondet had told about seeing sixteen corpses in a cellar.

At this time everybody was busy denying nearly everything. Nezondet was faced with still another witness who recalled something he had said about Petiot. This witness was Mme. Marie Turpault, a friend of René's mistress, Mme. Lesage. She had had dinner with Nezondet and his mistress shortly before Christmas, when Petiot was still in jail. She asked for news of Petiot. Nezondet promptly burst out, she said, with a remark very much like the one he had reportedly made to Porchon: "Petiot is a pirate! He is in jail and it would be best if he stayed there!" Asked for an explanation, Nezondet went on: "He was responsible for my spending almost a month in jail in May and June. His brother came to me a short time ago and asked me to build a wall to seal up part of a basement where there are cadavers in a pit—all bodies of persons killed by his brother—and a book and a diary in which his brother had a record of the names of the victims and the dates when they were murdered. Maurice Petiot had apparently just discovered the basement at 21 rue Le Sueur and his brother's work. I told Maurice Petiot I would under no circumstances help him in any way in this matter and that I would denounce Dr. Petiot as soon as the war was over or after the Germans were out of Paris."

This statement, confirming in small details the story Porchon had told, had a ring of truth. But when Nezondet was shown Mme. Turpault's sworn statement he insisted it was all pure invention, without the flimsiest basis in fact. When he was brought face to face with the lady, Nezondet continued to deny ever uttering such words. Then, the very next day, Nezondet decided that it would be safer to tell the truth. Yes, he had indeed told his girl friend and Marie Turpault and perhaps a few others that story about Maurice. And Maurice had most assuredly told him about the scene at number 21.

"It was in December," Nezondet recalled. "I had an appointment with Maurice Petiot at the Hôtel Alicot to discuss Maurice's delivery of certain radio parts I was to buy. Maurice arrived at 12:30 P.M., over an hour late. When I asked him what delayed him I saw that he was very shaken up. His face was pasty white, his voice weak and shaky, and his hands trembled. He said, 'I have just come from my brother's house.'

"I immediately thought he had discovered a clandestine radio or hidden arms and made some remarks along this line but Maurice reacted quickly.

" 'If it was only that it would not be so bad. This could get us all shot immediately!'

"I pressed for details and he went on: 'My brother's travelers' escaping from Occupied Paris start and finish at 21 rue Le Sueur. There seem to have been sixty victims. I saw a book in which my brother recorded the dates of the executions and the names of the victims. He killed them by some form of injection. My brother explained it in some notes in the book. There was a syringe, a hypodermic needle, and the poison. I found the whole thing by accident beginning with a pit full of bodies and quicklime—all of them were nude and seemed to have no hair or eyebrows or even faces.' Dr. Petiot's brother gave no further information or any names.

"During Dr. Petiot's imprisonment at Fresnes, Mrs. Petiot visited our home and I decided I had better tell her the horrible truth. I therefore told her what Maurice had told me about a month before. Mme. Petiot fainted, or almost fainted, three times during and after my explanations of what I had heard from her brother-in-law. There was no way to find out if she had any inkling of what her husband was actually doing but Mme. Lesage, who is a trained nurse at the Cochin Hospital, believes her fainting spells were put on. Incidentally, I never saw Mme. Petiot again, but I did see Maurice, her brother-in-law, who was very angry that I had told her. She had evidently discussed the matter with him. He reminded me that I had told him I would say nothing to anyone until the war was over or the Germans were gone.

"Maurice confessed to me that he still did not know what he

was going to do about the bodies nor did he ever tell me any more. He did tell me that he had collected all the suitcases and baggage at rue Le Sueur by a truck but did not tell me the destination of the suitcases."

This long confession sounded correct. It accounted for the stories told by both Porchon and Mme. Turpault. And it gave a good enough motive for Nezondet's effort to disown the talk—a promise, and a quite logical one—to say nothing until after the Germans were gone.

Nezondet, as probably the oldest and closest friend of Dr. Petiot, could be considered as an expert on the doctor. He sums up the situation as follows:

"The many mysteries, unanswered questions, and problems in the career of the greatest criminal in history are so complex and manifold that I cannot even try to resolve them. Dr. Petiot, both before and after the liberation, was protected by persons of different convictions and origins who knew the facts and knew that he was a criminal." (From René Nezondet's book *Petiot the Possessed*, published on May 27, 1950, but immediately suppressed by the French Government and copies picked up by the Paris police. One of Nezondet's own copies was obtained from Mme. Lesage in the preparation of this book.)

Aimée Joséphine Lesage, trained nurse, explained that she met René Nezondet during her vacation in the Yonne Valley in 1935, joined him in Paris in 1936, and became his common-law wife and later his wife. They were good friends with Marcel and Georgette Petiot and were frequent visitors at 66 rue Caumartin for dinner. "I can certify to my friend Nezondet's story that Maurice in a despondent moment told him about the sixty bodies at 21 rue Le Sueur which weighed heavily on our conscience. But we could not be sure that the doctor was not waging war on the Germans and French traitors so we decided to do nothing and to deny everything until the Germans were gone or the war over." This was her definite statement after twenty years. "I am certain I saved René's life," she added. After Petiot had been released by the Germans he of course found out from his wife and brother what René knew about 21 rue Le Sueur. In any case he phoned us and insisted that René meet him in his office at 21 rue Le Sueur and a date was set; however, Mrs. Lesage opposed and finally prevented

Nezondet from keeping the appointment. She maintained, with reason, that Petiot would certainly not have hesitated to liquidate anyone who could possibly expose him. One important item also contributed from this source was that there was no question that Petiot had helped the Resistance and Allied intelligence against the Germans and helped, on several occasions, the escape of some British fliers downed in Europe and of some Jews as well as others. It was common knowledge that Petiot belonged to some resistance apparatus. Contact with Mr. Alicot of the Hotel-Restaurant-Bar next to the Lyon railroad station revealed that Dr. Petiot seemed to be a bona-fide member, according to several sources, of the resistance net "*Agir*" (Action) based at Hôtel Alicot. Two persons stated that Petiot belonged to the net and had set himself up as the expert on escapees from Occupied France to North Africa and the Americas, and that perhaps through this resistance net he had received a number of travelers. These two explained that no one could come forward after the discovery of rue Le Sueur unless they wanted to turn themselves in to the Gestapo and that, after the liberation, the affair had such a stench that no one would admit any association with Petiot, much less having sent him any would-be travelers, especially anyone in the Resistance. One of these also claimed that he was certain Petiot did do intelligence work against the Germans.

Today on the wall of the hotel facing the station is a square metal plaque. It is seven feet above the sidewalk. It reads: "Here from 1941 to 1944 was the command post of the resistance net *Agir*. In its ranks . . . the following were lost for France . . ." Nineteen names follow with comments indicating that four were executed by the Germans, thirteen died in German prison camps, and two died after returning from them. So Dr. Petiot may have been a resistant of the *Agir* net even if he was not chief of the liquidation net Fly Tox. However, no one from the *Agir* came forth to defend him, even after the Germans were gone.

The Germans, however, were a long way from gone in early 1944 when Petiot was so unaccountably set free. Petiot insisted that there must have been a German hand that eventually betrayed him. "Would I," he asked the world, "after working with so much care and caution to dispose of the bodies of the collaborators and traitors who were my victims, have been so stupid as to stuff all this flesh into my furnaces and bring the whole neighborhood about my ears? Even had I been made desperate by my stay in prison, and been driven to the burning of bodies for a day, or even two, would I have kept it up for six days? [Witnesses testified that the nauseous smoke from 21 rue Le Sueur actually started on March 6 although March 11 marked the discovery of the charnel house.] And, more important, I was released on January 13, 1944. Why would I have waited until March to get rid of the bodies?"

No. The Seine was less than ten minutes away by bicycle. He still had his trailer bicycle and he would simply have made more frequent journeys. How many bodies had there been? Nezondet, quoting brother Maurice, said sixty at 21 rue Le Sueur—all stretched out—in December 1943. Yet on March 11, 1944, Dr. Paul found pieces of not more than twelve, perhaps fifteen, bodies. Could both stories be true?

Petiot eventually in his confidential admissions to Dr. Paul stated he killed perhaps as many as 150 persons—but had actually lost count—the bodies of whom he disposed of without a single mistake and without danger of identification or proof of cause of death. Was it his enemies—either Masuy and his Abwehr or Lafont and his French Gestapo—who had stuffed the bodies and fired the furnaces at 21 rue Le Sueur to expose Petiot's doings to the French police? Perhaps with the impending liberation he had refused to cut them in on his fees and ancillary profits.

To Petiot, then, the news that a nauseating smoke had been pouring from the chimney at 21 rue Le Sueur was a sign that he had been betrayed. No time to ponder on which of his enemies might have done this—in a sense, all men were his enemies. He had to destroy whatever dangerous records he had on hand at 66 rue Caumartin, then to check on what had been happening and how much the police had discovered at number 21. Another criminal might simply have used whatever time was allowed him to get as far from the police as possible. But Petiot always acted with audacity, even arrogance. He walked right into the arms of the police and depended on his wits and his incredible good luck to keep him from harm. His phone call to his brother to burn the papers was his first concern, remembering that Landru's notebook had cost him his head.

Having almost certainly told his wife to go at once to Auxerre, where he would meet her, he mounted his bicycle and pedaled furiously to see if anything could save the situation. Perhaps he hoped, as he sped through the darkening streets, that the police would at least hold off until he came with the keys. Then he might still be able to concoct an explanation that would keep them from nosing too deeply into what lay behind the doors. Even when he arrived and found them in the house he was not daunted in the least. He would be "the brother of the owner" until he thought of a way out. His justification was strong even in the case of Dreyfus, who, he knew from his informers and the victim himself, was scheduled for recapture and certain deportation and death in a German prison camp—he killed only the enemies of France in a way and those already condemned to a slower and crueler death. In the Dreyfus case both excuses applied, yet he knew he also killed for his own future and the security of his beloved family.

CHAPTER IX

The Murderer Lives at Number 21
a 1942 thriller movie
1944

The most popular detective novel in France, if not in Europe, at the beginning of the war, and a favorite of Dr. Petiot, was made into a movie in 1942 with Pierre Fresnay, Suzy Delair, and Jean Tissier as its stars. It was the story of a mass murderer who operated in midnight London, baffling Scotland Yard with a series of "clueless" killings, always done with robbery as the motive. The killer, whoever he was, always left behind at the scene of each killing a plain white calling card that bore no legend except "Mr. Smith." Eventually the police traced the man to a boardinghouse at number 21 Russell Square and this provided the book and the movie with its title: *L'Assassin Habite au 21.* (*The Murderer Lives at No. 21*)

It was inevitable then that this phrase should again become a catchword when the human remains were discovered at 21 rue Le Sueur. The London murders were both eclipsed and brought back to the memory of all by the Paris newspapers on March 12, 1944. A super Landru case had been unearthed and the French, who believe in *"cherchez la femme,"* soon converted the findings into headlines of "Fifty Women Murdered Then Burned." The fact was, however, that this assassin never lived at any number 21 at all but resided in the theater and night-club district where, even during the Occupation, many a man and woman roamed who wore a false identity or who operated in some clandestine byway of a subterranean world.

Petiot had always been a creature of the night and took to

this dark world as if he had been raised in it. A few hours after the alarm had gone out for his capture he had disappeared with not the slightest trace. Actually, his escape was made much easier by the fact that Frenchmen in that day were often called upon to give false answers to inquiring officials, to pretend they had not seen things that had taken place before their eyes, and to help cover up the traces of any hasty departures.

Unlike the murders of Mr. Smith in the movie, the victims had to be identified and this proved very difficult. It was soon discovered that the bodies at rue Le Sueur bore the very same characteristics of expert dissection as the unidentified cadavers and human debris found in and around Paris, particularly in the Seine, for many years. From 1941, when Dr. Petiot purchased 21 rue Le Sueur, to May 1943, when Dr. Petiot was arrested by the Gestapo, eighty-six unidentified bodies (fifty-one males, thirty-five females) or their parts were found in the river. During the same period 241 identified bodies were fished out of the river and many times that number were found elsewhere in Paris, but few of these were murders, just underground war casualties of one kind or another.

Years later, Dr. Paul, the Paris coroner, reminiscing about the Petiot case, told the author that after long private talks with Petiot and after comparing notes with experts of the Institut Médico-Légal he summarized Petiot as "the coldest fish and the most brilliant criminal, yet the most convincing talker that I ever met in my long career in the fields of crime and medicine." Dr. Paul added, with amusement, "Besides, I never heard of a doctor-surgeon-mayor-murderer in fact or fiction, much less one who was also a spy, or intelligence informer, writer, cartoonist, antique expert, mathematician or who calmly claimed possibly a hundred and fifty victims . . . he had lost count . . . but all justified in one way or another!"

Petiot never denied that the bodies or the human debris found in the Seine were traceable to him but denied having anything to do with the fire or the burning bodies at 21 rue Le Sueur. He did not, however, deny the bodies as evidence against him, but he refused either to identify any of the bodies or to give any indication as to how he killed them.

As far as the Institut Médico-Légal and its top experts—doctors Piedelièvre, Derobert, and Professor Sannie as well as Dr. Paul—

they failed to identify a single cadaver or piece of human debris, nor could they find a single clue to the cause of death of any of the Petiot victims. No sign of bullet, knife, blow, or strangulation was present and exhaustive tests of every kind failed to denote the slightest indication of any poison. There was no question that all of the bodies ascribed to Petiot demonstrated expert knowledge of anatomy and great experience and skill. In the case of the lifting of the mask or face from the skulls, this was a brand-new and original technique indicating creative genius as well as technical knowledge.

This discovery of the charnel house with mutilated bodies similar to those found in the Seine made the manhunt more extensive as well as efforts by the police to find all possible accomplices or scouts. The finding of the fifty or more suitcases at Courson further intensified the search for Petiot. Inspector Battut was in charge of building up the case against the missing assassin from number 21 while Inspector Poirier was in charge of the "Fox Hunt."

Probably the pivotal clue was the tracking down of a long-distance call made on March 11, 1944, at 2020 (8:20 P.M.), a phone call made by Dr. Marcel Petiot to Maurice Petiot at Auxerre from the Bézayrie Bar in Paris. (The concierge of 66 rue Caumartin swore she saw Dr. and Mrs. Petiot at their apartment at the exact same time.) Dr. Petiot was overheard directing his brother to "burn the papers."

The manager of the bar implied to the police that Petiot might be hiding with the Bézayries, who were Petiot's patients and friends. The Bézayries denied seeing Petiot since the discovery of the charnel house. Where Petiot actually hid from March 12 to March 24 no one will ever know. (Petiot in his notes states he was hidden out from the Paris police by his resistance unit Fly Tox.) On March 24 he moved in with Georges Redoute, a house painter at 83 rue du Faubourg St. Denis. He remained there until the day after the liberation of Paris, August 25, 1944. To Redoute, Petiot was a hero, head of a liquidation unit that killed Germans and collaborators. With a beard he had grown and wearing dark sunglasses, Petiot called himself Henri Valéry—with identification papers to prove it. Mme. Krabert, the concierge at number 83, remembered him well.

"Henri Valéry," she said, "rarely went out in the daytime. He only went out for food and books. Once there was a bad leak in the house and the fire department and plumber tried to get into the apartment where Valéry was staying. I had a very hard time convincing him that the men were not after him. He was very *engageant*, very nice in manner, and a convincing talker."

When Inspector Massu and his son visited 66 rue Caumartin to pick up any new leads the concierge there was very sad.

"Who would have thought it possible," she said, "a man so gentle, so nice, and so considerate—one of my nicest tenants and such a wonderful husband and father. Why he was constantly bringing presents to his wife and son. I don't believe it. It must have been only Boches he was killing. He hated the Germans."

Just then came a call on the doctor's phone for Massu. It was Dr. Paul. He told Massu he had just discovered that the cadavers of rue Le Sueur unmistakably matched many found in the Seine for years. . . . "And," added Dr. Paul with his well-known morbid humor, "I hope you can get a few more pounds of meat from the same butcher. . . . In the meantime, pleasant dreams!"

One interesting clue picked up by Massu concerned a bartender at a rather dirty bar next door to 66 rue Caumartin who stated he had frequently helped Petiot get his bicycle and trailer wheels over the sill of the frame of the large door of the court. That often the trailer was filled with furniture, statues, books, pictures, paintings but sometimes carefully covered with a tarpaulin and on those occasions there was a very peculiar smell that he had thought came from medicines or disinfectants.

There was mad activity at La Grande Maison, the Paris police headquarters of the Homicide Squad (*Brigade Criminelle*) at 36 Quai des Orfèvres. From the chief inspector's windows is the beautiful view of the quai, the Pont Neuf, and the famous restaurant Le Vert-Galant. This is the neighborhood of the famous huge horse chestnut trees. Here the victims of Dr. Petiot were being ascertained but so far there seemed no clues or hopes reported from the Fox Hunt.

The Paris newspapers in the meantime did not help the police but helped their German censors. News on Petiot replaced the bad news of Allied successes everywhere against both Germany and Japan. In the newspapers that everyone knew were Nazi-controlled, Petiot became "the greatest murderer of history."

Petiot, in the meantime, convinced Redoute that he was innocent of the crimes the papers were laying against him. Redoute asked Petiot to "swear on the head of his son Gerhardt" that he was innocent of these murders reported in the papers. No one in the world, Redoute knew, was dearer to Petiot than his only son. Petiot took the oath without blinking.

"I cannot swear I did not kill anyone," he said, "but I can assure you that the cadavers referred to are those of Germans and collaborators. The papers controlled by the Germans do not mention the cadavers my associates in the Resistance and I threw into the Ourcq Canal and in the Bois de Boulogne!"

Redoute charged Petiot nothing for room and board. He was proud to have a hero of the Resistance hiding with him. But there were many opportunists who had worked earnestly to inform the Germans against their neighbors and who, now, deciphering the unmistakable handwriting on the wall, began to inform *against* the Germans or provide them with false information. It is fairly definitely established that by 1944 there were more than 100,000 informers in Paris. One thing is certain: On December 28, 1943, the Gestapo in Paris had 26,000 strategically placed "carded" informers. In France, as in most other countries, there were many who desired only to wind up on the winning side, whether democratic, Fascist, or Communist. This did not mean that there were not millions of patriotic and loyal Frenchmen who were biding their time.

The Germans and die-hard collaborators, on the other hand, went berserk. In France alone the Germans killed 75,000 men, women, and children. In twelve days in the spring of 1944, Lafont and his French Gestapo arrested 4,766 persons according to actual records. Few of these lived to tell about it or were ever heard in any court. There is no question that these were among the motivating influences that convinced Petiot to kill for his country and to give a quick death to those scheduled for long and cruel deaths —especially where these actions meant security for himself and his family.

Redoute was a solid and loyal Frenchman. For all he knew he was risking his neck by putting up Petiot. But he never doubted that his clandestine guest was a patriot. Petiot told him details of arms parachuted into the countryside by British planes, of bringing these arms by secret routes into the city to put them into the hands of the underground, and how he had helped French and Allied intelligence and arranged the escape of some British aviators and Jewish families. Petiot told him that he, Petiot, had contributed to the costs of purchasing lime, medical instruments and supplies to help get rid of the bodies. Petiot told him he also served as a secret agent against the Germans. (It required very little departure from the truth to tell this story.) Petiot also told Redoute that the bodies would never have been discovered except that some traitor had sabotaged his work. As for the "triangular room" and the "periscope" and all the women's bodies, Petiot assured his host they were German-controlled newspaper exaggerations.

By this time Petiot had actually turned himself into a new person, for his simple disguise of heavy beard, longer hair, and dark glasses was perfectly effective, combined as it was with the supreme self-confidence he always had. When he walked out to make his purchases, he was no longer a fugitive—he was Henri Valéry, a hero of the French Resistance. When a young lady named Marguerite Durez, who Redoute had always considered as his "daughter," came to live in the Redoute household in May 1944, Petiot was introduced to her as Valéry and she never knew him under any other name, nor suspected that this charming gentleman was the fugitive whose picture had been in every newspaper.

During this period Petiot read and listened to BBC clandestinely. He was greatly impressed and knew the war was lost for Germany when France was invaded from the sea on June 6. The statistics alone, which he frequently repeated to his hosts and the concierge, were phenomenal to Petiot. Allied strength: 2,876,439 men, 5,000 fighter planes, 3,500 heavy bombers, 2,500 transport planes, 2,500 gliders, 1,000 other planes, first attacking force twenty American, fourteen British, three Canadian, one Polish, and one French division. This army made possible by U.S. industrial power moved rapidly. By June 27 Cherbourg and 50,000 German prisoners were taken. By August 14 another American and a British army landed at the mouth of the Rhône and the Germans were in retreat. Paris was certain to be liberated from outside.

As usual Petiot had strong ideas on many subjects, especially on politics, and aired them freely even in bars, bistros, and more espe cially at bookstores. "Marshal Smuts, of South Africa, is right," declared Petiot. "The defeat of Germany will leave America and Russia confronting each other, England will be permanently an enfeebled, degenerate, small island kingdom and will lose its entire empire. No matter what improvisations de Gaulle may make to try to give the impression he spells the balance of power between Russia and America, France will no longer be a great power. The Americans with their pioneer innocence will be no match for the machinations of the Soviets and the fifth column they will implant everywhere. The Communists are the best bet although I am sure not going to share any fortune I can build up with them. After all, Communism and Marxism are only ways and means of attaining power. If you don't believe me, Hitler, Mussolini, Stalin, Jacques Doriot all started as Socialists or Communists and wound up as dictators. De Gaulle knew what he was doing when, in Algeria, he insisted on full co-operation with the Communists and when he pardoned and called back Maurice Thorez from Moscow. But the first order of business is to lick the Nazis and liberate Paris."

By this time Henri Valéry was indeed active in the Resistance, as were many who, now that the Germans were on the run, suddenly found themselves filled with patriotism again. Petiot actually participated (according to him) in the liberation of Paris, engaging in the fire fights in front of Paris City Hall, in the Place de la Concorde, and in the Place de la République, where five fellow resistants were killed at Petiot's side. He had taken a rifle from a mortally wounded man, had acquired a revolver, and carried some German hand grenades. Actually, Paris was liberated solely and completely by the U.S. armies and their Allies, including one Free French division.

On August 25, 1944, Paris was liberated by a special and secret agreement between General von Choltitz, the German commandant, and the U.S. forces—a truce arranged by the Swedish consul. U.S. forces, with one token French division, were to enter the city while the Germans agreed to leave or surrender. The Germans further agreed not to fire unless fired upon and not to attack any buildings held by resistants. The only fighting was the result of

hatred and the reaction of thousands who had a guilty conscience
because they could not resist before. General Le Clerc's Second
French Armored Division had been released from U.S. General
Leonard Gerow's Fifth Corps to advance on Paris as a gesture to
French help but was badly needed for the continued advance of
the U.S. armies. In fact it had been detailed to protect the right
flank of the advancing Fifth Corps and was to leave Paris
promptly. Yet de Gaulle, who had no official recognition as head
of France, ordered Le Clerc to parade with him down the
Champs Élysées. When Gerow was informed of this he sent a
message to Le Clerc reminding Le Clerc that he and his division
were under Gerow's command and that he would follow his combat orders and not parade for de Gaulle or anyone else. Le Clerc
tried to avoid the issue by hiding out but one of Gerow's staff
officers found him in a restaurant near Les Invalides, Napoleon's
tomb. Le Clerc took the American to de Gaulle, who sent back
the following message to Gerow: "I loaned you Le Clerc, therefore it seems to me I can take him back for a few hours." It was,
strangely enough, mainly through U.S. effort and U.S. patience
and a parade of Le Clerc's division that marched the master opportunist de Gaulle into power and the leadership of a new
France.

   Dr. Petiot, under his false identity of Henri Valéry, did not,
therefore, as he claimed, help liberate Paris in any way, but he
was there. He tried to enroll in de Gaulle's G-2 rue St. Dominique because of his intelligence activities. He finally joined the
F.F.I. of the Tenth Arrondissement based on the Reuilly armory
and was commissioned a lieutenant. Petiot then began to come
back home to Redoute, wearing his F.F.I. brassard, and carrying
some trophy taken from the Germans. He was restless now to improve his financial status. News of the arrest of his wife and
brother had made him both angry and uneasy. Uneasy not entirely because his position was dangerous but because his income
would apparently be cut off for a long time. He could not practice
—unless he could somehow borrow the identity of a physician—
but his work with the F.F.I. offered excellent opportunities to lay
hold of items of real value. With his education and rather extensive experience in both undercover and underground work,
Valéry-Petiot by then was an avowed Communist. He soon be-

came a captain in charge of cleaning out "collabos." He had enrolled and was assigned to the *caserne* Reuilly a few blocks from the two buildings he owned on rue Reuilly.

One day a newspaperman approached him with a list of prisoners that were supposed to have been released by the Germans but had not been. Petiot-Valéry looked over the list and noted the name of a doctor he had heard about, Dr. Girard, who lived on boulevard Raspail. Immediately Petiot went to the address hoping, if all was well, to borrow the doctor's identity. His F.F.I. brassard made him welcome to the doctor's home where Mme. Girard told him that her husband had been jailed in the very early period of the Occupation, but had been free since March 1942. The doctor at that moment entered the room, noted the F.F.I. brassard, learned this tall, bearded, and fearsome man was Captain Valéry, and promptly offered the visitor a drink. They sat down and talked heartily together. Petiot told Girard that he felt the punishment of collaborators was much too slow and that "he had personally and out of sheer impatience, liquidated some sixty-six suspects by himself." (This incidentally was never looked into.) Dr. Girard had been at Fresnes prison, so he and Petiot exchanged reminiscences of the place. Petiot displayed his filed teeth, broken nose, and other evidences of torture and told how his head had been squeezed until blood came from his nose and ears. Then Petiot managed to ask quite casually if Girard knew of any other doctors who had been made prisoner. Perhaps, Petiot-Valéry suggested, *he* could arrange an exchange of prisoners.

Girard told Petiot of a Mme. Wetterwald, whose son, a doctor, had been deported to some prison camp in Germany. Several days later Petiot called on Mme. Wetterwald and told her Dr. Girard had suggested he visit her. He spoke to Mme. Wetterwald of the possibility of arranging an exchange of prisoners that would bring her son, François, safely home. Did she have his papers—military and college both? Eagerly, Mme. Wetterwald produced the papers, but the military identification card was missing. Please try to find it, Petiot asked her. It is important that I see it. I will come back in a few days. Two days later, when Petiot returned, Mme. Wetterwald produced the military identification card along with all the other papers. While she was not watching him, Petiot managed to extract the papers needed, left her the rest, and went away.

Now he had two solid identities—one his admittedly "false" identity of Valéry, which, he told his comrades, he had to assume because he was being sought by both Gestapo and by Nazi informers, and the other, his "real" identity, Dr. François Wetterwald. No one ever learned how he had managed to secure the papers of Henri Valéry or, indeed, who Valéry really was and what had become of him. He was, according to his papers, born in 1895, in Elbeuf (Seine-Maritime). Whether he had been a victim of Petiot's was never determined, nor did Petiot ever reveal Valéry's fate, if indeed he knew it himself. The real Dr. Wetterwald never returned to his mother or to reclaim his papers and reportedly died in a German concentration camp.

With his identity now doubly secure, Petiot found the F.F.I. a sort of happy hunting ground. It was routine for some of the more enterprising operators in the F.F.I., a few of whom had only lately been converted to their fiercely anti-collaborationist stance, to seek out wealthy collabos or those suspected of having aided the Germans and to shake them down, in some cases killing them. No past connection toward the Germans was necessary if the suspects were helpless and had negotiable properties to seize. One victim of such activity by Petiot was a woman named Juliette Couchoux, who owned a café-bar at 40 rue de Montrevil. Mme. Couchoux had a busy place during the Occupation, and had undoubtedly been forced to serve many Germans and collaborators. She certainly could not turn them away and at least fed her employees, but in doing this, had stowed away a comfortable profit, which Petiot, and others, knew about. In his position as Captain Valéry-Petiot, he was able to plan and execute a raid on her place. A lieutenant named Dubois, one of Valéry's subordinates and once a concierge, led the group that burst into her establishment and "confiscated" about three million francs' worth of jewelry. The jewelry was divided, with Captain Valéry, the commanding officer, getting the lion's share. A few days later, on September 13, 1944, Valéry had Mme. Couchoux arrested. She remained in jail without a hearing for sixteen days and was finally brought before Valéry. She had already, even before her arrest, complained that she had been robbed by Dubois. The imitation

Captain Valéry not only withdrew the charge but also advised her to sell her café immediately and go into hiding. Otherwise, he assured her, she would certainly be arrested as a collaborator. He even suggested that her life was not safe. But Mme. Couchoux was not to be scared out of her nest egg. Petiot thereupon had her committed to La Roquette prison—not sufficiently sure of himself to have her liquidated yet afraid to let her go. At La Roquette her papers and warrant for her arrest were deemed not in order so she was sent to an internment camp at Tourelles to await proper trial. There she remained until December 9, 1944, when she was released for want of any evidence against her. On January 5, 1945, Mme. Couchoux reported her entire experience to the Paris police. But by that time "Captain Valéry" had been identified and arrested and would soon be on trial for his life so the full story of the theft of Mme. Couchoux's jewelry and her personal experience with Dr. Petiot was never publicized.

The exploits of "Captain Valéry" in blackmail, robbery, and murder while in the F.F.I. were never fully known, much less reported or remembered. However, some facts are well known. France during the liberation had never known in her entire history a bloodier or more lawless period. This is what overshadowed the Petiot case and made no particularly great criminal out of Petiot, merely an opportunist of his time. The massacre that followed the liberation was far more savage than the revolutionary terror of 1789 or the Nazi liquidations during the German Occupation. There are no certain statistics, but Adrien Texier, Minister of the Interior, in charge of the police, and Colonel Dewavrin (code name Colonel Passy), General de Gaulle's chief of intelligence (himself arrested and separated from his job at a later date) both estimated that 105,000 Frenchmen were executed and perhaps twice that number arrested. Anyone with a grudge could work it off by denouncing someone as a collaborator. In most cases the money, jewelry, and valuables of those arrested or liquidated disappeared. Concentration camps were far more crowded by the French than they were by the Germans. Those who had collaborated changed their loyalty and in many cases killed their neighbors who knew of their collaboration. On the other hand the leading collaborators fled or disappeared like Masuy and his Abwehr group and Lafont and his French Gestapo. Hitler knew ex-

actly what he was doing when he ordered that Pétain be brought
to Berlin and that Paris be burned. He knew that this would bring
on chaos and lead to the Communist takeover of Paris and then
France. After all, this slaughter and even Petiot's liquidations
were in accordance with a law promulgated by de Gaulle in Algiers for the period of the Occupation and liberation. "There can
be no crime or felony if the crime or felony has been committed
in the interest of France." An honest error merely proved that
man was not infallible.

So, exactly what F.F.I. Captain Valéry, alias Dr. Wetterwald,
alias Dr. Petiot, did during this period as official prosecutor of collaborators to rehabilitate himself financially is difficult to ascertain. However some episodes were duly recorded.

Probably Captain Valéry's most noted adventure was the seizure of a priceless stamp collection that had been left in the keeping of the mayor of Tessancourt by its owner, a M. Baumgartner,
a Jew, who had to flee ahead of the Germans. Captain Valéry
learned of the existence of this property, which was, of course,
completely negotiable, in the course of arresting a noted alleged
woman collaborator, Mme. Bonnasseau of Tessancourt, an active
member of the L.V.F., an anti-Communist organization (League
of the French Volunteers Against Bolshevism). In Communist
eyes the L.V.F. was a Fascist organization and its members all fair
game. The Communists had, right after the liberation and
through their working agreement with de Gaulle, pretty well
taken over the security forces, the police, and the gendarmerie
charging, arresting, and even liquidating many officials and personnel who had held office or merely held on to their jobs during
the Occupation and could therefore be counted as collabos. However, in many cases, their only guilt was that they were anti-Communists or devout Catholics.

Matters got worse before they got better. General de Gaulle
named Mr. Airaud as inspector general and assistant commissioner of the Paris police as well as president of the Committee of
Expurgation to hunt down and liquidate traitors and collaborators. Mr. Airaud had been a member of a secret Communist apparatus and had previously been arrested by the Paris police but
had escaped. When the Nazis and Communists were Allies he
was reported to have conspired against France. Under his orders,

all members of the Paris police who had been anti-Communist during the war or before were immediately arrested and thrown in jail. Twelve hundred members of the Paris police were jailed, three thousand were separated. All vacancies were filled with young Communists. Even Georges Massu, chief of the Homicide Squad in charge of the Petiot case, was thrown in jail. Despondent, Massu attempted suicide in jail but was fortunately saved and later released. The police became a political force. The Paris police chief, A. Bussiere, was among the first arrested, tried, and condemned to imprisonment and hard labor for life. The final statistics: executed, seven (two without trial); prison terms, sixty-three; suspended or discharged, thirty-nine; retired without pension, 658; retired, 234; other punishments, 817; total tried by commissioner of epuration, 2,760. Needless to say, police ability to control crime and violent excesses or to solve the many problems of the Petiot case were greatly reduced during the period from the liberation until well after Petiot's trial. The large number of arrests and some of the trials did show that some of the Paris police were collaborators, further indicating that Petiot may well have had police protection from the Germans during the Occupation and from the Communists during the liberation since he played all sides.

When the party sent by Captain Valéry had reached Tessancourt, Mme. Bonnasseau had already been arrested and was being held by the gendarmes at Nantes. The F.F.I party—Lieutenant Jean Duchesne, Corporal Jean-Richard Salvage, and a civilian F.F.I. agent named Victor Cabelguenne—proceeded therefore to Nantes to gather in their quarry and while there learned from the local gendarmes that the unhappy lady had mentioned to them that a Mr. Boutillier, who lived at the Closerie des Saules in Tessancourt, knew all about a certain collection of rare stamps held by the mayor. As their orders from Captain Valéry were to find and seize the stamp collection and arrest the mayor, Duchesne and his party returned to Tessancourt. Henri Boutillier, it turned out, was the chief of the local F.F.I. Yes, Lucien Leuregand,* the mayor, he told them, was not only the richest man in the area but a notorious collaborator who had been responsible for the execu-

* In many Petiot books, the name given is Larrogance, but based at least on one record in Tessancourt, the name is Leuregand.

tion of one local resident, a M. Botelle, who died before a German firing squad on August 23, 1944.

It seemed therefore the positive duty of Lieutenant Duchesne to arrest Leuregand and to see that he answered for his crimes. This was covered by de Gaulle's general orders. They thereupon burst into the mayor's château and seized him. No one knows just what happened. According to the official story of the F.F.I. group from Reuilly, they went to the château prepared to conduct a hearing, an improvised court-martial, and brought along as supplementary "judges" Henri Boutillier, the head of the local F.F.I. contingent, and young M. Botelle, son of the man who had been executed. The mayor was given his chance to defend himself, according to this story, was duly found guilty, and, at midnight on September 16, was taken into a nearby wood, *les Aulnes*, and shot with rifles by the three F.F.I. men from Reuilly. The *coup de grâce*, they reported, was delivered by Lieutenant Duchesne—a pistol shot through the back of the head.

But other witnesses told a wholly different tale. On September 23 the police of Tessancourt found the mayor's body in the woods. Vermin had eaten away much of the head but it was still possible to discern indications of a beaten skull apparently resulting from repeated blows—seemingly from a hammer—and of two bullet wounds in the back of the skull, as well as two other shots in the body. It seemed most likely to the police that the mayor had been beaten senseless in his château, then dragged to the woods where several bullets were pumped into the back of his head.

According to the version of the raid published on December 11, 1944, in the newspaper *Défense de la France*, that is just about what happened. There was, the newspaper said, no trial and no discussion. The Valéry group simply broke into the château, beat the mayor with a hammer, shot him in the head, and dragged his body away. With a hand grenade, they blew the lock off the safe, seized the stamp collection, and robbed the house of every valuable they could find.

At any rate, the three executioners returned with their plunder to report to the man who had ordered the raid, Captain Valéry, at dawn on September 17, bringing back to the Reuilly armory Mme. Bonnasseau, two "Tessancourt witnesses," the stamp collection, and other valuables taken from the castle. Officially, they denied finding any money or jewelry although the mayor was known to keep jewelry and cash in his safe, which was empty after his "capture." The witnesses, Roger Centold and Jeanne Lepré, appeared to have been badly beaten. Was this to keep them from telling all they had observed? Apparently it was, for they told a somewhat different story when they got out of the hands of Petiot-Valéry and his minions.

Petiot, however, behaved with his usual dash, reprimanded his men for not having liquidated the witnesses, improvising rapidly to stay on his feet and still keep possession of the treasure his men had brought in. The cash and jewelry he divided among the participants, keeping, of course, a good share for himself. The stamp collection, estimated as worth more than $50,000, he dutifully "turned over" to Captain Grey, official custodian of collaborator properties at the armory. Captain Grey put the collection in his desk, and Petiot, when Grey was away for a moment, swiftly reclaimed it and hid it away where it would never be found. He then reported its "disappearance" but there was no intensive search made, for the armory was in a constant boil anyway, with everyone apparently trying to move in three ways at once.

This time Petiot had to depend on his luck and his persuasive tongue, which had seldom failed him. It was his good luck that caused Reuilly mayor and investigator Raphy to send the lieutenant of the Patriotic Guards to report his story to none other than Captain Valéry. Valéry was able, after a long man-to-man discussion, to persuade the lieutenant to forget the entire matter. It was a foregone conclusion, or so it seemed to Petiot, that the top chief, Colonel Roll-Tanguy, a well-known Communist, would stand by any men who had done no more than beat and rob a wealthy mayor and industrialist who had been named a collaborator responsible for the execution of a resistant according to the local F.F.I. According to an inventory, there had been $50,000 worth of cash and jewelry in the mayor's house.

So the pressure was lifted from Valéry-Wetterwald-Petiot for a time, although the Tessancourt incident was never forgotten. Before the end of November, warrants had been issued for the arrest of the men dispatched by Valéry to Tessancourt.

After that, although Captain Simonin of the F.F.I. remained

deeply suspicious of Valéry and was one of the first to pierce his disguise, the Tessancourt affair was laid temporarily to rest. Eventually a military tribunal did sit on the case and found Duchesne and Boutillier guilty of having murdered—by mistake—Mayor Lucien Leuregand of Tessancourt on the night of September 16–17, 1944. Salvage, Botelle, and Cabelguenne were acquitted. Duchesne and Boutillier, who had acted, the court decided, under extenuating circumstances, were sentenced to three and two years' imprisonment respectively. The sentences were promptly commuted and they went free. They had acted, after all, in keeping with the temper of the times and *en bonne foi*. The law protected the loyal Frenchman, even in killing someone he erroneously thought to have been a traitor to France. (According to Petiot's claims he also killed the enemies of France.)

Petiot did not have much longer to remain free himself, although he was not yet aware of any danger of discovery. Indeed, there is reason to believe that but for his own petty greed and vanity and what he later insisted (in his notes) was the carelessness of his lawyer—or was it carelessness?—he might have lived out his life in peace in Southeast Asia or some other distant land.

Petiot, aware perhaps of Simonin's suspicious attitude, had begun to act more warily. He was not often at the Reuilly armory and kept no regular schedule there. This, he explained to his associates, was because the French Gestapo and certain collaborators were still on his trail, afraid he would denounce them. He seldom stayed in one place for any extended period but moved to various hotels and apartments with different clients and friends. He became especially friendly and close to young Salvage, who was promoted to sergeant under "Valéry's" command. Salvage's mother, Yvonne Salvage, owned a furnished apartment at 22 rue Paul-Bert at St. Mandé although she herself lived on Court Debille. Salvage secured permission for his commander, Captain Valéry, to use his mother's spare apartment. Petiot stayed there for a few days. He had already applied to the DGER for a job in French Indochina. According to several reports, he made contact with Colonel Passy, head of de Gaulle's Secret Intelligence. He explained that he could be of triple value to the intelligence service there—first because he was wholly unknown in that area yet experienced in intelligence, and, second, because he was a physician and so could pursue a legitimate and highly useful profession while remaining a buried agent with access to people on the highest levels, and, third, that he had an old acquaintanceship with Ho Chi Minh, the Communist leader in Southeast Asia when they had both been students in Paris.

He was reportedly promptly accepted by the de Gaulle intelligence service and was told he could expect to be ordered to Saigon with a promotion to major at once. Naturally at this time Petiot decided to officially join the Communist Party, feeling that this would give him added strength. He was already a member of the Communist front organization, the Patriotic Militia. The Communists at this time, of course, were high in the councils of the Free French Government and in the good graces of Charles de Gaulle. Maurice Thorez, the head of the French Communist Party, who had once helped Petiot in his electoral campaigns in Villeneuve, became de Gaulle's number two man.

Valéry-Wetterwald-Petiot, in this era, was a commanding figure. His beard and his luxuriant dark-brown hair were well cared for. His uniform was neat. His posture, as always, was self-assured, even in the morning hours when he was only half himself. His dark glasses, hiding his eyes, added to the mystery and fearsomeness of his appearance. His bright F.F.I. brassard won him respect wherever he turned. Apparently some of his associates had begun to suspect that there was more to this man than he admitted, something even beyond Valéry and Wetterwald. But if any had really penetrated to his real identity, Petiot would have managed to persuade them that he was a victim of calumnies invented by the Nazi-controlled press. To the Communists, he probably implied or claimed to have been related to a Communist terrorist group or perhaps he had actually been so related. It would have seemed clear to anyone hearing the story that he must also have had some help from the Paris police to have gotten away so cleanly for so long.

Mme. Petiot was finally released from jail in October and Petiot was determined to make very cautious contact with her, no doubt to arrange to get some of his money or at least a stake to get another start in some new business. It was also Petiot's aim, after the liberation, to get in touch with the noted resistant Brossolette of whom he had learned much while at Fresnes prison.

Somehow he felt if he could ally himself with so famous and formidable a figure, he would be out of reach of the law. He did not know that Brossolette had jumped to his death from a Gestapo window prior to the liberation.

Petiot's vanity never diminished. And it may well have been that in persuading others of his innocence he had come to believe in it himself. At least he wore the self-righteous air of a man who was confident his actions were justified and it was this self-righteousness that destroyed him. (According to some psychiatrists, it was, perhaps, Petiot's death drive, a part of their diagnosis of his mental condition, that led him to practically turn himself in.) It is perhaps going too far to imagine that anyone with the Paris police could have planned the whole affair as a means of driving Petiot into the open, knowing that his vanity would not permit him to allow libelous accusations of the grossest sort to go unanswered. But the published article that forced Petiot to betray himself does seem to have been a complete fabrication. The name and actual existence of the alleged witness, Charles Rolland, who swore to the testimony, is suspect. He was actually never found. Therefore it and the editorial or article based on it seem an entrapment, and so it was. It was the work of an editor steeped in intelligence operations with a code name and experience in the French Resistance, and, more important, a deep understanding of a paranoiac.

The article appeared on September 19, 1944, in the newspaper *La Résistance* under the title of "Petiot—Soldier of the Reich." The article is based on the sworn statement of an unknown and never found Charles Rolland as made to Chief Inspector Massu of the Homicide Squad on June 24, 1944.

The tale recounted in the testimony contained such obvious fabrications and dates that were impossible, addresses that were incorrect, descriptions that were clearly false that it must really have raised the hair on Petiot's neck. It was so easy to prove this and that—and that, too!—were all damned lies. According to Petiot, only someone as stupid as Massu could have given any credence to the story. The witness at the police interrogation described himself as a veteran of the campaign of Tunisia. He had met Petiot, he said, in Marseille, in 1937, through a prostitute he, Rolland, ran into on the Cannebière. The prostitute, whose name

was Solange and who lived on rue Torte in the Old Harbor, asked
Rolland to have intercourse with her in front of a client who
wanted a "show." Rolland would make 100 francs. Rolland agreed
quickly enough, and in this way he met Dr. Petiot, for he, according to Rolland, was the client. The girl and Rolland put on a
show for Petiot and the girl then made love to them both.

After the performance was over, Petiot invited Rolland to meet
him at the Cintra Bodega café in the Old Harbor the next day.
They met at noon and "had a long talk."

"Petiot told me I had made a big mistake in enlisting in the
army and especially in the Fifteenth Infantry for service in Tunisia. I told him I had done it because I had been convicted of a
minor irregularity and had chosen the army in preference to the
house of correction. In confidence he offered me a job as his partner in the traffic of cocaine. I accepted. He delivered the stuff to
me at the bar and I delivered it to certain designated persons at
the American Bar on the Cannebière. I placed the cocaine next to
the water faucet of the washbowl in the men's lavatory. The client
picked it up there on signal from me but paid Petiot, who accompanied me."

This system, according to Rolland's testimony, went on for
three weeks, or until Rolland's unit was sent to Tunisia on January 3 or 4, 1938. Petiot, at that time Rolland said, was living at a
hotel on rue Panier under his own name.

"He told me both his name and his profession but he did not
give me his address in Paris."

When Rolland was discharged from the army for "physical incapacity" in 1939, the testimony continued, he went directly from
Marseille to Paris and did not return until October. At that time
he met Petiot in the Cintra Bodega bar and "he gave me his address in Paris as 23 or 21 rue Le Sueur. This was in October 1939.
There can be no doubt about it." (But there was doubt about it
for Petiot did not purchase the building at 21 rue Le Sueur until
July 1941 and even then he did not live there nor give the address
out to anyone.)

Rolland and Petiot met again, according to Rolland's testimony, in mid-January 1943 when Rolland, again in Paris, "found
Petiot's address" and went to see him at 23 rue Le Sueur. "No, I
am wrong [Rolland corrected himself], it was around the begin-

ning of 1940, before the German troops had entered Paris. It was about March fifteenth, after my birthday, that I had the sudden idea to see Petiot again. . . . I went to 23 [wrong number] rue Le Sueur in the Fifteenth Arrondissement [wrong arrondissement] . . . with a girl named Rose Berger, who lived in a hotel on rue Durantin. It [number 23] was a high building that was round in front and on the corner of a street. I asked the concierge, who gave me Dr. Petiot's apartment. I do not remember the floor. I think it was on the second floor." (He thought wrong, in every respect. There was no concierge. The house was not high, had no round front, and was not on a corner. The number was 21, not 23. Petiot had the entire building, not just one floor.

The recorded testimony went on:

"It was Petiot, himself, who opened the door. He was very annoyed if not angry when he saw me. He blamed me for coming to see him without having previously announced my visit. He ushered my friend and me into the parlor. I found his apartment strange, quiet, and without any servant. I did not see any clients either.

"It was then that Petiot asked me never to visit him without prior notice. He suggested sending me a *pneumatique* care of General Delivery at the post office at 7 rue Legendre telling me when I could visit him."

The *pneumatique*, according to Rolland's testimony, arrived several weeks later and invited Rolland to meet Petiot at the Café de la Paix. Here Petiot proposed they re-establish their partnership in the cocaine business. They made a similar arrangement to the one they had in Marseille, with Rolland getting the cocaine from Petiot at the Café de la Paix and leaving it in the men's lavatory in the basement of the Dupont-Bastille bar, with payment made to Petiot in some way unknown to Rolland. This arrangement lasted about a month. Rolland was arrested by the Paris police "toward the end of 1940," and did not see Petiot again until early January 1943.

"I visited rue Le Sueur again. It was near Grenelle. I took the Métro to the La Motte-Picquet station. [If he did, he did not land very close to rue Le Sueur. L'Étoile was the nearest Métro station to rue Le Sueur.] Petiot admitted me, but told me he did not want to see me anymore. When I entered his parlor this time

I smelled chloroform. He was nervous. He seemed in a strange condition and did not want me to stay. I told him things were not going well for me. He gave me five hundred francs and said, 'Leave quickly. I am waiting for some clients.' "

And now came the part of Rolland's testimony that must have bitten into Petiot's soul:

It was only this year [1944] at the end of February—about the twenty-fifth or twenty-sixth—that, having been in Marseille several days, I met Dr. Petiot by accident at the Café Cintra Bodega. He was alone. I was shabbily dressed, being down and out. We talked for a long time. I told him that I was going to join the P.P.F. [a French Nazi police force] at Marseille under a false name but that I was missing a work certificate. Petiot asked me what I was going to do in the P.P.F. I told him I didn't know what—it made little difference for in any case I would be sheltered from the French police. Petiot obtained a false work certificate for me from the Red Cross through Dr. Blanc, the medical director of the Sanitary Department of Marseille and an old friend of his. [Petiot noted that he did not know any Dr. Blanc or any Dr. Noir.]

He then decided to enter the P.P.F. at Marseille. I even took him to the site of their headquarters at 42 La Cannebière. There he enlisted under the name of Marcel Sigrand, having identification papers to match. He asked me to tell no one about his new affiliation and cautioned me that we were in the same boat. I saw Petiot almost every day. We ate together at the tavern Catalans in the Old Harbor.

On March seventh he left for Pointe-St.-Esprit [Gard] in an anti-resistant Nazi unit under a German Army officer, Captain Draeger. There Petiot could take any identity, since he now had German papers and was dressed as a German. He took guerrilla training in the château, then participated in operations in the hills. This last information was further confirmed to me at P.P.F. headquarters in Marseille on June third.

Rolland described Petiot as "about forty-three" (he was actually forty-seven) and five feet ten inches tall (correct) with dark-brown hair (also correct). But he wrote that Petiot "always wore a mustache." (He never did until he let his whiskers grow to become Captain Valéry.) He also said that Petiot wore glasses, but he wore no glasses until after he had become Valéry, and then he wore only dark ones. Rolland also mistakenly described Petiot as having slightly graying hair around the temples, but Petiot's dark hair, even when grown out to alter his appearance, showed not a trace of gray.

The whole story was so far removed from fact, and yet so convincingly set forth with irrelevant details that made it sound like a real experience, that it could not have been better calculated to drive Petiot into some frenzied action. And Jacques Yonnet, its author, the editor of *Résistance*, was a well-known resistance and intelligence officer under the code name of Lieutenant Yborne.

Without taking time enough to measure the possible conquences, Petiot set out to answer this accuser and witness and the editor who had woven such a false picture of him. Still smoking with indignation, Petiot wrote his reply in longhand on eight pages of letter paper, weaving fanciful details even more expertly than Rolland had. His months of confinement with other members of the Resistance at Fresnes prison had enabled him to express himself concerning the French underground with all the glibness and authentic jargon of an insider.

"Dear Mr. Editor," the letter started. "All accused persons should be considered innocent until proved guilty," he began sententiously. ". . . Because of law and justice I have the right to defend myself and to ask you to print my answer. . . ."

Dr. Petiot, the reply set forth, was a member of the Resistance under the code name of Dr. Eugène and the code number 46. "He is chief," said Petiot of himself, of a very active net called "Fly-Tox" working in collaboration with his client and friend Cumuleau, chief of the group *"Arc-en-ciel"* (Rainbow)—working against the Todt Agency and the German Army and its helpers and seeking intelligence information on German industry, inventions, etc., to be communicated to the Allies to shorten the war.

Petiot then undertook an involved, hasty, and confused explanation of the "liquidations" he had performed, liquidations, he said, of "Germans and collaborators and Gestapo agents." He indicated that there were, in the Resistance, men who, knowing his true identity, were actively trying to find ways to make known the "truth" about him without compromising themselves. Who these were, he gives no hint except to say that "some have important positions."

When he signed that letter Petiot signed his own commitment to the guillotine, for he had made it clear that he was to be found under a new identity, active as an officer in the Resistance. The shrewd editor, Jacques Yonnet, would very soon be able to run him down. He was greatly aided in the search by Petiot himself and by Petiot's lawyer, the noted Maître Floriot, to whom Petiot mailed the letter. He mailed it in Paris, promptly narrowing Yonnet's search area. And he sent it in longhand. He may have told himself that Floriot, a criminal lawyer, would have sense enough to have it all copied on a typewriter before sending it to the editor; certainly he would not forward the envelope with the postmark. But he gave no such instructions. So Floriot, instead of mailing a copy, telephoned Yonnet and insisted that Yonnet come and get the letter, envelope included, at Floriot's office. This was positively sworn to by Yonnet!

After that it was but a matter of days. The cunning and experienced editor and intelligence officer had a very simple investigative task. First to get a sample of Dr. Petiot's handwriting, easily available from the police. He summoned Professor Édouard de Rougemont, the greatest graphologist in France, who immediately and positively identified the handwriting of the letter to the editor as that of Dr. Petiot.

"He continues to do his utmost for the cause of France without question or argument. A friend had to bring me your newspaper so that I could read it. Having lost all but my life, I will continue to serve and make sacrifice under another and false name. However, let us hope that the easy tongues and facile pens will finally know the truth that should be so easy to guess. Please forget the heavy-handed lies of the Boches that two cents' worth of good French sense should see through."

Later Petiot was to berate himself—for sending it in longhand, for mailing the letter in Paris, for not waiting until he was on his way to Indochina and then having it mailed by someone else; finally, for not choking down his anger and tearing the letter up. But it was too late to call anything back. Yonnet (code name Ybarne), an experienced resistance fighter and holder of the Legion of Honor and the Resistance Medal, decided very quickly that Petiot was to be found in the newly organized F.F.I. in Paris, undoubtedly, as implied in the letter, as an officer, probably as a doctor. So he asked that the handwriting be circularized to all units and compared against that of all F.F.I. officers in the Paris area and particularly with officers who were also doctors of medicine. Two days later word came back that a similar handwriting had been found—in a report from the executive officer of the G2 of the First Infantry Regiment of the F.F.I. at the Reuilly armory, a man who had enlisted in September 1944. His name of course was Captain Henri Valéry, but he was really Dr. Wetterwald, M.D. Strange that he should not have had a suspicion that his lawyer might have caused his arrest in order to take over his hidden fortune in millions of dollars of cash, jewels, and furs.

Petiot had carefully planned to move out of France and then perhaps have his beloved family follow. He had, according to reports, explained to several persons that he had been accepted by the DGER for service in Indochina—was to be commissioned a major in the Medical Corps, with departure by ship for Saigon around the first of November 1944. So the end of October represented perhaps a small margin of time before an escape and a new life and rehabilitation with a good chance of the ultimate transfer of at least a part of his rather considerable fortune.

His letter to the editor destroyed all his past luck, or perhaps merely brought up the bad break that was long overdue. In all fairness to Maître Floriot, perhaps he had become convinced that a free Petiot was too dangerous and deadly an animal and that his escape might mean more unlimited killings. However, friends and members of the Petiot family believed that the hidden objective behind perhaps 150 murders could have been the motivation for Petiot's lawyer's strange conduct in connection with the letter. Did Maître Floriot know where Petiot's cache of spoils, estimated by some as worth over ten million dollars, was located? Or could the very sizable real estate holdings and estate of Mme. Petiot and young Petiot be a target for legal bills? In fact, could Floriot be the explanation for the fact that the Petiot spoils were never found? This also would explain why Maître Floriot never pleaded insanity for his client, who had been found 100 per cent insane by the French Army after World War I.

The author was made far more curious in the fact that after some talks with Mr. Yonnet, he had attempted to interview Maître Floriot on many occasions, explaining that he wanted especially to discuss the Yonnet letter but failed ever to get an interview with Floriot, although Floriot was very careful never to actually refuse an interview—he always was too busy or just leaving on a trip or called away at the last minute. Even an effort to have Floriot invited to lunch at the U.S. Embassy along with the author failed, for Maître Floriot sent his regrets at the last minute and did not show. Then, after Floriot's death, efforts to assess or learn about his will, estate, or fortune proved impossible and seemed under very special and unusual safeguards. Could it be possible that the Floriot estate included any millions of dollars from the killings of "The Great Liquidator" collected for his defense that failed?

Now that Petiot had been positively identified as Captain Valéry by his lawyer's action, all that remained was his arrest. Sergeant Salvage, alone at the Reuilly armory, knew where Captain Valéry was to be found, and Simonin was eager to make the arrest. Petiot had no warning whatever of his fate. It was 10:45 in the morning of October 31, 1944. Petiot, as Captain Valéry, had spent a quiet but, as usual, late night reading at the apartment owned by Sergeant Salvage's mother at St. Mandé, a Paris suburb. The St. Mandé-Tourelle station of the Paris Métro is but three stops removed from the Reuilly-Diderot station that is closest to the Reuilly armory. As he descended into the subway he saw the three uniformed men waiting on the platform below, but he failed to react. He was aware that one of them, a DGER man, was holding a pair of handcuffs out in his two hands. It was Captain Simonin. Petiot's morning-fogged mind had just taken this fact in and he realized that the others were F.F.I. men from the Reuilly armory. "You are caught, Petiot!" Simonin shouted. "Unless you deny who you are, I arrest you in the name of the law!"

CHAPTER X

Dr. Petiot, alias Captain Valéry, alias Dr. Wetterwald arrested by Simonin, alias Soutif, and a DGER order disappears
1944

Petiot did not deny that he was Petiot. He hardly murmured a protest as the handcuffs were snapped on his wrists. The other two men in the arresting party seized his two arms to hustle him off to the nearest police station. At that point the entire party—the prisoner and his three captors—was lost in the sea of secret red tape, interviews, and interrogations without benefit of the press or lawyers. All that was done and said and all that was asked and answered may never be known. One highly reputable witness, and only one witness, now dead, claimed that Petiot had orders from the DGER as Major Wetterwald, M.D., to report for transportation to Saigon within forty-eight hours. These orders were seized by Simonin and disappeared. Eventually a five-page statement was issued, signed by Petiot, and attested to by the arresting officer, Captain Simonin.

In this statement Petiot offered far more fanciful and far more specific details of his resistance activities than he had in his letter to the newspaper. He also repeated an assertion he had first made in that letter—that the cadavers found at 21 rue Le Sueur were not victims of his, but rather had been placed there by his "enemies" (presumably the rue Lauriston group). But that left the question of who had eviscerated them and dissected them—all with such medical skill.

The lime pit, he said, had been closed up by workmen at his orders and it was the unnamed enemies who opened it and depos-

ited the corpses therein. He had sent for more lime because the
bodies were in such an offensive state. He had not called in the
police because he had "more important work to do"—i.e., pursue,
capture, and liquidate more Germans and collaborators. He did
not, at this time, excuse himself for killing Jews who would have
been killed anyway by the Nazis. He insisted that all were German agents or collabos. Whenever he was pressured for details
concerning his Fly Tox group, he sought patriotic reasons for refusing to answer, to give any names of his associates, or any information about them.

I am actually and currently the Investigations Officer of the
Reuilly armory for the 1st Infantry Regiment F.F.I. with the rank
of Captain. I entered service at the beginning of September. I reported to the Commanding Officer of the Regiment Colonel Ruaux
whom I believe has, for some time, known my true identity.

Having been discharged from the Army for physical disability in
the 1914–18 war I did not participate in the war operations
1939–40. I had a fine medical practice that earned me over
500,000 francs per year [approximately $32,000]. In 1941 I ac-
quired a building in Paris, 21 rue Le Sueur, which I planned to con-
vert into a combined home, medical office and private clinic after
the war.

But from 1941 I tried to find ways and means to be helpful. First
I demoralized German officer patients, next I established contact
with the Resistance and they regularly sent me French workmen
from Germany who had been sent back for incurable wounds or dis-
eases. Besides treating them, I was able to gather outstanding intelligence information on what they had seen or heard while in Germany. In this way I was able to give the Allies data on a secret
weapon, code name "Boomerang."

[He did know that the great Pierre Brossolette must have been
aware of him, for he "definitely entered into the Resistance apparatus of Brossolette."]

I was put into contact with him by an individual whose name I
never knew but who introduced me to a secret agent who came
from London to organize a Resistance organization in Franche-
Comte. He put me into contact with the group or net "Action"
[Agir] of the Pierre Brossolette organization. [This was the actual name of the well-known net, based on Alicot's Hôtel in Paris.]
The chief of this group was Cumuleau, sometimes spelled C-u-m-u-

l-o. His net was called *"Arc-en-ciel"*—Rainbow! Cumuleau looked
like me and we were often mistaken for each other. He was about
the same build and he was dark and had brown hair like me. My
net Fly Tox must be known to Brossolette. [Petiot did not know or
was pretending not to know of Brossolette's suicide.] My code
name was well known to the Germans and many others as "Dr.
Eugène." I had used this code name before when I made contact
just at the time when diplomatic relations between the United
States and Germany were broken—with a Mr. Thompson, a
member of the U.S. Consulate in Paris. I had made contact with
this man in the hope of communicating to the United States a secret weapon I had developed by which a person could be killed
from a distance of about 30 meters (98.4 ft.) without any noise.
Thompson had sent me to a Mr. Muller, one of his subordinates,
who had written up a report on my invention based on confidential
information supplied by me. This report was several pages in length
and I signed it with my code name of "Eugène." I remained in
touch with Mr. Muller by telephone for several days and before he
and the other U.S. personnel left Paris and the U.S. Consulate was
closed.

Petiot's mind, always agile, seemed to remember or create explanations—that his net Fly Tox specialized in the discovery and
execution of informers, plants, and agents of the Gestapo and active collaborators. He gave what he said were details of the Fly
Tox methods of liquidating spies and collabos:

> We would arrest the suspects, posing as members of the Gestapo
> in order to invite their confidences and in order to get them to tell
> us of their pro-German activities and accomplishments. They by
> their own admission, in defending themselves from German accusa-
> tions, would trap themselves. The examinations of these persons
> were in my apartment building at 21 rue Le Sueur. Once we had
> established the guilt of our suspects beyond any doubt we would
> proceed with their execution, either by shooting them with a re-
> volver or by using my secret weapon. The cadavers were immedi-
> ately transported to the Marly Forest or to the St. Cloud woods.
> The exact location of the cadavers I cannot remember.
>   I definitely swear that I never left any of our [Fly Tox] cadavers
> in my building on rue Le Sueur. As a matter of fact I had stored in
> this property a large part of my belongings and investments in an-
> tiques and the building represented an important part of my estate.

The entire neighborhood had been almost all expropriated by the Germans, I therefore expected that at any time that they would take over my place. They had a garage in front of my building and they had one of their houses of prostitution next door.

Petiot also in his statement pleaded inability to supply the names of any of his victims and refused to name any of his associates. "We did not particularly care about the exact and legal identification of the persons we executed," he declared. "All we were actually interested in was that they were enemies or traitors who had to be liquidated."

Petiot even suddenly forgot the name of his old friend the hairdresser, Fourrier, at whose shop he met some of his victims. He was arrested by the Gestapo in May 1943, he said, in the after math of a trap involving a go-between, Guelin, a friend of Count Chambrun, in which "a Jew named Dreyfus was put in touch with a hairdresser whose name escapes me." He had told the hairdresser, Petiot admitted, about the possibility of providing an escape for anyone wanting to get out of Occupied Paris and that he "might make himself some money" from someone very desirous of escape. Here Petiot was casually skirting close to the truth so as to account for testimony that might otherwise have sounded damning. The fact that Dreyfus actually *was* a German plant must now have seemed heaven-sent coincidence to Petiot. He was able to inform his questioners sternly:

"The Gestapo were using him [Dreyfus] to track down an underground escape route and probably to reach and arrest Lucien Romier." After the hairdresser had been arrested he had denounced Petiot. The constant attempt to identify his efforts with those of respected and beloved leaders of the Resistance really served more to irritate his questioners than assuage them. They knew things about the resistance leaders that Petiot did not know. That his "client" and supposed double, Cumuleau, was a blond, for instance, that he never used the name Cumuleau at the time Petiot pretended to have known him, and that his real name was Charbonneau, and that he was already dead, killed by the Gestapo.

Petiot spoke proudly of the tortures to which he had been subjected by the Gestapo of rue des Saussaies and at the Fresnes prison. He was proud also to explain that he had been sent to the headquarters of the German Counter Intelligence, namely to Masuy's torture chambers at 101 avenue Henri Martin, but gave no information. And then, in another typical gambit of the experienced liar, he confided to his questioners:

"During my imprisonment," he said, "I noted to my surprise that at various times the Germans seemed to give me many excellent opportunities to escape. I did nothing, but wondered why."

Was this Petiot's way of allowing the inquisitors to conclude that he must have been set free so the Gestapo could use him to lead them to the members of his dreaded Fly Tox group?

"I remained at Fresnes prison for eight months," he related, "and was interrogated many times on the activities of my group, Fly Tox, and on my secret weapon. They got nothing out of me." As for Yvan Dreyfus: "He remained at my home at 21 rue Le Sueur and I am completely ignorant as to what eventually happened to him."

After being released from jail I went to Auxerre to visit my brother for some time and then returned to Paris. I meant to get even with the Germans for my imprisonment and torture and to increase my patriotic and resistance activities. I tried to establish contact with the intelligence service or G2 activities of Pierre Brossolette. I also tried to establish liaison with the British Intelligence Service by an intermediary. I became "Special 21" and I once again communicated my secret weapon to a group that promised to relay it to the governing committee of the Resistance. I was also in touch with an American secret agent planted in the Abwehr headquarters at the Hôtel Lutetia.

It was necessary, too, that he supply some rational explanation for the horrors uncovered at 21 rue Le Sueur and to justify his own failure to come into the open once the Germans had left.

I passed by rue Le Sueur only to find that my ultraviolet-ray machine, my infrared machine, an electrical furnace, some five pots, and a forged iron rod and other articles had disappeared. In the court, behind the garage, a pit that I had had sealed by workmen had been reopened. I found that this pit was filled with cadavers pell-mell and with the cadavers were the missing articles just mentioned. The bodies were fresh and I am certain they were put into the pit while I was in jail. The cadavers smelled horribly and this is the reason why I telephoned my brother in Auxerre and asked him to send me some quicklime without explaining why I wanted it. [This, it will be noted, was incorrect as the smell was minimal as all the entrails and intestines had been removed.]

I had given orders to my friends to get rid of the cadavers, but my friends merely put them in the garage and covered them with lime. Most of the cadavers were burned in the hot-water furnace.

Now he was able to tell a straight story with only small deviations from the truth:

I asked the police to hush up the entire matter while waiting for the chief of police or some principal officer to arrive. . . . However, acting on the advice of one of the police officers, I left without waiting for the arrival of any of the brass and, of course, the Germans and the Gestapo who had just released me. The next day I telephoned the police officer at a telephone number he had given me and he advised me to disappear, which advice I took. . . .

Now apparently he saw a sound explanation for his inability to offer many names of associates or tell too precisely just what groups he was connected with: "As a result of these happenings, I requested an even more active role in the Resistance but I was kept pretty much in complete isolation from any activities or groups of organizations because I had become a threat to their security. I had become so well known that I could easily compromise my friends. . . ." Clearly he was indicating that his "friends," whoever they might be, knew his real identity and understood that he had been liquidating only Germans and collaborators. But his questioners had already asked him if he had identified himself to his commanding officer in the F.F.I., Colonel Ruaux, as Petiot. No, he had not, Petiot admitted. But later on, said he, he was certain some fellow officers knew who he was and understood that lies were being told about him. But before joining the F.F.I. he had participated in the street fighting in Paris. Petiot explained:

I did it individually, as I did not at that time belong to any military group or unit. Mr. Marius of 6 rue Aldouy, to whom I revealed my true identity during the attack on the last German defenses, Place de la République in the boulevard St. Martin, can testify as a witness to my presence there at that time. Shortly thereafter I joined the F.F.I. under the name of Valéry, first in the Tenth Arrondissement, then at the Armory at the Quai de Valmy. It was there that I requested transfer to a G2 or intelligence assignment, believing that this would finally put me in touch with Pierre Brossolette, whom I had never met face to face.

I went to General de Gaulle's headquarters, rue St. Dominique. They sent me to 10 rue St. Dominique, then sent me in turn to 251 boulevard St. Germain. It was during these efforts that I finally enrolled and was accepted in the F.F.I. at the Reuilly armory. I was appointed a lieutenant in the G2 office and soon became deputy chief of intelligence of the regiment under command of Major Raphy. Shortly afterward, I was promoted to captain by the Commission for the Revision of Ranks at Vincennes.

At this juncture, Petiot emphasized a point he thought might tell strongly in his favor:

"I became a member of the Communist Party about ten days ago. I had never previously been a member, but I became sold on this party because of its important part in the Resistance. . . ."

Captain Simonin, who attested to all these statements, also reported to his chief, Colonel Dewavrin (code name Colonel Passy), and to the Paris police further added that he had searched his prisoner and found on his person the following items:

1. 31, 780 francs in cash.
2. An identification card bearing the name of Henri Valéry, born February 20, 1895, at Elbeuf (Seine-Maritime). A picture of Petiot in full beard was pasted on it.
3. An identification card of the French Army bearing the name François Wetterwald. This also carried a picture of the bearded Petiot.
4. An identification card of the French Army bearing the name Captain Henri Valéry.
5. A passport bearing the name René Cacheux, evidently ready for use if necessary.
6. A letter giving Captain Valéry authority to investigate and to arrest the enemies of France.
7. Papers indicating that F.F.I. Captain Valéry, alias Dr.

Wetterwald, had been appointed Judge Advocate to pursue, try, and sentence collaborators at the Reuilly armory. With these were various authorizations and requisition forms in blank.

8. A Communist Party membership card made out to Captain Henri Valéry. This card had been issued eight days earlier.

9. A membership card in the Patriotic Militia—a Communist terrorist organization.

10. A card of membership in the France-U.S.S.R. Friendship Committee, a Communist-front organization.

11. A ration card belonging to Virginia Bonnasseau, the café owner who later charged Valéry and his men with having raided her café, arrested her, and stolen several million francs on the grounds that she had been a collaborator.

12. A ration card made out to a child named René Valéry. But this had clearly been actually issued to René Kneller, 4 avenue du General Balfourier by the Administration Office of the Sixteenth Arrondissement, the "Kneller" having been scratched out and Valéry crudely written over it.

13. A revolver, caliber 9 mm. (.35 mm.) fully loaded.

Notable in this list (based on the official police record) is the absence of any mention of the papers or orders assigning Captain Valéry or Major Wetterwald to Saigon, or his transfer from the F.F.I. to the DGER. Of course, the revelation that de Gaulle's intelligence service had been taken in by Petiot and was ready to send him as Major Wetterwald to Indochina on November 2 would have caused some very red faces at the DGER headquarters. Whatever the reason, Captain Simonin failed to turn in these papers or Simonin's superiors neglected to list them. Officially, no such papers were found on Petiot or were included among the articles listed as found on him.

After his interrogation by the military, Petiot was turned over to the police and sent to La Santé Prison in the Fourteenth Arrondissement, located between the insane asylum and the Cochin Hospital. The prison at that time was crowded with collaborators, traitors, German agents and informers, black-market operators, and a lesser consignment of thieves, burglars, and pickpockets than usual. But Petiot was the sole prisoner to be housed all by himself in cell number seven, block seven. He did not mind the solitude. In fact, he preferred having a room to himself, but it did not ease his mind to learn that this cell was usually reserved for prisoners awaiting execution—and that it had once been occupied by Landru, "the Bluebeard," before his public execution at Versailles.

Petiot had been quickly divested of his handsome F.F.I. uniform and clothed instead in one of his own gray suits, which soon acquired a thoroughly lived-in look, but he lost none of his self-confidence. On the contrary, as soon as he had adjusted to his misfortune, he seemed to become more brash by the day. He insisted that he and his Fly Tox net had liquidated scores of Germans and collaborators. He retained the same brilliant attorney who had piloted him safely out of his prosecutions for narcotics trafficking and the sequestration of witnesses. Petiot had no doubt that René Floriot would save him from the guillotine. Floriot would help him explain his liquidations as being for France and in connection with the Resistance. Petiot began to act like a man outraged.

"My victims were all traitors!" he declared.

If anyone wondered then why he had led the police on such a chase for all those months after the liberation, he would give the reply with a sort of "between you and me" demeanor: "I had more important things to do than merely defend myself from false charges! I had to defend France!" His patriotism practically boiled out of him, although his record during the liberation seemed to again point toward unknown or unrecorded acts of terror for the aggrandizement of his purse.

When Judge Goletty, who had been appointed investigative judge (comparable to our preliminary prosecuting attorney), suggested a possible charge of twenty-seven murders prior to the liberation, Petiot reacted with indignation.

"False!" he cried. "I killed sixty-three persons. That is, my group and I did." And much later when Judge Leser, who was to preside at his trial, again mentioned the figure of twenty-seven killings, Petiot commented with an air of complete unconcern: "You must be joking, sir, why twenty-seven when I have liquidated sixty-three persons?" Later and more or less in confidence he stated to Dr. Paul that he actually had killed some 150 persons, although he had actually lost count. Dr. Paul later jokingly told the author that he had never disclosed this to the press for it would have tended to make all the authorities, including himself, look worse in their failure to identify the body of even a single victim or the cause of death of any victim.

One outstanding fact, forgotten or purposely omitted, is the lack of any definite statement by Petiot about his espionage activities or intelligence gathering. However, the answer is quite easy to understand. No one who had co-operated with Petiot would have even admitted any association whatsoever with him, now that he was shown up as a mass murderer. Dozens of persons had already been arrested as scouts or accomplices and suspects related to Dr. Eugène's escape apparatus. Rumors had arisen with respect to Petiot's possible payoffs and relations with French resistance units, British intelligence, the German Abwehr, the French Gestapo, the German Supply Service, the Paris police, and the Communist underground. All were now being connected with wholesale murder. No one talked anymore where Petiot was concerned . . . nor would anyone admit giving or receiving any information, much less valuable information of any kind from him.

The long series of interrogations that precede a trial in France began for Petiot on November 2, 1944, the very day he had been scheduled to sail for Indochina, where he had hoped to live out his life under a false identity as an intelligence officer and a physician. What one is constrained to wonder is whether the Vietnamese would have appreciated this doctor of the workers and now avowed Communist who had come to practice among them. Would he have been caught up in the intrigues then brewing that would lead to the dissolution of the French Asian Empire? Or would he have merely found new ways to fatten his estate while acting as a physician and as an intelligence agent for de Gaulle?

In Paris, in November 1944, the investigative judge was concerned with the question: Was Petiot really an active resistant? Had there indeed been such a group as Fly Tox of which he was leader? When the liberation came, it seemed that nearly everyone belonged to a patriotic organization of some sort. Like converts at a revival, each one sought to outdo the other in bearing loud witness to his own heroism, so it was difficult indeed to separate the real resistant from the newly hatched or the completely false.

There was, perhaps, no one in France who could have called the roll of all the legitimate organizations as so many had worked independently of each other. So it was entirely possible that Petiot's extermination group had been real and it was necessary to dig deep to find the truth.

"I have been a member of the resistance movement ever since the Germans first arrived in Paris," he told his questioners. "At first I only furnished false medical certificates to Frenchmen to prevent their deportation to German labor camps or to do war work. Then I was put in touch with an anti-Franco, anti-Fascist group of Spaniards in Lavallois. But I unfortunately cannot give you any details or any names. [How often this same unfortunate inability possessed him!] All these people worked incognito with code names such as Gómez, Álvarez, Ruiz, Rodríguez, and the like."

With these divers unnamed Spaniards Petiot asserted he "did some interesting things." But again he found himself in the same unfortunate fix: unable to divulge a single detail. He could not even provide exact dates for his contact with this group.

It may have been talk of this sort that caused his listeners to discount every bit of information he offered them. On that account, they overlooked an extremely interesting revelation—Petiot had apparently secured more than a sniff of one of the most profound secrets of the war: the V-1 and V-2 rockets with which Hitler hoped to bring Britain to her knees. He had referred to this as project "Vengeance"—also as "Boomerang." Little did the world realize, although Petiot made much of it, that the flying rocket might well win the war, especially if it could have become combined with another development in the atomic field which the Nazis were working on at the Kaiser Wilhelm Institute and which later was connected with the heavy-water production in German-occupied Norway.

The interesting fact that Petiot never found out was that this new "flying" weapon was based on U.S. patents and the work of an American, Dr. Goddard, improved and further developed by the Germans.

"The Resistance," Petiot declared, "would send me prisoners released by the Germans. . . . They were supposed to go to rue Cambon to a German organization but instead they were sent to me to treat and also to give information of value to the Resistance or to our allies. I had special persons to whom I was supposed to relay the information to and they were connected with the French Cinquième Bureau." Again, however, Petiot was unable to tell any names. He believed, he said, "that an Alsatian started it all but I never met him." He stated that he could "give an example of the intelligence he was able to turn in concerning a new and secret weapon."

Petiot had heard the two code names, "Vengeance" and "Boomerang," and later V-1 and V-2. Petiot originally located the production of this new weapon, a rocket with a propeller and with wings, or fins, about thirty-five miles southwest of Berlin near the Elbe River and then later moved to Peenemünde.

While this may be repetitious because of the complications of the Petiot story it is worth noting at the risk of duplication. A complementary reaction of J. Edgar Hoover through M. Ladd, one of his deputies, and the FBI liaison officer, was tendered to the War Department General Staff Intelligence Division's Espionage unit, the Secret Intelligence Branch. It was asked, it will be remembered, to use every effort to keep the Abwehr thinking that their agents who were in fact controlled agents of the FBI based on their having been spotted by Petiot were not controlled. According to Ladd the clandestine communication with the Abwehr was currently through a clandestine radio set located, it will be remembered, in the Hotel Astor at Times Square in the center of New York City. The FBI had been surprised that a U.S. espionage organization had been able to penetrate into the top management of the German Abwehr, in the Western Hemisphere, located in Paris, but would have been more surprised had they known that the penetration into the Abwehr installations at the Lutetia, Meurice, and Lotti hotels in Occupied Paris was through a Paris medical doctor-informer with an unknown but close relationship with the Abwehr executive Masuy. However, what must be pointed out is that the incorrect information that delayed the Nazi atom-bomb project at the Kaiser Wilhelm Institute was pivotal. First, it deprived Hitler of the superexplosive element to combine with the V-1 and V-2 rockets with which to win the war and which later Dr. Petiot had also smelled out. Next, forgetting about the rockets, it enabled the United States alone to develop the atom bomb with which to win the war, although used against the Japanese only, as the Germans were defeated first. The source of the highly technical information almost led to an administrative fight in Washington. All in all, this is perhaps the most extraordinary fact about the complex story of Dr. Petiot that is still unknown and would probably be difficult to prove . . . but then there is still no positive proof that Dr. Petiot was in fact the great liquidator and actually killed anyone . . . nor has the Petiot plunder or the Petiot fortune ever been found, yet he practically confessed to all.

All kinds of proof existed that Petiot could not be dismissed as a mere weaver of fairy tales. Could Petiot be telling the truth? Much later in his career and after the liberation, his wrongdoings seemed clearer and simpler. For instance, the story of his ordering the murder of the mayor of Tessancourt and the confiscation of cash and jewelry and an unusual stamp collection seems for the first time to definitely and positively incriminate Petiot directly. There can be no doubt who ordered the raid on Tessancourt as the orders were not only signed "Valéry" but were typed on Valéry's own typewriter . . . even with a description of the hiding place of the stamp collection in the rear of the clothes closet in the mayor's bedroom.

After making some rather convincing statements about his resistance activities and particularly his intelligence work, Petiot underwent perhaps the most intensive questioning, and most thorough, since he had been in the hands of the Gestapo. Two highly respected and experienced resistants took turns quizzing him. They were lieutenants Brouard, alias Brette, and Ybarne, alias Yonnet, of the French counterintelligence. Yonnet was the man who had written the editorial in the newspaper *Résistance* that had, with the help of Petiot's attorney, flushed Petiot out from behind his disguise. The aim of this interrogation was to ascertain, as fairly as possible, if Petiot's Fly Tox story and his claim that he had been an active resistant were true. They reported in detail what Petiot had told them and they appended their own comments.

Petiot had told them that "*Arc-en-ciel*" was an "action group." It was no such thing. It was not a group at all but a subnet of the net "Turma," which was connected with the B.C.R.A. (Bureau Central de Renseignement et d'Action) in London and it was engaged exclusively in the gathering of information—never in sabotage or liquidation or action of any type.

Petiot could not tell them anything of Cumuleau's function in the underground nor did he know what had become of the man, even though every active resistant knew that Cumuleau had been killed by the Gestapo. Instead, Petiot took refuge in an irritating dodge to which he often had recourse. He said he had been treating Cumuleau for a disease he could not discuss "out of deference to Mme. Cumuleau." This he seemed to feel would cause his questioners to tread softly and to deal delicately, but it really succeeded only in angering them.

In the course of the questioning, Petiot, like a hunted fox, doubled and backtracked, changing his story sometimes and sometimes trying to crisscross his trial. Fly Tox had been an "action" group for liquidating informers, he said. Then, in another story, it had been a group organized to "supply false papers." It had worked with a man from the Argentine Embassy, said Petiot, a man named Desaix, known as "DeC" who had access to papers issued to South American nationals who wished to extend their stay in France. Such papers would allow men and women to visit Spain or Portugal, whence it was a simple matter to escape to South America. Ybarne and Brouard noted, however, that there was no need of an organization merely to supply false papers.

Again and again the questioners sought a single name of any fellow member of the Fly Tox group. Petiot would name none. Well, what was his code number? Number 46. But a two digit number had no meaning in the underground. And who, they asked him, had given him this number and his code name? Here Petiot fell into a disastrous trap.

"I don't remember," he said. That, however, was not the answer all bona-fide members of the Resistance were trained to give. The standard jargon password when that question was asked was to say "A guy who did nothing but that." This catch phrase was established in all clandestine groups. A different answer meant the person was a fraud.

And what about Brossolette? Petiot was asked, for this was the name Petiot liked to conjure up. I never met him, Petiot admitted. No, of course not, for Brossolette was dead.

As to the bilateral messages sent out from time to time by the

BBC—messages known to almost all members of the Resistance—
Petiot admitted he knew nothing of them. And finally, what
about his false papers of Henri Valéry? Petiot claimed that the
papers had been secured from a resistance group. The investigators knew well enough how Petiot had come by the Dr. Wetterwald papers. Names of his Fly Tox net? Names of any fellow resistants? He would name none but had one final answer that, in
light of later events, may have caused faces to redden.

When Petiot hid behind secrecy, his interrogators called attention to the fact that all persons, nets, groups, or apparatus, such as
"Rainbow," "Turma," "Action," etc., were listed in the records of
"Fighting France" at 76 avenue Henri Martin, Paris, with full
identities, code names, photos, even, in some cases, fingerprints.
Petiot said: "The persons who released these lists are either crazy
or criminal, for among the officers of the DGER under 'Colonel
Passy' are ex-members or informers of the Gestapo as well as collaborators, and if the Germans come back, now or in the next
war, the persons named in these lists will be executed."

Although this was a disclosure and argument difficult to overcome, yet it seemed the usual excuses of Petiot until it came out
some time later that Captain Simonin of the DGER, who had
arrested Petiot and first examined him, had been, as Soutif, police
inspector of Quimper, himself a German agent and collaborator
who was publicly denounced as one by the same newspaper, Résistance, that had caused Petiot's arrest. No libel suit followed but
Simonin, alias Soutif, did not show at Petiot's trial and threatened
suit against a later book that came out on the Petiot case. The
final explanation may be that Soutif, alias Simonin, may have
been a highly patriotic and courageous double agent and in any
case was cleared by the general amnesty after the war.

The voluminous report on the interrogation of Petiot and the
results of extensive investigative procedure terminated with the
unanimous conclusion of the experts:

"The claims of the prisoner are ignorant, stupid, unbelievable,
and certainly false. Our interrogation proves that Petiot at no
time had any serious or bona-fide relationship or serious contact
with the Resistance." Signed, Military Security Experts Brouard
and Ybarne (code names). However, there was evidence that took
years to surface—that Petiot did play all sides, including the Re-

sistance, and did definitely aid Allied intelligence, although, at the same time, having a close relationship with the Abwehr, the French Gestapo, and the Communist terrorist underground forces. Testimony proved that Petiot had aided Jews, resistants, and English Air Force personnel to escape from Nazi Europe, not via 21 rue Le Sueur. It was also proven that when prospective customers of Dr. Eugène's were neither collaborators nor Jews marked for arrest by the Gestapo, their money was returned and they did not go to Dr. Eugène's 21 rue Le Sueur terminal.

But now came another question. Was Petiot sane? He had a history of mental illness—an army discharge and pension for 100 per cent mental incapacity, later reduced to 50 per cent. He had been released from two charges of theft—one of the petrol at Villeneuve and the other of the book in Paris—on grounds of mental illness. Certainly his deeds and his accomplishments marked him as abnormal and his real or simulated kleptomania suggested that he had always been emotionally unstable. An army medical report had even specified that *he needed a guard or an attendant whenever outside of an asylum.* He had been retired on a permanent pension from the army with what the army doctors described as "depression, epilepsy, and dementia praecox." Even the Gestapo record at rue des Saussaies after his release and dated January 1944, stated that he was not mentally responsible for his actions, or was this another form of protection afforded him by his German friends?

Then, last but not least, was the report from the board of experts composed of Claude, Liagnel-Lavastine, and Genil-Perrin of December 19, 1936, which wound up by stating that "any further actions or charges involving the subject should definitely not prevent him from being legally responsible for his acts."

So on December 18, 1944, over a month and a half after Petiot's arrest, Judge Goletty arranged an examination of a doctor by doctors—a conference between head shrinkers and an expert in mental gymnastics on the feigning of mental aberrations. The judge appointed a board of the greatest experts available to study Petiot's mental condition and they reviewed all the evidence bearing on Petiot's sanity. The board consisted of three of the top psychiatrists in France: Dr. Heuyer, who had pronounced Petiot insane at the time of the petrol theft in Villeneuve and who was now director of the Special (mental) Infirmary of Paris; Dr. Gouriou, director of the Psychiatric Hospital of Villejuif; and Dr. Genil-Perrin, director of the Henri Rouselle (psychiatric) Hospital, who had dealt with Petiot once before. It was their task to report to the court and to the prosecutor whether or not they believed the prisoner was sane under the provisions of Article 64 of the Penal Code. They would also report if their psychiatric and physical examinations showed any mental or physical abnormalities that would mitigate in any measure his responsibility for his acts. The board was authorized to meet and examine the prisoner at La Santé Prison.

When, in late December, the board met with Petiot, he immediately seized the initiative. Dr. Genil-Perrin had taken part in an examination eight years earlier which resulted in a report that said, among other things, that Petiot, although morally unbalanced and a "constitutional delinquent," had no mental troubles or psychopathic symptoms to warrant his confinement. But it had added, ominously, "any further actions or charges involving the subject should be judged without reference to his past history and should definitely not prevent him from being considered legally responsible for his acts."

Jaunty, defiant, sarcastic, his dark eyes aflame, Petiot as usual assumed the strategy of taking the offensive as the best defense throughout the examination. He did reply, however, to a few questions and took a brand-new position in regard to the doings at 21 rue Le Sueur.

"My property at rue Le Sueur," he said, "served the Resistance in many ways. At one time there were over sixteen hundred pounds of arms hidden there!"

As for taking part in any scheme, apparatus, or conspiracy to help fugitives escape from the Nazis, that had been merely a pretense to entrap spies. "All the persons brought to me by Fourrier [he now recalled the name] were *allegedly* desirous of escaping from Occupied Paris and were escaping after double-crossing the French Gestapo. They were all members or former members of the Gestapo. [He had obviously decided to emphasize his advantage in having liquidated the gangsters of rue Lauriston and the Gestapo plant Dreyfus.] I merely came to get them at Fourrier's and turned them over to another who interrogated them near the Madeleine."

The bodies found at 21 rue Le Sueur, in whatever state, did not include any of these pretended escapees, he insisted, with the possible exception of Dreyfus.

"You people just don't know what it's all about!" Petiot exclaimed. "Do you think for one minute that I could have trapped and killed gangsters like Jo the Boxer by myself? He was taken by my resistance group to the woods where all the executions were held. Remember, you forget it was I who was imprisoned and tortured by the Germans at Fresnes for eight months, then the bastards framed me with the bodies they stuffed into my house." Did the Germans, also, the doctors may have wondered, eviscerate and dissect those bodies with surgical skill? And did they bring in that store of hair—far more than the present bodies could possibly have accounted for?

But the examining board was also interested in how a simple neighborhood doctor could have amassed the fortune that Petiot obviously possessed. "We understand you have over fifty *immeubles* [real estate properties] worth millions?"

"I did not acquire my fortune from my alleged victims," Petiot asserted. "I made five hundred thousand francs per year from my medical practice. I spent hardly one hundred thousand per year. My wife is very frugal and my servants very cheap. Then my second-hand and my antique business brought me profits. A rug I purchased for seventeen thousand francs I sold the same evening I purchased it and received sixty thousand francs. Then I made money on my real estate operations."

"Of the sixty-three persons I liquidated," Petiot went on, "thirty were Boches in uniform. [But why, among the incredible store of men's and women's garments traced to Petiot, were there no German uniforms?] Ten of the dog tags of these thirty Germans are in the hands of my lawyer." Maître Floriot, however, never came up with any.

And why did he not turn himself in once the Germans were gone? Why keep the whole police force chasing after him?

"I did not turn myself in," said Petiot scornfully, "because the purge of collaborators is a fake. The informers of the police are the same as those who informed for the Gestapo. [Here Petiot had a good deal of truth on his side.] All the hunters for collaborators were themselves collaborators, or else they are merely gangsters who kill alleged collabos to steal from them. [The mayor of Tessancourt?] At the Reuilly armory everyone knew I was Petiot. To consider me guilty must prove you are either morons or criminals! When I joined the Resistance I was ready to make any sacrifice. Well, I suppose I asked for this sacrifice too. Now I am labeled both as a murderer and as a monster!"

Physically, Petiot was found in fine health except that his reflexes were slightly delayed. He did have a small cholesterol spot in his left eye—the *arcus senilis*—not unusual in a man approaching fifty. The scar of the grenade fragment, relic of World War I, was found on Petiot's left foot and duly noted.

After Petiot was excused, the doctors discussed their findings over a long period. Petiot had made a deep impression upon them and they wanted to deliberate at length before issuing any findings. Petiot's intelligence, not to say his cunning, was obvious from the start. That he evidently had studied psychology and psychiatry and human behavior was apparent. The pathology of homicide and forensic medicine were not strange to him. He had also clearly done extensive reading in mental disorders, sexual deviates, and abnormal syndromes, and must have learned every possible indication of mental imbalance. His history, in the army, at Villeneuve, in Paris, even when in the hands of the Gestapo, showed a clear pattern: Whenever he was in serious trouble he exhibited symptoms of mental illness that served to win his freedom. Even the Germans, when they released him, indicated that they had found him not possessed of all his mental faculties. When he was adjudged unbalanced on stealing a book and was confined in a sanitarium, his "cure" was rapid. And Petiot was a most persuasive man.

Finally the board brought forth their findings. He had, they reported, no sign of any mental trouble whatever, but was unusually intelligent and energetic, with a strong character. He was, to judge by his conduct, completely amoral and with perverted standards of conduct. The many diagnoses of his condition, both in and out of the army, had been controversial and contradictory, the board found, and posed some question as to the authenticity of the subject's own symptoms. In short, they found Petiot completely

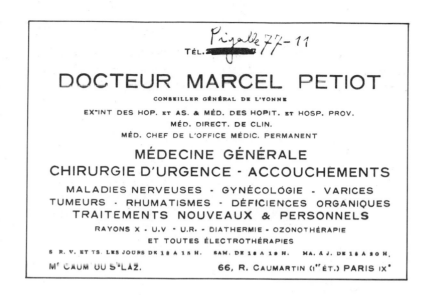

TÉL. *Pigalle 77-11*

DOCTEUR MARCEL PETIOT

CONSEILLER GÉNÉRAL DE L'YONNE

EX-INT DES HOP. ET AS. & MÉD. DES HOPIT. ET HOSP. PROV.

MÉD. DIRECT. DE CLIN.

MÉD. CHEF DE L'OFFICE MÉDIC. PERMANENT

MÉDECINE GÉNÉRALE

CHIRURGIE D'URGENCE · ACCOUCHEMENTS

MALADIES NERVEUSES · GYNÉCOLOGIE · VARICES
TUMEURS · RHUMATISMES · DÉFICIENCES ORGANIQUES

TRAITEMENTS NOUVEAUX & PERSONNELS

RAYONS X · U.V · U.R. · DIATHERMIE · OZONOTHÉRAPIE

ET TOUTES ÉLECTROTHÉRAPIES

S R. V. ET TS. LES JOURS DE 18 A 18 H.   SAM. DE 18 A 19 H.   MA. & J. DE 18 A 20 H.

Mᵉ CAUM OU Sᵗᵉ LAZ.   66, R. CAUMARTIN (1ᵉʳ ÉT.) PARIS IX°

Dr. Petiot's card with telephone number written in by him.

DOCTEUR MARCEL PETIOT

MAIRE DE VILLENEUVE-SUR-YONNE

Official memo paper of Dr. Petiot as Mayor of Villeneuve. Found in garage of his house at Villeneuve in 1966.

Doodlings and signature of Dr. Petiot. Acquired by the author.

Cartoon drawn by Petiot in jail. Secured by author.

Dr. Petiot confers with his Chief of Defense, Counsel Floriot, during the trial. Dr. Petiot's police guard is also in the picture. Paris Presse

The Palais de Justice and its marble front as the Petiot case court begins its move to 21 Rue LeSueur. UPI

des
Sympathiquement
à Monsieur Leser
Petiot

— à vous
qui m' avez fait ces loisirs...

Les recherches ont été exécutées
par le "Docteur EUGENE", ex-Chef du Groupe de Résistance
Les colonnes de chiffres ont été alignées   FLY-TOX .
sous le commandement du "Capitaine VALERI
9 a la 1ère Armée, 1er Régiment de Paris
Les erreurs dans les opérations ont été commises
par le Docteur Marcel PETIOT ...

Petiot's autograph "Very sympathetically to M. Leser. Petiot."

Dr. Petiot plays host to the court trying him in a tour of his house at 21 rue Le Sueur. The large contingent of police is to keep back the huge crowds who want to attend the Petiot circus and could not get into the trial itself. U.P.I.

The rue Lauriston French Gestapo management just before their execution on December 27, 1944. Extreme left, front row: Paul Clavie; left, rear row: Pierre Bonny (with glasses); Henri Lafont, fourth from left; Alexandre Villaplane (with a beret) a Rugby champion. Others among this group: André Engel, Louis Hare, Louis Pagnon, and Charles Delval. Clandestine picture taken by one of prison guards.

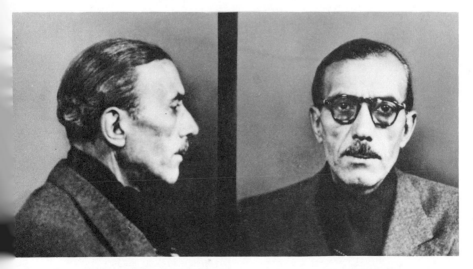

Deputy chief of the French Gestapo, ex-Chief Inspector Pierre Bonny.

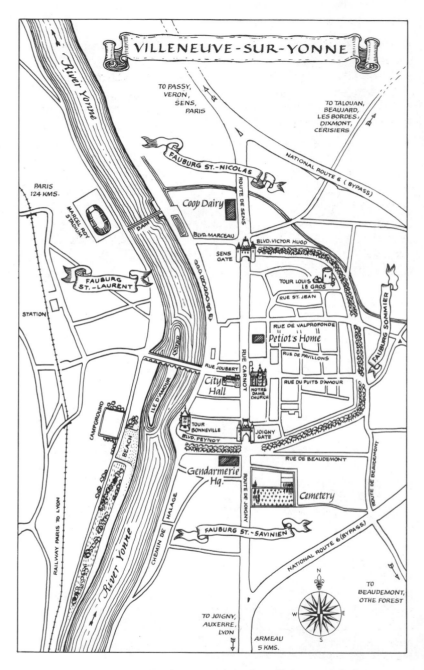

Plan of town in which Dr. Petiot practiced medicine, served three terms as mayor, made out all death certificates as medical examiner, and served his apprenticeship as a murderer. Agence Marbois.

and entirely responsible for his own acts and that his abnormalities, if really existent, could not in any way diminish his legal responsibility nor mitigate the penalties for any transgressions.

Despite these findings, most observers expected Maître Floriot to have his client plead insanity in order to escape the guillotine. Such a plea would make Petiot seem, in the public eye, something definitely less of a criminal. Because of the violence of the Occupation and the even more murderous liberation, Petiot's public image never assumed the proportions it would have in normal times. Besides, on the matter of sanity it was well known that Judge Leser, who was to preside at the trial, had great scorn for, and little confidence in, psychiatrists and was not likely to give too much weight to their findings. He had been known to remark, jokingly, that both Cenil Perrin and Gouriou were as crazy as any of their patients. As for Dr. Heuyer, his position as the man who had years earlier declared Petiot not responsible for his acts would render him vulnerable indeed on cross-examination. But there was no insanity plea. (Dr. Heuyer years later refused to be interviewed and when pressed reacted violently against any discussion of the Petiot case, indirectly admitting perhaps that he had been fooled, the *first* time, by Petiot's clever faking.)

But the gathering of evidence was brought to an almost dead halt when it came to providing a *corpus delicti*—the solid substance of the crime. Some body, some part of a body, had to be found that could be definitely labeled as the remains of a Petiot victim. To accomplish this was the duty of the Paris coroner, Dr. Paul, and the Institut Médico-Légal. He and Dr. Petiot had met before but never had they crossed words as in a pretrial encounter.

The endeavor to locate and identify some shred of flash provided an opportunity for Petiot to make a number of excursions throughout the city, always handcuffed and under adequate guard, but able to enjoy some contact with the public. On the occasions when the populace had some notice of his appearance, there was always a crowd to greet him. Hatless, wearing his just-out-of-fashion overcoat, his dark hair often falling on his temples, and shorn of his heavy beard, Petiot made a fascinating figure. He was affable, never ducked his head in the manner of so many prisoners, and turned his smile this way and that, while his eyes blazed with their usual fire.

Many who met him at this time were actually attracted to him in the same manner as one is attracted to a hooded cobra standing to strike, sensing in the insane light of his eyes and the bitter cynicism of his smile a nature so vicious, yet so deadly efficient as to be admired. One of the doctors at the Institut Médico-Légal found that talking to Petiot gave him goose pimples. Strangely enough, while not handsome, Petiot had a certain fascination for women, although he either awed or frightened them. Dr. Paul was completely at ease with the man, as he was with everyone, and tried hard to engage Petiot in a doctor-to-doctor discussion of his methods of eliminating his victims, especially those he willingly admitted killing. But Dr. Paul, despite his undeniable charm and easy manner, could not penetrate Petiot's determination to yield up none of his secrets.

Petiot's visit to the Institut Médico-Légal was made without notice to the press, so the small cavalcade of cars that carried "the Great Liquidator" to the Paris morgue drew up almost unnoticed in the cobblestoned courtyard behind the institute, where hearses, ambulances, and police cars, swinging from the Quai de la Rapée, approach the service entrance of the morgue. Outside this bleak and unadorned entrance mourners often gather to escort the body of some homicide victim after an autopsy, but when Petiot and his caravan drew up there was no crowd there at all.

The building itself, bleak and bare as its walls are, is, nevertheless, an imposing structure, looking out across a garden on its side to the Seine River, and over a garden in front to the approaches to the Austerlitz Bridge. The corridors inside are long, solemn, and poorly lit. The institute represented the first scientific medical criminal detection organization in the world. Here, medicine, physics, chemistry, and science were first harnessed to crime detection. It was also here and with the Paris police that Bertillon developed the infallibility of fingerprint identification.

Cold statuary adorns the niches along the walls. There is a library and a museum, but the public is not welcomed in either. In rooms along either side, nude cadavers lie with name tags on chest or abdomen.

Petiot was interviewed here by Dr. Paul and the Institut Médico-Légal experts Dr. Piedelièvre, Dr. Derobert, and Professor Sannie. These men were, without question, the most learned in all

France in forensic medicine and they had dealt with some of the most bloodthirsty killers France had known, but Petiot was something else again. Dr. Paul, however, was not the least intimidated. He rather welcomed this meeting and was eager to try to wring from Petiot some of the details of his crimes.

Easily the most charming of the four, Dr. Paul was a round-faced man with a continual twinkle in his eye. Despite a somewhat dramatic manner, he was sincere, friendly, and casual in his approach. His lifelong intimacy with the horrid side of human faring had developed in Dr. Paul a macabre sense of humor. He delighted in jokes about corpses and homicides and was known to have urged the police, when they supplied him with the first portions of the victims found at 21 rue Le Sueur, to hurry and send him another shipment of "meat."

Dr. Paul's accomplishments were impressive indeed. He was often referred to as "the man of one hundred thousand autopsies." He had a genius for smelling out a murder when a suicide seemed indicated and in deciding through some strange sixth sense just what test was needed to bring the truth to light. He had earned honors and decorations from every country in the world. But he never learned from Petiot, or from minute examinations of the bodies either, who the victims were or how they had been killed. He had almost always been able to get an accused murderer to explain his crime. He tried his approach with Petiot:

"Let's forget who your victims were. As a doctor, just tell me how you killed them. We are both scientifically interested and should be able to discuss the matter confidentially and professionally."

Petiot by this time had had all the questioning he wanted.

"I have nothing to say," he insisted, "except that I liquidated many enemies of our country and disposed of their bodies. I did not set the fire at 21 rue Le Sueur nor were the bodies found at rue Le Sueur mine. I have nothing else to say."

Dr. Derobert also interviewed Petiot along with Dr. Piedelièvre. Derobert was small in stature but erect, trim, and haughty in his carriage. He had gray-blue eyes. His heels came down with a firm clack as he walked across a room. His graying hair and beard were neatly trimmed and handsomely patterned. He, as well as Dr. Paul, was an admirer of American methods and particularly of Dr.

Milton Halpern, then deputy chief medical examiner of the city of New York, and later the chief medical examiner. Dr. Derobert reported to Judge Goletty as follows:

"We failed completely in identifying any single body or any part of a body. We also failed to find any cause of death with respect to the cadavers we labeled as Petiot's victims. I am convinced of the characteristics involved in these so-called Petiot bodies." (Years later Dr. Derobert wrote a technical monograph on *The Identification of Cadavers and Human Debris*. It was published in Italy. Its first seventy pages are devoted to the Petiot corpses.)

"A very skilled hand had cut up all these bodies with the same techniques. The techniques and skills showed great and intimate knowledge of the human anatomy. All bodies were first eviscerated. The organs or entrails removed are the first to decompose and often the easiest to get rid of and the least dangerous with respect to identification. The hands and head were always cut off. The face mask was always skinned and the ends of the fingers always sliced to assure that no identification would be possible. The removal of the face mask from the skull in one operation followed by the scalp, hair, and ears was always identical."

Dr. Derobert also observed two other "trademarks" that indicated the bodies had been handled by someone well versed in medical-school dissection methods. For one thing the bodies were always cut up and worked on from the right side. This was standard procedure in medical school. Then too there were marks on the right thigh of each cadaver where the scalpel had been plunged in, as in a pin cushion, to remain while the dissector took a break. This too is standard procedure in medical school where it is bad form ever to set a scalpel down flat, where it may be knocked off to do an injury to a foot or leg or where it would certainly cause a near deadly infection from decomposed blood or other putrified body liquids.

There were, also, the typical cigarette marks on the thigh, where the inveterate smoker, grown overfamiliar with working on dead bodies, would stump out a cigarette. A dead body always contains much water, which extinguishes the fire.

Of course these signs were no proof that it was Petiot who worked on the bodies. What they did show was that a skilled doctor or an expert in human anatomy who was also a heavy smoker, as Petiot was, had done the dissecting. The same hand, according to Dr. Derobert, had cut up all the bodies gathered from the Seine River and many places in Paris between the end of 1941 or January 1942 and March 12, 1944, *including those found at 21 rue Le Sueur.*

Dr. Derobert adjudged Petiot "the greatest individual murderer in modern history." He had no doubt of Petiot's guilt but felt that, had he been less careless and overconfident, his crimes would all have been "perfect." But the avaricious nature of Petiot and his wife, Derobert theorized, led Petiot into stupid blunders, particularly his hoarding of that store of clothing and toilet articles found in the suitcases stored with the Neuhausens. Essentially, these articles provided the only evidence the prosecution could come up with. The Institut Médico-Légal not only failed to identify a single body but could not in any single case suggest the time or the cause of death. Even the vast amounts of jewelry, gold napoleons, and cash and furs that Petiot was known to possess or to have acquired were never found by the police.

Describing his own meetings with Petiot, Derobert spoke of the "insane quality" of his glance and his tendency to swing from wild rages to perfect calm, when he would respond in a deliberate, reasoned, and sarcastic manner. Derobert felt goose pimples in Petiot's presence and a growing horror and fear as he talked with the man. Yet he was to grant that Petiot had "a certain charm, was extremely persuasive, extremely intelligent, and good at repartee, with a sharp sense of humor." But when Derobert tried to discuss medical subjects with him, Petiot drew back. Derobert then tried to talk about sadism. Here Petiot obliged him and remarked, "The Marquis de Sade satisfied his sex instincts by merely beating, biting, and pinching women. I fuck them."

Dr. Piedelièvre (did Petiot resist making a joke about a "hare's foot" when he heard this doctor's name?), professor of the medical faculty and director of the Institut Médico-Légal, endeavored to loosen Petiot's tongue on the subject of killings by describing to him the famous Vacher case of the late 1800s. Vacher was the army sergeant who had killed four boys, six girls, and an old woman, all sheepherders, and had sexually molested the bodies after disemboweling them. It seemed a story that might appeal to

Petiot's well-known preoccupation with the macabre and the perverse. But Petiot did not respond. He knew all about Vacher.

Dr. Paul tried a different tack. He showed Petiot through the institute museum, with its gruesome exhibits and relics of extraordinary crimes. Here was a large bottle in which a set of male sex organs, the penis and testicles, were preserved in alcohol. These had come to the institute through the mail, from a man who had cut them off himself, then boxed, wrapped, and mailed them—apparently in a mad desire to become the central figure in a sensation. After the mailing of the package, the poor wretch had collapsed on the post office steps from loss of blood and had died two days later. It was also two days before the package reached the morgue, but the officials nonetheless had accepted the donation and preserved it.

Petiot also was shown another strange exhibit—a carbonized human hand, fingernails and all, holding a carafe of water. This was a memento of a strange accident, in which a miner, coming home late, had somehow caused a gasoline lamp on his table to explode, setting a violent fire, and had then grabbed for the carafe in a vain effort to put out the flames. When the firemen arrived they found the miner's body already burned beyond recognition although the hand and wrist had fallen away from the body and remained in perfect preservation still clasping the neck of the carafe. (Both these exhibits can still be seen in the Museum of the Institut Médico-Légal in Paris.) Petiot simply refused to take part in this doctor-to-doctor intimacy and continued to keep his own counsel on the subject of his liquidations. He did manage to awaken a certain sympathy in these men who could not suppress respect for the quickness of Petiot's mind, his outstanding medical knowledge, and his dissecting skills. They seemed to agree, despite what the specialists might have said, that Petiot could not have been sane when he committed his crimes.

The search for the *corpus delicti* and other corroborating evidence turned up a few oddities. Among Petiot's effects, for instance, were a rubber stamp and a box of printed visiting cards bearing the legend: "L. Duplan, 185 rue Beliard." L. Duplan, it developed, had died a natural death in February 1942 and his furniture had been auctioned off at the Salles des Ventes. Petiot had purchased a desk at that auction and obviously had found cards and rubber stamp in the desk and had hung on to them.

More mysterious was a birth certificate of Max Wolkowicz, dated June 9, 1931, indicating birth in Paris on July 2, 1902. Investigation brought out these facts: father, Bernard Wolkowicz; mother, Lea Klinger Wolkowicz; police record—four convictions, two on narcotic charges. Arrested by the Germans on February 9, 1944. Imprisoned in Drancy concentration camp and believed deported to German-occupied Poland.

His connection to Petiot could not be found. Could he have escaped the Germans and found his way to 21 rue Le Sueur before March 11, 1944? Could he be one of the bodies in its court pit? How did Petiot wind up with his birth certificate? This could never be determined. But if Petiot had not been dealing with the man regarding escape from Paris, how would he have come into possession of the birth certificate? There would have been just enough time, had Wolkowicz escaped from the Germans, for him to have joined the ranks of dissected fugitives found in the Seine River or at 21 rue Le Sueur before the betraying smoke started to pour from the chimney. His name was added to the ever-growing list of possible if not probable Petiot victims which later was abandoned by the police as too numerous to be attributed to even the Great Liquidator.

There seemed no question of the fact that more people were killed by Petiot than were ever ascribed to him. The police earnestly endeavored to search out any they had not learned about. The enormity of their job can be judged by the fact that no less than 60,000 men, women, and children had disappeared in Paris during the Occupation, many of them Jews. There was no list of those who had vanished and even if there had been it would have been impossible to try to track down each individual. Some undoubtedly had escaped. Some had been killed in the constant underground guerrilla warfare, many had been executed out of hand by the Germans and their bodies buried with no attempt at identification. And of course some had been painstakingly cut into pieces by Petiot. Yet by January 1945 some eleven alleged accomplices, scouts, and members of his family were released for want of evidence.

The Paris police undertook a novel experiment. On November

10, 1944, announcements were placed in the newspapers and carried over the radio inviting all whose close friends or relatives had disappeared between January 1, 1942, and March 11, 1944, to appear at a certain place and try to identify some of the effects found in Petiot's houses or hidden in the Neuhausen home. This venture was not a success. While it was reported that some two hundred persons had been identified as owning pieces of clothing or jewelry in the display, it turned out that some of the people thus "identified" as Petiot's victims had actually been killed by the Nazis during the Occupation or by the Communist reign of terror that followed the liberation. No one in the Western world has any idea of the Communist massacres in France, Germany, Czechoslovakia, Hungary, Rumania, not to mention, later on, liberated Southeast Asia.

Early reports indicated Petiot would be tried for fifty-one murders. Petiot insisted officially to the police and examining judge that he had executed sixty-three persons, and the authorities, unofficially, agreed that it was more like 150—a figure once referred to by Petiot himself but only to Dr. Paul.

Even before Petiot had been taken the police were tracking down his supposed accomplices—not only his wife and brother but also several scouts who had directed fugitives his way. Long before Petiot's arrest most of the scouts, or suspected scouts, had been seized and interrogated: Fourrier, Francinet, Porchon, and Nezondet. But one major figure eluded them—Eriane Kahan. This lady, mistress of that sleazy figure Dr. St. Pierre, and mistress as well of a German Luftwaffe sergeant named Wesling, had directed to Petiot some of his most remunerative clients and had recruited for him actively. Had she been wholly innocent, the police reasoned, she would have turned herself in on learning the truth about Dr. Petiot. Or at least she would not have dodged away, concealing herself more ably than even Petiot himself.

The police found Eriane Kahan by means of an anonymous letter from Auxerre, the author of which was never discovered. Whoever he or she was, the letter led the police to quite a number of travelers she had sent "on organized trips to overseas points through a doctor originally from Auxerre." (Many persons concerned with the case believe Mme. Petiot wrote the letter.) The anonymous writer identified her as "Dr. Eriane," who lived on rue

Pasquier in Paris. The police were soon able to find that a forty-eight-year-old Rumanian woman named Eriane Rudolfina Kahan had lived at 10 rue Pasquier but had dropped out of sight when the gruesome discoveries of 21 rue Le Sueur were reported in the press. The police then spread their search throughout France, but they found no trace of Eriane until April 24, 1944, when a food-ration card bearing her name was presented for renewal at the office of the Food Administration in the Eighth Arrondissement. The man who presented the card was promptly interrogated by police. He proved to be a Rumanian named Kurt Kunstlich, a translator for the French Radio-Electric Company.

The ration card, said Kunstlich, was given to him by a German noncommissioned officer named Wesling. Wesling was soon picked up and declared that Kunstlich was lying. When Kunstlich was confronted by Wesling (all this being before the evacuation of Paris by the Germans, of course), Kunstlich admitted that the card had, instead, been handed to him by another translator, one Marin. This gentleman was then brought in and identified himself as Étienne Robert Marin, who lived at 21 rue de Rémusat in the Sixteenth Arrondissement. According to the story Marin told the police, a nurse who worked in a medical clinic in the same building had given him the ration card with two hundred francs and asked him to take it to the concierge at 10 rue Pasquier, who would get the next month's card, leaving this in exchange, as before. Marin knew the nurse only as Irene but he had seen her in company with her boy friend Wesling at dinner with another girl, a Miss Bonnay, and with Kunstlich and a Dr. Després. Unable to make the trip at once, Marin had given the card to Kunstlich, who, instead of bothering with the concierge, had gone directly to the Food Administration office.

Hot on the trail now, the police questioned Dr. Louis Pierre Després, director of the Rémusat clinic at 21 rue de Rémusat. Yes, he had indeed dined in company with a practical nurse named Pascale, with Marin, Kunstlich, and Wesling. Miss Pascale had come to the clinic in company of a patient who was to be operated on, a Mme. Manfredini, who lived at 32 rue Pierre Le Premier. Mme. Manfredini had stayed at the clinic until April 22 and the nurse had remained a day longer. Where she had gone to he could not say.

Next, the police questioned the concierge and learned from her of the three families that had been directed by Eriane to a Dr. Eugène, later recognized as Petiot in the newspapers—the Valberts, the Baschs, and the Bastons. But the track of Eriane Kahan was lost and the police could follow it no further until after the liberation. Actually Eriane had, by this time, fled Paris and, identifying herself as a resistant with a price on her head, found refuge first with some friends named Pictin, living on rue de Centre at Pecq (Seine-et-Oise). She moved then to Mme. Mouroc's at 3 rue de Docteur Blanche in the same town, and soon afterward to the town of Antony (Seine) where she lodged with a couple named Gaudry at 11 rue des Clématites. Everywhere her story was that she was a member of the French Resistance with a price on her head by the Germans.

By the time of the liberation, Eriane was back in Paris, living first with a Mme. Lemarchand, 78 rue de Passy. Then she rented an apartment at 7 rue du General Appert in the Sixteenth Arrondissement. Here she used the name of Molto and here the Paris police found her at last, in November 1944, after Petiot was already in their hands. Like the other scouts, however, Eriane was cleared for lack of evidence. The suspicion remained in many minds that this well-groomed lady well knew what sort of operation Petiot was conducting. But there was no proof whatever that she knew, any more than the other scouts had known, that the fugitives were really destined to begin their journey on rue Le Sueur.

By this time the prosecution was concerned with another minor point—the handwriting on the various letters and postcards that had been received from the Petiot victims after their disappearance. The Paris police had already, in the matters of Mme. Khait and Marc van Bever, looked into this matter of the handwriting and had submitted the letters in question to France's greatest handwriting expert, Dr. Édouard de Rougement. De Rougement, it will be recalled, found that the letters had been written by the people whose names they bore, but that they were obviously written under stress. Still, in the van Bever case, the lawyer and long-time friend of the van Bever's family sharply disagreed and insisted the writing was not van Bever's at all.

Now more letters were submitted to de Rougement by the police and by Judge Goletty. First, there was the letter purposely handed to "Yonnet" by René Floriot, the one that betrayed Pe-

tiot to the police. Professor Rougement had already identified this
for Yonnet. Then there were the letters supposedly written by Dr.
Braunberger to his wife, one of which his wife said looked as if it
had been by her husband, but with the feeble and trembling
fingers of a man of eighty. Along with this, of course, de Rougement received a verified sample of Braunberger's writing. De Rougement also was given a letter supposedly written by Denise
Hotin to her husband after her disappearance, and with this he received a sample of a letter known to have been written by Denise.

De Rougement's study was painstaking and his opinion detailed
and definite. "All the letters," he said, "were written by the persons whose names were signed."

In the letters of the "victims," however, de Rougement found
certain signs of "disintegration, of a strange lack of physical co-
ordination." The writing also, the expert said, showed a condition
"comparable to some form of stupor or intoxication." It could, he
explained, mean that the letters were dictated under some form of
coercion, for the writer seemed to lack conviction in what he was
writing.

"In the case of the handwriting of Mme. Khait," he said,
"there are marked differences in the height and slant of the letters. These differences are accompanied by variations in the thick-
ness of the strokes due to a jerky rhythm or pressure in writing.
There are indications of intense emotional disturbance. . . ."

De Rougement went on to point out that a rising line in handwriting denotes a state of excitement or tension, while changes in
direction of the slant are accepted as indicating a contradiction
between the words being written and the real thoughts of the
writer. In the Khait letter, when Mme. Khait wrote that she, as
well as her daughter, was a drug addict, there were sharp changes
in directions of the handwriting. Again the changes, when she
wrote that Petiot was not to be blamed, showed that she was writing not her own thoughts but what someone was dictating to her
under duress.

The van Bever letter, too, said de Rougement, showed the same
characteristic shifts in direction when he confessed to being an addict. And Denise Hotin, when she wrote that she had never had
an abortion because she was never pregnant, revealed that the
statement was not truthful.

As for the Braunberger letters, these, said de Rougement,

showed even greater pressure and mental disturbance. Fear and tension were so great that individual letters within words were disfigured and the writing faint and distorted. The instructions to his wife about leaving and having their furniture moved to Petiot's house revealed a conflict with the true thoughts of the writer and indicated dictation by someone else.

In almost all the letters the authorities had already noted the oddity of the signatures—the full name and even the title, despite the intimacy of the letters—obviously to make it clear to an outsider that these letters were written by the people in question. And in every instance the content of the letter was such that it could only have been of use to Petiot. It was quite clear then that, *if* the letters were indeed dictated, there was only one person who could have dictated them.

Petiot admitted that the cards and letters from Jo the Boxer and his associates had been written by himself. And there were those who held, despite de Rougement and other experts, that all the letters had been forged, too. Petiot was skilled with a pen and there seemed no reason why he could not have imitated the handwriting of all his victims. But de Rougement offered this definite and final conclusion:

"The letters of Mme. Khait, Jean Marc van Bever, Mme. Hotin, and Dr. Braunberger, all written after their disappearances, were written by them, but in an abnormal condition and under duress and in the last case close to a total breakdown.

"The letters, especially those of Dr. Braunberger, seem to have been dictated by a third party."

The authorities never did decide exactly how Petiot managed to force his victims to write letters. The police at one point thought morphine might have been used. They were obviously not familiar with the properties of mescaline or peyote, as Petiot was, a fact brought out for the first time in the research for this book. (Inspector Massu in his book *L'Enquête Petiot* suggests that Petiot might have injected strychnine into his travelers to kill them and states this poison would leave no trace or sign even in an autopsy; yet forensic chemistry experts and texts indicate many autopsy tests that afford sensitive discovery of strychnine, all known since the Dr. Neill Cream Scotland Yard case in 1892.)

The comments of the handwriting expert were extremely important to the case and the letters themselves helped point the finger at Petiot. But on the other hand Dr. Rougement stated that, based on his handwriting, Dr. Petiot was unquestionably insane.

Unable to provide a simple and incontestable *corpus delicti*, the prosecution had to rely on an overwhelming mass of circumstantial evidence to show beyond doubt, through establishment of a common pattern, that all twenty-seven killings (the final and very limited number included in the indictment) had been performed by the same hands, and that those hands were unquestionably those of Marcel Petiot. A paranoid "tendency" toward "repetitive behavior" seems evident.

There was, for instance, the *modus operandi* of the roped trunk. Poor Louisette's headless body had been found years before in a roped trunk in a field near Dijon.

Much later, another body in a roped trunk was found floating in the Seine in Paris and still another was discovered at the railroad station in Mandé in the South of France. All these bodies had been eviscerated and decapitated and dissected in the same manner and with the same skill. They offered no contrast whatever and could all logically be ascribed to the same hands.

Then there were the letters. All of them—from lover to his sweetheart, from mother to her daughter, from husband to wife, from wife to husband, from client to lawyer, from gangster to fellow gangster, from refugees to relatives—some dictated by Petiot, some written by Petiot, but all with precisely the same format and with the same purpose. The dissection and disposal of the bodies of the victims likewise followed identical designs.

Again and again the prosecution, in the person of Judge Goletty, came back to question Petiot, to see if he was ready to reveal the names of the people he admitted killing. The press, too, put its own pressure on Petiot, and on the court. Petiot was perhaps no worse than the Nazi extremists and the Gestapo of the Occupation or the Communist terrorists or patriotic killers of the liberation; but the isolation, the unfriendly treatment, began to have their effect on Petiot. The judge's scathing sarcasm and coolness of manner all began to tell. Petiot's cockiness and wit began to sag and his temper to flair up.

Judge Goletty would ask him, as he had asked him before:

"Can you supply me with a list of the sixty-three persons you admitted killing?"

"I must note," Petiot would snap, "that I never said I personally eliminated sixty-three persons. I stated and again specifically state personally that I liquidated two Germans under circumstances I described to you. Personally I was incapable even of killing a rabbit. I was once obliged to exchange a live rabbit for a dead one for cooking purposes. The men in the Fly Tox group killed all whom they thought it was their duty as Frenchmen to liquidate. It is regrettable that they did not liquidate more."

Finally Petiot had begun to contradict himself. On October 30, 1945, just one year after his arrest, he announced that he would answer no more questions. "I await anxiously the opportunity to explain everything to the public at my trial," he said. And it goes without saying that the public, with equal eagerness, awaited the trial too.

In jail from October 31, 1944, to his trial, which opened March 18, 1946, Petiot's greatest interest was the reading of newspapers with respect to world events and happenings in Paris. He delighted in telling his guards about all the collaborators who, having become "September Resistants," were now in high places. However, his enthusiasm became joyful when he read, on November 30, 1944, one month after his own arrest, that the entire top ranks of the French Gestapo had been arrested, and more especially, Lafont and Bonny. These two were hidden out with their families with carefully prepared new identities on a farm purchased as part of their escape plan. Lafont and Bonny, and their families, with five to ten million francs in cash and jewels, were apprehended as a result of information supplied by one of the many double agents—persons who may have changed sides many times or may have been loyal Frenchmen all along. Joseph Joanovici gave the information of Lafont's and Bonny's whereabouts to Chief Inspector Morin of the Paris police, who made the arrests. Although Petiot could not have been happy about it, Lafont, one of the richest collaborators in Paris, was defended by Maître Floriot. Petiot was surprised and pleased at the speed of justice and the very prompt trial of the French Gestapo members on December 12, 1944, and their execution "en masse" on December 27, 1944.

He did seriously comment, however, on the fact that they had been executed "honorably" by a firing squad for being both criminals and traitors to France, while it looked like he would be guillotined for saving France the trouble of executing some of the same group as well as other traitors. There was, of course, considerable truth in this statement.

Petiot searched the newspapers every day and asked his guards and everyone who visited him, and particularly his lawyer, for news of some of the people whom he categorized as the top enemies of France and deserving of liquidation. Masuy was, of course, foremost in his mind, then Algeron, Jean Luchaire, Guy Crouzet, and Georges Prade—all four publishers or editors of collaboration newspapers sympathetic to the Nazis, who, incidentally, had violently attacked him as a mad fiend and sadistic killer of women. With even more venom he wanted news of the "unhealthy pair" —Otto Abetz, ambassador of Hitler to Paris and France and de Brinon, ambassador of Vichy France to the Third Reich and the latter's wife. He also shared an interest with everyone else in France in the fate of old Marshal Pétain, the dupe who many people believed had been betrayed by Winston Churchill in a secret agreement to take France out of the war but to fight at a later date, and Pierre Laval, the real villain in France's quick surrender.

In a kinder and merely curious vein, Petiot was interested in Magda Fontanges, his old Opéra district patient when she was trying to break into the theater and whom Floriot had gotten off scot-free after her attempted assassination of the French ambassador to Rome. Petiot kidded Floriot about a reported romance between Magda and her defender, warning Floriot at the same time that he believed, as a doctor, that Magda was very mentally disturbed, if not unbalanced. It was already well known that she had entered into German service and later that she was being sought for arrest.

Petiot was elated at the execution of Pierre Laval on October 15, 1945. His father-in-law, a restaurant owner, had often told him what a thief Laval had been in the wholesale grocery business, which had earned him the title in France of "le sale épicier" (the dirty grocer). For Pétain, Petiot felt as many others did that the World War I hero had been a dupe but not such a stupid or guilty one, for many claimed he had a secret agreement with

Churchill, as was later established according to many by the go-between, Professor Louis Rougier. But, as usual, according to Petiot, the British had double-crossed the old man's effort to take France out of the war so it could rejoin the war with some strength at the proper time. Certainly Pétain and the Vichy Government helped the Allied cause secretly, as Petiot well knew because of his intelligence and underground contacts. The American landings in North Africa were made with minimum losses because the Vichy foreign service officers in North Africa were secret agents for the U.S. Army at the risk of their lives.

While he felt sure that most of the top collaborators and also Magda Fontanges were in Germany, he was certain Masuy and Brandl were in Spain with great fortunes. He was surprised and amused when Magda was found hiding out in France and arrested on March 23, 1946, and defended by Maître Floriot. By the time Petiot went to trial, Luchaire, Crouzet, Algeron, Prade, and de Brinon and Mme. de Brinon had all been found and arrested. All of them, except de Brinon, were defended by Floriot. In some of the last-minute interrogations of Petiot by the prosecution staff or the police, someone asked him how come he, an active resistant pleading that he liquidated only Germans and collaborators, had as counsel a man who was defending so many traitors. His answer was very typical of his peculiar psychology. "If Maître Floriot can get back some of that money they stole, and put it back into circulation in France, he will be doing some good because their cause and defense are so poor they will all be shot anyway although they should be guillotined."

Despite Petiot's announcement that he would do no more talking, the investigators did question him once more on November 3, 1945, when Petiot complained bitterly that he had never been allowed to see what the police had found in the suitcases from 21 rue Le Sueur. These suitcases would indeed have been a very weak point in a trial in the United States for they had been through many hands and had been opened and examined many times before they were to be used as evidence. Instead of being sealed promptly when they were found, they were taken to Paris and pawed through by any number of investigators and later looked over by hundreds of persons. It would have been possible to make all sorts of substitutions, insertions, and removals in the contents

between storage and discovery and between discovery and final presentation as an exhibit at the trial.

Petiot's position now was rather different from what it had
been at his previous trials. In his earlier cases before Judge Olmi
he had been able to awe the judge somewhat, with his position
and with his obvious, but undefined, connection with the Occupation authorities. He did not, however, overawe Judge Goletty.
Rather the opposite, Goletty treated him with contempt and sarcasm and Petiot was finally unable to hold his own against him.

Authorities had different theories, not only about how Petiot
dealt with his victims but also about the number killed and the
extent to which his relatives were involved. Chief Inspector
Georges Massu, who had been the first to examine the lime pit at
21 rue Le Sueur, was convinced that the entire Petiot family had
guilty knowledge of his doings. Massu had interviewed Léone Arnout, who was housemaid for Georgette Petiot's father, Nestor
Lablais, and later became his "companion." Léone, said Massu,
was a sort of courier for the Petiot family and, when Petiot's troubles began, was used to carry urgent messages from one household to the other. She told Massu that Monique Petiot, wife of
Dr. Petiot's brother Maurice, had instructed her to tell the Neuhausens to hide from the police the suitcases that had come from
21 rue Le Sueur. There were also two witnesses to confirm that
Georgette Petiot knew all about the suitcases and had visited the
Neuhausens and examined them. Other witnesses told Massu that
Georgette had been told about the bodies at rue Le Sueur long before Petiot had been set free by the Germans.

But Massu was not upset that Petiot's wife, brother, and other
alleged accomplices had all been released before the trial began.
He never felt he had sufficient evidence to convict them. He considered he had completed his job with eminent satisfaction, to
bring to trial the most important criminal of the century. Massu,
however, was not to savor his satisfaction long. With the liberation
and the influx of the Communist forces into the de Gaulle government, Massu was fired as head of the Homicide Squad and
thrown in jail as an anti-Communist—specifically for the arrest of
a reportedly Communist resistant during the Occupation. So
Massu can hardly be blamed for being overly careful about arresting Petiot, known to have been elected mayor by the Communists

and Socialists. After his arrest by the Communist-controlled Paris police Massu became despondent and attempted suicide. Fortunately, his attempt was unsuccessful and he lived to be cleared and reinstated but not as head of the Homicide Squad. Much later he was hired by the CIA, which also took over Nazi General Gehlen's Eastern Abwehr Secret Intelligence organization, the very same outfit to which Masuy and his operations in Paris belonged, and which leaked important intelligence information to Petiot.

After the Communist takeover of the Paris police, with executions and arrests of all anti-Communists and Catholics without trial, the Petiot case was handled by several police executives. After Massu was Pinault, then M. Tanguy. Then came the most able and best-informed police officer ever connected with the Petiot case. René Desvaux took over soon after Judge Goletty was appointed and charged with preparing Petiot's prosecution.

Desvaux, who soon established a close relationship with his prisoner, was certain that Petiot might well have liquidated 150 persons. He also believed that if Petiot had been more careful and had not yielded to his avariciousness and that of his wife and to his overconfidence he could never have been convicted. He believed that both Petiot's wife and brother knew what was going on and that Maître Floriot had "set up" Petiot and then refused to try to save him from execution by an insanity plea!

Desvaux was also convinced that Petiot, through his persuasiveness and his gift for improvisation, was able to play all the opposing forces against each other. Desvaux believed that Petiot was secretly tied up with Masuy and the Abwehr of avenue Henri Martin and also was dealing with Lafont—or at least with Bonny and Clavie—whom he knew, but that Petiot also played with the Communist terrorist underground and the Resistance. It was Desvaux's conviction that Petiot may even have killed a few German military personnel and certainly talked defiantly to them when he was a prisoner, chiefly to impress the resistants. Desvaux also believed that Petiot had been very useful as an espionage informer against the Nazis.

Desvaux propounded the theory that after Petiot had double-crossed one of his German allies, the Germans—possibly Masuy—started the fire at 21 rue Le Sueur in order, literally, to smoke Petiot out into the arms of the police. "Otherwise," said Desvaux, "why would a man who had successfully eliminated the bodies of his victims start a fire in a house stuffed with bodies in March 1944 for no good reason?"

Petiot, said Desvaux, was an all-out opportunist. When he saw that the Communist Party was gaining in strength with de Gaulle's co-operation and the strange support of the U.S., Petiot immediately joined not only the party itself but before that a number of Communist-front organizations. But he had no real devotion to any cause, said Desvaux. "His only love and loyalty was first for himself and then for his family."

His family undoubtedly returned his loyalty but Petiot took care never to incriminate any of them. Desvaux believed that Mme. Petiot thought her husband to be a courageous member of the French Resistance but was also fully aware of the financial advantages of his liquidations.

While Petiot's confidence had flagged somewhat under the continued questioning, he had full faith in his lawyer. He also counted heavily on the testimony of Colonel Dewavrin (code name Passy) of the DGER, who, he claimed, would prove that he was a true resistant. He had been encouraged when the indefatigable Yonnet, who had run down Petiot by means of Petiot's "letter to the editor," had exposed DGER Captain Simonin as a collabo.

Petiot and his counsel were convinced that Dewavrin would have to testify in support of his loyalty as a Frenchman and a resistant, for otherwise Dewavrin would not have selected him to be sent to Saigon as an agent of the DGER. (This was denied by Dewavrin and no proof ever delivered.) Dewavrin would also have to explain why Captain Simonin of the DGER, who arrested Petiot, was, in fact, the Nazi collaborator Soutif of Quimper. Unfortunately for Petiot—and somewhat to the amazement of both the prosecution and the defense—neither man appeared at the trial.

Even without these witnesses, Petiot's case was far from open and shut. Maître Floriot, who defended some of the most notorious and richest Nazi agents, officials, and collaborators in France (Lafont, Masuy, Mme. Fontanges, Algeron, Jean Luchaire, Guy Crouzet, Georges Prade, Otto Abetz, Mme. de Brinon, the latter, whose husband was executed, was found to be innocent) performed well in defense of Petiot and more than once seemed to score heavily against the prosecution.

The trial would hardly have been deemed a fair trial in this country—and perhaps not even in France. The public had been aroused to a frenzy against all killings and against Petiot, whose crimes seemed to grow more horrid with each retelling. He was not granted the sympathy he might have won if his arrest, imprisonment, and torture by the Gestapo had been known or he had been presented as mentally sick. But there was a great deal of controversy, questions, and even contradictions in the trial and in Petiot's career and hundreds of people both in Villeneuve and Paris still believe that Petiot was a "good guy" framed or used—or both —by more guilty persons. Many believe the only real winner in the Petiot case was René Floriot.

Petiot's own behavior, reported fully in the press, did not temper the public outcry against him. His name became a byword and his public image—defiant, sarcastic, unrepentant—underlined his ruthlessness. Yet many thought he had a special and strange appeal. The police, of course, had long been convinced that he had been literally getting away with murder because the Germans had countenanced it. The investigating judge engaged in bitter verbal duels with him. The various police investigators all agreed that his actual crimes far outnumbered those for which he had been indicted. And the public wanted nothing less than Petiot's head, although many recognized the fact that he was but a product of a bloody lawless era.

It was a marvel, then, that he came as close as he did to slipping out of the guillotine. The trial lasted sixteen days and involved three tons of evidence, 660 pounds of documentary submissions, ninety witnesses, twelve teams of lawyers, and was concerned with only twenty-seven murders, although the accused officially admitted to sixty-three "liquidations" under oath at his trial and "some 150 although he had lost count" to the Paris coroner "in confidence." Most living criminologists today agree that this trial, and its subject, were the most sensational and unusual of modern times.

CHAPTER XI

First week of Petiot trial
March 18–25, 1946

The Petiot trial that began March 18, 1946, ushered in the first peaceful springtime Paris had known for six years and attracted a holiday crowd come to view a living waxworks figure, a real-life Dr. Jekyll and Mr. Hyde. The fact that it was a man's life at stake did nothing to dampen the carnival atmosphere. So many tens of thousands had died. So few families still lived who had not felt their own brush with death. So many thousands of Frenchmen, on a starvation diet, had been literally worked to death in the Nazi slave-labor camps and factories. Many allegedly liberated by the Soviet armies had again been enslaved with some killed by the Russians. What if one more man should die to quiet the conscience of a nation and the shame of a country with past military glory that had been blitzkrieged to defeat in weeks and undermined by Communist saboteurs at first loyal to Russia's alliance with Nazi Germany.

From 1938 to 1945, the German Nazis had imprisoned and killed over four million persons. Their original allies, the Soviets, had murdered many more. Auschwitz, Dachau, Neuengamme Majdarek, Lublin, Buchenwald, Sachsenhausen were just a few places where mass killings of every race and nationality took place. At Katyn Forest, the flower of the surrendered Polish Army had been massacred by the Russians. In Auschwitz the average life of a prisoner (on 750 calories a day) was four months. In this camp's hospital, 131,000 died. German industry worked slave laborers until they dropped dead. Fifty thousand men from Auschwitz were given to I.G. Farben and many to Siemens and other well-known German industrial complexes. Nazi prisoners, in 1945, numbered over a million. Then came peace, but revenge was not forgotten. On January 3, 1946, William Joyce, "Lord Haw-Haw," broadcaster for the Nazis, who laughed at the British, was tried and hanged. Traitors and collaborators, except for Communists, were executed everywhere. The Soviets had switched sides. General Mikhailovitch was being hunted down to be liquidated by the Communists although he had been a loyal patriot and violent resistant against the Nazis and had asked for protection first from . the Allies and then from the U.S. alone. Purges in every formerly occupied country liquidated thousands—many innocent as well as guilty persons—but by 1946 mostly by trials. Even Vidkum Quisling had a trial before his preordained execution. In Russia and Central Europe and the Balkans the Communist executions of Catholics and anti-Communists were going on.

The number of persons killed without trial in France during the liberation if anything very definitely exceeded the number killed during the Nazi Occupation. Anyone who was a devout Catholic or had opposed the Communists or the Socialists or came from a titled or rich family was a likely target for sudden death. Both periods were bloodier than the massacres of the Dark Ages. According to a U.S. correspondent with the U.S. army that liberated France, in an article in the April 1946 issue of *The American Mercury*, U.S. Army Intelligence estimated that 50,000 persons were executed by the Communists in 1944 in the South of France alone. In November 1944, Adrian Tixier, French Secretary of the Interior, stated that official statistics indicated that France had suffered 105,000 victims of executions without trial during the first part of the liberation. No trial for murder after such a period could therefore be determined by cold and dispassionate justice.

The very day that the Petiot trial began news came from the British that one of their Nazi prisoners, Rudolf Hoess age forty-five, had confessed to the killing of over two million persons in the Oswiecim labor camp (better known as Auschwitz) on order of Heinrich Himmler and 500,000 more on his own authority as commandant. The British added that they had positive evidence indicating that Hoess was responsible for many more . . . mostly but definitely not restricted to Jews. Hoess, when asked if he believed in God, replied, "Most emphatically no!"

Besides the thousands who had fought in the Resistance against
the Nazi Occupation troops, and the many thousands more who
had hastened to join the patriotic forces once patriotism had become safe again, there were the countless everyday Frenchmen
who had holed themselves up in their workaday lives, treading the
safe path from home to work and home again and closing their
eyes and ears to all unpleasantness. It was their consciences that
demanded some final act of contrition.

There was a satisfaction in being able to join with other decent
people to demand, in angry and violent tones, the destruction of a
creature who seemed to epitomize all the brutality the country
had struggled against for years and then for a time had itself suc-
cumbed to. The French Communists had practiced sabotage and
fought clandestinely first with the Nazis then against them. Some
French in the Pétain Vichy setup were still loyal Frenchmen biding their time to cut the throats of their Nazi masters including
the very aged Pétain, while others, like Laval, were definitely
traitors and deserved and earned their quick deaths.

But there were people, too, who came as they would come to
any horror show, avid for stories of sadistic excesses, of slow tortures, of orgiastic killings, bloody dismemberment, and screaming
victims. There were reporters from all over the world, and imitation reporters from everywhere who had wangled press passes to
ensure themselves seats for this, the greatest public show since the
war began. In the court, besides these, there were lawyers, the
prosecutor and his assistants, the defense counsel and his assistants, and lawyers representing every one of the few named victims
come to seek civil penalties—a sort of court of reparations as well
as a criminal trial, as is usual under French law. In many countries
in Europe, libel is both a criminal and civil offense.

The trial was held in the Grande Salle des Assises, in the beautiful and imposing Palais de Justice on the bank of the Seine
River. The courtroom, as wide as a concert hall, was given extra di-
mension by the large murals that carried the eye into the far distance but for this trial the huge room was not one quarter large
enough. Many spectators had to stand and many who came were
crowded out. Many holders of press cards, some secured through
influence of one sort or another, were forced to take seats, or even
stand, directly behind the accused and receive the full force of the

prosecutor's sarcasm. The press were there in force—reporters and photographers from New York, Buenos Aires, Rio, Montreal, London, Berlin, Moscow, Cairo, Capetown, Hong Kong, and Tokyo. There were not seats enough for all the lawyers and they had to spread into places usually held by spectators. Prosecution exhibits were ranged in glass cases in front of the judge and jury box and the mountain of luggage, gathered in by the police and traced to Petiot, was stacked along one side behind the jury box. Suitcases, some bursting open, handbags, and hand luggage of every description, reaching nearly to the ceiling, made the court look like the baggage room of a busy railroad station.

From the very first day, celebrities crowded into the hall, drawing even more spectators by their own presence. There were movie stars, such as Paulette Dubost and Josette Day, radio personalities, war heroes, famous industrialists, and well-publicized playboys. It was like the opening of a stage play or the first night of a movie spectacular. And then there were the off-duty police (some former secret agents of the U.S. Army) some, one may suppose, come to see a long-time antagonist but all anxious to see him lose his head.

There was no doubt that Petiot himself would be the star of the show, but he was not present immediately. The presiding officer of the court, or judge—"M. le Président" as he is called in France—was himself an impressive figure. He was Marcel Leser, a portly man of dignified carriage and the round, pink-cheeked face of a cherub. The picture of kindness and good nature, he was relaxed but self-assured and firm. He was quick at repartee and his sense of humor was often in play. Still, he seemed the perfect choice for a trial that teetered on the edge of becoming a vaudeville show. Judge Leser's black robes set off his imposing stature in fine style and gave him exactly the air of reasoned and reasonable authority the circumstances required. Notwithstanding his kindly look, no one could possibly mistake the judge as weak. Not once did he let either the defendant or his flamboyant counsel take matters into their own hands. (His dignified handling of this great criminal trial singled him out as France's finest criminal judge and he was to be chosen to preside over another sensational trial, that of Bernardy de Sigoyer, in December of 1946.)

The chief prosecutor, the "procureur général," was Pierre

Dupin,* a slender, graying man who could have melted into a crowd in the Métro and have been quickly forgotten. He was tall, yet not exceptionally so, and he had no single feature that would stick in an observer's mind. But it would have been a mistake for the defense to have supposed there was anything about him, beyond his appearance, that was mediocre or negative. He was tireless, shrewd, and tenacious. While he could not engage in repartee with the slashing wit of either Petiot or Judge Leser, and while he lacked the platform presence and oratorical flourishes of defense counsel Floriot, he was able to follow a thread of logic through a cloud of confused details and refute a cunningly contrived set of falsehoods by a simple setting out of the facts.

Then there was Maître René Floriot, counsel for the defense, head of a battery of young attorneys with identically curled hair who were known to the press as "Floriot's boys" (Ayache, Cousin, Jacquet, and Libman). Floriot was a dramatic figure. Heavy-set and dark, he wore his hair cut about even with his ears, giving him an extra and imposing expanse of temple and jaw. His hair was well-groomed, brushed straight back, and parted on the left side. His face was set off by a pair of extremely heavy, black tortoise-shell glasses, movie-producer style. He was always cleanly and freshly shaven and his clothes, of a conservative cut, were nevertheless obviously expensive and expertly tailored. The standard

* This judge and other lawyers and principals in this trial were frequently interviewed by the author many years after the trial and were very co-operative and helpful except for the defense counsel Maître Floriot, who avoided meeting with the author even when invited to lunch by the U.S. Embassy to meet with the author. No reason or excuse or any actual refusal was given by Maître Floriot for his failure to meet with the author although, fortunately, some of his assistants were helpful. It was the belief of several persons close to the case that Maître Floriot's avoidance of the author was because he had somehow learned of the author's activities in World War II and he was afraid he would be asked too many questions on his Nazi and Nazi collaborator clients and why he sent Petiot's original "letter to the editor," which positively led to Petiot's capture under his up-to-then successful aliases. In fact it was reported that Floriot knew that some high-level Paris police had been U.S. Army secret agents working for the author and that the author had been told by Jacques Yonnet how Floriot had actually caused Petiot's identification under successful aliases and his final arrest. The judge, M. Leser, was probably the most co-operative and helpful source and told the author that he, the author, seemed to know Petiot better than Petiot knew himself. Judge Leser even gave the author some of his notes made during the trial on the promise that they would be used to help the author but any publication using his notes could be releasable only after the judge's death.

black robe and white cravat of France's formal court attire gave his appearance a dash that set him apart, a featured player in a full-length movie. He was aggressive, dominating, full of vitality.

Pierre Veron, lawyer for the estate and family of Mme. Khait and her daughter, Raymonde Baudet, was the only authentic resistant in the cast. He stood inches over the average Frenchman, had the rugged profile of a leading man, and the chest and shoulders of an athlete. Veron had been a major of the Maquis, operating with the army of U.S. General George Patton during its sweep westward into Germany. His unit served as Patton's right flank outguard, and he had earned many medals for his bravery in action.

A Hollywood movie producer in the temporary service of the U.S. Army who had attended the trial said that there were three men who could have played their own parts on the screen: the judge, the accused, and Pierre Veron. Most spectacular of all, of course, was Petiot. His very entrance into the courtroom was a sensation and his first gestures were those of a man who seemed to revel in his part. But before he entered, the jury had to be chosen. From twenty-seven candidates examined, seven laymen were to be selected. Then two magistrates were included, trained lawyers of the state who had been agreed upon by both defense and prosecution. This is the French method. It has the special advantage of including in every jury two men who are learned in the law and can answer questions or offer explanations without recourse to the judge. When the jury had been chosen and seated the courtroom began to stir. Then the room fell silent. A few people, badly situated, began to stand up and crane their necks to see what was taking place. Those behind them cried out, as at a football game: "Down! Down in front! Sit down!" It was Petiot, just entering.

Haughty, erect, and, for once, faultlessly groomed, Petiot insisted that his handcuffs be removed. He had no desire to face his public in the posture of a criminal. The gendarme removed the irons just before Petiot stepped into the prisoner's box. Petiot then settled himself with great aplomb. His hair was neatly combed back. He wore his finest suit, gray with a lavender pin stripe, beautifully fitted to his husky form. He carefully adjusted the knot in his cravat and, of course, rubbed his hands together. He was calm, confident, curious as to the make-up of the crowd.

Then the flash bulbs began to burst all around him and he automatically raised both arms to shield his eyes. He caught himself quickly, lowered his arms, and lifted his head to offer the photographers an advantageous pose. He smiled and looked directly at the cameras. Then, at last, he lifted one hand in a gracious gesture, seeming to say "Gentlemen! Please! That's enough for now!"

Petiot had a file of papers which he now placed on the desk before him. He looked calmly around the room seeking the faces he knew. He saw his wife and his son, Gerhardt, who was now almost eighteen. He smiled. Then he continued to stare at the crowd, fascinated by the assortment of men and women who had come to observe him at bay. And the crowd, every last one of them, stared back in his face. Those deep-set but wide-opened eyes with the unearthly fire burning deep inside! Those who had learned to think of him as inhumanly cruel saw the cruelty in his mouth. But some found him handsome, physically fascinating, well set up. Others saw him as a dangerous animal whose closeness stimulated physical fear. But all found him dignified, nervous, emotionally repressed, and hypnotic.

The press described him variously as "a super star with sex appeal," "the incarnation of Satan himself," or "the devil's poet." No one seemed able to discern the color of his eyes. But all observed the wide brow and head of the intellectual, the satanic, dark, and heavy eyebrows, and the deep pouches under his eyes. Before long all eyes had fastened on his hands. The hands not of an intellectual or a doctor but the hands of a butcher! Large and dark, with out-curving thumbs, bony fingers, and roughened skin. Powerful hands but certainly not those of a physician. "The hands," wrote some reporters, "of an assassin, the hands of a strangler."

Petiot, listening to the reading of *l'acte d'accusation*—a full statement of the charges traditionally read at the opening of a trial in France—would occasionally brush back the hair that fell on his temples, first with one hand and then the other. The specific charges were premeditated murder and robbery of twenty-seven victims, twenty-six by name. He had heard all these charges before. Indeed, when Judge Leser had warned him, in chambers prior to the trial, of the fact that he was going to be tried for twenty-seven murders and would be executed if found guilty, he

had made the remark to the effect that the judge was surely joking. "Not twenty-seven. I liquidated sixty-three persons, but all
enemies of France!"

"Very well," said Judge Leser. "But we will start with twenty-
seven and that may do for the others as well."

The charge set forth that all of Petiot's activities at 21 rue Le
Sueur had been part of a diabolical murder plot and that his office
and apartment there were nothing but a murder factory. It cited
the building of a wall to prevent neighbors from looking into the
court; the hall and triangular death chamber with its one very
secure door and one false door; the fake bell and iron hooks on
the wall; the peep hole equipped with the Lumvisor; the lime pit;
the lime; the use of the two furnaces; the large sink and the dissecting table . . . and the drain directly connected with the famous Paris sewer.

The victims for whose deaths Petiot was finally being tried were
categorized as follows: fifteen Jews (all marked for certain death
and wanted by the Gestapo except one, Dreyfus, who was proven
to have been at least technically a plant of the Gestapo to trap Petiot's escape apparatus); three witnesses against Petiot in police
matters; and nine "questionable characters," French Gestapo renegades—all gangsters and all definitely and positively Nazi collaborators and their molls. All of the men in the last group were
wanted by both the French police and German Gestapo.
Strangely, the victims were all named except the very last one,
who was an unknown and unidentified girl. The approximate time
of her disappearance was given as December 1942 or January 1943.
Here also, as in the cases of the twenty-six other victims, Petiot
was charged with stealing her clothes, jewelry, money, and identification papers.

The prosecutor set forth in the charge Petiot's background of
thefts, robberies, and dope traffic, and explained that a board of
experts had found him sane and responsible for his acts. On this
final score, the prosecutor himself was not really convinced. He
rather indiscreetly had set forth before the trial that he did not
see how a man with psychological troubles as a child, adjudged
mentally incompetent to serve in the army in World War I, adjudged sufficiently sick mentally to receive a 50 per cent (originally a 100 per cent) disability pension and deranged enough, on

one occasion, not to be held responsible for theft, robbery, and resisting arrest, could still be held liable for a series of murders. M. Dupin expressed this feeling not only before the trial began but during the trial and afterward.† It was his duty, however, to press the charges as they were set forth.

The *acte d'accusation* setting forth the charges was twenty pages long and the audience soon wearied of it. It covered every detail of Petiot's career—his childhood and school years, his service in World War I, his confinements in asylums and psychiatric clinics, and finally his days in medical school. Petiot brightened visibly when his achievement of a "superior" grade on his thesis was mentioned, and he listened with obvious pride as the prosecutor told of Petiot's success as a country doctor and a politician.

"You enjoyed a tremendous popularity and were elected mayor several times and that is understandable as you are a very personable fellow," commented the judge.

"Thank you very much," quickly answered Petiot, smiling.

It being the French method in criminal trials for the presiding judge to first "examine" the accused, the first day of the trial provided many opportunities for Petiot to match wits with Judge Leser and he must have felt that he was scoring solid points, for the audience rewarded him often with loud laughter. At times, however, they booed Petiot heartily.

When Judge Leser asked Petiot about the mysterious disappearance of his "servant and mistress Louise" at Villeneuve, Petiot replied with broad sarcasm:

"Ah, yes. My first murder. But I assume that of course you have proof or at least a witness. Seriously I can tell you that she married a doctor and is in perfect health. She lived happily ever after!"

The judge then leaned across his desk to look Petiot directly in the eye.

"What about your stealing gasoline and tires from the town? Also electricity? And the cross from the cemetery?"

---

† In an interview with the author, prosecutor Dupin definitely stated he believed Petiot to be positively insane but a genius in cunning. A quote of Dupin: "A man who also according to his army record had fired a revolver at someone for no known reason and had once been determined by an army medical finding as needing a bodyguard or guardian whenever out of the security of an insane asylum."

Petiot was not the least ruffled. "Just political gossip! Except the cross. That caused me great trouble from all the bigots and hypocrites in my town. And don't forget, while I admit I was responsible for the disappearance of the cross, no one can prove it and nobody has ever found it. And believe me, I didn't swallow it!"

The judge persisted: "But you *were* convicted for tapping electricity?"

"Yes, I was convicted, but that does not prove me guilty. Not in our political world!"

This sally also drew a satisfying laugh from the audience and Petiot obviously was enjoying himself. But the prosecutor, M. Dupin, interrupted the judge's examination to see if he could force a more definite admission of guilt. For the first time, Petiot's self-control gave way.

"Stop!" he shouted to Dupin. "I do not want ever to be put in a position of seeming to be guilty!"

The judge broke in to take matters back into his own hands. He turned to the time when Petiot had opened his practice in Paris and had sent out those rather improper promotion pieces.

"Those were the prospectuses of a charlatan," the judge commented.

"I thank you for your recommendation," said Petiot quietly. "But I request that you do not volunteer your personal opinions."

Maître Floriot, always on the alert, his chin jutting out and his eyes seeming to flash behind his glasses, leaped to the fray:

"The first requirement of this court should be complete impartiality," he said sharply. "I request the withdrawal from the record of your designation of my client as a charlatan."

"I did not actually call the prisoner a charlatan," said the judge gently. "In fact, was not Dr. Petiot a city medical examiner?"

Petiot, mollified, turned with great satisfaction toward the jury. "Yes. And I still am," he said.

Later in the examination, Petiot was again able to win, at least for an instant or two, the sympathy of his listeners. The judge had taken up the question of Petiot's wealth, which seemed inordinate for a simple practitioner.

"You proudly claimed that you made an astronomical income?" The judge made a question of it.

"No," said Petiot readily. "Not astronomical. From three hundred to five hundred thousand francs a year." (Approximately $20,000 to $30,000.)

The judge smiled. "But I see," he went on, "that you declared on your tax returns only twenty-five thousand francs a year. And that is indeed far from astronomical."

"Well, yes," Petiot confessed. "I followed the tradition of all us Frenchmen and of my profession. When a surgeon earns ten million francs, he reports a hundred thousand." Petiot then raised his voice to make sure his listeners did not miss his next point. "This also definitely proves that I am French. After all, I did not want to look like a sucker!"

A definitely sympathetic chuckle then sounded from the audience and a few distant corners even gave out a scattering of applause. Tax evasion as well as avoidance was obviously a popular pastime. (French tax evaders, when caught, rarely go to prison.) Responses of this sort may have encouraged Petiot to take the offensive. This had always been his best defense in all his trials and interrogations. He felt he might win the listeners—and the jury—if he could somehow turn the tables on the prosecutors. He knew, for instance, that Judge Leser was a holdover from the Vichy regime and had taken an oath of allegiance to Pétain, whose trial had recently ended with a finding of guilty and a sentence of death, the sentence being promptly commuted to life imprisonment.

Petiot soon saw an opportunity to strike back when the questioning turned to his earlier arrests. What about the book he had stolen from Gilbert's?

"I was looking for a book to help me with my invention to cure chronic intestinal laziness," Petiot explained blandly. "It was raining. I put the book under my arm and walked out without paying. You know inventors are always absent-minded and are often considered crazy."

"But it is you," said the judge intently, leaning across the bench to point directly at Petiot, "who always pleads insanity whenever you have any troubles with the law."

Petiot shrugged and offered a sarcastic reply:

"One never knows if one is crazy or not. After all, insanity is comparative . . . and sometimes close to genius."

Judge Leser disregarded this comment and pressed on:

"And you have been mixed up with dope traffic and with the strange death of one of your patients?"

Petiot seemed to bristle now. He lifted his eyebrows sharply and rubbed his hands together.

"The autopsy," he replied bitingly, "showed my hypodermic injection had nothing to do with her death. As a matter of fact, I telephoned Dr. Paul, whom I knew, to ask him about the autopsy on my patient. He said, 'If you worry about the conditions under which everyone dies you will never have time for anything else!' Of course," Petiot added, perhaps hoping for another reaction from the crowd, "everyone knows Dr. Paul liked his little jokes."

But neither the crowd nor the judge responded, and the latter forged ahead into more sensitive areas. What about the triangular cell, the supposed gas chamber, the iron hooks, the talk of torture? Petiot began to smolder.

"That is simply a newspaper fairy tale. The triangular chamber, the viewer, they were for my X-ray room. That is why the walls were abnormally thick instead of there being a lead shield. The false push button for the bell was old and was left because the wiring could not be found to take out. And the false door was simply there for protection against humidity, as wood absorbs dampness. As for the hole the journalists say was where I introduced poisonous gas, that was for electric wires for the X-ray machines. And for that famous viewer, that was pure fabrication. The viewer was to aid me in controlling my patients and their X-ray pictures."

"And the cadavers?"

Petiot now let his temper go.

"I had nothing to do with them!" he shouted. "When I got out of Fresnes I found them planted in my place on rue Le Sueur!"

"And the lime pit?"

Petiot was apparently ablaze with indignation. But he spoke clearly and proudly.

"That is where my comrades of the Fly Tox resistance apparatus got rid of some of the bodies of Germans they had liquidated."

Here M. Dupin seemed to see his opportunity and he leaped in with the question Petiot had always dodged.

"What comrades? Give us the names of your associates."

"I will never give the names of my comrades!" Petiot cried. "They are no more guilty than I am! Several wanted to come here to testify for me but I would not let them. They deserve the Cross of the Liberation for having liquidated thirty Boches. Instead, you would put them in jail!"

"If they will come forward," said Dupin firmly, "I'll guarantee to give them the Cross!"

But Petiot had seen his chance to swing into the offensive.

"Absolutely not!" he said. "I'll give no names until there has been a *real* purge completed, when no one who took an oath to serve Pétain can hold a position of authority and . . ."

The judge lifted both arms in disgust and irritation, then let them drop despairingly.

"Do not raise your arms like that!" Petiot snarled, pressing his attack.

The judge was icily calm. "I will raise my arms whenever I please," he said. "But now let's talk about your activities in the Resistance."

Petiot seemed to welcome this opportunity. He took up his story with gusto, perhaps feeling that he would now carry audience and jury with him:

"I began my resistance from the first arrival of Germans in Paris. At that time there was no Resistance. . . ."

To Petiot's dismay, the crowd drowned him out with their sudden booing and catcalls. Obviously it did not pay to belittle the men who had fought underground—even if not from the beginning. There *had* been a resistance, they were saying. When Petiot could be heard again he hastened to give details of his own daring deeds. There was his secret weapon that killed silently at twenty-five yards. There was the time he planted explosives in German railroad cars and had handled *le plastique* in the Chevreuse Valley. A British officer, parachuted into the Franche-Comté to organize resistance, had first demonstrated to Petiot the proper way to use plastic explosives, he said.

"His name?"

Petiot never knew his name but he was to be asked this question again. And what else had he accomplished for the Resistance? Well, he had been of great assistance in gathering intelli-

gence for Cumuleau. Ah, yes. Cumuleau. The investigators were
well aware that Petiot's description of Cumuleau was incorrect.
But they offered him a chance to walk into the trap again. This
Cumuleau. What color hair did he have? Petiot, as before,
guessed, and as before, he guessed wrong. But men did sometimes
change the color of their hair. He was shown a set of pictures.
From these could he pick out Cumuleau? He could not, although
Cumuleau's actual photograph was among them.

Petiot was not helping his case with either the audience or the
jury but, when the lunch break came, he was still the star of the
show. Some of the foresighted spectators drew sandwiches from
their pockets and held tight to their seats while they ate their
lunch. Others persuaded their neighbors to guard their seats for
them, then went down to the courtroom lunchroom in the building to seek refreshment. Outside the courthouse, hawkers peddled
the book by Petiot which he had written during his imprisonment. Not a defense, nor a confession. Nothing to do with the
trial or the charges at all. It was a book called *Le Hasard Vaincu*,
dealing with the mathematical laws of chance and of combination
and permutation. It was heavy going indeed for a person not well
versed in mathematics and it was not nearly so original as it pretended to be. (The title, *The Conquest of Chance*, might have
been selected by an American publisher.) All the same, the book
sold rapidly. For those who entered the courtroom during the
lunch hour, Petiot descended from the defendant's box and graciously signed his autograph on the flyleaves of the books as they
were handed to him.

The Petiot show was living up to all expectations. It was more
entertaining, for a certainty, than a morning at the cinema and
the most exciting moments were still to come.

One of the best moments did come when Judge Leser returned
to the subject of the secret weapon. Petiot now had grown wary.
As often, when he had no answer to give, he flaunted his patriotism before his questioners.

"If I gave you this information, it would be leaked and used tomorrow in the next war by the Germans, who attacked us in 1870,
in 1914, and in 1940. In fact, the less I tell you about my resistance organization Fly Tox or the net Rainbow, the better for
France!"

At this point, the handsome and striking figure of Pierre Veron uncoiled itself from the attorney's section and advanced toward Petiot. As an attorney for the family of two of the victims he had a right to question the prisoner. Looking like the Resistance incarnate, and known to nearly everyone as a true hero and an expert on underground warfare, he faced Petiot directly.

"Now that you have said you have had instruction and experience in the use of *le plastique,* pray give us detailed information and specific facts about its use."

Petiot could not answer directly. He stumbled and evaded. Veron pressed for specific answers. His questions became more and more technical and Petiot was obviously far over his head. Finally Floriot jumped to his feet to rescue his client from the morass.

"After all," he protested, "this is not an examination for L'École Polytechnique you are giving."

Veron was unperturbed. He nodded to Floriot.

"Yes," he said. "It is an examination. But it is a resistant's examination." He turned back to Petiot. "One thing you have not made clear—your use of the plastic with the German potato-masher grenade, the one with the wooden handle."

Everyone knew, of course, that as a combat officer with the guerrilla forces Veron was intimately acquainted with weapons of this type.

"Well," said Petiot, rushing brashly ahead, his irritations growing, "as I told you before, I wrapped the plastic around the German grenade, then I would throw the combination at German soldiers, especially German Army motorcyclists and Gestapo personnel in jeeps, especially when they passed through the Bois de Boulogne or some other open place, so as not to kill any of our own people." Perhaps sensing the feebleness and fragility of this reply or perhaps responding to the open skepticism on Veron's face, Petiot flared out in anger—and made one of his many serious tactical blunders.

"Your questions and the manner in which you allow me no time to answer and your misquotations of me are shysterlike!" he shouted. "You have no right to ask me questions. You are the lawyer only for Jews and traitors!"

The rank discrimination of this statement could not have

helped him with the court, jury, or spectators. The audience reacted with howls of derision, boos, whistles, and hissing. It took several minutes of gavel pounding before Judge Leser could restore order. After this disastrous interlude, Petiot held himself in check and became more cautious in his replies. He was asked about Pierre Brossolette, whose name he had used so often in spinning his yarns of his resistance activities.

"I never knew Brossolette personally," he said quietly. Soon afterward, Judge Leser, who was determined to prevent a long trial, adjourned the court and announced it would reconvene the next morning.

But the judge was reckoning without the lawyers. There were twelve teams of attorneys altogether, including the representatives of many of the families of the victims, and each was determined to keep clean the reputation of his client's relatives. Then there was Floriot, with his backfield of four young men with almost identical hairdos. This quartet—Ayache, Cousin, Jacquet, and Libman—caught the attention of the journalists for the manner in which each of the four had been assigned and had studied one fourth of the case, so, together, they had a greater command of the entire case than anyone else. With their help, Floriot was destined to throw the prosecution into much confusion and score some major points for Petiot.

The second day of the Petiot trial was even more of a sellout than the first. The doings of the first session had been widely celebrated in the press and by word of mouth, so many who missed the first day had promised themselves they would be in on the second sitting. Outside the Palais de Justice there was a sort of ticket exchange where entry permits signed by the presiding justice were resold openly by those to whom they had been issued. Inside there was even less standing room than before and again the journalists, real and make-believe, had to find seats or standing room behind the prisoner's box. And this time, even the prisoner's box was occupied. When Petiot was brought in, he found, seated in his place, a young, attractive girl in a red dress. Petiot was charmed. With the gallantry that he could assume so easily, he smilingly bent toward her and whispered a few flattering words. Finally she stood up and made a place for him and he thanked her graciously.

Today, Petiot seemed more relaxed. As Judge Leser resumed his examination, the very first question got back to the heart of Petiot's resistance activities.

"How did you recruit the members of your liquidation team and how did you determine who deserved to be liquidated?"

He told how he used the auction center of Paris, La Salle des Ventes (where no one could say he had not been frequently seen), as a general headquarters and assembly point for members of his group. Dodging the question of how he chose the members of his group, he told how they operated: "When we spotted an informer or collaborator, we would arrest him by saying, 'We are German police, follow us.' Then we would interrogate them rapidly and take them in a jeep to Marly Forest."

"What did you do with the bodies?"

"We buried them for better security."

"Give us some names of your associates or some names of your victims."

Petiot had apparently made up his mind to control his outbursts. He made no patriotic speech this time but merely shook his head. Then Dupin, with an air of hopelessness, pointed out to Petiot his gross contradiction:

"You have told the police your executions were at 21 rue Le Sueur. Now you mention a car and woods. Once more, were you or were you not present at the executions?"

"Oh yes," Petiot replied quickly, seeing an opportunity now to drop a small bombshell that he had been saving, and one that would perhaps wipe out all his troublesome contradictions. "I may have admitted many things that were not true when arrested by that famous resistant captain of the DGER—who was afraid to show up at this trial"—Petiot had raised his voice to make sure no one missed his point—"because he also worked for the Gestapo under his real name!"

Maître Floriot, bulldog chin thrust forward and lips curling in a sneer, quickly joined the attack, to make sure the name was brought out:

"Yes, my client was arrested by that famous Captain Simonin. Where is he? He was served with papers along with Colonel Dewavrin. And why don't you have him appear—as Simonin, or under his *real* name—Soutif!—Gestapo collaborator police inspector of Quimper responsible for the execution of a score of French resistants!"

Dupin could justifiably have been somewhat shaken by this sally, for he, too, was puzzled by the failure of either Simonin or Colonel Dewavrin to appear, but Pierre Veron was ready to strike a blow.

"Did you not," he asked Petiot, in a firm tone, "say you wrapped plastic around a German grenade, pulled the pin, and threw the potato-masher hand grenade at Germans on motorcycles and in jeeps proceeding at normal speeds through the Bois de Boulogne?"

"Yes," said Petiot.

"And the explosion killed them all?"

"Yes."

"Then you are trapped! Because, while an American pineapple hand grenade takes only three seconds to explode, after pulling out its pin, the German hand grenade is slower—it takes seven seconds. Therefore if you pulled out its pin and threw it at Germans on motorcycles or in jeeps, by the time the grenade and plastic exploded the Germans would be out of range. How can you explain that one? And how can you still insist that you were a resistant with training and experience in plastic, in explosives, and in grenades?"

Petiot was not the least discomfited but replied with a note of triumph, as if it were Veron, rather than he, who had been caught in a misstatement:

"Oh, I did not kill Germans with plastic or grenades, but with my secret weapon!"

Veron smiled. "Fine," he said. "Tell us about your secret weapon."

"You don't think for one moment," said Petiot indignantly, "that I am going to reveal any secrets that are of value to France?"

There was no outburst of applause at this appeal, nor did Floriot step in to rescue Petiot. Floriot was asleep! Or was he pretending to sleep to avoid Veron, who was obviously the hero of the hour? Floriot, having jokingly pointed out somewhat earlier that he was the only one in court who had not claimed membership in the Resistance, was in no position to match his patriotic record with Pierre Veron's, especially after his defense of so many collaborators and Germans.

Veron, meanwhile, pursued Petiot by insisting that he tell how he had killed his victims, how his secret weapon worked, and urging him to give at least *one* name of a member of the Fly Tox group. Without his lawyer to protect him, Petiot finally had to refuse to answer any more questions. He tried to make light of it all by waving his hand and laughing. "Your trap to make me look bad has failed," he told Veron.

It is doubtful if anyone in court agreed with him. Far better for Petiot if the jury rather than Floriot had slept through this dismal exhibition.

After this the judge and the prosecutor both pressed Petiot to give them details of his escape route and about his travelers. Once more they exposed the contradictory stories. Petiot, as the questions drove him into more obvious evasions, began to play for the sympathy of the listeners by referring constantly to his arrest and torture by the Germans. Self-pity filled his eyes with tears and tightened his throat. Finally he had to put his head down in his arms on the desk in front of him and give himself over to sobbing. He raised a tear-stained face at last to the jurymen, and told them, between choking sobs:

"I saw my comrades dead at Fresnes, the victims of German cruelty. I took tremendous chances then and in fighting on the day of liberation in the streets. My acquittal is certain. . . . I have the greatest confidence in you, gentlemen of the jury."

Then Petiot dropped his head once more into his folded arms and broke into a violent fit of weeping. When he had recovered himself, he went on to tell how he had hidden from the Germans after his release. He did not, however, explain his being set free at a time when men and women were being executed on mere suspicion of opposing the Occupation forces. He explained how he became a member of the F.F.I. as Captain Valéry, in charge of investigations at the Reuilly armory to purge France of its traitors and collaborationists.

"I arrested the Duke of Rochefaucault," he related proudly, "the Count of Roche-Guyon, a Mme. Bonnasseau, Mr. George Fox, an executive of N.V. Philips, a Muller . . ."

But the court would not permit him to wander too far off the track. The judge and prosecutor wanted to hear about 21 rue Le Sueur. It had sound reason to doubt Petiot's reliability in identifying collaborators or resistants.

"I was released from Fresnes," Petiot went on, still sobbing, "to find 21 rue Le Sueur stuffed with corpses about which I knew nothing but that members of my resistance group left there." This was a new line, as he also claimed the bodies had been planted there.

Finally Petiot was driven into an admission concerning the disposal of the bodies. Yes, it was true that, under pretext of needing the stuff to clean out the apartment and kill bedbugs, he had asked his brother to bring a load of quicklime to rue Le Sueur. Then his associates had evidently decided to hasten the process by burning the bodies in the furnaces.

Petiot again expanded on the theme that he had been a resistant from the beginning and that he killed far more persons—at least sixty-three—than he was being tried for but that they were all Germans or collaborators. But the killings, for some strange reason, did not seem the main concern of the trial. It was as if that matter had been already decided on and attention could now be given to such matters as stolen papers, relationships between witnesses and the Gestapo, reliability of testimony, and the question of who was and who was not a collaborator. Even the prosecution seemed to steer clear of determining how the many victims, named and unnamed, may have met their deaths.

Mr. Dupin pried into the alleged thefts of identification papers by Petiot while he was acting as medical examiner. He had, said Dupin, many times lifted the dead man's papers while making out the death certificate.

"False!" Petiot shouted. "I kept the papers of only one dead man, those of Harry Baur, the comedian tortured to death by the Germans. [Baur's card, number 1402866, was found by police at 27 rue des Sous-Murs in Auxerre, another one of the many Petiot properties.] Are you going to accuse me of trying to pass myself off as a famous comedian?"

The prosecutor then switched to a question about another alleged victim, Denise Hotin. But Petiot merely replied that he did not know what the prosecutor was talking about. He was asked then about the dope-traffic cases involving Raymonde Baudet and Jean Marc van Bever.

"You must know," Petiot replied bitterly, "that dope addicts are cheats and liars. Baudet had one of my prescriptions forged and her mother, Mme. Khait, lied." This had been previously proved in the preliminary hearings.

But what about the letters supposedly sent by Mme. Khait and Jean Marc van Bever?

"I know nothing about those," said Petiot. The prosecutor then revealed the fact that all the letters had followed a set pattern. All had been clearly designed to exonerate Petiot. But when he was shown the letters in his examination preceding the trial, the prosecutor revealed, Petiot refused to give any explanation. Pierre Veron, who was representing the Khait family (later he was also to appear for the Dreyfus family), then stood up to point at Petiot and declare that Mme. Khait had been a witness whom Petiot had to get rid of, lest he lose his license. Petiot took this charge with great calm. He gazed mildly back at Veron.

"You know, Maître Veron," he said, "you have lots of talent. I congratulate you. . . . I will send you some clients."

Veron, who was never caught off balance, came back swiftly:

"It would be much less dangerous for you to send me clients than for me to send any to you!"

The crowd burst into loud laughter at this and kept on chuckling. The three lawyers meanwhile—Dupin, Floriot, and Veron—engaged in an uneven battle, two against one, on the subject of the Khait disappearance. She had left the wash boiling on the stove. . . . The discussion went on and on, with never a reference to the accused, who sat ignored in the box. Finally he protested.

"Have I not the right to speak also?" he broke in. "After all, I am the star of this show, not just a spear holder." The audience showed its appreciation of this interruption, but Judge Leser, noting that it was already 5:45 P.M., immediately declared an adjournment.

The third day of the trial began with a firm statement by M. le Président that he was determined not to let matters get out of hand. They were running behind schedule and he was going to see to it that from now on standard procedure was followed, so there would be no more delays. The crowd, however, which seemed to increase day by day, was not going to allow him to stick to that resolve. They were here to see the show.

The subject first raised by the prosecution this day was the disappearance of Jean Marc van Bever.

"A dope addict!" Petiot exclaimed. "And a bad one! So he disappeared. So what am I supposed to know about it?"

Then what about the furrier Guschinow, a rich man?

"That is one person whose escape I did arrange," said Petiot. "I turned him over to Robert Martinetti, who was an experienced guide for escape routes to Spain. Guschinow got to his destination, Buenos Aires, and I received letters from him from the Alvear Palace Hotel there. If I had any valuable furs belonging to Guschinow it is because he gave them to me for saving him from Auschwitz, the German death camp in Poland."

The thought of his kindness to Guschinow brought fresh tears from Petiot, and once more his speech was broken by sobs. In the meantime, Floriot and his boys had prepared a booby trap for the prosecutor.

"Did you send an investigator or commission to Buenos Aires?" Floriot demanded of Dupin.

"You know perfectly well I did not!" Dupin replied. Floriot loudly expressed his shock at this dereliction, then let it go. He would refer to it again. But he would not refer to the fact that he had not checked in Buenos Aires either and that Guschinow's former partner had sent many fruitless queries after him. Floriot was out to score points now and on this day he scored several good ones.

In the course of the day, Petiot, at least once, shocked the spectators and presumably the jury with his apparent cold-bloodedness. Whether points were scored or not, the knockout appeared still inevitable. Both Petiot and Floriot tried to keep punching aggressively throughout the session. Questions were asked about Dr. Braunberger's disappearance, and Petiot brushed them off:

"I saw him for only ten minutes in my entire life, at a luncheon for the communion of his daughter."

And the lawyer for the Braunberger family wanted to know how it happened that everyone he dealt with, who was trying to escape, wrote letters back that followed an identical pattern—and all, according to the experts, were written under duress. Petiot, however, was not giving explanations. He was out to prove that his alleged victims were all agents of the Gestapo or somehow involved with the Nazis. Above all, he was not interested in letters.

"All I am interested in," he said to Maître Perles, the Braunberger attorney, "is seeing you try to tie in your affair with me or with the others. Since your effort will fail completely to involve me, so will the others." Having had time to brood upon his angry gaffe of the previous day, Petiot now sought to repair the record. "Incidentally," he went on, "I want to be certain that everyone understands that I am not anti-Semitic, I considered Dreyfus an exception. If I have become so today, it grows out of the unfairness of my prosecution."

Now the questions turned to the group known to the French newspapers as "*Les Mauvais Garçons*"—those gangsters and former members of the French Gestapo and their girl friends. These killings Petiot had admitted—the only ones he enthusiastically confessed. And it was not going to be difficult to show that they had indeed had Gestapo connections. There was, however, one other fact about them that offered no help to Petiot's case—they were all heavily loaded with loot—cash and jewels—and were fleeing both the French and German police. They had all taken their mistresses along, also loaded with their life's savings, and these too Petiot admitted killing. If he was going to liquidate the enemies of France, well and good. But the women? Did he have to liquidate those as well, he and his gallant associates of Fly Tox? Why kill Gisele Rossmy, and Annette, the Little Bedbug, and Joséphine Grippay, the Chinoise, and the poor nameless girl no one could describe?

The prosecutor put this question to Petiot, and Petiot, with hardly a moment's thought, replied with bitter sarcasm:

"What would you have wanted me to do with them?"

At this callous retort, the whole courtroom recoiled almost visibly. Floriot quickly broke in to explain that his client had already admitted getting rid of these gangsters and their mistresses.

"They were mistresses of Gestapo agents," Petiot added. "They would have denounced my associates and me."

Three of the men worked for the Gestapo, Floriot explained, and the fourth ran a licensed whorehouse for the German Army.

These men, said Floriot, had left in couples, exchanging women. He implied that the device of exchanging mistresses was proof of a Gestapo plant. Petiot described Estebeteguy as a friend and an associate of Lafont and Bonny and part of the French Gestapo at rue Lauriston. This was almost the only point in the trial at which the judge and prosecutor tried to learn details of how these nine people met their deaths. Petiot turned aside these inquiries. Beaming with self-satisfaction and putting on a show of mock revulsion, he said, for the audience rather than the judge:

"My, but you people have a sadistic curiosity!"

Then he went on, with a show of great patience: "I was not present but I can only tell you they were killed by being bludgeoned with a cudgel made from rubber hose stuffed with a subtle mixture of lead, sand, and pieces of a bicycle frame."

At this, the prosecutor made some comment on his own respect for life and human dignity. Floriot was quick to seize the opening.

"You respect the life of members of the Gestapo of rue Lauriston?" The prosecutor was thrown into confusion by this. It was not politic at that season to admit any feeling of human sympathy at all for enemies of France, Gestapo, collabos, informers, or what not. Even a Catholic priest who had called for Christian charity at Notre Dame during the Communist excesses that followed the liberation was forced out of his church.

Judge Leser quickly declared a short recess and Dupin had time to recover his balance. When the court was called to order again, the questioning concerned the Jewish couples Petiot was accused of eliminating, the Wolffs, the Anspachs, and the Bastons, or Basches. Petiot promptly identified them all as Gestapo agents intent on exposing the Fly Tox apparatus and all properly executed by his associates and buried in the Marly Forest.

"The Wolffs," the prosecutor declared, "were Jews fleeing from German prosecution. They were one hundred per cent resistants and anti-Nazis."

Petiot looked unbelievingly at the prosecutor, as one looks at an idiot, and replied scornfully:

"They were Germans. So were the Basches . . . same route. Same treatment." The lawyer for the family intruded them to insist that the Wolffs had left Holland on June 12, 1942, and had been in constant flight from the Germans. Petiot, shouting him

down, cried out: "They came from Berlin!" And Floriot, with one
of his "boys" whisking out the proper paper at the exact moment,
then read a report by Police Inspector Battut which said that the
Wolffs had entered France on a visa officially stamped on their
passport in Berlin. And where had they stayed while at Lyon?
Why, at a hotel where the first two floors were occupied by the
Germans!

"Oh, yes," Petiot burst in. "They were hiding from the Germans the way I hid from my wife in bed when I was a newlywed.
I would get under the sheet naked and call to her, 'Try to find
me!' "

All these people—the two Wolffs, the three Basches, the two
Anspachs, and the two Stevens, said Petiot—were sent to him by
Erlane Kahan in connection with the Gestapo's efforts to find Fly
Tox. Kahan, he insisted, was a Gestapo agent. "If Kahan had sent
me a hundred Jews or a hundred Gentiles," he declared firmly, "I
would have liquidated every one of the hundred first. Then Kahan
would have been next."

On that ringing declaration, Judge Leser closed the third session of the trial. It had been a very successful one for the defense.
Their strategy of attack had succeeded in tarnishing the reputa-
tions of at least eighteen of the twenty-seven with whose deaths
he was charged. Floriot's brilliant tactics and his excellent research
had staggered the prosecutor more than once, but perhaps it was a
victory that meant ultimate defeat for Petiot. The points he
scored were like the flicking jabs of a boxer—technically brilliant
but of practically no value in a fight to the finish, as this fight was.
It might even have been better had there been fewer points scored
that day, for it was a day when it would have been perfect strategy
to plead insanity.

Petiot's chilly disregard for human life, his cold-blooded indifference to the fate of the five women he admitted killing, revealed the basic viciousness of his character. With the prosecutor already convinced that Petiot was unbalanced, and with the
living proof of his insanity right before their eyes, court and jury
might well have been quick to grant that he might better be
locked up for the rest of his life.

But Floriot and Petiot, having held one winning hand, obviously decided to play for the whole pot. They would attack and

attack and give the prosecution no respite. Or Floriot, perhaps knowing where the spoils were hidden, preferred his client to be executed!

On the fourth day, after more details on both the Gestapo and the Jewish travelers, the questioning dealt with Dreyfus. Here was one victim whose connection with the Gestapo could not be denied. Here there was documentary proof that Dreyfus had agreed to be a plant to uncover a resistance escape apparatus even if to double-cross the Germans.

Petiot, to open the session, immediately undertook to seize the initiative. Without any prompting, he began to tell the court a story:

"A certain general . . . Victor, I believe . . . was parachuted into the neighborhood of Lyon. In order to find him, the Germans mobilized into their intelligence service four hundred prostitutes. . . ." Perhaps Petiot had chosen a subject of intense fascination to the spectators, but it held no interest whatever for Judge Leser. M. le Président broke into the story at once to remind Petiot that the court wanted to hear what he knew about Dreyfus.

Well, yes, Petiot explained that he met Dreyfus through two "pretty shabby characters," Chantin and Guelin. He had wanted to help Dreyfus, too, until he discovered that the young man was part of a Gestapo plot to trap him and his Fly Tox apparatus. He beat them all, he proclaimed with pride. It is true that the next plant, Beretta, got him arrested, but he had outwitted the Gestapo. What became of Dreyfus, said Petiot blandly, he did not know.

"There is a German record," said Floriot quickly, "starting in 1943 that proves Yvan Dreyfus was an informer for the Gestapo that far back. So let's not get soft on the fate of Yvan Dreyfus."

Veron, now representing the Dreyfus family, was outraged by this statement and so was Judge Leser.

Pierre Veron then offered the court a quick summary of Dreyfus' true career: a return from the sanctuary of the United States in order to fight for France in 1939, a fight that Petiot took no part in, even though he was in France already. Then, after the armistice, Dreyfus was arrested by the Germans when he was trying to reach England in order to join de Gaulle. This, for the time being, seemed to complete the Dreyfus story.

Next, Petiot was questioned about the Knellers—the father,

mother, and little boy. Here there could be no attack on Kneller's patriotism: he had joined the Foreign Legion to fight for his adopted country. He was neither gangster nor Gestapo agent and had no connection with Eriane Kahan, but Petiot, all the same, took the offensive.

> Kneller was a patient of mine. I don't remember for what. But I do recall I always had lots of trouble with him, collecting my bills. He never paid. He owed me two thousand francs. Then he wanted to escape with his wife and child and I furnished him with false identification papers making them both single—he a Belgian, she an Alsatian. Yes, they had a child. He was very nice. . . . As they had little money, they gave me their furniture to pay for the papers. The neighbor and concierge made a fuss when I came to get it. [The jury must by this time have been more than mildly repelled by the insatiable, not to say insane, greed of the man—jewels, cash, clothing, furniture—everything!]
>
> I got them tickets to Orleans. They slept at 21 rue Le Sueur, then left. I received a card from them two months later. Mrs. Kneller wrote that her husband was sick. She wrote to several friends after her departure.

And now the delicate question. The little boy. Spectators and jury must have been asking themselves: Was there any reason for killing the little boy?

"What about little Kneller's pajamas in the Kneller bag found after it had been moved from 21 rue Le Sueur?"

Petiot was completely unruffled and he answered the question in an offhand manner:

> Oh that must be the pair of pajamas the child slept in the night before they left 21 rue Le Sueur. They did not want to take any dirty clothes with them, especially with the identification of the initials K.K. I always warned all people I helped escape to get rid of anything with names or initials and all their identification papers so as not to contradict their new identities. And why would I want to keep the kid's pajamas?

Dupin now felt he had closed the trap. For the first time in the trial he stood up and delivered a hammering attack directly at Petiot:

This particular matter is your undoing! It is this family that completely breaks up your system of defense! The best proof is that in connection with the Knellers you have consistently refused to answer the questions of the police and the prosecutor's questions, and all questions on the Knellers in the pretrial examination.

"False!" cried Petiot. "I answered all questions on the Knellers!"

Floriot too had come to his feet to utter the same cry—"False!" —in a voice that rattled the courtroom. "As a matter of fact," he went on, "we have never even received an inventory of what was allegedly found in the suitcases, and . . ."

Now Dupin interrupted in a loud voice:

"Judge Goletty in his examination *did* present the inventory— *frequently!* And Petiot refused to answer any questions."

"Why tell this court incorrect facts?" Floriot shouted back. "Find me one page of such a file . . . !" The wrangle went on, with Floriot daring Dupin to call Judge Goletty to the stand. Finally Judge Leser silenced them both by declaring a short recess in order that Judge Goletty might be consulted. When the court reconvened there was no explanation of what had gone on behind the scenes. But the two lawyers were quieted down and Judge Leser announced that Judge Goletty could *not* be called as witness. Thereupon Maître Floriot officially admitted in open court that an inventory of the articles seized by the police had indeed been offered to Petiot. Petiot, however, had never seen the contents of the suitcases, still piled precariously behind the jury box. He would be given a chance to look them over, along with the witnesses.

The examination of the accused was now complete, without any further effort to delve into the fate of the Knellers. Again the court and prosecution seemed to draw back from a full examination of the crimes themselves—the killings. Was it because they felt that these had been established past denying? Or were they sensitive about the lack of a single identifiable body?

The next order of business, following the French procedure, was the parade of witnesses—ninety of them in all. First came the police officers, and they made a sorry show indeed. Were they overawed by the reputation of Floriot or cowed by that battery of bright young men each with his file full of written records? Whatever the reason, once on the stand, they hemmed and hawed, they contradicted each other and contradicted themselves. They groped for words or blurted out replies without thinking. But this day there was time for only one.

He was Officer Pinault, to whom Petiot had been first turned over by the arresting party, led by Captain Simonin; Simonin, who actually was Inspector Soutif of Quimper, publicly denounced as a collaborator.

Pinault established the fact that Petiot had hidden out in the apartment of Georges Redoute, who accepted him as a resistant. He also testified about his own interview with Lafont and Bonny of the French Gestapo, both of whom had been executed two years before the trial. Neither of them had admitted knowing Petiot, although there was no question that Petiot knew Bonny and Paul Clavie . . . at least the latter. Estebeteguy, it was admitted by both, had been a good friend and associate of Lafont, who had had to get rid of him for "indiscreet actions." Lafont, who had been defended by Maître Floriot, had failed to identify any of the pictures shown him—of Petiot, of the scouts, or of Eriane Kahan. He had later equivocated on knowing Kahan in the hope of staying alive until Petiot was tried. Here ended the fourth day of the trial, with Petiot apparently having not lost any ground.

The fifth day was a spectacular one. Had it occurred in the United States it would almost certainly have led to a mistrial. On this day, at Petiot's invitation, the whole court—judge, prosecutor, lawyers, jury, and journalists—journeyed to 21 rue Le Sueur to enable the jury to decide if the crimes could or could not have taken place there. Petiot insisted on being host to the court to show them that 21 rue Le Sueur was not at all a charnel house or a place designed for murder. Before the sight-seeing trip began, Professor Sannie, director of the Legal and Police Identification at the Natural History Museum of Paris, held a short briefing session, complete with diagrams, to acquaint the travelers with what they might behold. The lecture dealt chiefly with the ground floor and the basement as it was there that the criminal doings allegedly took place.

The procession, which formed at 2 P.M. outside the Palais de Justice, consisted of fifteen cars, preceded and flanked by police motorcyclists. With sirens howling, the long cortege rolled through the streets. The whole city knew that Petiot would be on parade today and it seemed as if at least half the city were watching, for sidewalks along the route were jammed and windows were crowded with spectators.

When the cars pulled up at number 21, the little street was soon tightly crammed with excited men and women, all hungry for a glimpse of Petiot. Where was he? Shouldn't there be a police patrol car? Or a prison van? To everyone's surprise, Petiot, hatless and in a gray overcoat with the collar turned up above his ears, stepped out of the second limousine. Two plainclothes policemen, their felt hat brims snapped down in front in standard motion-picture style, hustled the prisoner through the crowd. They went directly into the courtyard of the building where Judge Leser was already waiting. The courtroom contingent gathered around him, and M. le Président raised his hand high.

"Gentlemen!" he proclaimed. "We will now start with the doctor's office. Professor Sannie, we are ready to follow you."

With judge, prosecutor, and jury pushing ahead into the office, the accompanying throng—journalists, photographers, even the wives and relatives of court officials, took to wandering through the house, like souvenir seekers after an earthquake. The house was already in disorder enough—dirty, with furniture pushed helter-skelter and wallpaper peeling off. This invasion just trebled the confusion. Many crowded close to view somberly the hole in the stable wall which some said had contained the viewer that enabled Petiot to watch the death agonies of his victims. Judge Leser was already inside the dark little room and the crowd could hear the question he addressed to Petiot:

"Why did you have this wall built?"

"It was here I was going to have my X-ray chamber."

Then Floriot's ringing voice:

"The viewer has been taken out! Where is the viewer? If you lose any of the articles or their official seals of sworn police witnesses, you cannot present them in evidence!"

There seemed to be no immediate reply to this. Then Petiot, the gracious host, turned to one of the jurors and asked him if he knew what was meant by a "viewer." Before the startled man could say yes or no, Petiot pressed the explanation upon him.

You can tell the other jurors that the viewer in question was not a periscope but a sort of telescope that allowed me to see very clearly only a certain limited part of the room. Only where Judge Leser is now standing. This room was for an X-ray chamber. I had intended to put an operating table into this room and the viewer was to study my patients from the outside without their knowing. I purchased the viewer, not at the Paris fair, but from the manufacturer, Lumvisor.

Petiot's Lumvisor is now in the Paris police museum but an exact companion of it was found in Nezondet's belongings.

The only light in the little room was a single candle held by some official. Through the hole in the wall, Judge Leser's head could be seen. Then suddenly the face of Petiot, ghastly pale. He was beginning to reel. Was it fear? A sudden surge of remorse? Or was it rather the fact that he had taken only one meal—a bowl of soup—each day for the last few days? Perhaps it was merely the closeness of the room, for as soon as Petiot was brought out into the courtyard again, he recovered.

"Thank you," he murmured. "I feel better although I felt very badly a minute ago."

A fireman with a flashlight then led the official party down to the basement. Professor Sannie pointed out where he had found pieces of cadavers. "It is here at the bottom of these steps that I discovered pieces of cadavers. Next to the two furnaces you see there was half a human body, split in the middle. In the larger furnace were human remains burning and sizzling with human juices and blood oozing out from the heat."

Petiot smiled wanly. Then as he started up the steps, his knees began to give way again. He had to cling tight to the rail to keep from falling. Only Floriot seemed to show any interest, to say nothing of sympathy, for Petiot's plight. He and the police helped Petiot back into the courtyard where the fresh air revived him sufficiently to allow him to continue with the official sight-seeing party again.

Petiot began to reply at length to the questions Judge Leser was asking him about the remains that had been found here—the pile of quicklime containing bones, and bits of flesh, a great quantity of hair, the remains of a jaw, a shredded arm. Petiot was then asked to descend into the lime pit where more lime and more bodies had been found. He made the descent, but once at the bottom, he reeled, staggered, and almost collapsed. No feigning this time. He was milk-white in the face and ready to fall. He was brought back to the fresh air with nothing special accomplished. When he recovered completely, one of the jurors asked him a question:

"Could not the triangular room . . . also serve as a prison cell?"

"No," Petiot answered patiently. "If you lived here you would know that the walls are built of thin plaster blocks that will not withstand much pressure. The room is not very secure and it would have been impossible to kill anyone in this small place." Full of confidence again, he turned to Judge Leser and asked: "Would you tell me how I could kill anyone in there?

"If I had told you I had never killed anyone, I would understand your stubbornness! But I admitted willingly that I executed many persons. So here or there should not concern you. These stories and your embellishment of them are going to make us appear as imbeciles to foreigners." By "us" he meant of course all Frenchmen. Once more he seemed to be dodging into his ultimate retreat—patriotism.

There was one point that might have been made during this visit had Petiot and his lawyer not been so preoccupied with other matters, or was it another error of the defense . . . ? It was a point that troubled the jury, the presiding judge, the prosecutor, and the opposing lawyers, and especially the police: There was, in the alleged triangular death and torture chamber not a single sign of struggle, or the slightest trace of any efforts to batter down the doors, the real or the fake, or to kick or punch through the plaster walls (some very thin indeed) or to use force of any kind on the doors or the doorknobs. Not a single mark, not a dent, not a crack in the plaster. Yet it seemed altogether natural that, were a man or woman to be trapped in there, even in his death agonies, he might use all his remaining strength against a door or wall. Yet neither Petiot nor Floriot took advantage of this fact to cast doubt on the prosecution's theories.

At 4:10 P.M. the visit had been completed and Judge Leser led the court party back to the limousines. This time Petiot had to run a veritable gauntlet of men and women who had closed in

around the entrance. He thrust his way along between the policemen, half smiling as the crowd set up a roar:

"Death! Death to the murderer!"

It would seem to anyone versed in American methods of justice
that intimidation of this sort visited upon the jury must certainly
have justified declaring a mistrial. But there was to be a more
flagrant episode than this connected with the United States without there being any admission that the trial had been less than
fair. Back at the Palais de Justice, at 5 P.M., Professor Sannie took
the stand to tell what he thought of the explanation Petiot had
made about the triangular room.

"Absurd and ridiculous," said the professor. "You can see there
is hardly room for the small bed, and I do not even mention an
X-ray table with X-ray apparatus."

After this, the court returned to the regular order of business—
hearing from the police witnesses. The last witness of the day was
Chief Inspector Massu, former head of the Homicide Squad, who
had since been demoted. Massu appeared with a bandage on his
left hand and wrist, where he had slashed arteries in his suicide attempt when arrested by the Communists as an alleged collaborator.

Floriot quickly threw Massu off balance by sharp questioning
about the improper handling of the suitcases from 21 rue Le
Sueur—the lack of proper seals or the breaking of seals. Massu immediately lost his temper and gave vague and contradictory answers. He admitted his investigative procedures had been incomplete. He forgot important points. Floriot was able to save the day
for Petiot by winding up with a practical confession from Massu
that his search and follow-up at 21 rue Le Sueur had been a fiasco.

The newspaper *Figaro*, commenting next day on Massu's performance: "Why is it that nine out of ten policemen on the witness stand make such pitiful figures . . . ? Inspector Massu's exhibition yesterday holds the police up to ridicule."

The next session, on a Saturday, began at 1 P.M., and the attendance was the greatest yet.

Petiot entered the courtroom in a depressed mood. Instead of
two policemen at his side, he had four. He studied the crowd
this time with great interest, perhaps aware for the first time that
they were incurably hostile. It took him several minutes to pick

out, from the swollen mob, his own relatives and friends. He appeared very tired and weak. He had hardly eaten since the trial began.

There was a new policeman on the stand today—Inspector Battut of the Paris police. His testimony was long and detailed, while his way was beset with traps that Floriot sprang on him. Little that was new came out of his tedious story of finding the suitcases and trying to identify the victims. He was intent, however, on emphasizing one fact that seemed to him of great importance: that was that the Germans had great interest in the Petiot case, directed the Paris police's investigations, and required regular reports. As for Mme. Kahan, he was positive that she had never been a member of the Gestapo. Otherwise, why would the Germans have asked him to find and arrest her? Floriot would not accept this estimate and insisted on further details. Dr. St. Pierre, who was Mme. Kahan's acknowledged lover, or one of them, had made a "confidential" effort, said Battut, to persuade the Paris police either to abandon their search for Mme. Kahan or, if they did find her, not to turn her over to the Germans.

Well, did not Petiot, after his arrest, which was after Paris had been liberated, denounce Mme. Kahan as an agent of the Gestapo? No such thing, said Battut. Well then, was it not known that the Wolffs, and the Basches, whom Mme. Kahan introduced to Petiot, were themselves members of the Gestapo, or Gestapo agents? On this point Battut was doubly emphatic.

"I can positively swear under oath that they were not," he said.

As for Dreyfus, he knew only what he had read in the police record. Floriot leaped upon this statement and tried to force an admission that Battut knew Dreyfus had agreed to act as a Gestapo plant. Battut stubbornly held his ground. Then why were not the suitcases from rue Le Sueur shown immediately to the families of the supposed victims? Battut calmly reminded the attorney that the police were then under German orders and the Germans, presumably, had no urge to co-operate with the families of escapees. Well, the Germans had been ready enough to come to Massu's office and identify the shirts of Estebeteguy. Even Lafont had come down to check these. (Maître Floriot knew this, since he had been defense counsel for Lafont.)

Whereupon, wholly without warning, came one of the shocking

moments of the trial. Battut replied that he was not fully informed about that identification but he knew that Lafont had
come down to check on the disappearance of his agents who had
participated in the Hautefort theft. "Except for Lombard. He had
disappeared."

Half rising from his seat at this juncture, Petiot shouted in a
voice that seemed to ring with implications: "Are you *sure?*"

There was a subdued murmur from the spectators. Then, as if a
choir master had given a signal with his hand, in sudden unison a
great gasp arose. *Mon Dieu!* Were there then twenty-*eight*
murders? (In his prison notes [in 1946] Petiot confessed to liquidating Lombard although Lombard was alive and in jail in 1966.)

But Maître Veron arose now to bring out the fact that Guelin,
who had introduced Dreyfus to Petiot, was himself being held for
"intelligence with the enemy"—in other words for treason or active collaboration—and so was hardly a man who could condemn
Dreyfus on his unsupported word. Battut was not sure. Again and
again he had to fumble in his recollection and come up with
empty hands. Floriot scornfully commented on the lack of respon-
siveness of some of the answers, but this time it was the policeman who scored a point and drew a sympathetic laugh from the
audience.

"Yes, sir," said Battut. "But then I do not have four assistants
and a battery of secretaries to help me."

Police Inspector Pascaud, the next witness, was a real disaster
for the prosecution. He did not know—no one knew—who had
opened the suitcase (exhibit number thirty-four) presumably
belonging to Dr. Braunberger. He did not know what had become
of Dr. Braunberger's shirt and cuff links. Then who *did* know? A
shrug. The almost criminal carelessness with which this important
evidence had been handled was now obvious.

Police Officer Casanova came next but he did not speak of love.
He spoke instead of dead men in Marly Forest—two bodies that
had been dug up and identified. They could not possibly have
been victims of Petiot or of "Fly Tox" or any resistance group.
They were the bodies of Fauvel and of d'Auger, two French Gestapo agents from the rue de la Pompe who were positively killed
by eleven other Gestapo agents under the orders of Dr. Berger.
The witness was positive of that. Petiot had no comment.

Now came a witness in the uniform of a French paratrooper, wearing medals. No one was going to label *him* Gestapo agent. He had been a fellow prisoner of Yvan Dreyfus at the Compiègne concentration camp and had known Dreyfus well. The paper Dreyfus signed? It meant nothing. "I would have signed such a paper myself," said the witness, Captain Henri Boris, "if it had meant a chance to escape to England and fight the Germans."

Had he heard of Fly Tox? Absolutely unknown at the co-ordination center of general headquarters, Boris affirmed. Then Petiot got into the discussion and there followed a three-cornered colloquy among Petiot, Veron, and Boris. The subject turned to *le plastique* and Petiot asserted that he had gotten his supply of plastic and instructions on how to use it from a parachutist who had come direct from London.

"Oh good!" said Boris. "Tell me his name. I will definitely know him. I was chief of the parachutist service in London."

Petiot was clearly in a trap. But he wriggled out glibly and without embarrassment. "I do not know his name or his code name or first name or his address. He was almost caught and left for Corsica and committed suicide." How often and how conveniently for Petiot had witnesses vanished from the earth! This further coincidence was just too much for court, jury, or spectators. There was a howl of laughter. Even if this story had been true, it could never have been established under these circumstances. The judge mercifully turned away to a wholly different topic—the disappearance of Denise Hotin. This particular case was to be a complete triumph for Floriot, thanks largely to the chief witness—Jean Hotin, widower of the vanished girl. Hotin was bumbling, embarrassed, uneasy, unsure of his facts—a typical slow-witted country boy, one might have said. He had learned, he testified, that his stylish and pretty young wife had gone to Dr. Petiot for an abortion in June 1941, soon after their marriage. In June 1942, in order to silence village gossip, she had returned to the doctor, hoping to get a certificate that she had been treated for a lung congestion. Then she disappeared. M. Hotin mumbled and repeated himself. His father, the mayor, had been much distressed by the gossip. Then the disappearance. That seemed as if it might have been a murder by Petiot. The doctor had already been accused of causing the disappearance of two witnesses against him in a narcotics case.

Well, had he gone to see the doctor? Yes, he went to 66 rue
Caumartin. He arrived at 4:30 P.M. The doctor's office hours did
not begin until 5 P.M. So Hotin dared not ring the bell or go upstairs. Besides, there was his own work to finish—and a train to
catch. "So I left." The audience could not suppress its snickers at
this picture of the complete country jay, afraid to "disturb" the
doctor who might have told him what had become of his missing
wife. Then, when Floriot brought out in his questioning that
many months had gone by before Hotin had even thought to look
for his wife and he had done nothing at all after failing to see the
doctor, Hotin was reduced to a mass of hopeless embarrassment.

And now he was a widower, yes? Ah, yes, a widower. And it was
as a widower that he had remarried? The witness gave an embarrassed sigh. Yes, he had rather quickly remarried.

Then was not this disappearance really a sort of divorce? You
seemed to have so little faith in the fact that your wife was dead
that you testified she had abandoned you! And this testimony was
corroborated by a magistrate of your village. The mayor himself.
A man very conversant with your family affairs. Indeed, your own
father!

And why not ask Petiot about her? You were only a hundred ki-
lometers from Paris. And you did not decide on making this trip
until six months later? Of course you could not call on the doctor
out of office hours!

And then the matter of the abortion. When was it that your
wife told you that she was pregnant and wanted an abortion? By
this time Jean Hotin was utterly confused.

At this moment, Judge Leser, who had very nearly drowsed off
during the weary and uninformative recital, became suddenly alert
and asked abruptly: "Let's see. When was the date of the marriage?"

This brought a loud laugh from all the listeners which set Hotin's face and neck on fire with embarrassment. Ruefully he left
the stand and hastened to hide himself. Petiot smiled with a very
satisfied and confident air, for there had certainly been little to
connect him with the disappearance of Denise, the city girl, from
her home and board with her husband and in-laws. It appeared
that she was even expected to work in the fields at Neuville-Garnier. No one after this exhibition could possibly have found Petiot

guilty of *that* murder. But there were more witnesses still. For the defense counsel later in the trial came back to the Hotin case, possibly to get the jury's minds away from some damaging testimony on another matter. But Judge Leser had had enough of the Hotin case and he hastened to excuse the witness. "There is too much gossip in that village," Judge Leser told the jury.

Before this took place, there had been the Guschinow case and a witness from Villeneuve. The man from Villeneuve, the final witness at the Saturday session, was variously identified in the press but in truth he was Urbain Gouraud, a former member of the *gendarmerie* in Villeneuve and Petiot's nemesis, who had been transferred at the request of Dr. Petiot, who was then mayor of the village. Gouraud, who later served in November 1945 as captain in command of the French *gendarmerie* acting as occupational military police at Badekreuz-nach, Germany, revealed an unremitting vindictiveness against Petiot. He evidently had felt many times in Villeneuve that he had the doctor dead to rights but never developed quite strong enough proof to arrest Petiot when he was at the height of his popularity and political power. Floriot, detecting the bitter hatred that motivated every remark, gave the captain his head and allowed him to reveal himself as a man so everlastingly prejudiced against the doctor and so determined to even the score that his testimony was thoroughly tainted. "Petiot was an adventurer . . . an opportunist without any principles. . . . His maid-mistress's body is at the bottom of some abandoned well. . . ." So wild and so fervent were his accusations and so clearly did he bear a grudge against Petiot that Floriot almost rendered him thanks when he was done. It was another score for Petiot.

But Petiot, despite his scoring of points, seemed to be growing physically weaker by the day. Some reporters felt he was being beaten down by the weight of the testimony and was on the verge of collapsing and confessing his misdeeds. Actually Petiot was faint from hunger. For six days he ate only the one slim meal a day—a piece of bread and a bowl of soup at night. By midafternoon he would be tottering close to collapse.

When the second week of the trial began, portentous events took place. Among the lesser matters was the appearance in court of H.R.H. Prince Rainier of Monaco, who someone, much later, was to call "the hereditary proprietor of an amusement park." But this amusement park had nothing to match the Petiot circus where deeds were done every day that would have horrified the entire Bar Association in America. Strangely enough a new incident was contributed from New York City. On this day it was revealed that members of the jury had already decided Petiot was a monster deserving death. A story appeared in the New York *Herald-Tribune* on March 20 that seemed to provide certain grounds for a mistrial when it was read in Paris. The headlines read:

PARIS BLUEBEARD CALLED DEMON BY TWO JURORS.
TERM GUILLOTINE "TOO SWIFT."
Judge says: "He is a Terrifying Monster."

The story then proceeded:

Dr. Petiot was described as a "super-intelligent madman" and "a demon" by the Judge and two members of the jury as his trial opened its second week at the Palais de Justice. . . . The jurors lingering in the sun-drenched courtyard before entering the gloomy trial chamber declared: "He is guilty and the guillotine is too swift a death for such a monster."

The story was written by David Perlman, the *Herald-Tribune*'s Paris correspondent. It was most certainly read by Maître Floriot and he could not have been unaware that it provided the basis for a motion for mistrial, but Floriot, again with unexplainable logic, was content to allow the judge to discharge the two offending jurors and thriftily allow the two alternate jurors to take their places. This stripped the jury of any substitutes in case of sudden illness, but it saved a great many francs for the government and much of the judge's time. After this, how could what remained of the trial be deemed "fair"? If two jurors were ready to be quoted on this opinion, what of the others? And had the judge indeed lent the weight of his authority to a verdict of guilty before all the evidence was in? Everyone who knew Judge Leser was certain he would never have made any statements during the trial.

No matter now. The trial went on. Petiot, having taken a little more nourishment over the weekend, was on the attack again while Floriot was intent on scoring more points against the prosecution. With several regular meals and, on Monday morning, al-most an American breakfast of *omelette fines herbes* with some half-dozen croissants, Petiot came out of his corner throwing punches.

First to appear on the witness stand on Monday was Mme. Guschinow, wife of the missing furrier who had been "the only one besides the Knellers," according to Petiot, who he had helped escape. The Guschinow attorney took over the questioning. He expressed "surprise" that Guschinow had remained three days (by Petiot's account) at 21 rue Le Sueur, and that he had forbidden his wife to accompany him.

Petiot was scornful. How could the man be surprised at some-thing so completely logical?

"I could not take care of him at rue Caumartin where I had my wife, servants, and clients. Besides, I had to give Guschinow his papers and his instructions for the voyage."

"You are indeed very intelligent," commented the Guschinow lawyer, Maître Archevegue.

"Intelligence is a matter of comparison," said Petiot quickly, earning chuckles from his listeners.

Well then, Archevegue went on, what about these vaccinations and inoculations for a trip to Argentina?

Once more the scorn dripped from Petiot's tones:

"That is stupid. There are no rules in Argentina requiring vacci-nations and certainly not inoculations. All that stuff about my giving injections is so much newspaper talk."

But Mme. Guschinow had testified that her husband told her "Petiot is taking care of everything" and that he was worried only about the injection the doctor told him he must have. . . .

Petiot broke into this: "I had been giving him injections for a year. Why should he be worried? The witness is lying!"

Here the judge himself stumbled into a booby trap. "The wit-ness made her statement under oath," said he.

"No, your honor," Petiot shot back. "The witness was not sworn in!" For the first time in the trial the judge seemed to lose control of his temper. His face turned deep red and he clenched the side of the box, apparently ready to explode with anger. Floriot quickly raised his right hand and stood up to forestall the explosion. Gently, apologetically, he told the judge:

"Mme. Guschinow was not sworn in because she is an interested party in this trial—one of the civil witnesses with a claim for damages." The judge subsided. Score one more half point for Petiot.

On the handwriting of the missing people, which experts had said indicated the writer had been bewitched or bedeviled, Petiot was firm. Nothing strange about it at all. Normal handwriting of a sick man on the day after a long trip. But Mme. Guschinow insisted she had never seen any of the letters Petiot was supposed to have received from Buenos Aires. On the contrary, Petiot declared, he had given her several of the letters. Furthermore, he demanded of Mme. Guschinow and the entire courtroom, had any of Guschinow's clothing or jewelry ever been found at 21 rue Le Sueur? No! Well then what?

"But the suitcase," Mme. Guschinow put in. "The one he had bought especially for the trip. That was there."

"But," said Petiot, "I told you about that myself. The suitcase was too heavy. A passenger could not pass through three frontiers with any such load as that. I persuaded Guschinow to exchange the suitcase for a lighter one. . . . And incidentally," he went on quickly, "why did not Mme. Guschinow leave with her husband when I offered to take both, or refuse to join him when he sent back word for her to come?" He seemed to be hinting that Mme. Guschinow had a boy friend.

"My health . . ." Mme. Guschinow explained weakly. "My business . . ." "My doctor . . ."

With the lady now apparently in retreat, Petiot pushed his advantage. Did she know what the disease was her husband was being treated for, what injections he was getting? Had Guschinow ever told her? The broad implication was that it was, of course, a venereal disease—another good reason for her to want her husband far away. Petiot had no chance to follow up this attack, however, for the judge decided they must be getting on with the trial. Otherwise, he sighed, we will be here until July! But one fact had not been wiped off the slate or explained away. Guschinow *did* have over three million francs in cash and jewels with him when he left—not to mention some furs he had turned over to Petiot for relay to Buenos Aires through the Argentine Embassy.

Guschinow's partner, Jean Gouedo, now explained that he had helped Guschinow prepare for his trip. He had seen the contents of the suitcase: jewelry, pearls, watches, the cash, including $2,000 in American currency. And his partner had taken five of the most valuable sable skins to sell in Argentina. Not at all, said Petiot. Those had been a gift to Georgette, Petiot's wife, in gratitude for all Petiot had done. (Not mentioned was the million-franc fur collection turned over to Petiot for relay to Argentina.)

And now Floriot was ready to come back to the point of the failure to make any investigation in Buenos Aires. It would have been "elementary" to have shown pictures of Guschinow to hotel employees! Some of the employees would certainly have recognized him. And the state had not done this? How sad!

"Cheap tricks to impress or influence the jury!" the prosecutor cried. Floriot had plenty of chance to request or suggest this at the examination before the trial. Why had he not done so?

Floriot raised his own voice to a shout: "No one is dead and no one has disappeared!"

No one? With all those bodies, those arms and legs, that human hair, that burning skull, men and women who had never been seen again? The ludicrousness of Floriot's remark struck spectators, jury, judge, and attorneys, even the usually solemn court attendants, all at the same moment, and there was a concerted outburst of laughter. Floriot was staggered to silence by the unexpected effect of his remark. He had not meant it that way! When the room quieted down, Floriot, his voice lowered now, went on in an apologetic tone. "No one is dead nor has anyone disappeared in the *Guschinow* affair. You [pointing to the prosecutor, Dupin] must first make an investigation in Argentina and at least verify the fact that Guschinow is missing there."

It was after this setback that Floriot returned quickly to the Hotin case to rack up some quick points and to remind the jury that there was never any direct evidence against Petiot.

Witnesses on the disappearance of this young lady were heard: Mme. Mouron, whose eighty-year-old mother, Mme. Mallard, had helped and sheltered Denise at their home when she was sick with a "lung congestion."

"Are you sure it was a lung congestion and not an abortion that was involved?"

"Positively not an abortion . . . you can well imagine that at eighty my mother was not going to serve as a midwife." With this finally out of the way, M. Cadoret was called. It had been he, with Mme. Cadoret and their son, who had met Petiot through Robert Malfet and Eriane Kahan. He was an interior decorator, his wife a psychiatrist. . . . He told the story of how Mme. Cadoret had been first shocked by Dr. Petiot's strange but expert knowledge about the strong hallucinatory drug peyote, now known as mescaline. Also of how Mme. Cadoret had been repelled by Petiot's dirty hands, and particularly by his intense interest in money, which did not seem at all natural for someone involved in the Resistance. Then his talk of injections and false papers did not ring true.

"We decided not to go," said M. Cadoret. "Later we escaped through another underground route. When we came back to Paris after the liberation we found we were listed as victims at 21 rue Le Sueur."

Floriot first questioned M. Cadoret about Mme. Kahan. Yes, the witness admitted, she seemed to have many friends among the Germans and seemed to be recognized by German soldiers. Petiot asked Cadoret what price had been quoted him for his escape. Did he not get his money back? M. Cadoret agreed that it had been returned, all 50,000 francs.

"I had a long conversation with Kahan about this," Petiot interrupted. "Don't you recall being asked for ninety thousand francs?"

The witness did not remember that amount.

"This is very important," said Petiot earnestly. "It is what saved your life!"

But the courtroom did not grasp what Petiot was driving at. Their hisses drowned out his voice and it was several moments before he could explain. "When Cadoret said it cost too much I knew he was not an agent or a plant for the Gestapo, even if he was connected with Kahan. Before that I had believed he was. From then on it was I who refused to arrange his escape or have him come to rue Le Sueur to be liquidated by my Fly Tox group." Having offered what he apparently felt was a convincing and complete explanation, Petiot then addressed M. Cadoret in an almost intimate manner, inclining his head graciously. "And how is

Mme. Cadoret?" he inquired blandly. "I hope we will have the pleasure of seeing her here at the trial." If Cadoret shuddered at this remark, he did not show it. He left the stand without any reply.

The next witness was a former patient of Petiot's whom Petiot had saved from deportation to Germany as a slave laborer. Petiot had given him a certificate stating that he had syphilis. And was this not a false certificate? Petiot inquired. The witness, Jean Scarella, maître d'hôtel at a restaurant, smiled wryly.

"I certainly hope so," said he. But he went on then to explain that after saving him from deportation, Petiot tried to persuade him to escape to America but told him he would have to bring "one hundred thousand francs and some jewelry" and "to bring his wife too, because she will bother me by asking for news about you."

"I was all for leaving," said Scarella, "but my wife did not want to go."

Judge Leser then excused the witness and thus ended the first full week of the Petiot trial.

CHAPTER XII

Second week of Petiot trial
March 26–31, 1946

Tuesday, March 26, was the eighth day of the trial. It ushered in its second week and presented its very special features. It was the day of the technical experts—the doctors, coroners, anatomy experts, psychiatrists, psychologists, and graphologists. The prospect of gruesome details of dissection and possible torture ensured full attendance at the Palais de Justice and brought the usual long, patient lines of the curious who waited for hours before the doors were opened.

The star today was the most famous medical witness in all of France, perhaps in all of Europe, Dr. Paul, who had been featured in many previous murder trials, most notably that of Lover Landru. This was the romantic murderer with a faithful wife and a loving mistress and glorified by many books, plays, and two class A movies, a George Sanders presentation and the Charlie Chaplin (*Monsieur Verdoux*) version.

This time Dr. Paul could provide nothing conclusive, for, unlike the Landru case after World War I, there was no diary or any bits of flesh or bone that could be ascribed to any individual known to have disappeared in Paris during the period of Petiot's activities. Not a single victim was ever identified, only assumed to be a victim because they were missing. Dr. Paul could not even provide specific dates for the killings nor could he describe the methods used to do the victims in. Perhaps human progress between two world wars was too much for the Paris coroner. He provided nothing more than suppositions based on condition of the flesh and the similarity of the method used in dissection. He could only say with assurance that all the remains had been human. This, too, was the conclusion of his associate, Professor Clavelin, of the Museum. But could he then say how many bodies had been found at number 21? Not exactly . . . Only that there were at least ten, probably thirteen, but perhaps as many as fifteen. But there was such a very great amount of hair that undoubtedly there had been many more victims there or elsewhere. . . . The fire and lime and the Paris sewer and the Seine River might account for many more! Years later, in retrospect, Dr. Paul claimed there could well have been twenty or thirty at rue Le Sueur!

"And of all this hair," Floriot inquired, "was there any that was white?"—there being several white-haired people among the alleged victims of Petiot. "No," the coroner granted, "not one scrap of white hair." Still he was able to offer some conclusions about the people whose parts had been gathered up and brought to him:

"There was probably an equal number of men and women. The largest man was exactly one meter eighty centimeters tall [five feet, eleven inches]. There was positively no fractured skull, no bullet wounds, nor any signs of stabbings, no broken bones from beatings. Nor could any trace of poison be found." That left, of course, death by poison gas or by suffocation. Or what about death by an injection or by a hypodermic?

The doctor laughed. "Perhaps," he said. "But I am not in the habit of gargling or choking on conjectures."

The doctor was, however, also able to affirm definitely that the cutting up of the bodies had been the work of a skilled technician with a complete knowledge of anatomy. Many of the bodies found in the Seine during the "Petiot period," he affirmed, bore surgical marks resembling, in workmanship, those found on the bodies at rue Le Sueur. There had been an actual "stuffing of the Seine" with bodies and parts of bodies during the Occupation. Many of them seemed to show the same characteristic marks as those taken from rue Le Sueur. A medical doctor undoubtedly cut up those bodies. "And I am horribly afraid," Dr. Paul added, "that it may have been one of my former pupils. I recognize one of my teachings—that when you want to change instruments or take a rest or a smoke, to prevent an accident you should just plunge your scalpel into the nearest thigh of a cadaver. Most of the unidentified bodies, both from the Seine and from rue Le Sueur, all with their heads severed, showed scars where a scalpel had been plunged into the right thigh—almost proving that the dissector was right-handed." All *identified* bodies (which were far more numerous) found in the Seine, if dismembered (and very few were), had no similarity in expert carving technique.

But Petiot, Floriot pointed out to the witness, had had neither practice nor actual instruction in dissection as a medical student.

"That astonishes me," said Dr. Paul innocently. "He did a superior job of dissection without that advantage."

This answer astonished Floriot and unsettled him for a moment.

"I beg your pardon, sir!" he exclaimed. "You mean that the *dissector*—not Dr. Petiot—was excellent in the art of dissection."

Dr. Paul accepted this correction with a self-satisfied grin. He was obviously pleased at having put one over on the crafty defense counsel.

There were other medical experts, including M. Grippon, director of the Toxicological Laboratory of the Paris police. He agreed there had been no trace of poison but asserted that this was no proof that the victims did *not* die from poison. He suggested, too, that they might have been killed by the use of gas in the triangular room at number 21. The room was not, Floriot reminded him, hermetically sealed. A mere piece of cloth over the space under the entrance door, Grippon replied, could have turned the room into an acceptable gas chamber. And what kind of gas? a juror inquired. Any kind, Grippon said, except illuminating gas. There was no gas connection in or near the house on rue Le Sueur. But in Petiot's home at 66 rue Caumartin a large store of drugs had been found, including narcotics worth an unbelievable cash sum. And there were many empty narcotics bottles found at 21 rue Le Sueur.

But had he found a single bottle of poison at Petiot's office? Floriot demanded. Grippon gave an unexpected reply: "Yes, lots of morphine which, given in large doses, is fatal."

"So is water!" Petiot interjected, scoring one more small point.

The psychiatrists came next. Their findings were well known. Petiot was sane but morally deficient. Dr. Genil-Perrin asserted that the board definitely believed, after examining the accused,

that he was fully responsible for his actions. Dr. Gouriou emphasized that the board of experts had found Petiot to be a "dishonest and perverted character . . . a faker and malingerer . . . not a
crazed monster, only a sinner with a very deficient moral education." As for his medical education, Gouriou had made a study of
Petiot's record in medical school. "He had an average mark for
dissection." This drew further laughter from the audience, who
had found the sparring match with the experts amusing from the
start, with both sides excelling in repartee. Gouriou, who seemed
very antagonistic toward Petiot, continued, "The only extraordinary mark on Petiot's record was 'superior' for his thesis but this
is not unusual, for a thesis can be bought. I have every reason to
believe that Petiot did not really author his thesis." No mention
was made either by these experts or by defense counsel of Dr.
Cesare Lombroso's "genius paranoiac."

Floriot did not fail to point out that one of these same experts
had found Petiot insane years earlier for appropriating some gasoline as mayor of Villeneuve and now found just the opposite. And
had they not, Floriot inquired, been struck by the behavior of Petiot's sister? The doctor (a psychiatrist) responded thoughtlessly
that Petiot's sister showed no sign whatever of mental weakness.
Floriot's eyes, behind his glinting glasses, seemed to acquire fresh
sparkle.

"How sad!" he said. "Petiot had no sister!"

This brought a roar of laughter and undoubtedly helped persuade both Floriot and his client that they had the opposition on
the verge of rout. Next in line were the handwriting experts and
Floriot found them easy meat. Yet their testimony was damaging
for they underlined the points already made about the repetitive
pattern of the notes from Petiot's victims and the probability that
the notes had been written under duress. And was it really possible then, Floriot wanted to know, that they could tell when the
writer of a note was expressing his true thoughts? Yes, indeed.
Floriot, meanwhile, had been scribbling something on paper. He
now thrust the paper upon the expert.

"Then tell me," he urged, "if what I have written corresponds
to my private conviction." The expert looked at the paper and
declined to answer. The audience broke into loud laughter and

Floriot sat back, beaming again. He had written that the graphologist was "a great servant who never makes mistakes."

These points all having been added to the score, the prosecution might have been rated far behind. But there were witnesses on the way who, without clever repartee or legerdemain, would strike some staggering blows for the state. First came the French military intelligence expert, Jacques Yonnet, known also under his code name as "Lieutenant Ybarne," who had set the handwriting experts on the trail of Petiot with the help of Floriot, who had handed over Petiot's letter in answer to Yonnet's accusations in his newspaper. The handwriting had been compared with all possible F.F.I. officers in Paris and thus found Captain Valéry, alias Dr. Wetterwald. Yonnet told the story of that search and added some conclusions of his own, based on his own acknowledged and extensive experience in the underground: There was no "Fly Tox" or anything like it. Petiot never knew Cumuleau at all. Petiot was never a member of the "Rainbow" group. All he had done was pick up enough of the underground jargon and superficial details of resistance activities while he was in jail to enable him to spin a fairly convincing yarn. And his release by the Gestapo, after the payment of a trifling bribe by his brother, was more than suspicious. Had there been any ground for even suspecting he was a resistant, he'd have been shot—and quickly. On the contrary, his release proved he worked with the Germans somehow—somewhere!

These comments drove Petiot into a blind rage and he shouted profane denials. Promptly, Veron, with the enemy aroused, jumped into the fray himself, for he too was an acknowledged hero of the underground. He addressed his questions to Petiot:

"You have said you killed thirty-three agents or plants of the Gestapo and thirty German soldiers for a total of sixty-three liquidations. You also told us how you made two Germans disappear in June 1940. Now tell us about the twenty-seven others."

Petiot offered no reply but insults and curses. He was almost inarticulate with anger. He finally calmed down enough to say:

"I cannot explain any details of murders for which I am not even charged." Nor would he offer any explanation of why the Germans released him. It had not yet, apparently, occurred to anyone, not even to Floriot, who consistently refused even to question his client's sanity, that perhaps the Gestapo let him go because Petiot had made them believe he was a harmless but perhaps useful lunatic.

Next came Lieutenant Brette (code name "Brouard," another underground intelligence officer), who had confirmed what Yonnet had offered. The session then came to a close. It was 7 P.M.

By this time nearly everyone who had attended the trial was convinced of Petiot's guilt. But there were those who questioned the fairness of the trial. And nearly all, even the newspapermen, were bemused by the persistent mysteries. Still nobody had been identified and one victim in the indictment was even unnamed! No exact dates had been supplied for the killings, nor any cause of death assigned. Not one body of any single victim had been identified! And still there was no clue as to what had become of the mountain of treasure—the cash, the jewelry, the furs. Nothing had been found. Petiot, all agreed, was a devoted, loving, and unselfish husband, father, and brother, bent on keeping his family from harm and on building their security. But in every other way it seemed that he evidently could be as bloodthirsty as a raging beast—a caged curiosity worthy of exhibition. A human vampire, measuring five feet, eleven inches and weighing 165 pounds. And yet many believed he was a violent French Communist patriot turned into a mad dog by the cruelty of two world conflicts. Why was his highly competent attorney avoiding the only obvious defense—that of insanity? Did he have the spoils and was he setting up his own client?

The attraction at the ninth session was the scheduled appearance of the accomplices, the scouts who had rounded up clients for Petiot and steered them into his hands. There was the roly-poly hairdresser, Raoul Fourrier, at whose shop the victims first met Petiot. There was the comic creature with the prominent Adam's apple, stage-named Francinet, actually René Pintard, the motion-picture make-up man. There was Albert Neuhausen, who had been asked to hide the more than forty suitcases transported to Auxerre from 21 rue Le Sueur. There was Roland Porchon, too, a man who had been close to the Germans and who had obviously made many more introductions to Petiot than he was ready to admit or were ever brought out at the trial. And finally there was the family: Petiot's brother Maurice, who talked himself right into the shadow of the guillotine, and Petiot's wife, Georgette, who may have known everything or may have known nothing. Of course, in all fairness, they could both have easily been led to believe that the liquidations were part of the war, just patriotic and dangerous deeds of which they needed to understand no details.

Fourrier took the stand, seemingly afraid for his life. He would admit nothing except that Petiot had asked him to help find people who wanted to escape from the Boches. It was Francinet who did all the recruiting.

Francinet had underground connections and found clients quickly. The first was M. Jo—Jo Jo the Boxer. He sent a gangster friend and a girl to try out the route ahead of him. Fourrier looked anything but the conspirator on the stand, frightened, hesitant, with a rather kindly face. When the questions grew too pointed he would offer a standard excuse for knowing so little: "I was arrested with Petiot by the Germans and released with him eight months later." The lawyers for the victims all assailed him with questions designed to show that their clients had had no connection with the Germans. But Fourrier merely grew confused and managed to confuse his listeners. There were some clients who had definitely had connections with the Germans and some who had not had.

Francinet offered little more. He had known certain people from having met them in bars and night clubs. Yes, he had introduced Jo Jo ("the Boxer") and Pierischi ("Zé") and Estebeteguy ("the Basque") to Fourrier. He had made no effort to investigate their fates. He had been shown a letter by Fourrier in which Jo Jo reported his safe arrival in Buenos Aires. Petiot had admitted forging this note, but it is doubtful if he realized how devastating an admission that was. Safe arrival outside of Nazi-occupied France was a standard feature of the letters he did *not* admit to forging. Would the jury add the two opposite claims?

Both Francinet and Fourrier insisted that they took no commission, indeed made not a sou through these introductions. Probably no one believed them. They unquestionably believed they were helping people escape from the common enemy.

Francinet, too, was overwhelmed with questions by the lawyers in the civil suits and he did no more than Fourrier to lessen the confusion.

But now came the man who may well have set the seal of doom on Petiot. It was René Nezondet, the Villeneuve friend of Petiot's young bachelorhood, the man for whom Petiot had found a job when he turned up broke during the Occupation; the man who went to Fresnes prison when Petiot did; the man who had come to Petiot's home the night of his arrest bringing theater tickets for the family. While they were in jail together, Nezondet testified, Petiot had told him: "When you are released, tell my wife I love her and tell her to go—she knows where—and dig up she knows what." Here was the first breath of something many in the court had begun to ponder on—the hiding away of the treasure. But there was no more. Many, including members of the Petiot family, wondered if Maître Floriot had the spoils hidden away or had been told where they were hidden by Petiot toward an assurance of his fee. It was established again that upon the arrest of Petiot and Nezondet, the suitcases had been spirited away from rue Le Sueur and taken to Courson, where Mme. Petiot was reported to have visited and apparently had looked over their contents.

After his release, Nezondet testified—and on this testimony, even though it was hearsay, the whole case may well have pivoted —that Maurice Petiot, in December 1943, when his brother had been jailed by the German Gestapo, had been very late for an appointment with him and arrived greatly disturbed. When queried by Nezondet, he explained that he had seen things in the basement of 21 rue Le Sueur that could get them all shot by the Germans. "I found some sixty bodies and my brother's record of their identifications and my brother's notes on the secret of a poison hypodermic syringe. There were many Germans with their uniforms, no doubt Nazi deserters. I burned their uniforms and destroyed their identification tags." Nezondet claimed he had told Maurice that he would report the matter to the police when the war was over or when the Germans were out of Paris. Here was the closest thing the trial had provided to any direct connection between any killings with Dr. Petiot and 21 rue Le Sueur. It may have resolved the last doubt in the minds of the jurors, for Nezondet was sincere, straightforward, and seemed to have no private ax to grind. Yet the German uniforms would support Petiot's claim of being a great patriot. Brother Maurice, who followed him and flatly denied every detail of Nezondet's story, was surly, combat-

The mobile guillotine of the French government being dismantled in the yard of the Prison de la Sante, reportedly after the execution of Dr. Petiot. Time: 6:30 A.M., May 24, 1946. In normal times the portable guillotine is sent to various towns when needed. Courtesy of the Prison de la Sante and the Paris Police.

Photograph of the skull of "The Great Liquidator of the Occupation."
Although his skull was found, the $14 million Petiot treasure is still
unfound.

Beginning of first page and close of last page of eight-page handwritten "letter to the editor," sent via mail by Petiot to his counsel, René Floriot, who turned the letter over, including the return address, to the editor (who was working with the Paris police), thereby fingering Petiot in his successful aliases and his location and which led to his immediate arrest. Note official Paris police seal.

Paris Bluebeard Called 'Demon' By Two Jurors

Term Guillotine 'Too Swift'; Judge, in Office, Says He 'Is a Terrifying Monster'

From the Herald Tribune Bureau
Copyright, 1946, New York Tribune Inc.

PARIS, March 19.—Dr. Marcel Petiot, charged with the murder of twenty-six persons, was described today as an "intelligent madman" and a "demon" by the judge ad members of the jury, as the second session of his trial opened at the Palace of Justice.

Presiding Judge Marcel Leser and two of the seven jurors voiced their conviction of Petiot's guilt just before the session began.

"He is a terrifying monster, an appalling murderer," the judge exclaimed in his office. The jurors, lingering in the sun-drenched courtyard before entering the gloomy trial chamber, declared: "He is guilty, and the guillotine is too swift for such a monster."

Petiot, again taking a verbal battering from the prosecutor and attorneys for the families of his alleged victims, was a much calmer figure after a last-minute conference with his attorney, Rene Floriot, in which he was obviously warned to avoid the outbursts that had marked the first day's session.

Under questioning from Judge Leser, Petiot described at length his position as leader of the "Flytox" resistance group. He told a jeering court how he had killed two Germans with a secret weapon and for the first time named one of his victims—Adrien Estebeguy, known as "Adrien the Basque."

Prosecutor Pierre Dupin again tried to drag from Petiot the names of his resistance conspirators. "Give me names, give me names," he chanted.

"I will give you names when I am acquitted," Petiot replied. "I have great confidence in the jury, and when they acquit me, you will have your names."

Speaking in a conversational tone Petiot told how he and his resistance comrades" lurked near Gestapo headquarters during the German occupation and singled out French stool pigeons for vengeance.

"When we had selected our

man," he said, "four of us would grab him and say we were German police. Then we would load the Boche agent into a car or small truck and take him to a convenient place like the Forest of Marly."

There, Petiot said, they questioned their victims as to their complicity with the Germans Then they shot them and buried the bodies in a hidden ravine.

Petiot insisted he himself had killed only two men, both Germans In each case, he said, he used his secret weapon, which made no noise and could be used with impunity in the middle of a crowded Paris street.

At this point, Pierre Veron, attorney for the family of Yvon Dreyfus, one of the victims shouted: "How could you possibly have killed two German motor cyclists without any one ever remembering anything about it?"

"I will not answer you," Petiot screamed. "You are a double agent."

"I'll smash your face," Veron shouted back.

It was indicated yesterday that the defense will seek to establish that Dreyfus had dealings with the Gestapo and thus was marked for death by the "Flytox" group.

As Petiot subsided, trembling Veron made one last thrust. "You yourself," he cried, "are sullying the name of the glorious resistance." A storm of applause greeted his words.

Continuing his story, Petiot told how he finally was arrested by the Germans and thrown into Fresnes Prison. "They hung me up by my jaws," the swarthy doctor said "They twisted my fingers. They filed down my teeth, and finally they gave me the electric bathtub treatment."

Petiot gave the court an involved explanation of how his "underground railroad" smuggled Jews and other fugitives from the Nazis into the free zone of France thence into Spain and to Argentina. The prosecution asserts that his victims, some of whom were found in the furnace of his Rue le Sueur home, included fifteen Jews who had paid him large sums on the promise of a voyage to freedom.

Belgium Bars U. N. O. Blo

BRUSSELS, March 19 (UP)— Premier Paul-Henri Spaak, in his inaugural address before the Chamber of Deputies, said today that Belgium will refrain from joining any political bloc directed against any member of the United Nations.

IS, March 19.—Dr. Marcel Petiot, charged
the murder of twenty-six persons, was
cribed today as an "intelligent madman"
a "demon" by the judge ad (sic) members
he jury, as the second session of his trial
ned at the Palace of Justice.
residing Judge Marcel Leser and two of the
n jurors voiced their conviction of Petiot's
just before the session began.
He is a terrifying monster, an appalling
derer," the judge exclaimed in his office.
urors, lingering in the sun-drenched court-
before entering the gloomy trial chamber,
ared: "He is guilty, and the guillotine is too
for such a monster."
etiot, again taking a verbal battering from
prosecutor and attorneys for the families of
alleged victims, was a much calmer figure
a last-minute conference with his attor-
Rene Floriot, in which he was obviously
ed to avoid the outbursts that had marked
rst day's session.
der questioning from Judge Leser, Petiot
ribed at length his position as leader of
Fly Tox" resistance group. He told a jeer-
ourt how he had killed two Germans with
cret weapon and for the first time named
f his victims—Adrien Estebeteguy, known
drien the Basque."
secutor Pierre Dupin again tried to drag
Petiot the names of his resistance con-
ors. "Give me the names, give me
s," he chanted.
will give you names when I am acquitted,"
replied. "I have great confidence in the
and when they acquit me, you will have
ames."
aking in a conversational tone, Petiot
ow he and his "resistance comrades"
near Gestapo headquarters during the
an occupation and singled out French
pigeons for vengeance.
hen we had selected our man," he said,
of us would grab him and say we were

German police. Then we would load the Boche
agent into a car or small truck and take him to
a convenient place like the Forest of Marly."

There, Petiot said, they questioned their victims as to their complicity with the Germans.
Then they shot them and buried the bodies in a
hidden ravine.

Petiot insisted he himself had killed only two
men, both Germans. In each case, he said, he
used his secret weapon, which made no noise
and could be used with impunity in the middle
of a crowded Paris street.

At this point, Pierre Veron, attorney for the
family of Yvon Dreyfus, one of the victims,
shouted: "How could you possibly have killed
two German motorcyclists (sic) without any one
ever remembering anything about it?"

"I will not answer you," Petiot screamed.
"You are a double agent."

"I'll smash your face," Veron shouted back.

It was indicated yesterday that the defense
will seek to establish that Dreyfus had dealings
with the Gestapo and thus was marked for
death by the "Fly Tox" group.

As Petiot subsided, trembling, Veron made
one last thrust. "You yourself," he cried, "are
sullying the name of the glorious resistance."
A storm of applause greeted his words.

Continuing his story, Petiot told how he
finally was arrested by the Germans and thrown
into French Prison. "They hung me up by my
jaws," the swarthy doctor said. "They twisted
my fingers. They filed down my teeth, and
finally they gave me the electric bathtub treatment."

Petiot gave the court an involved explanation
of how his "underground railroad" smuggled
Jews and other fugitives from the Nazis into the
free zone of France, thence into Spain and to
Argentina. The prosecution asserts that his victims, some of whom were found in the furnace
of his rue Le Sueur home, included fifteen
Jews who had paid him large sums on the
promise of a voyage to freedom.

A view of the Petiot trial. Judge Leser ; a police officer in the witness box; Petiot speaks to the judge.

Jailed and incarcerated in special camps:		Convicted to death but pardoned:	
Police Prefet	1	Retired without pension	658
General Directors	4	Retired with pension	48
Directors	5	Revoked with pension	21
Deputy Directors	2	Retired	34
Division Chiefs or Commissioners	6		
Commissioners of Arrondissement or Head of Spec. Serv.	22		
Neighborhood Commissioners	13	Total punished	1,732
Suburb Commissioners	10	Total tried before Commissioner of Epuration	2,760
	63 total		
		(date: August 1944)	

Suspended—not jailed:

Directors	6
Deputy Directors	3
Division Commissioners	8
Commissioners of Paris suburb	22
	39 total

Convicted to death:

Director General	1
Director	1
Police Commissioner	1
Police Commissioners without trial	2
	5 total

THE NEW YORK TIMES.

RENE FLORIOT, 73, CRIMINAL LAWYER

Defender, With 3 Executions in 52-Year Career, Dies

Special to The New York Times

PARIS, Dec. 22—René Floriot, France's most famous criminal lawyer, died of a heart attack last night at the American Hospital in the suburb of Neuilly. He was 73 years old.

Mr. Floriot, who began practicing here in 1923, was credited with a spectacular score of three executions of clients in the many thousands of cases that he handled during his 52-year career.

One of the three executions was that of Dr. Marcel Petiot, the mass murderer of 24. During the German occupation in World War II, Dr. Petiot lured Jews to his house with the promise of smuggling them out of the country, then killed them, burned them in his oven and kept their jewels and money.

Mr. Floriot's first success came in 1936 with the acquittal of two brothers accused of having stolen 20 million francs in a train robbery. Barely a week later, a road accident in which the brothers were involved led to the discovery that they had indeed committed the crime.

Aided Mussolini's Mistress

Other cases included the defense of Magda Fontanges, a mistress of Benito Mussolini who shot and wounded the French Ambassador in Rome, whom she thought responsible for her having fallen in disfavor with the Italian dictator. Mr. Floriot got her off with a year's prison sentence.

After the Liberation, Mr. Floriot defended Otto Abetz, Hitler's deputy in France. Abetz escaped the death sentence and was given 20 years at hard labor.

On the other hand, Mr. Floriot failed to save the life of Jean Luchaire, a leading newspaper publisher who had collaborated with the Germans and who was executed for high treason.

Mr. Floriot was counsel for the defense of two Paris officials involved in the Ben Barka affair, the kidnapping and presumed murder of the Moroccan left-wing leader Mehdi Ben Barka here a decade ago.

He was sometimes accused of defending "just anybody," but he would answer that he was "always on the side of the victim."

His Weapon was Logic

The lawyer, a powerfully built man with a leonine head who wore horn-rimmed glasses, was credited with having revolutionized his profession. Up until the 30's, most French lawyers were rhetoricians who relied on moving judge and jury by appealing to their emotions. Not so M. Floriot, whose delivery was low key because his weapon was pure logic. A compulsive worker, he would spend all the requisite time to study a case, and then had it studied by an increasing number of assistants, each of whom specialized in a legal discipline.

Mr. Floriot wrote books on famous trials in French history, on pleading, on the legal aspects of crime under German occupation, on judicial error and on cases in which he was involved.

He was a bachelor, and his single hobby was African safaris. He was a commander of the French Legion of Honor.

One of the three executions was that of Dr. Marcel Petiot, the mass murderer of 24. During the German occupation in World War II, Dr. Petiot lured Jews to his house with the promise of smuggling them out of the country, then killed them, burned them in his oven and kept their jewels and money.

Obituary of Dr. Petiot's counsel twenty-nine years later in the United States claiming twenty-four Petiot convictions in lieu of twenty-six.

ive, and an admitted liar. Besides, he might well have been in on the conspiracy—his help with the lime and with the suitcases, the unexplained manner in which his own wealth greatly increased!

Nezondet and Maurice were brought face to face in the courtroom and neither yielded an inch. Nezondet heard what he had heard. Maurice insisted his brother was a brave resistant, liquidating the enemies of France. But then why the lies? And why persist in them until he had to face witnesses who had evidence he could not deny? He seemed to many as guilty as the doctor himself and there were many who could not understand the failure to prosecute Maurice. Maître Veron, for one, practically denounced Maurice as a fellow conspirator of his brother. Nothing, nothing would force from Maurice a word that would damage Marcel. The ties that bound the Petiot family together were beyond the powers of this earth to break or weaken. To the end, Maurice stubbornly insisted: "I never saw any bodies or anything unusual at 21 rue Le Sueur."

He transported the lime because his brother asked him and for the purpose of cleaning the place. He removed the suitcases after hearing of his brother's arrest, to prevent the Germans from using them as evidence against his brother. He believed his brother to be a very brave resistant liquidating the enemies of France.

Roland Porchon, who came next, seemed as unsavory a character as had so far been produced. He had grown rich in a trucking concern that did much business with the Germans during the Occupation. He had had connections with the Todt organization, with the Service Otto, and with Masuy. He had been a rag man, a garbage collector, had a police record, and looked, according to at least one who saw him then, "like a gangster." He identified himself as "an industrialist."

Porchon had known Petiot from his days at Villeneuve. He had directed some people to Petiot, including a couple named Marie. Marie was next on the stand. He had been ready to leave but became suspicious "when Petiot told me that if I took only five hundred thousand francs, it would not go far and that I should certainly take all my fortune . . ." But Petiot, asked if he had meant to liquidate this couple, only looked bewildered. He could not apparently establish any quick connection between the Maries and the Gestapo or any Germans.

"I do not recognize this gentleman," he murmured. "I never had anything to do with him. What has this got to do with my trial?"

As pointed out most effectively by a Paris newspaper columnist, on this same day and at this same time, while Petiot was defending himself and the Maries testified, von Ribbentrop was being cross-examined by the Nuremberg Tribunal and unearthed further evidence against Hitler, Himmler, and Bormann (who in the end served Stalin)—all of whom, like Petiot, were responsible for mass murder. As Petiot laughingly remarked, attending the Nuremberg trials were representatives of Stalin responsible for the murder of millions and the Katyn massacre.

But now came three witnesses to support René Nezondet's testimony—his girl friend, Mme. Lesage, her friend, Marie Turpault, who had once been a patient of Dr. Petiot, and a neighbor, Mme. Octavie Lombre. Mme. Lesage testified that she had been present when Nezondet told Georgette Petiot about the bodies at number 21. Georgette, said Mme. Lesage, who was a trained nurse, had pretended to faint several times. She was sure it had all been pretense, and that the revelation had been no real surprise to Georgette at all. Of course, she, like Maurice, may well have thought the doctor was killing Germans. They testified too, as Porchon had testified, that the Paris police seemed unable to proceed against Petiot because of the interference of the Germans. They knew about Petiot well enough and knew what was going on at number 21 but found that Petiot was protected by one or more German sources—most probably the French Gestapo—the rue Lauriston group of Lafont and Bonny, or the Abwehr and Masuy of avenue Henri Martin, or both . . . perhaps for a cut in his profits, perhaps as a double espionage agent.

Of interest to the audience and jurors, too, was Mme. Lesage's later claim that she had saved Nezondet from himself becoming a victim of Petiot when the doctor had urged Nezondet to come there after Petiot had been released from Fresnes by the Germans and after hearing that his brother had told Nezondet about the bodies. She had a presentiment of danger, she averred, and she would not let René go.

Mme. Lombre and Mme. Turpault supported Mme. Lesage's

story based on conversations they had overheard between Nezondet and Lesage at the time.

The civil parties' attorneys of course were then turned loose on
all these witnesses. One of the few effective questions asked was
asked of Maurice Petiot. "Were you not surprised to find that in
all those suitcases and among all the clothing that you hid for
your brother or that he had at 21 rue Le Sueur there was not a
single German uniform or Gestapo identification card?" Contrary
to his alleged statement to Nezondet on this score, he had nothing to say.

But in most cases the lawyers seeking damages for the deceased
managed to confound each other and utterly confuse the courtroom with their involved and repetitious questioning. At one
point, when the questioning had grown particularly involved, Petiot stood up in his box and took his head in both hands.

"The further this trial goes," he moaned, "the more confusing
it becomes."

"*Voilà*," said Judge Leser. And the whole courtroom dissolved
in good-natured laughter. The judge motioned Petiot back into
his seat. Immediately thereafter he ended the confusion by recess-
ing the court for the day at this relaxed and amusing point.

On the tenth day (March 28), Eriane Kahan herself was to be
the star, and again the spectators waited avidly for the door to
open. This was better than a circus, for each performance offered
a new attraction. And this lady, often referred to as the "Rumanian Redhead," had been long sought for and long awaited. Was
she indeed a Gestapo agent then? If this could be proved, perhaps
Petiot would have a chance after all. But if she was not an agent
of the Germans—even if she was a prostitute or the next thing to
it, an adventuress, or a grasping and greedy opportunist who lured
people into Petiot's hands for profit—that could be the end of the
last hope for Petiot. His whole defense seemed based on showing
that, because this lady was a German Gestapo agent, all the Jews,
both men and women, who had come to Petiot had been either
collaborators or Gestapo plants trying to discover and apprehend
his underground escape apparatus.

Mme. Eriane Kahan made a striking appearance. She wore a
well-fitted and beautifully tailored suit that was the ultimate in
fashion—wide lapels from waist to neck, trimmed with otter fur.

A matching toque of otter fur was set at a saucy angle on the back of her head. A jabot of silk was fastened with an oval broach. Her hair, all waves and curls that burst out luxuriantly from under her hat, was an amazing color—not red, not pink, but a sort of rose, as if both blond dye and red dye had been used on it. Her face was rather heavily made up, almost as if for the stage, and dark sunglasses gave her the appearance of a movie star. She looked, to many who saw her that day, like Greta Garbo. Her face was not that of a murderess or an adventuress. It was pretty and gentle, with a soft and passionate mouth. She kept crossing and uncrossing her shapely legs. She was a woman, one would say, in her middle thirties. The whole courtroom gasped in astonishment and admiration when she gave her age as fifty. Her voice was deep, even guttural—but very sexy. Her eyes were shielded by the dark glasses because they had been giving her trouble.

She, too, she told the court, had been a victim of Petiot, not an ally at all. A Jew in Paris, under the Germans, she had hidden out with friends on rue Pasquier. Dr. St. Pierre, her doctor—who was also her former lover—had introduced her to Petiot, not as Petiot but as "Dr. Eugène." Indeed she had never known his true name until after the charnel house had been discovered and his picture had appeared in the papers. Her only motive had been to help people escape from the Nazis. The Baston couple, for instance. They had thought of Petiot as a god. "Just think," they had said to her, "a Frenchman coming to the aid of foreign Jews and risking his life for them without even knowing them!" As she told this, Eriane Kahan looked Petiot directly in the face. Her deep voice trembled with anger.

"The Bastons were very nice people," she declared. "Everyone liked them. They were not only anti-Nazi but they were fleeing for their lives from the Germans."

She, herself, she told the court, had begged Dr. Eugène to help her escape too. But he had urged her to stay and help him, for she was "doing important work." He would get her away in time. In fact, she would go when he himself escaped.

But why then, if she was innocent, had she gone into hiding?

"I am Jewish," Eriane Kahan repeated. "I felt that I was doubly wanted by the German Occupation authorities. So I hid. I thought of notifying the authorities but Maître Floriot advised me not to do anything."

Maître Floriot smiled, a tight-lipped smile. He would have his innings soon.

"I have papers to prove I am a loyal Frenchwoman and an active member of the Resistance," Mme. Kahan declared. Was everyone at the trial then either a resistant or a Gestapo agent or a double agent or someone who changed sides as did the Communists? But Mme. Kahan made her declaration firmly and most people in the courtroom probably believed her. The prosecuting attorney declared that "all information on Mme. Kahan was favorable." All information? But the police report named her a liar and an adventuress. Did the prosecution then have certificates to show she was a member of the Resistance? Floriot seemed ready to drive home the sword. He turned to Mme. Kahan.

"Did you ever collect money for the travelers you introduced to Petiot?"

"No," said the lady flatly. There was plenty of evidence in police files to show that none of the scouts had gone unrewarded. Yet every last one of them had testified he or she had never received a sou. (Years later, many finally admitted, in interviews for this book, that they not only received commissions but were given valuable articles from time to time by Petiot—gifts, said the doctor, from grateful escapees.)

And now as to Mme. Kahan's relations with the Germans, from whom she had been "hiding" at rue Pasquier. Was not her boy friend, her lover, a member of the German Air Force?

"He was not a German, he was an Austrian," said Mme. Kahan with a touch of indignation.

"So was Hitler!" Petiot cried. And the spectators laughed appreciatively. Floriot smiled approval at his client and counted one more good stroke for his side. "And did not Mme. Kahan's landlady, Mme. Goux, sometimes entertain German soldiers?" "Yes?" "And this was the house where she was acting as a resistant and staying out of the way of the Germans?"

Promptly, M. Dupin, the prosecutor, came to the rescue. The prosecution, he declared, had just received a "new" file on Mme. Kahan from Inspector Poirier of the police indicating that he, Poirier, had "testified incorrectly" on certain details involving the lady. Floriot was irritated. How could there be a "new" file? There was only one file. Things could be altered suddenly this way. Dupin, himself angered now, declared that Floriot was overstepping the limits of his proper role.

"I am your adversary," said Floriot.

"Yes, but your position is without honor. . . ."

That was not the thing to say to Floriot. He was especially gunshy because of the numerous rich Germans and collaborators he had defended. Everyone knew he was money-crazy and all of his Nazi clients paid fortunes to him. He blazed with anger and seemed about to pitch into Dupin in a man-to-man encounter. Judge Leser hastily leaned forward and, in a fatherly tone, tried to get Floriot to explain himself further. Floriot demanded the right to reply first to Dupin. Dupin quickly asked for a short adjournment.

"That is too easy a way out!" Floriot shouted.

Nevertheless, Judge Leser declared a short recess and Eriane Kahan had several minutes in which to regain her composure. After the recess Dupin apologized to Floriot for any personal remarks that might have injured his feelings. Floriot continued the examination then, pressing Kahan to give details of her relationship with the Occupation authorities.

Yes, she admitted, she had visited Gestapo headquarters in German cars. Yes, she had been greeted on the street, it was true, by German soldiers. But only because her Austrian boy friend was among them. Beyond that Floriot extracted nothing of importance although he badgered her through sixty-two single-space pages of small, typewritten testimony*—about fees quoted to the Cadorets (75,000 francs, she said, raised from 50,000), about her "property assets in Italy" (her sister and brother-in-law had been furnishing her with a regular allowance from Italy, she said, which

---

* Actual minutes of the trial used as part of this book were obtained in a most unusual but legitimate manner by the author with help from the former German Occupation authorities and before seizure by the French Government of all Petiot records. Access to the official records of the public trial, usually available in a democracy, was requested through the U.S. Embassy by the author three times but according to the official answer will not be accessible to the public until 1996—fifty years after the trial according to an old French law, so the minutes obtained shortly after the trial by unofficial means would seem the only possible record available.

was verified by this court). She also received occasional checks
from a Dutch boy friend. Floriot subjected her to every possible insult and innuendo—so much so that years later (1966) Maître
Veron, in an interview with the author, stated that Mme. Kahan
had been subjected to very unsportsmanlike—if not shameful—
treatment.

Dupin broke in on the testimony at one point to assert that
there was a French intelligence file to prove that information
Eriane had secured from her Luftwaffe boy friend and other
sources had proved of sufficient importance in several instances to
be sent by clandestine radio to England. But Floriot had already
sprung a major surprise by quoting a "file" of his own—a file in
the possession of the Paris police he said that definitely proved
Kahan was a traitor and collaborator. It was file number 16582, he
said, and had been completed on April 3, 1945. The judge
promptly ordered the prosecutor to secure that file. It was not produced until the final day of the trial and it showed no such evidence as Floriot had set forth. The failure of this bomb to explode did not condemn Petiot, for by then he had been hopelessly
enmeshed in his own contradictions and hasty improvisations, and
it did not help to clear Mme. Kahan or to make her testimony
valuable. Floriot had very cunningly raised considerable doubts
about Kahan's character based on two definite misstatements that
she was either trapped or knowingly convinced to make. First, she
asserted that she never expected or collected a commission on the
fees paid by the travelers. Second, she maintained that she did not
hide out after the liberation. No one on the jury or in the courtroom believed her on either of these issues. Definite evidence had
established the contrary. Could she also have been playing both
sides, as many did . . . the Gestapo included? Or could her
relations with the Germans have been based only on a love affair
with a Nazi Air Force sergeant?

When the aggressive and heartless cross-examination of Eriane
Kahan was finished, it did leave some blemishes on her testimony.
It had been shown she had lied when she said she had not gone
into hiding after the liberation. And the presumption of guilt in
her close association with Germans was still strong. This was the
Petiot strategy and that of his defense counsel not only with
Eriane Kahan but with every prosecution witness—to put the wit-

ness on trial and make him defend himself against charges of collaboration with the enemy. But throughout the long examination
Petiot had been brooding on a matter that had been passed over
long before—a reference to his dirty hands!

"Supposing I did have dirty hands, as mentioned by a witness. I
did not dirty them by raising them to take an oath of allegiance to
Pétain!"

This direct thrust at the judge as a collaborator brought a quick
flush to his face.

"I will not permit you to be insolent," he said to Petiot.

"To whom?" Petiot inquired bitingly. "To Pétain?"

"You know very well," the judge said, trying to retain his calm,
"that all magistrates and judges had to take an oath to Vichy
under unusual circumstances." The judge then excused Mme.
Kahan from the stand.

After Kahan came a whole group of well-meaning ladies. Mmes.
Gang, Chalet, Moulier, and Goux. (Mme. Gingold, responsible
for the whole chain, may or may not have appeared but she left
Paris shortly after and took every possible means to avoid ever
being connected in a story where she innocently had been the central figure involved in the mass murder of nine persons.) All these
witnesses testified, unequivocally, that the three Wolffs, two
Baches, two Anspachs, and two Stevens could not possibly have
been agents or plants of the Gestapo but, on the contrary, were
innocent Jews fleeing for their lives from the Germans.

As seen in retrospect, all of these witnesses agreed that it was
the moneys and jewelry that the travelers were carrying on their
persons that were the only passport to 21 rue Le Sueur.

Then came Charles Beretta, the *mouton* who had led Dr. Petiot into the hands of the Gestapo. To assail his character and
prove his connection with the Germans would be no task at all.
He had been brought down under guard from Fresnes, the same
prison in which Petiot had been held by the Germans. Beretta
was held on a charge of "intelligence with the enemy"—i.e., treason. He was a witness because of his proximity to the disappearance of Yvan Dreyfus, possibly Petiot's last victim at 21 rue
Le Sueur, but certainly the last of the twenty-seven victims he
was being tried for. Beretta tried to be down to earth and
straightforward as he told his tale. He had no interest in Petiot or

the Petiot trial or in Yvan Dreyfus. He saw merely a chance to plead his own case at length before the public. He was rather well dressed in clothes of a conservative cut and he might have made a strong impression on the court but for his slurred and slangy speech, interspersed with four-letter words. He was no match at all for Floriot, who quickly exposed his duplicity and wrung out confessions of his work with the Gestapo. Finally, poor Beretta, harried past hope, turned to the courtroom and spread his hands:

"I was caught in the middle!" he cried.

Floriot, savoring his easy victory, nodded in sympathy. "Don't exhaust yourself *mon vieux* or worry too much. We understand."

Beretta stepped down and Petiot's side seemed to have made another gain. But Petiot was not rejoicing. Suddenly the spectators, who had been concentrating on Beretta, realized that Petiot had put his head in his arms again and was silently weeping. Why? Had the appearance of this man reminded him of the one stupid misstep that brought about his exposure? If he had only avoided Beretta's trap, had sensed the duplicity of the man— would there have been any smoke at number 21, any discovery of the charnel house, any flight, any disguises, any contradictory stories, only a number of unidentified bodies in the Seine and a fortune hidden away to await better days? Or was he crying because he realized for the first time that traitors and collaborationists like Beretta would finally be freed and pardoned while he faced the guillotine for killing people he sincerely believed were the enemies of France?

Guelin appeared, too, also a prisoner from Fresnes under guard, and, like Beretta, he had come to plead his own case. He also was charged with treason. He was an articulate man, a former lawyer, an able administrator, but, breathless at this priceless chance to justify himself in front of a crowd of his countrymen, he simply talked too much and too long. His listeners wearied, they lost his points, they could not follow his arguments, they merely wished him to be still. He had been a great resistant! He had, even in his capacity as theater director, had his performers sing "*La Marseillaise*" in front of four hundred SS storm troopers! It was only because he considered Dreyfus a loyal Frenchman that he had agreed to help. He had been intent on saving the life of Dreyfus although admitting he had planned to divide the ransom with his friend, the German Gestapo chief.

"I have looked forward to the opportunity every day I have been in jail," he pleaded, "to come and explain my actions before French justice. . . . I beg you let me tell my story and I beg you to listen to it."

But Petiot, back in control of himself and ready to fight, stood up and pointed an accusing finger. "You are a traitor and you served the Germans and you know it!"

Guelin, seemingly stricken with terror and remorse, now began to weep as he told his story, the big tears falling unchecked down his face. But the sharp questioning of Floriot angered him and put a sudden end to his sobbing. He turned quickly on his attacker:

"You are a lawyer for the collaborators and for the traitors and for the Germans!" he cried.

"That is why you asked me to be your counsel!" Floriot shouted.

Guelin blazed right back at him:

"Your place will not always be as a lawyer and as a nonviolator of the law!"

This show of anger was no help to Guelin. Mercilessly, and with the aid of his assistants, who kept passing papers to him precisely when needed, Floriot cut Guelin to pieces. He brought out that he had an identification card as a German Occupation official, a permit to carry firearms, a Gestapo membership identification card that gave him not only authority but protection and co-operation from the German police. Guelin denied it all but his cause was hopeless. Petiot's case was forgotten and another prosecution witness was convicted of collaboration. The audience got one wry chuckle out of this testimony when Guelin explained that Mme. Dreyfus had paid three and a half million francs in gold for her husband's release and that he, in turn, had supplied Dreyfus with 150,000 paper francs to use as his fee for Petiot. Every Frenchman could see the irony there, as every Frenchman to this day knows the difference between gold and paper. There were a few half-admiring snickers at the gall of Guelin in raising his price several times over. Of course Petiot and his scouts had also raised the passage price of travelers, depending on the wealth of the clients, from 25,000 to 150,000 francs per person without considering the residual or ancillary profits collected at 21 rue Le Sueur.

Police Officer Pehu, the other intermediary in the Dreyfus case, did not take the stand until the start of the eleventh day. He too seemed intent largely on justifying himself. He did have one good mark to start with: He had been discharged by the Vichy Government for "nonconforming." But Floriot soon convicted this man too, showing that reports by Pehu had been submitted to the Gestapo. When Pehu tried to deny this, Petiot once more stood up in the role of Avenging Angel and pointed a finger at the witness. Solemnly and positively he declared: "This Pehu is the man who broke my nose with his fist at the Gestapo headquarters at rue des Saussaies."

There were more witnesses now to testify to the innocence of Dreyfus, which suddenly seemed more of an issue than the innocence of Petiot. Floriot endeavored to confound them all, but he could not eliminate the circumstantial evidence that would not be downed. Dreyfus, with Petiot, had, after all, eluded the tails the Gestapo had placed on them. How could that be explained, unless Dreyfus had told Petiot of his role and the two had co-operated to accomplish a real escape? The contradictions of Petiot were there for all to read and Maître Veron did not fail to point a finger at them. Petiot at one point said that he had left Dreyfus alive and well in an upstairs room at number 21. At another time he said that Dreyfus had been killed by "my associates" and good riddance to him. He had also testified that he never knew what happened to him.

Nearly everyone in the courtroom was deeply affected by the appearance of Mme. Dreyfus, Yvan's widow, a frail girl in black who spoke in a calm and steady voice but with eyes red from weeping. She made a striking appearance in a black veil that fell from the black toque to below her chin. A white blouse and single strand of pearls added to the almost masculine severity of her dress. Her shoulder-length hair was set in tight curls around her small hat but fell in gentle waves.

Quietly she told the whole story of the dealings with the various intermediaries and the manner in which the requests for money accelerated. She described her own horror at learning what kind of agreement her husband had been forced to sign. She had first thought the release was to have been without conditions. She had made the final payments into Guelin's hand outside Fouquet's. There were many wet eyes in the courtroom as she told of her meeting with her husband: "We were to leave together but Guelin told me one last formality at the rue des Saussaies was necessary, for my husband had no papers. He went the next day and I never saw him again."

Floriot brought her very close to fainting with the questions he posed, designed to create at least a small amount of doubt in the minds of the jurors. He asked first if her husband had suitcases when he left. No, Paulette Dreyfus replied weakly, Guelin was to take care of all of that. And were there not two letters of agreement—one to not take up arms against the Germans, and another? Yes, there were two. Then what was the other agreement?

Mme. Dreyfus was deathly pale and seemed about to break down. But she took a firm hold on herself and replied: "To give or find out information on a resistant organization involved in the escape of persons from Occupied France."

The Dreyfus story within the Petiot case was, as all others, confused. The eleventh day of the trial added no startling facts or testimony proving or disproving Petiot's guilt. As a proven collaborator of sorts in connection with his written agreements, according to the law of war, Dreyfus was fair game for Petiot. To make the story ironic was the fact that if 3,500,000 francs (about $80,000) had not been paid by his wife as ransom, Dreyfus might have survived the German camps and the war. Even past that point, if Dreyfus had followed his agreement with the Germans he would have lived and caused the arrest of Petiot. But, because he was a true patriot, he must have told Petiot that he was an unwilling plant and they were being tailed and thus earned his place in the triangular room.

After Mme. Dreyfus came Fernand Lavie, son of Mme. Khait, and another client of Maître Veron, who was now trying to establish the civil claims or damages of his clients, namely, for the murders of Yvan Dreyfus and Mme. Khait. Here there was another small triumph for Petiot. Lavie went over the whole story of his half sister's and his mother's dealings with Petiot, of his half sister being a dope addict, of the tampered prescription and Petiot's threatened arrest . . . the blank injections, the accusations, the appointment that took his mother out of the house and from which she never returned. There was a discussion once more of the letters, purportedly from Mme. Khait, and clearly designed to clear Petiot of blame. Lavie had seen the van Bever letters, too, and had thought they and his mother's letters had all been written by the same hand.

Floriot, when his turn came to question the witness, seemed to play with fire for a moment for he asked what had become of Mr. Khait, the witness's stepfather. As Khait had been arrested by the Germans immediately after screaming threats at Petiot, and never heard from thereafter, this did not seem good tactics. It might remind the jury of the probable connection between Petiot and the Germans. Nevertheless, Floriot asked Lavie if his stepfather still lived. "I don't know," said Lavie.

Floriot then brought out the great confusion in dates that seemed to indicate Mme. Khait had been seen alive by several people long after she was supposed to have disappeared. He managed to suggest, too, that she had affairs with other men that might have made it convenient for her to abandon her husband without warning. With all these doubts well planted in the minds of his listeners, Floriot struck his strongest blow. And where was the real principal in this matter, Lavie's half sister—Raymonde Baudet? Why was she not present to bear out these stories?

M. Dupin, caught off guard, could not conceal his embarrassment.

"Is she not at Poitiers?"

Lavie, still on the stand, replied: "I am without news from her. All I know is she is not in the city."

Dupin offered lamely: "She must know she is expected here at the trial in the Cour d'Assises de La Seine and that her presence would be most welcome."

Floriot, beaming as if he had just been handed a bagful of bank notes, said nothing. He did not need to. But he did not have the final word in this matter. That belonged to Maître Veron, who reminded Floriot: ". . . you will perhaps have eliminated two reasons why your client should not be given the death sentence. But twenty-five other reasons will be left."

With the completion of the eleventh day of the trial, the press made public note of the fact that Petiot's guilt no longer seemed the issue. The prosecution witnesses had all been put in the position of pleading their own innocence and most of the testimony concerned the behavior during the Occupation of these men and women who had been summoned to bear witness against Petiot. Had they been collaborators or patriots, resistants, or mere opportunists? Floriot's tactics of accusing every witness and blackening his character had gotten the whole trial off the track, and no one, except the spectators, seemed concerned with the means used to kill the victims ascribed to Petiot, the dates of the killings, the identity of the dead, or the possibility that any might still be alive. There had been missing persons enough in Paris that might be traceable to Petiot for well over twenty-seven more murder charges that had no connection with the ones now at issue. Yet the court steered clear of pressing any direct inquiry into the details of the crimes themselves. Petiot had admitted some of the killings but his stories of how he had disposed of the bodies were flimsy and incomplete. No one, however, chose to delve more deeply. The defense still unbelievably refused to plead him insane.

On the twelfth day, Mme. Braunberger took the stand to testify on the disappearance of her husband. She had to admit at once to the long delay (almost three months) in reporting his disappearance. And she confessed that she had never charged Petiot with murder until a shirt and hat she identified as her husband's had been listed among the items removed from 21 rue Le Sueur. The shirt and hat were taken from the glass case in the courtroom and identified by the witness. Petiot was questioned about them. He refused to answer. Judge Leser grew angry.

"I give you the definite order to answer that question!" he told Petiot, leaning over the bench toward the defendant.

"I will answer that question," Petiot replied calmly, "after the other witnesses in this affair have been heard."

Mr. Perles, the lawyer for Mme. Braunberger, protested: "That will give you time to think up an answer."

Judge Leser grew more sharp. "Petiot!" he snapped. "I again order you to answer that question."

"I have already told you," said Petiot, "I will answer in half an hour. *Mon Dieu*, I am not going to go away before then. How can I?"

What neither the judge nor the unwary lawyer realized was that Petiot this time had a real bomb to drop. He would explode it when the time was ripe. And so the recital went on—the story of the early phone call, the trip to L'Étoile Métro station, and the letters—plenty of letters. Raymond Vallée told of the letters he received and of his mystification that Braunberger should know about 21 rue Le Sueur. Petiot at this point, fuming with rage, began to revile his wife's cousin. But Judge Leser managed to quiet the row and get on with the questioning.

The servants of the Braunberger household told their stories and also identified the shirt and hat. After that Petiot was ready for his carefully planned maneuver. He spoke with all the conviction, logic, and appeal that won him two elections as mayor of Villeneuve.

"There is no possible reason for me to have liquidated this old man," he asserted. The old man, he pointed out, had neither money nor jewels and was hardly the victim a kidnaper would choose. As for the shirt, the police identification bureau indicated that the initials removed from the shirt were probably not P.B. at all, and that it could not have been worn by a person who was killed. Nor did collar and cuffs jibe with the style and size favored by the doctor. When all these points had been made, Petiot scornfully flung the shirt into the very face of the clerk of the court.

"Therefore," he concluded, "do not talk about this shirt anymore. And that should end the Braunberger matter!"

The judge himself was so stunned by the performance that he immediately declared a short recess, perhaps to reassess his own attitudes.

During the intermission the guards led Petiot into a small anteroom and there he was promptly surrounded by autograph seekers, some having bought copies of the book *Le Hasard Vaincu* outside the building and some bringing pictures of Petiot to be signed. Petiot accommodated them all, with graciousness and endless patience. Even Judge Leser received his own copy of *Le Ha-*

sard Vaincu, complete with autograph on the title page which read:

> *Very sympathetically*
> *To Judge Leser*
> *Marcel Petiot*

After the intermission, the Kneller case was gone over again with all the witnesses who had received notes and postcards from the Knellers telling their stories. But only M. Jorin had saved one of his letters and had hung on to some of the Knellers' jewels. Petiot made no effort to refute any of this testimony. He stuck to his story that he had helped the Knellers escape, had turned them over to a professional *passeur* and had last seen them all alive and well.

Then Mr. Stafanaggi, the attorney for the family of Joseph Piereschi, known as "Zé," interrupted to ask Petiot a question out of the blue—a question that had been raised before:

"Why were you released from Fresnes by the Germans and under what circumstances?"

Fresh from his small triumph, half believing he was about to win his case, Petiot was out of patience. Trembling and white with rage, he replied: "I do not admit your insinuations based on your unfair and cowardly efforts to blacken my character. On Monday you will hear from my cellmate at Fresnes."

But lawyers in the other civil suits would not let up. Mr. Charles Henry of Marseille, attorney for Paulette Grippay's family (she was the one known as "La Chinoise"), made a direct attack on Petiot. In his thick South of France accent, which some in the courtroom could hardly understand, Henry vowed that he himself would prefer charges against Petiot for intelligence with the enemy (treason), that such charges would take precedence over any murder charges and would require his being tried on those charges first.

The other civil parties' lawyers took the same stance, in one way or another, asking why the Gestapo had been so quick to let Petiot go free when he might, more logically, had he been a true patriot, been shot or shipped to a concentration camp. Petiot ultimately answered them all at once in a voice that rang in every ear:

"I was tortured by the Gestapo but I never talked. You lawyers of the alleged victims, you are acting very poorly in attacking me at the last moment. In other words, you are all bastards!"

In practically perfect unison, the lawyers for the civil parties all replied with the same word: "Thanks!"

And Petiot, who would never yield up the last word if he had breath left, shouted back: "You are entirely welcome!"

Whereupon Judge Leser wearily announced the recess of the trial until Monday morning and in a voice hardly louder than a whisper wished all his associates and the jury a good rest over Sunday.

The trial had now run two weeks. There was one week more. On Monday, April 1, by coincidence April Fools' Day, the defense would start. The case for the prosecution had been presented. However, as usual with everything connected with Petiot, it was incomplete and full of mysteries and unanswered questions.

To the police the prosecution's case was startlingly short of additional specifications, each representing another murder Petiot might well have committed but where there was no proof, not even the thin connection of any meeting with Dr. Petiot or Dr. Eugène or his scouts or the finding of some article of clothing belonging to the missing and possibly murdered person . . . and, of course, not a single identified body!

First there was Mme. Eugénie Carroue, born Dumont, reported a victim of Petiot's by the newspapers and the police. She was reported missing by Eva, her daughter, on March 9, 1943. They lived together at the Hôtel d'Amboise near the Opéra Comique. After a short trip to the country the daughter did not find her mother at home nor did the daughter ever hear from her mother again. Every possible attempt was made by the police to connect the disappearance of Mme. Carroue—and a box of jewelry and gold coins she possessed—with Dr. Petiot but without success. Mme. Carroue was well-to-do.

Then a Mr. Franz Teulings reported to the police the disappearance of two brothers, the Van Geldens, Dutch Jews who escaped from Holland one jump ahead of the Germans. They came to Paris to try to escape to America. One of the brothers had taken the name of Karl van Klaveren so when shirts were found at 21 rue Le Sueur with the initials K.K. (also for Kurt Kneller), Mr. Teulings was certain that the brothers' plan to escape to America terminated in the triangular room. The Van Gelden brothers, like Mme. Carroue, were never heard from or seen again.

An anonymous letter to the Paris police began an all-out search for a Pole named Leon Potarjnikoff, a friend of a Mme. Mireille Pointeau. This man arrived in Paris just after the war started. The police found evidence that he had been in Marseille in 1942 but left on October 22, 1942. Both Potarjnikoff and Mme. Pointeau were at one time patients of Dr. Petiot. Although Mme. Pointeau tried to identify some article left at 21 rue Le Sueur as belonging to her friend, none was found. Mme. Pointeau claimed her friend Leon had some faultless Siberian emeralds but neither the Pole nor the Siberian emeralds were ever found. The police, on the one hand, and Petiot's interrogations, on the other, did not produce any clue to support any charge.

Then Lechopier, the friend of Petiot who had frequently taken suitcases for Petiot to various addresses he later did not remember, added to the police search. Yes, he had sent to Dr. Petiot a Polish Jew, Samuel Blatt, that he had met in the Melun jail. Blatt was never found although there was no other evidence to connect his disappearance to Petiot.

It is important to remember, however, that Petiot, in admitting to sixty-three victims in court under oath during his trial or confidentially referring to some 150 to Dr. Paul, used the term "liquidations," which was consistent with the theory of his defense that right or wrong he had executed persons he believed were traitors or enemies of France.

Where the prosecution's case was weakest was in the unanswered questions. Where was the Petiot treasure, conservatively estimated at $14 million in jewelry, cash, gold, and furs? How had the Petiot family acquired fifty-one real estate holdings worth millions? Who wrote the victims' letters? What mysterious influence did he wield with the Occupation authorities, with the French Gestapo, with the Abwehr, and with Masuy? Why was he released by the Germans on payment of no more than a token ransom? What were the subject and nature of his two long interviews with Masuy of the Abwehr while a prisoner of the rival Gestapo? How many suitcases had *really* been taken from 21 rue Le Sueur as against the number taken to Courson? Where did Petiot acquire the fortune in narcotics found in his office by the police?

Who destroyed the records of his first narcotics trials? Was this, too, an instance of German interference on his behalf? Why did not the French police, after Petiot had been freed by the Germans, follow up their investigation of the disappearance of van Bever and Mme. Khait?

Petiot, of course, both in his relayed conversations and in his relayed notes, was as mysterious and contradictory as was his career and life. For instance, in his notes and at his trial he more than intimated that he had killed Lombard, who was found alive many years later, and he also once claimed killing a prominent German secret agent, Oscar Heisserer, whose head was mailed to General von Stülpnagel, the German commandant of Paris. Yet much later, after the liberation, the killing of Heisserer was found to be the work of a well-known resistant and had no possible connection with Petiot. The remainder of the body of Heisserer was later recovered by the Paris police but immediately collected by German authorities from the Paris morgue. The dissection of the body was not even done by a practicing butcher much less by the skilled surgeon of the Seine River and rue Le Sueur cadavers.

CHAPTER XIII

Third week of Petiot trial
April 1–7, 1946

Monday, April 1, marked the first day when there was no great crowd waiting for the opening of the Petiot trial at the Palais de Justice. It was the day when the parade of defense witnesses began. In a trial like that of Petiot's one might expect the appearance of at least one of the alleged victims very much alive to prove that at least one of the murdered persons had not been done in. The police would even have been pleased if one of the many missing they believed were victims of Petiot . . . but where no evidence had been found to support a charge . . . actually appeared to testify that he or she had escaped from Nazi France via rue Le Sueur but was alive and well. Instead of this, the defense presented only witnesses to testify that Petiot was a good man, a great doctor, an agreeable neighbor, a kind man incapable of murder or cruelty, and a patriotic and anti-Nazi Frenchman.

And the most impressive defense witnesses were to testify that Petiot was unquestionably a gallant resistant who defied the Germans and suffered much in the cause.

That day was also the first true spring day of the year and the first peaceful spring after seven years of war. Paris streets were bathed in the young sun and the new leaves had begun to appear on all the trees. Sidewalk cafés were crowded again and women in bright clothes walked the boulevards. As a result many people stayed away from the trial. Defense witnesses promised no gruesome details, no tears, no shouted denials. All that was left to chill the blood now was the sentence of death which everyone, except perhaps Floriot and Petiot, confidently foresaw. Meanwhile, who

would abandon Paris in the springtime just to attend in a stuffy
and overcrowded courtroom, the making of polite excuses for
murders in series?

Some thirty men and women of all ages and conditions stood
up in court this day to describe Petiot as their doctor, their mayor,
their benefactor, their savior, even their god. There were store-
keepers, mechanics, farmers, and an electrician just back from
Buchenwald, an "honest man" who said he was Petiot's doctor, a
conductor on the Métro, a *modiste*, an artist. Variously, they
attested that Petiot embodied all that was good. "As far as the
plain and humble people of Villeneuve and the workers could see,
'their Dr. Petiot' had been always a loyal Frenchman—one hundred per cent and even two hundred per cent a Frenchman. At
Villeneuve he did nothing but good things!" Someone laughed at
this, thinking no doubt of the maid-mistress who had disappeared
or the thefts that had even been acknowledged. The witness
turned quickly in the direction of the laugh and cried out:

"That makes you laugh, does it? Well, let me tell you that even
today at Villeneuve everyone misses the doctor. The town owes
him a lot—the maternity ward, the prenatal training school for ex-
pectant mothers, the sewerage system."

One worthy gentleman, Mr. Marcel Pothier, insisted under
oath that Petiot's troubles at Villeneuve were the result of a plot
between a drunken competitor who took to the bottle because Petiot was a better doctor and one of Petiot's staff at the city hall
who had also become an alcoholic. One witness was so remarkably
deaf that he could hear nothing the judge shouted at him. "Say I
swear!" the judge would yell, and the poor old man would pull pa-
thetically first at one ear and then at the other and repeat in the
almost toneless sounds of those who cannot hear their own voices:
"I am deaf!" His voice was so faint that he was placed at the rail
just in front of the jury. The press was unable to hear a single
word he uttered.

"It is the professional politicians, many of whom were collaborators," said Mr. Mur, another witness. "They framed Petiot, who
is a complete patriot and not a murderer!"

M. François Comte, a merchant from Villeneuve, testified as to
his long affection and respect for Dr. Petiot, both as his doctor
and as mayor.

In Paris, Petiot had over a thousand patients and many came forward with touching stories. "The good doctor never took money from the poor." "In 1942," a Mrs. Harant testified, "he supplied my sister and two British officers escaping from German imprisonment with false identification papers." "He even helped them escape at the risk of his life." "He was a resistant from the very beginning." "He helped many Jewish families escape from the Gestapo." "He gave out false health disability certificates to save Frenchmen, Jews, and refugees from the Nazis and from deportation to German work camps."

The unquestioned star of the day, the one witness who was convincing, impressive, and ringingly authoritative, was Lieutenant Richard l'Héritier, a cellmate of Petiot's at Fresnes. In the trimly tailored uniform of an officer of the Parachute Corps, the lieutenant wore the Resistance Medal and the Croix de Guerre with two (palms) citations over his top left pocket and parachutist's wings over his top right pocket. He had, he testified, shared a cell with Petiot for five months and had then been deported to Auschwitz but somehow survived and came back. A third habitant of the same cell as he and Petiot had died from beatings and malnutrition when Petiot was there.

L'Héritier was a handsome man, his blue eyes remarkably deep and clear, his face youthful, open, sincere, his clothing freshly laundered and pressed, his hair gleaming with pomade. He gave his testimony in clear, positive tones, without garrulousness or evasion. He first described how he had been dropped by parachute over France from London in 1942 and had been captured by the Germans. His effect on the courtroom was electric. There was not a doubt in his mind about Petiot. He knew the doctor as an authentic, loyal, and all-out resistant. Petiot had told him about his Fly Tox liquidation group long before it was needed as an excuse for murder and had also described the workings of his underground railroad to help persons, and more especially downed Allied pilots and Nazi refugees, get out of Occupied Paris. L'Héritier commended Petiot's intelligence, his knowledge of underground warfare, and, particularly, the excellent advice Petiot gave him on how to avoid talking or giving away any resistance secrets under torture. He told how Petiot had organized a system for getting messages from within the prison to the outside.

"Petiot," he asserted, "actually gave me the code names and addresses of aid stations, hideouts, and cutouts of the Resistance in Paris in case I was able to escape. Unfortunately, I never had the chance to use these for I left Fresnes under heavy guard to be deported to Germany. Dr. Petiot in some of his conversations convinced me of his value as an espionage informer and source of intelligence of great value to the West. In fact, he told me stories of his intelligence reports of great interest to me and with no defensive purpose. There is no question in my mind that if he relayed the intelligence information he told me about it would have been valuable."

"Dr. Petiot," he continued, "was both courageous and witty. His manner of talking to the Germans, even after they beat and tortured him, raised the morale of all the prisoners."

"You spent five months with Petiot," Floriot put in. "Do you believe that during five months under Gestapo imprisonment a man can hide or fake his real feelings or beliefs?"

"I do not believe anyone could be fooled by one's cellmate at the end of five months in a situation like that."

The many lawyers and the judge pressed him in different ways to tell what he truly thought of Petiot and his operations, for here was a true resistant as authentic as Pierre Veron himself.

"My opinion?" l'Héritier replied. "It is, first, that Petiot did not operate alone; second, that Petiot was a man with strong political views and consequently was a resistant, but not necessarily an official resistant and certainly not a resistant with the Western Allies. Third, I believe that his superiors or his party gave him orders which he followed in his own way. Fourth, I believe that any party or organization that admitted to association with Petiot now, as an assassin, would never win any elections. Fifth, I believe that any source of intelligence information or any legitimate receiver of information from Petiot would now deny any contact with Petiot now accused of being a mass murderer. Sixth, I believe that Dr. Petiot might well sacrifice himself for any political or ideological cause he believed in. Last, and most important, and one thing I am certain of, is that he had an intense hatred of the Germans. I know this. I saw it."

When l'Héritier had completed his forthright statement, so full of implications, Petiot arose in his box to address a direct question to his former cellmate:

"Do you think any sensible person could ever accuse me of working with the Gestapo?"

"Absolutely not! I assure you that, no matter what the result of this trial, I will always be proud to have had Dr. Petiot as a cellmate, a compatriot, and friend!"

This portentous comment made it clear to nearly everyone that l'Héritier, like most others in the courtroom, expected the death sentence for Petiot. And while l'Héritier had been careful not to use the word "Communist" at any point, his clear suggestion that Petiot's apparatus was connected with some underground other than that of the Western Allies left no doubt in the mind of even the least perceptive spectator in the room that he believed Petiot had been conducting his liquidation factory—and perhaps his loot-collecting service as well—under the direction of the Communists. More than one person must have asked himself if perhaps the Communists as well as the French and German Gestapo and their gangster minions were not also engaged in robbing the dead and the deported to finance their own activities. Everyone in court also knew that France had been infested during the latter part of the Occupation and the beginning of the liberation by terrorist Communist bands.

After l'Héritier had set these new and alarming doubts afloat, another cellmate of Petiot's, one Jean Courtois, who was also a bona-fide resistant and guerrilla hero whose brother had been killed by the Germans in August 1944, added his assessment of the doctor:

"Petiot was without any question a real resistant and a courageous one. There can be no doubt of this to all who should know, namely, those who were real resistants." (Were Yonnet or Veron then not "real" resistants? It was a question that confused many.)

Still another resistance hero then came forward to add new dimensions of courage to Petiot's record. She was an exceptionally courageous lady herself, a Mme. Germaine Barré, a former dressmaker who, while working for British Secret Intelligence, had successfully infiltrated the German Gestapo to become a secretary in the office of Dr. Yodkum at the Paris Gestapo headquarters at rue des Saussaies. She testified that she had been present when Dr.

Yodkum, a top executive in the Paris Gestapo, asked Petiot for 300,000 francs as the price of his release and she had heard Petiot reply:

"I don't give a damn whether you release me or not. I have stomach cancer and so have not much time to live anyway."

Thereupon, according to Mme. Barré, Yodkum telephoned Petiot's brother (who, it turned out, was the one who *really* had cancer and a short life expectancy) and arranged for a 100,000-franc ransom.

During most of the giving of testimony this day, with old friends and patients, political comrades, sharers of suffering, and distant admirers bringing him tributes, Petiot put his head down again and again and wept continually.

On the next day, which was the fourteenth day of the trial, Paris still bloomed and its boulevards still beckoned, so there were even fewer in attendance than the day before, with empty seats showing for the first time, even in the section that had not been reserved. But there was really no strong attraction on this day either. This was to be the day in which lawyers for the civil parties would try to establish claims against Petiot for murdering their clients. This is an unusual feature of French law. Theirs was a boring, difficult, perhaps even impossible job. In all the trial and investigation there had been only the flimsiest bits of evidence—a hat, a shirt, a child's night clothing—to indicate the possibility, but certainly not to establish beyond any reasonable doubt, that this or that particular person had met his or her death through Petiot's felonies. Yet the lawyers had to strive to make as close a connection as possible between Petiot's activities and the missing client and also to rub the client's reputation clean of all the tarnish Petiot and his attorney had managed to fling, to underline as best they could whatever circumstantial evidence offered that could point to Petiot's guilt in each instance.

This made for repetition, for the belaboring of petty details, for endless scratching of the record to unearth one more bit of corroboration. After all, the connections between the disappearances of the victims and Dr. Petiot were all purely circumstantial. Maître Archevegue for Mrs. Guschinow; Pierre Veron for the Khait family and for the Yvan Dreyfus estate; Claude Perles for Mrs. Braunberger; Maître Stafanaggi for the Piereschi estate—they all, by necessity, wandered over the same ground, pointed in the same direction, and eventually began to put the listeners to sleep. They even put Petiot to sleep as well as his attorney, Floriot. Petiot did come awake from time to time to amuse himself by clever doodling with paper and pencil but, at one point, a photographer was able to catch him and Floriot in slumber and the picture was published with the title "Everybody Sleeps at the Petiot Trial."

Beyond doubt the dreariest moments of the trial came when Mr. Charles Henry, lawyer for the family of Paulette, "La Chinoise," who a few days earlier was going to call into question the jurisdiction of the court, presented a windy and largely irrelevant peroration in an effort, he said, "to cast light on the entire case." Spectators, some of them awakened by the increasing outrage in the speaker's voice, began to call on him openly to be quiet, to sit down, to stay on the issue.

Petiot, finally, unable to restrain the prompting of his cutting wit, stood up, raised his hand, and, with a broad smile, told the judge: "I would like to remind the court that I am not paying for this lawyer's efforts or time!"

For this, Maître Henry turned not on Petiot but on his lawyer and began to berate Floriot in bitter terms. The judge had to request him sharply to "leave Maître Floriot alone." Finally, Maître Henry ran out of words. When he was finally done, the judge could not quite believe that he could have been so consistently irrelevant. With mild sarcasm, Judge Leser inquired: "And what about your client?" Completely missing the sarcasm or even the meaning of the question, Maître Henry assured the judge: "I am finished, your honor. I do not insist on anything further."

After this dreary episode, the courtroom was treated to a sharp, concise, and effective summation by the only woman among the lawyers—Mme. Andrée Dunant, attorney for Gisele Rossmy, one of the gangster girl friends. Her task was simplified by the fact that Petiot had admitted killing Gisele. Without histrionics or any effort to underline the obvious, Mme. Dunant repeated what Petiot himself had said—that he killed the girl because "he did not know what else to do with her." On the basis of this killing alone, Mme. Dunant pointed out quietly, the court could do no less than send Petiot to the guillotine (and assess the Petiot estate for 50,000 francs for Gisele's family).

Yes, the woman attorney in the Petiot circus had certainly succeeded in showing up her male associates acting for the civil parties.

On the fifteenth day of the Petiot trial, crowds once more filled
the courtroom. For, on that day, the prosecuting attorney, Procureur Général M. Dupin, was to at last begin his summing up
for the prosecution and demand Petiot's head. Among the lawyers
still to be heard for the civil parties was Pierre Veron, the resistance hero, who represented the family of Mme. Khait and that of
Yvan Dreyfus. His speech was sure to be bold and bitter, almost
certain to bring a response from Petiot. And it was this baiting of
Petiot, by both Veron and the prosecutor, that promised the spectators a day of excitement.

Mr. Jacques Bernays first made a presentation for the Wolff
family, followed by Mr. Gachkel for the Bache estate. Their main
theme was not directly against Petiot, but was to the effect that
their clients could not have been, as Petiot maintained, agents of
the Gestapo or collaborators but, on the contrary, were Jews
fleeing desperately for their lives. After an intermission, Mr. Lévy-
Lyon introduced himself as representing Lutz Kneller of Bolivia,
brother of Kurt Kneller, who, with his wife and seven-year-old
boy, escaped with Petiot's admitted help from Paris. It will be
recalled that Petiot claimed to have aided their successful escape,
although they were never found. The Knellers had been the last
to be added to the list of Petiot's victims.

"I am certainly an attorney for one of the civil parties arriving
at the very last minute. However, it is also at the last minute for
Petiot. He, like the Germans, succeeded in uniting families, but
uniting them in death."

Then came Veron, the movie hero-like attorney, and he set out
at once to destroy whatever benefit Petiot might have derived
from the undeniably impressive testimony of Lieutenant l'Héritier. Petiot a resistant? He was an imposter! He did not know the
organization, the armament, nor the members of the Resistance.
And as for Yvan Dreyfus, whom Petiot named an agent of the
Gestapo, his record of heroism and loyalty spoke for itself. In this
case, there was duplicity on every side. Yodkum had solicited a
bribe and had kept the lion's share. Of the three and a half million francs put up by the Dreyfus family, only a million, Veron

revealed for the first time, had actually found its way back to Nazi Germany. The rest had been divided among Yodkum, Duqueker, Guelin, Pehu, and even Petiot, who had received the "escape fee" but failed to find any fortune on his dead traveler.

And what of Petiot's explanations? Which was to be believed? He said at one point that he had left Dreyfus at 21 rue Le Sueur "occupying one of the rooms upstairs where he lived in full freedom." More recently, he had said in court that his associates killed Dreyfus "and they did right." No, it seemed clear that Petiot had murdered Dreyfus as he had murdered others, and for the same motive—money or to protect his profitable operation.

Step by step, Veron demonstrated that Petiot's claims to be a resistant were false. He must not, Veron urged, be allowed to hide in the folds of the flag of the Resistance for which 300,000 heroes have died. Veron said:

> It was not for a Petiot, that Gabriel Peri, Brossolette, Colonel Marchal, and many others laid down their lives.
>
> I do not know for sure if Petiot was, in fact, connected with the Gestapo or the Abwehr, but one thing is certain, namely, that the smoke from the chimney of rue Le Sueur will join in the skies of Europe with the smoke that came from the crematories of Auschwitz and the other Nazi camps.
>
> No, Petiot was never connected with the French Resistance and he has placed himself beyond human society. He must be eliminated forever by being condemned to death.
>
> He tried to fool us into believing he was a resistant. We are not that foolish. Death must be his finish!

At this, the spectators broke into the most uproarious applause of the trial. So great was the din that it completely drowned out the shouts of Petiot, who stood in the box, his face contorted with rage, and vilified Veron at the top of his lungs. Veron looked at Petiot and laughed.

"Anything you say is of no consequence," Veron said. "I will, nevertheless, attend your execution."

It was now twenty minutes past five. The spectators were exhilarated, almost breathless for the kill, but it was obvious that Procureur Général Dupin would not be able, in the time remaining, to complete his summing up for the prosecution. The summation for the prosecution was to be handicapped by being split into two parts. Nevertheless, he began with the certainty that he could not finish that day. His presentation lacked the emotion of Veron and the oratory of Floriot but, nonetheless, it was effective for he dealt sincerely and specifically in facts. His tone was calm, his manner direct. The audience did not miss a syllable.

The archives of this court, recorded and preserved for more than a century, do not offer a single example of a case so horrible as the one before us. . . . Twenty-five years ago a trial before this same court established a record in criminal law. It was the Landru case. Landru had killed eleven women, his eleven fiancées. . . . The whole world believed that never again would anyone see or hear about a more nightmarish trial. . . . But everyone was completely wrong, for today Landru has been surpassed!

Yes, to find as many cadavers, to see as much blood, to witness as many killings one must go to the other side of the Rhine . . . to Buchenwald or Auschwitz or Dachau. . . . But today it is not a German who is seated in the box of infamy. It is a Frenchman. . . .

Petiot heard all this apparently without emotion, busily making small marks on his pad of paper. In fact he was sketching a portrait of the prosecutor to have it ready when M. Dupin had completed his talk. But the talk had a long way to go. The prosecutor reviewed Petiot's entire life, characterizing him calmly as "a simulator, an illusionist, an imposter, and a liar." He was not a resistant at all, he said, or anything like it. He was, instead, "a gangster who worked neither for nor against the Resistance. He was indifferent to any side. He played all sides and many roles. He is a criminal and an assassin."

Before M. Dupin could go into the details of Petiot's killings, it was too late to continue and court adjourned until the following day. The court did not have a morning session on April 4, but started at 1 P.M. This was a warm day, but the April sun wooed no one away this time from the Petiot trial. This was the final day, when the sentence of death was to descend upon the accused. How does a man react when he is told he is going to have his head chopped off? It was to discover this that the crowds pushed, even fought, their way into the courtroom until the place held more people than the guards could control. There were, once again, famous men and women from every world—from the theater, the sports arenas, the cafés. And the police, too, in civilian clothes and on their own time, gathered in numbers to see their bugaboo meet his fate.

Petiot, despite the tension, was dignified in the box, even haughty, as he looked out over the audience and waited for M. Dupin to begin to recite the Petiot crimes.

M. Dupin had already covered the long, long list of lies and contradictions that had appeared in the various examinations of Petiot before the trial and in his testimony. He had illustrated once more the revealing pattern of the Petiot notes. Whether they came from doctor to patient or to his wife; from lover to mistress; from housewife to lawyer or husband; from refugees to their families—the notes all sounded alike and made the same point. And, of course, all were crudely identified by the full-name signatures, no matter how intimate the letter might have been. Dupin called attention to the fact that Dr. Braunberger had, strangely enough, signed his letter to his wife "Dr. Braunberger"; that van Bever had signed his letter to his mistress "Jean Marc van Bever."

Now the prosecutor began to sort out the Petiot victims into three groups, according to their origins and the motives for the killings. There were fifteen escaping Jews who had money or other valuables to steal. There were the three witnesses who had to be gotten rid of lest they endanger Petiot's career. Then there were the nine gangsters and collaborators with their mistresses, who brought uncounted—but a great deal of—loot. But cruelest of all the murders and the one in which the multiplicity of circumstantial evidence was so overwhelming as to almost overcome all probable coincidence was the killing of the Kneller family—father, mother, and little boy. No one could hold that Kneller was a collaborator or a Gestapo agent; his record of patriotism spoke for itself. And the clothing found at 21 rue Le Sueur made the connection with Petiot conclusive. There were two women's dresses and a terry-cloth robe along with household linen, all positively identified as having belonged to Mrs. Kneller. There was the shirt with the K.K. monogram, also identified beyond question. And there were the pajamas of little René, made out of one of his father's shirts. There was the appearance in the Seine of the body of a seven-year-old boy at just about the time that René had disappeared. And there was little René's ration card, crudely altered to carry the name of Valéry, found in Petiot's possession at the time of his arrest.

Both in his police interrogations and at his trial, Petiot repeatedly denied liquidating eight of the twenty-seven persons but admitted he killed nineteen enemies of France. "I helped the Knellers, Guschinow, Braunberger, Mme. Khait, van Bever, and Hotin. What happened to them after I introduced them to a 'guide' I don't know."

His general "cover story"—that he was an executioner of Gestapo agents and traitors—could not be stretched to justify the Kneller killings.

M. Dupin then turned to the killing of the couples brought in by Eriane Kahan. "Let us admit," said he, "that Erianc Kahan was a member of the Gestapo."

This remark brought an outcry of both shock and surprise from Mme. Kahan herself, who was seated near the front of the courtroom and had come with all the others to see the end of Petiot. M. Dupin hastened to mollify her:

"This is merely an assumption, because, contrary to the accusations of the defense counsel, Mme. Kahan has never been subject to any charges as a collaborator and has no file, as claimed by the defense."

It was at this point that the prosecutor brought out the fact that the mysterious file—number 16582 referred to by Floriot—had been obtained and that it contained these words: "The authorities hereby certify that Eriane Kahan is not sought under any charge by the Department of Justice." All the same the prosecutor, to be "sportsmanlike," was willing to assume that Mme. Kahan had worked for the Gestapo. But why then, he asked, did Petiot treat her in such a friendly and respectful manner? Why introduce her as his confidential secretary? Why urge her to continue her "important work" when he was killing anyone—men, women, children even—because they "had relations with the Germans" through her?

As he made this point, there was so much commotion in the courtroom that the judge had to recess the court for a few moments while the guards endeavored to restore order. After the interruption, M. Dupin expanded on this theme: If Petiot killed people just because Kahan brought them in, why did he spare Kahan herself? Why invite her to visit him and why visit her?

"No, there is only one thing Petiot considered—namely, that Kahan brought rich clients for him to assassinate and to rob them —nine in the fifteen days from December 15, 1942, to December 30, 1942."

Then Dupin reviewed the Dreyfus case and defended the memory and loyalty of Dreyfus. "Captain Boris, officer hero of the Resistance, had this to say about the letter Dreyfus signed: 'I would have signed far more and made further commitments if I had to get away from the Germans in order to get a chance to fight them!' "

In terminating a review of Petiot's victims he covered the cases of Mme. Hotin, Mrs. Khait, and van Bever where the motive was pure self-preservation. Then he spoke of the group of immoral characters and members of the French Gestapo. But here also Dupin called attention to the fact that the killings were for personal gain and robbery and certainly not for patriotism and involved the murder of five girls who were neither German nor members of the Gestapo.

Despite Petiot's insistence that the bodies found at 21 rue Le Sueur had been planted on him by his enemies, Dupin argued that they all showed unmistakable marks of the hand of the dissector who had handled the many other bodies fished out of the Seine and all ascribed to Petiot. He made it clear, too, that although the state charged Petiot with twenty-seven murders, and Petiot himself had said there had been sixty-three, there were very likely a good many more.

From this theme, Dupin slipped naturally into 21 rue Le Sueur, the Petiot-made factory for murder and the expert cutting up of cadavers found both there and in the Seine. The complete list of the twenty-seven victims involved in the trial was read, although the impression left with the court was that Petiot undoubtedly had successfully liquidated many more.

Finally M. Dupin, despite his own private doubts on this score, reminded the jurors that a board of eminent psychiatrists had found Petiot completely sane and responsible for his acts. Therefore, he concluded: "Your conscience and mine, gentlemen of the court and jury, is protected. Petiot, the great liquidator of the Paris Occupation, the monster of rue Le Sueur, is entirely responsible for his acts. . . . Let justice follow its proper course and let us see that Petiot quickly rejoins his victims."

Just as Dupin made this final statement, Petiot, having at last completed the sketch he had been working on, cried out: "The procurer of the French State!" and held up the portrait. The tense courtroom broke into roaring laughter. Dupin, not at all disconcerted, simply pointed to Petiot and declared: "Believe me, Petiot, the role of name-caller does not suit you." Then Dupin turned around and very calmly sat down while Judge Leser nodded toward Floriot.

René Floriot, the greatest criminal lawyer in France if not in Europe, on April 4, 1946, at 3 P.M. was to present the climax of the Petiot trial, the summary for the defense.

"It took you gentlemen of the prosecution, my adversaries, fifteen hours to prove the guilt of Dr. Petiot. This would indicate his guilt is not so clear or so certain. Please be assured that it will take me far less time to disprove his guilt. All I need to do is to simply rectify a few essentials, especially as this case and trial have been badly twisted around and placed on an improper basis. Twenty-seven disappearances have been blamed on my client. The accused, together with me, denies eight and admits nineteen. If any single one of the eight is proved a victim of my client, I admit defeat. If the nineteen others of the Gestapo were killed, then I may bow my head, but those nineteen were executed in the name of the Resistance and the name of France. Also, I call attention to the fact that unless all twenty-seven cases are proved beyond a reasonable doubt, my client will have to be acquitted."

Floriot then established beyond any doubt that the nineteen missing were gangsters, collaborators, or, in one case, that of Dreyfus, technically at least, a proven plant of the Gestapo to entrap Dr. Petiot's escape railroad. All introduced to Petiot by a person with a close personal relationship with a Nazi and who even visited the Gestapo headquarters in Paris. . . . Floriot then turned toward Veron.

"Dear fellow attorney and patriot, Veron. You have many decorations and credit for being a hero of the Resistance but you cannot possibly exclude Dr. Petiot from the Resistance when you see before you the result and proof of Dr. Petiot's imprisonment and torture by the Gestapo for seven long months."

It was indeed Floriot's turn and all agreed that he spoke magnificently, argued effectively, illustrated lucidly, and drove his points home with great authority. His summing up for the defense started at 3 P.M. But he had to ignore many contradictions, several damning facts, and all sorts of obvious implications. His talk was not a short one, about six and a half hours, yet every ear in the whole courtroom was attentive to his every word. Although his analysis of the evidence was often complicated and his arguments involved, his reasoning was always clear. His prose was polished and his delivery, although at times a touch theatrical, was never anything but sincere. The typewritten text of his summary was 339 pages long and very carefully guarded but to prove the fact that this is written on the basis of Floriot's own summary, each page of the typewritten record contained a left-hand margin of 8.3 millimeters.

Floriot first of all made much of the prejudicial atmosphere of the trial—and certainly none could deny the truth of his charges. The press had seen to it that before he ever appeared in court, Petiot was labeled a monster, a sort of human tarantula, who sucked out of his victims their money and valuables, if not their blood. And yet, said Floriot, had the press seen fit to feature the established fact that Petiot had been allowed on March 11, 1944, as a recognized resistant, to make his escape from 21 rue Le Sueur, after he had delivered himself right into the hands of the Paris police, the entire public attitude toward Petiot might have changed. And, even more important, had the press reported his arrest and torture by the Nazis from May 1943 to January 1944 as a resistant and operator of an escape apparatus for Jews, resistants, and British airmen and enemies of the Reich, Petiot might very easily have been originally transformed in the newspapers into a hero instead of a monster. But the press, originally controlled by the Nazis, instead chose to concentrate on the horrors of rue Le Sueur and tried to link every murder and every newly discovered corpse to the missing owner of the building. The discovery of the suitcases served only to provide the papers with another take-off point for stories on human depravity and wholesale slaughter for robbery. Without the 21 rue Le Sueur fire, possibly contrived by his German enemies to finger Petiot, everybody and every missing person would not have been blamed on Petiot.

Whereupon, once the liberation had been accomplished, and it was possible to learn about the gruesome atrocities the Nazis had perpetrated, the public naturally associated Petiot with the Gestapo monsters. For had he not, like the Gestapo, tortured and murdered his Jewish victims? And the press had made the connection even more direct with their story in *Ce Soir* entitled "Petiot, Agent of the Gestapo" and the story by Yonnet in *La Résistance* with the title "Petiot, Soldier of the Third Reich." Both these were probably full of gross errors. The fact that Petiot himself could lay claim to being a resistant had never been brought forth until Petiot was already on trial and already more than half condemned. Although many people began to see that Petiot did not belong to the Gestapo, no matter what, Petiot had to be prevented from proving that he had ever performed any act for the Resistance. Even the role of an informer or source of intelligence information would embarrass his contacts and the Resistance and, later, the brand-new French Government so it never surfaced.

Floriot then had the task to show that Petiot did *not* have a criminal background, that he could own the building and still not operate a charnel house, and that he was definitely a resistance fighter. Establishing these positive points was perhaps even more fearsome a task than even Floriot had envisioned. It was possible to go back over Petiot's life and present him as the beloved family doctor, the workers' doctor of a small village, the progressive and popular mayor, the former combat soldier who asked to be sent back to the front after he was wounded. And the record might be used to show that he had been a brilliant medical student, a successful doctor and politician, and a dedicated public servant who had often treated the poor without a fee, a man who had made enemies among the influential who had framed him on a theft charge and driven him out of office. In Paris, too, the record could demonstrate that he was both a successful and self-sacrificing doctor. . . . There was only that one flaw—the narcotics charge to which the court lent so little importance as brought out by Floriot that it fined Petiot only 2,400 francs ($60).

But what of the mental troubles in the army? What of the mysterious deaths in Villeneuve? What of the charging of fees and ex-

penses to the village? What of the stolen gasoline? And what
about the witnesses in the "minor" narcotics charges who disappeared and were never seen again? These matters, large and troublesome in the minds of the jurors, were all carefully avoided by
Floriot.

As for 21 rue Le Sueur—yes, Petiot had admitted that the triangular room was sometimes used as a cell. But it was to be an X-ray
room as well. And he had admitted that some of his executions
were performed there. So the décor, said Floriot, is "extraneous."
Persons did indeed visit 21 rue Le Sueur. Were they all murder
victims? Could not other people have committed murders there?

But what of the dissecting of the victims, the expert opinion
that the same hand had dismembered them all? What of the
strangely repetitive letters? What of the human debris found in
the furnace room and elsewhere? Floriot did not answer these
questions, but they remained to weaken his case with his listeners.

To prove Petiot had been a resistant, Floriot and his "boys"
(the French newspapers used the English term "boys" to describe
these assistants) had outdone themselves. There was testimony to
show that Petiot was violently anti-German; that he supplied false
certificates to prevent the arrest or deportation of Frenchmen and
Jews by the Germans; that he acted heroically while a prisoner of
the Germans and was beaten and tortured unmercifully; that he
had contacts with the Resistance and could well have operated
one or several groups of the Resistance that might well have been
unknown in Paris or London. There were, after all, Floriot reminded the court and jury, several types of resistant—official, semi-
official, unofficial, and even unheard of. Floriot meticulously
avoided any mention of Soviet apparatuses or Communist terrorist units not recorded in London or with the Free French.

The entire case boiled down to this, said Floriot: Petiot was accused of twenty-seven killings. He admitted nineteen and pleaded
not guilty to eight. Those in whose killings he admitted having
participated proved to be German collaborators or Gestapo
agents. But Petiot did *not* kill Hotin, van Bever, Khait, the three
Knellers, Guschinow, or Braunberger. If it could be proved beyond a reasonable doubt that Petiot did kill one of those, said Floriot, then Petiot should be convicted. There must have been some
who promptly decided that he must then be found guilty, if only

for the death of the Knellers, which he could neither justify nor explain nor successfully deny. Yet the Knellers, with the Gestapo one step behind them and with the Gestapo visiting their apart ment before their disappearance, could have been executed by the Gestapo after Petiot turned them over to a "guide." The clothes and identification papers could very well have been left at 21 rue Le Sueur. (Why would anyone in their right mind keep the clothes and identification of persons they murdered?)

Floriot made a valiant effort to justify the killing of Jo the Boxer, his friends and their mistresses, but the mere reading of the police records had no great effect, for their villainy had been taken for granted. It was not for that, certainly, that Petiot had rid the earth of them. Nor was Floriot able to prove that all nineteen were active collaborators and that all, including the women, were actually agents or plants of the Gestapo. On the contrary, it seemed clear that the French Gestapo and the German authori- ties were actively hunting for four of them. And in trying to show that the group of "Gestapo plants" was threatening the existence of Petiot, he sometimes acted as if words he had recently spoken could be wiped from a listener's memory. Floriot suddenly de- clared that the Fly Tox organization was an escape agency—not a liquidation apparatus at all. Here the defense crossed itself up, for Petiot had always maintained that Fly Tox was a liquidation ap- paratus and that it, and he, killed Germans and collaborators. Al- most the only "proof" Floriot could offer that these gangsters were involved in a Gestapo plot was that they criss-crossed their mistresses, sending each girl out with a man she did not belong to. (Then why, some jurors may have wondered, did not the other "Gestapo plants"—the three couples introduced by Eriane Kahan —also swap their partners about?)

Nor did Floriot establish the fact that, even being a resistant, Petiot had any right or authority to liquidate those he admitted killing. He could only quote that peculiar French law, created es- pecially for the struggle for liberation and promulgated in Algiers, that was itself of doubtful standing: "There is no crime or felony where the crime or felony has been committed in the interest of France." However, when honest errors had been made it had saved many a killer during the liberation. There was no reason why Petiot could not demand his right to be patriotic.

It was also difficult for Floriot to offer definite proof that *all* of the admitted victims—even the women—Jewish or not, were Gestapo agents. This was more than at least one juror (who talked about it years later) could swallow, and he made up his mind at that point that Petiot must be found guilty.

Floriot and his "boys" were far more successful in taking each alleged murder and showing that, one after the other, they all lacked a clear enough connection to Petiot to establish his guilt beyond a reasonable doubt. In a different time and in perhaps a different country, Floriot's lucid and incontrovertible arguments on this score might have set Petiot free, for it was true that no one had come to court who had either seen a killing nor was there an identified corpse, nor was there one shred of direct evidence that Petiot had killed anyone—even those he admitted liquidating.

All the weak points of the evidence used against Petiot were painstakingly examined. Floriot even recalled the details of the Raymonde Baudet case—the forged prescription—which could certainly not be laid to Petiot, and the lack of any proof at all that Petiot had planned a traffic in narcotics. But by this time the battle was well lost. The holes he had left unfilled and unexplained just would not vanish from the jury's recollection.

He went back, too, to the supposed reappearance of Mme. Khait, twelve to fourteen months after she was supposed to have vanished, and he recounted the story of the assault upon van Bever by the family of a girl friend and told, too, of van Bever's supposed reappearance. Again he emphasized the lack of a corpse in these "murders" or in that of Denise Hotin. In fact, he emphasized that not a single body of any one of the twenty-seven persons had been produced.

There were many other weak spots in prosecution testimony, and Floriot restressed them all: Mme. Guschinow's tale of her husband's "worry" over an injection when he had been getting injections from Petiot every day for weeks; the fact that there was really the guide mentioned by Petiot, a Robert Martinetti, and that the Knellers had no wealth and so could hardly have been prospects for robbery; that the two bits of clothing—the shirt and the pajamas belonging to the Knellers—and little René's ration card—could easily have been left behind; that the Gestapo visited the Kneller apartment before their escape, indicating the family might have been intercepted en route (if so a little boy's body in the Seine found on August 8 could mean he had been killed some time after he left Paris with his family and with a guide); Kneller's having been prosecuted for issuing bad checks had hardly been the act of a wealthy person; that Petiot could not have written the note to M. Jorin because he did not know Jorin; that Dr. Braunberger, too, was without money or jewels or any valuables and left his apartment with "only his doctor's bag and the clothes on his back"; that a German soldier had called at his apartment looking for him; that the hat and shirt "identified" as Braunberger's could not have been worn by him; that the suitcase seals had been broken—who knew when or where; that one suitcase supposedly belonging to Braunberger because it held his clothing also contained Petiot's pipe, his desk blotter, his camera, his flashlight, his diary with professional appointments, and nothing of Braunberger's but his shirt—no vest, no jacket, no trousers.

Floriot's story of the effort to identify the Braunberger hat held every listener in close attention, for it had been a painstaking job of detective work. To begin with, the hat carried the label of "Berteil, rue du 4 Septembre," although Mme. Braunberger had testified that her husband's hat was from Gelot. She explained this discrepancy by saying that while he had bought it at Gelot, he had had it repaired at Berteil, Gelot's having been closed in 1942. But Floriot showed that Gelot put their name not on the sweatband but inside the hat where it would still show even if the sweatband had been changed.

Furthermore, Gelot was the only hatmaker in Paris that sold only made-to-order hats and therefore they kept on file the measurements of all customers. Floriot sent for the "trace" of Dr. Braunberger's head shape and size and found a difference of two and a half centimeters (one inch) between the trace and the hat in question. Dr. Braunberger obviously could not have gotten it on his head.

The clinching facts, however, were these: Gelot did not close in 1942 at all but was open all through the Occupation while Berteil, where Mme. Braunberger said the hat had been repaired, closed permanently in 1939, never reopened, and never would. Floriot learned, too, and proved it by the records, that the hat bought by

Dr. Braunberger from Gelot was not a flat felt, like the hat in evidence, but a *chiné*—made of rough or hairy felt. Samples had been brought into court and did not match the hat in evidence.

When Floriot had completed this smashing demonstration, utterly destroying the "identification" of the hat, the entire audience stood and applauded, as if he had performed a record-breaking high jump or had caused a live rabbit to disappear. The applause lasted for seven minutes. Yet there was probably not a single member of the audience, other than those closely connected to Petiot, who did not remain convinced of Petiot's guilt. Hat or no hat, the pajamas, the ration card, and the little dismembered body still remained sadly unexplained. Yet all those were only circumstantial evidence, but twenty-seven murders, all connected with one person, seemed significant.

Floriot had been on his feet for six and a half hours. He had masterfully picked apart the weak spots in the prosecution's case. In a really extraordinary fashion and in each separate case he clearly demonstrated that there was insufficient direct evidence to find Petiot guilty beyond any reasonable doubt. In other words, according to Floriot, since no single murder or group of murders could be definitely proved, the court and the jury could not find Petiot guilty of two, twenty-seven, or sixty-three murders. Not even young Kneller's disappearance could be translated into a Petiot killing by any solid evidence. Petiot turned the Knellers over to a *passeur* one step ahead of the Gestapo; young Kneller's dirty pajamas had been left at 21 rue Le Sueur, his ration card that would have identified him was taken by Petiot and kept—but if Petiot had killed him, would he have kept his card? The body in the Seine could have been that of one of 20,000 other little boys. Coincidence, yes. Evidence, no! Floriot kept hammering away that Petiot had killed nineteen enemies of France of the twenty-seven murders he was charged with, but not a single one of the remaining eight.

Floriot then explained how Petiot had often helped persons who turned against him. He easily established that Petiot had tried to help van Bever cure his girl friend's addiction and that Raymonde Baudet's boy friend had forged Petiot's harmless prescription and that both had gotten Petiot into trouble. He quoted Dr. Petiot's statement of principle:

"As a doctor, and true to my pledge, I feel strongly that a doctor is not a judge or a god, if there is one. My duty is to save lives, reduce physical pain, assist the crippled, and relieve the mentally ill. If a mother does not want a child and an addict wants dope, why not help them!"

One extraordinary part of Maître Floriot's summation that to many almost overcame the case against the accused was that pertaining to Denise Hotin, the most glamorous of his alleged female victims. Floriot reminded the court that the first murder in the prosecutor's case was that of a pretty model and salesgirl at the world famous Lancel in Paris. However, Floriot stated that he was both worried and confused because any accusation against Petiot in this case did not make any sense and could not stand up on the facts and the testimony presented to the court.

Judge Leser and many others were undoubtedly very impressed with Floriot's uncontestable summary and the presentation at least on this one charge and Judge Leser was so impressed at this point that he had declared a short recess.

Floriot, and even prosecuting attorney Dupin, were therefore not too surprised when three DGER and the other expected witnesses did not show although it would appear that their absence was more costly to the defense.

At the conclusion of the seven hours covering the summary for the defense and the evidence of the innocence of his client of the eight murders he denied and the proof and evidence that the nineteen other murders were definitely for the Resistance and for France, Floriot turned directly to the jury and concluded his summary: "I have completed an appeal to your intelligence and your reason, I now am going to appeal to your heart. Can you really believe that this devoted doctor, who treated gratuitously a child with leukemia all night and all day and for many nights, as brought out in testimony, could be capable of killing little René Kneller? Can you really believe this resistant who, when arrested and tortured by the Gestapo, let them file all his teeth down, pressed his skull until he bled out of his nose, mouth, and ears without talking, that he could kill Jews escaping from the Germans? Lieutenant l'Héritier, a patriot, a hero, and survivor of a German concentration camp swore to you that no matter what your decision, he would remain proud for the rest of his life of having been a companion, a co-patriot, and a friend of Dr. Petiot. I also, no matter what your decision, will ever remain proud of having defended Dr. Petiot before you. I place him and his future in your hands. I am certain that you will answer a 'no' to all the questions the court will request from you." With that, Floriot, exhausted, staggered to his chair and sat down.

The entire audience and members of the court remained absolutely silent in deference to the unusual and extraordinary defense presented by Maître Floriot. All the hatred that had been present in the court for sixteen days seemed to have evaporated. Petiot, his head in his hands on his desk before him, cried in sharp, regular spasms.

"Petiot! Have you anything to add to your defense?" asked Judge Leser softly but firmly. (French law gives the last word to the accused.)

Petiot sat up, wiped his eyes of tears, then stood up and, facing the jury with the air of a military hero who has only done his duty, said:

"Gentlemen, you are Frenchmen. It has been proven to you that I eliminated agents of the Gestapo, you know what is left for you to do!"

Judge Leser then explained to the jury about answering the questions that would be submitted to them. He then recessed the court.

There were 135 questions prepared by the court that were presented to the jury (two magistrates and five civilian lay members) to deliberate on. Court was closed. The jury retired to consider its verdict. It was 9:30 P.M. but no one wanted to leave. Nearly all who came had expected a long session and had brought food along. Men and women throughout the courtroom, sitting or standing, took sandwiches from bags or briefcases or packages and ate them. Others made their way to the courtroom café where many of the spectators, some of whom had not missed a single session, sat around large bowls of sauerkraut with platters of cold meat and glasses of beer.

The jury, too, decided they would be unable to deliberate on an empty stomach and asked for food to be brought in. A local bistro supplied a lavish meal with excellent wine for all seven of them—

and the bill went to Judge Leser. The judge, somewhat taken aback at this, paid the bill. He did not receive reimbursement from the state until eighteen months later and, because of this delay, the cost of the meal was paid for by the patient taxpayers of France. (This would have drawn a happy laugh from Petiot.)

At ten minutes before midnight, on April 4, 1946, the jury sent word that they had answered all the questions. Five minutes later they filed back into the courtroom. Judge Leser reopened the trial. Petiot, arms sprawled out across his desk, was sound asleep and had to be shaken awake by Floriot. He sat up quickly and watched intently as the jury offered their answers to the questions. Of the 135 questions, they answered "no" to only three. The three negative answers indicated that they had absolved Petiot of the murder of Denise Hotin, but they found him guilty of all the other twenty-six killings.

Petiot stood, apparently unmoved and completely silent, as Judge Leser sentenced him to death. The journalists ranged behind him were paler and more distraught than he. The sentence spoken, Petiot rubbed his hands together in his characteristic gesture, frowned slightly, then made a grimace of anger. His eyes seemed slightly dilated and brighter than ever, but more from mad rage than fear. The prospect of death evidently held no terror for him.

The trial then droned into a weary anticlimax. The court and jury again retired for deliberations on the amount of damages and interest to allow to the civil parties. Court was then reopened and the awards were read off, all chargeable to Petiot or to his estate, for the wrongful deaths of Mme. Khait (50,000 francs); Dr. Braunberger (700,000 francs); Paulette Grippay (100,000 francs); Piereschi (10,000 francs); Gisele Rossmy (50,000 francs); Anspach (80,000 francs); and Yvan Dreyfus (880,000 francs). The awards totaled 1,870,000 francs. Petiot was also charged with the costs of the trial. These were carefully accounted for and read into the record: 312,361 francs and 50 centimes, plus 250 francs for "mailing charges." Petiot, no man to belittle the value of a franc, could not suppress a smile at the thriftiness of this accounting. (Grand total: 2,182,611.50 francs, or now approximately 436,522.30, U.S. dollars depending on the fluctuation of the dollar value of the

French franc.) He also may have smiled knowing what difficulties the collection would be—from his wife!

The business of the trial was ended. Judge Leser formally closed the court. Petiot, as calmly as if he had just lost a minor suit for damages, leaned over his desk to sign the appeal his lawyer handed him. The crowd was reluctant to leave. Everyone looked back at Petiot, who was now being taken away by his guards. Petiot, too, looked back over the courtroom in the direction of his family and cried out in a firm voice:

"I must be avenged!"

And his fight was not over. Besides his appeal for reversal, Petiot filed on May 13 two charges of false testimony and perjury—one against Mme. Braunberger and the other against her maid. He also preferred charges against the jurors who had told the American reporter of the *Herald-Tribune:* "Death is too sweet for Petiot."

There remained to decide only the method of execution. The official Paris guillotine had been badly damaged in bombardments and the men responsible for its care and upkeep were threatening a strike. Would Petiot have to be shot like a military offender? No. It developed that the portable guillotine was intact and ready for use. M. Desfournaux, chief engineer and operator of the guillotines, usually referred to as "Monsieur Paris," announced that he was ready. He would personally drop the block and blade on the neck of Dr. Petiot.

The press, meanwhile, had been commenting endlessly on the trial and on the dozens of questions still unanswered. None seemed to doubt Petiot's guilt, but one writer made a sage comment: "If Floriot had been given a chance to defend Petiot for the twenty-seven murders one at a time before different juries, there is no question that he would have won out on all." After all, there were no identified bodies and no direct testimony of a single killing, nor even the cause of death of a single cadaver attributed to Petiot.

It was the heaping of horror upon horror, the dreadful weight twenty-seven disappearances and the bodies at 21 rue Le Sueur and in the Seine that turned Petiot into a monster even before the trial began. One juror, discussing the case ten years afterward, said that he had made up his mind "after one week of the trial that Petiot was a monster and that everything Petiot or his counsel said after that helped prove I was right. It was Petiot that had to be liquidated."

But this same juror, twenty years after the trial, had this to say: "Now as I look back on the whole affair, I am certain Petiot did not have a fair trial and it is just possible that he was a misguided soul suffering from overaggressivity and exaggerated patriotism in a bloody atmosphere and did kill many persons, including nineteen involved in the trial, honestly believing they were collaborators and not the eight that he helped and who subsequently disappeared."

The press also propounded the many questions that had been left unanswered and some even unconsidered: How did Petiot kill his victims? What had become of the missing police records on the Villeneuve killing of which Petiot was suspected? Who had filched the record of the finding of a woman's headless body on an abandoned farm from the Dijon police files? Why was there no longer any record of an early abortion case in Paris related to Dr. Petiot? Where did Petiot get his fortune of narcotics seized by the police at 66 rue Caumartin and an even greater fortune of dope he supplied to ninety-five addicts he "treated"? Where and how did Petiot get his peyote? Several times he had hinted of getting it from Germany. Was this tied up with his possible connections with the Abwehr and Masuy and the Otto Service or with the French Gestapo? He frequently referred to Barmen and Darmstadt, the sites of the Merck laboratories. Merck was a major European supplier of mescaline sulphate prior to World War II. A German scientific reference book found at 21 rue Le Sueur states that peyote was used as a stimulant and intoxicant in night clubs in Paris in the 1930s and that the structure of mescaline was so simple that it could be made by any organic chemist and the structure was deduced in 1870.* This confirmed Petiot's notes and their reference to his use of this drug in connection with his liquidations and, more particularly, as to how he got his victims to

---

* According to a forensic medicine expert, mescaline was isolated in 1896, synthesized in 1914, and its effect studied in 1913, and that by 1944 its use could be detected in human urine if looked for in time.

write letters dictated by him before he killed them. He even included the chemical formula $C_{11}H_{17}NO_3$.

Did Petiot ever sample his "jam" (narcotics) or try peyote or mescaline himself? Did Maurice Petiot know what really went on at 21 rue Le Sueur? Did Georgette Petiot, the doctor's wife, know what was going on? To whom belonged the strange clothes constantly being packed and taken away from 66 rue Caumartin by Mrs. Petiot, according to Geneviève Cluny, a former maid, later a Catholic nun and reliable witness? Why did the French police not continue their investigations of the missing witnesses in Petiot's narcotic-traffic charges after he was released by the Germans?

And, more important, why did Petiot, during the trial and in police interrogations and in his prison notes, claim that he had executed Charlot when, in fact, Charlot was alive and reappeared after the war and again was in trouble with the law and was arrested in the 1960s? Petiot also claimed in police interrogations and also in his notes that he had killed Oscar Heisserer, a German spy, whose body was allegedly found cut up like those found at rue Le Sueur and in the Seine, but in two different suitcases at two different Paris railroad stations. Petiot bragged about sending Heisserer's head by mail to the German commanding general. But this killing had nothing to do with Petiot. The man was actually executed by a prominent resistant who dissected the body and packed it in the suitcases, then shipped the head to the German commandant of Paris, General von Stülpnagel, who hastened to snatch the rest of the body out of the hands of the Paris coroner, Dr. Paul. Had the Germans left it in the morgue someone would have noticed that the dissection, or butchery, had been done by an amateur. Petiot would have dearly desired to have had this killing laid at his door, for it would have confirmed him in the public's mind as an underground fighter for France.

How many persons had Petiot killed out of over 60,000 persons missing in Paris during the latter part of the Occupation and the first part of the liberation? Was there really a "Fly Tox" apparatus and could it be possible that Petiot was innocent and some of the victims, like the Knellers and Denise Hotin, would show up someday? How had Petiot, almost alone in the annals of crime, avoided leaving any single piece of direct evidence or a single body that could be identified or even show cause of death? But probably the most dramatic question was—where was the Petiot treasure from Dr. Eugène's operation, estimated at $14 million, and how much of the Petiot estate, including fifty-one real estate holdings worth millions, was legitimate and how much plunder from his murders?†

All that seems reasonably established is that no appreciable reimbursements or payments on the court's assessments against the Petiot estate were ever made. Petiot, unlike most murderers, had contrived to arrange that his family would keep most of his plunder. What were Floriot's fees and how they were collected may never be known, although some of his jealous rivals and those who disliked him for his defense of so many Nazi collaborators spread the report that Floriot had known where the Petiot plunder was hidden or had actually been given it to keep. Efforts to find out about Floriot's will, estate, art collection, charities, trusts, etc., after his death seemed surrounded by a high iron curtain. These same rivals of Floriot also pointed out that had Floriot pleaded insanity and won, Petiot's funds and plunder in all probability would have been taken over by the court with greater difficulty to collect his fee in whole or in part. It must be remembered in this respect that there is positive proof that Floriot, a great criminal lawyer, nevertheless did in fact deliver Petiot's "letter to the editor," an obvious entrapment which caused Petiot's arrest. Also in this same respect, one wonders why Floriot did not plead insanity for his client. Perhaps it was because Floriot hesitated to be responsible for Petiot's freedom as too dangerous to society. On the other hand, perhaps Floriot had been given or in-

† It must be remembered that the earlier results of the thefts of Dr. Petiot were given or loaned to his father-in-law to help finance the father-in-law's real estate, butcher, and restaurant businesses and investments, with Mme. Petiot inheriting her father's estate as his only heir. Also, Petiot invested his money and no doubt some of his plunder in some fifty-one real estate holdings, usually in his son's, brother's, or wife's name. Also, it must be remembered that Dr. Petiot undoubtedly made considerable money from his successful medical practice aided, according to reports, by his abortion and dope traffic and large profits from his legitimate antique business. So in addition to the hidden booty or plunder of the last few years of killing, there can hardly be any known way of dividing the good money from the bad and evidently no great effort was ever made to do so, nor can the records be seen for fifty years.

formed of the location of Petiot's plunder. This is why many persons tried to obtain information on Floriot's estate, but were unable to get any answers. Why should Floriot have anything to hide, especially after death?‡

‡ René Floriot died December 21, 1975, as noted all over the world in obituaries in the press, such as the one in the New York *Times* of December 23, 1975.

CHAPTER XIV

*The execution of Dr. Petiot and what happened
to his rivals, accomplices, and fellow criminals
the Petiot books, stories, and legends that followed
Saturday, May 25, 1946—and after*

La Prison de la Santé, where Petiot was incarcerated, is called by
the cynical French "The Prison of Health." It is a dark-gray
splotch on the edge of the Fourteenth Arrondissement, a quadran-
gle of stone buildings with tiers of cells surrounding a small cob-
blestone court where the guillotine is set up for executions. (The
execution of "Bluebeard" Landru was public after World War I
but Petiot's was private after World War II.) Huge walls of gray
stone, weather-beaten and darkened by years of dirt and grime,
surround the buildings and the entire block they occupy. The
walls are secure. They are six feet wide at the top, twelve feet
thick at ground level, and twenty-nine feet high.

There had been repeated rumors after Petiot's trial that the
Communist deputy of de Gaulle, Maurice Thorez, had recommended clemency and the lifting of the death sentence on the
basis of an unfair trial in a negative "climate" and because Petiot's crimes might well have been errors of judgment arising from
overenthusiastic patriotism. Thorez, however, never referred to Petiot as being a Communist or the possibility that Fly Tox was a
Communist terrorist unit. Petiot's principal visitor was none other
than Chief Inspector René Desvaux, an experienced and dedicated police officer whose entire life had always been centered in
his job. Desvaux had been head of a resistance organization during the Occupation and he felt that if ever Petiot were to talk it

would be as a result of an appeal to his intelligence or because of his love for his family or to improve his image as a patriotic Frenchman. However, progress was very slow and beyond Petiot's constant doodling and the writing of his notes, which he had hoped would be his autobiography but now realized he could not finish, no very significant information or communication was obtained from him except as he approached the day of his execution. He, then, on three separate occasions, made oral comments which Desvaux duly reduced to writing and relayed to his superiors. (Much later, Desvaux became one of the author's sources.) They were:

"I cannot tell you or anyone else the real truth for, if I do, it will mean that my loved ones—my family—will suffer."

"If I am executed, strangely enough, I'll be buried in Ivry, at the cemetery where the human beings liquidated by the state are buried. It is a beautiful and serene spot with the green grass and the shade of trees. Alongside of me, and I hope significantly, will be 860 Parisians shot by German firing squads from 1940 to 1944. Among the bodies will be that of Lucien Micaud, who died for France on August 21, 1942. He was shot by the Germans but was only twelve years old." (These facts were checked out and are true.)

"According to the Communists, there is no God but every man is his own god and all men must divide everything up. Yet, as I approach death, I am certain the Communists are opportunists and are sophisticated in merely using an impractical but nice-sounding theory to gain power. After all, remove individual incentive in man and you have a vegetable; remove the hope of a future in a hereafter and you have an animal. Although I have never believed in God, since my family does, may God bless them and keep them from any harm resulting from anything I have ever done. I must admit, however, as I approach death, as an atheist, that there is a disturbing question for me as a physician and scientist. There must be a Supreme Being or a God and a hereafter, for, otherwise, what happens to us—to our soul or self or mind or thinking being—when our body changes to water and dust and gas? Nothing is indestructible in the universe, nothing ends in nothing. Also, why have I been hounded from my birth to my death with priests and churches and cathedrals and crosses? How

could the Catholic Church have survived the Dark Ages? . . .
There will certainly be a priest at my execution. Yes! I am afraid I
may even take the last rites—for my family, for my wife, for my
son."

With respect to some of Petiot's acquaintances or possible associates, they were always of great interest to Petiot and the subject
of constant questions, although he did not outlive them all. He
had already rejoiced at the execution of Lafont (defended by Floriot), Bonny, Clavie, and other members of the French Gestapo
in December 1944. As for Algeron, Jean Luchaire, Guy Crouzet,
Georges Prade, de Brinon, and Mme. de Brinon, all, with the exception of de Brinon, were defended by Floriot. Only Jean Luchaire was tried and executed before Petiot's trial, while Mme. de
Brinon was released for want of evidence after a brilliant defense
by Floriot. After Petiot's trial, Algeron was sentenced to death,
then pardoned. Guy Crouzet was sentenced to life imprisonment
at hard labor but pardoned after twelve years. Georges Prade got
seven years, de Brinon was executed, and Otto Abetz, former ambassador of the Third Reich to France, also defended by Floriot,
was sentenced to twenty years at hard labor but was liberated after
nine years. Every one of them had attained great wealth during
the Occupation.

Magda Fontagnes, former Petiot patient, the would-be actress
from the Opéra district and once mistress of Mussolini, turned
German secret agent 8006F and Nazi propaganda operative with
Algeron, Luchaire, and Crouzet, was not found and arrested until
March 23, 1946. Her trial was on January 30, 1947, and, of course,
her defense counsel was Maître Floriot, who put on a brilliant defense. Her sentence was fifteen years at hard labor but, with the
help of Floriot, she was released in 1954. Then, as Dr. Petiot had
warned, her mind began to crack and she stole an Utrillo from the
house of Floriot, who promptly had her arrested. She then threatened his life and he used the full measure of his influence to keep
her in jail. She was finally released in 1960 and went to live with
friends in Switzerland; she committed suicide on October 1, 1960,
probably to the great relief of her erstwhile defender.

This left only one—probably the most cunning, the richest and
the most powerful of all of Petiot's associates or later rivals—
Georges Christian Masuy, whose real name was Georges Henri

Delfanne. Masuy's fortune could not even be estimated but was probably over $25 million. He had fled to Spain with his friend Otto Brandl, former head of the German Supply Service in Occupied Europe, also a multimillionaire, who died in Spain. However, Masuy was not too welcome in Spain and, after sixteen months, he made a bad move to Germany under a well-prepared false identity, that of Otto Bauer, a German, but was arrested in April 1947 by the U.S. Army, turned over to the French, and tried and convicted on July 24. As this was over a year after Petiot's execution, no one, not even Maître Floriot, queried Masuy about his relationship with Petiot.

Masuy was executed on October 1, 1947, by a firing squad, but not before an almost successful effort to buy himself off. His price —the turning over and the operation by him of a vast and well-organized secret German Abwehr intelligence system, particularly in Eastern Europe and the U.S.S.R. as well as among the Communist apparatuses and parties in Western Europe, all set up and working, plus untold gold and treasures hidden away in various countries by Otto Brandl, a fortune worth $90 million. Masuy also talked about an immediate delivery of certain Russian codes and ciphers. As he put it, "I am worth several fortunes alive, but absolutely nothing dead." French Intelligence authorities, as well as the British, all secretly joined in a "Let's Save Masuy" movement. For a time there was great interest in accepting his offer but, pressured by the Communists and Maurice Thorez, the last-minute delay was ended by the sharp reports of a firing squad and the death of an efficient and ruthless underground and espionage organizer.

Masuy smiled ironically and faced death with indifference, leaving an autographed picture to Colonel Remy, director of the French Secret Intelligence Branch: "To one man I never could catch, with admiration for him and his agents." Masuy was the last of Petiot's rivals, or, more probable, the last of his accomplices. Masuy's execution was sixteen months and five days after Petiot had departed. When one remembers that the U.S. and, later, Mr. Allen Dulles and the CIA made a deal and financed General Gehlen to the tune of some $20 million, although Gehlen had been a loyal member of the Nazi General Staff and Hitler's Chief of Secret Intelligence for the U.S.S.R., it is surprising that France did not save Masuy's life. The only answer is that the United States was more anxious for secret intelligence penetration of the Soviet Union and Communist organizations than was France at a time when Communist Maurice Thorez was de Gaulle's deputy. (Gehlen, of course, was a professional military intelligence officer with no criminal record, but unlike Admiral Canaris had always been loyal to Hitler.)

On Saturday, May 25, 1946, several hours before dawn, in heavy fog and mist, police in large groups began arriving at La Santé prison in Paris, where Petiot was asleep in his cell. Beginning at 2 A.M., they arrived in personnel carriers and in jeeps to station themselves outside the prison gates and walls. In the misty darkness police took their places around the nearby cemetery at Ivry where Petiot's body would be buried. Never before had such security precautions been taken for the execution of a single person. In the prison courtyard, the mobile guillotine had been set up. In cell seven, block seven, Petiot slept on, until, finally, at a quarter to five, with the dawn just beginning to thin out the darkness, he was awakened by the entry of a small group of people. They included Pierre Dupin; René Floriot; the prison superintendent; the prison chaplain, Father Berger; Magistrate Meiis, who had been one of the two magistrates on the jury and who had come as a representative of Judge Leser; Dr. Paul; two guards and several other individuals in minor capacities. M. Dupin officially announced to Petiot that his last appeal had been denied and that he was now to be executed. He asked if Petiot had any special requests.

"Yes," said Petiot, quite calmly. "I want a little time to write a farewell note to my wife and one to my son, to be delivered to them by my counsel."

Dupin approved this request. Petiot was still in handcuffs and leg irons, which were attached by a chain to an iron ring in the floor. The guards unlocked these bonds. Petiot washed carefully and dressed himself in his best suit—the gray suit with the lavender pin stripe, the one he had worn at the trial. Then he sat down at his small table and began to write. The others stood in silence, watching him. After a time, someone whispered to Dr. Paul, asking how long they might have to wait.

"I don't know," the doctor whispered back. "But I once remember a condemned prisoner writing letters for four hours while everyone waited."

Petiot, however, completed his letters in twenty minutes and handed them to Floriot. There was no expression of worry or fear on Petiot's face. It might have been the beginning of a business day.

Father Berger advanced then to offer Petiot the last rites of the Church. Witnesses cannot agree on what then passed between them. Some say he thanked Father Berger but refused. The majority of those present agreed that when the chaplain approached Petiot, he raised one hand to signify his refusal but that Father Berger had then told him that Mme. Petiot wished him to receive last rites. "In that case, Father," said Petiot (according to several witnesses), "proceed." The chaplain then administered a rather abbreviated version of the last sacraments. According to one witness, not only did Petiot bow and then kneel before the priest but, in the end, quietly, and with resignation, crossed himself, seemingly giving in, finally, to God. Petiot then smoked a cigarette while murmuring last-minute instructions to Floriot. That finished, he turned, without bravado or any sign of fear, toward the prosecutor and said simply:

"Gentlemen, I am ready."

Before leaving his cell, Petiot was offered the traditional glass of rum provided for all condemned prisoners in France just before execution. He quietly refused this final kindness. Then the group, led by one of the prison officials, walked with measured step out through the hallways and into the cobbled courtyard where the guillotine stood. "M. Paris," the executioner, gently asked Petiot to loosen his collar. Then Petiot smoked his final cigarette. Now, if ever, was the time for an ultimate confession or revelation of what had gone on behind the doors at 21 rue Le Sueur. Dupin asked Petiot if he had any final remarks to make. The answer was published all over the world: "*AUCUNE. Je suis un voyageur qui emporte tous ses bagages avec lui!*" (None. I am a traveler who is taking all his baggage with him.)

Petiot's hands were tied behind his back. He was led toward the guillotine. His smile now was contemptuous and his eyes still showed no fear. The guards of the execution detail seized him roughly and seated him, tied him in place, and shoved his head into the lunette. At precisely five minutes past five, the weighted blade and block fell with a peculiar thud. Dark-red blood from the severed arteries spurted in several directions for as far as six feet. The head had tumbled into a large basket and the stub of the neck, slipping out of the lunette, still pumped out quantities of darker and thicker blood. Some witnesses said that when the head fell into the basket, it still wore a contemptuous smile. It was certain that Petiot remained cool and disdainful to the very end. Said Dr. Paul, who had seen many men die:

"In my forty years, I never before saw a condemned man with so much scorn and indifference to death."

A British correspondent, writing of the end of Petiot, said that the use of the guillotine rather than the firing squad was at least a sign that France was getting back to the normal ways of peace. But Petiot, oddly enough, would have preferred the firing squad. He considered this a more honorable way to die even though it was the death awarded to traitors and spies of the stripe of Lafont, Bonny, and Clavie. It may have been that he thought of himself, to the end, as a patriot deserving a military death or as a revolutionist who should not have died as a common criminal. Perhaps even in that deranged brain, the executed man did consider himself a doctor, mayor, spy, and patriot, dying for a Communist France to be—even though, as a paranoiac, believing in nothing and critical of everything.

A few minutes after the execution, Petiot's body (and his head, too, it is supposed) was carried in a hearse to the Ivry Cemetery. Two motorcycle policemen provided an escort and the policemen stationed at the cemetery took care that no unauthorized persons were present to note the spot of burial.

The Petiot funeral paralleled that of Landru's, except that Landru's body was carried in a horse-drawn hearse. The cemetery, a small one filled with lovely shade trees and surrounded by a high white wall, is the final repository for the remains of many executed criminals. The body of an executed criminal is first buried here in a spot marked only by a number, the number being known only to officials. After ten years, the body is disinterred and the criminal's family may claim it in order to have it buried elsewhere. If it is not claimed, it is dumped into a common grave without a marker.

Petiot's wife asked permission to attend his funeral but was refused. When the body was disinterred in 1956, however, she made no effort to claim it and it was dropped forever into the mass grave with many nameless and headless corpses, like the corpse of a Petiot victim. The head, however—and that is another story—may have been separated from the body, perhaps like the heads of his victims. Some police and prison officials insist steadfastly that the head was spirited away in a canvas bag from the courtyard of La Santé, a bag used to bring the head of another man from the Paris morgue. When Dr. Paul was asked about this some years later, he turned aside the question with a chuckle and stated that he and his colleagues would have liked to have the Petiot head for study—to see, for instance, if there was a tumor on the brain and to satisfy themselves that the state had not put a sick man to death. It would have been a simple matter, too, he remarked, to find a skull somewhere about the Paris morgue that could have been substituted for Petiot's. There is, however, another oft-repeated story in the Petiot case which has not been forgotten after thirty-two years. According to this report, when the body of Petiot was exhumed in 1956 from his secret numbered grave and was not claimed by his wife or son and therefore reinterred in the common pit of executed criminals, the Ivry Cemetery workers smuggled out the decapitated head and gave it as a token of their esteem to one of the principals of the trial.

There are not many things connected with Petiot that are really beyond question. Even the authoritative testimony of Captain Boris, who questioned Petiot's knowledge of *le plastique*, was disputed by a man who wrote a letter to Judge Leser during the trial. The letter rang with expert knowledge, truth, and sincerity. Petiot, said the writer, could have been a resistant, could have used plastic without knowing too much about it, and could have killed his victims under the sincere impression that they had collaborated with the Nazis.

That this letter made a strong impression on the judge cannot be doubted (he gave the author a copy). But it simply could not outweigh the mountain of evidence that piled up against Petiot, or the effect of his own evasions and contradictions. A study of the handwritten notes made by the judge during the trial indicates that the forged ration card belonging to René Kneller may have been the single most important bit of evidence in the judge's mind.

Of the testimony of the psychiatrists, he wrote down: "The psychiatrists unanimously find that he is sane and therefore responsible for his acts." And about the handwriting experts, he set this down: "Letters of van Bever, Khait, Hotin, and Dr. Braunberger were in the authentic handwriting of the victims, but under some strange hallucination or unusual influence and evidently dictated or suggested by one and the same party—Petiot."

Whether these were the points that swayed the jury as well cannot be known. It seems certain that the jury was affected to some extent by the public clamor and the almost universal identification of Petiot as a new but super Landru, a monster, and a kindred soul to the Nazi and Communist mass killers. The French Government did not seem particularly proud of the Petiot trial. Its obvious lack of fairness may have been one reason or it may be that it was sensitive about the degree to which many respectable figures were revealed as partial collaborators as, indeed, were all who tried to hold an official job during the Occupation. Or who were loyal to the Vichy Government. Whatever the motive, the fact is that the de Gaulle government of France sequestered the trial records—although not until they had been seen and parts of them copied or reproduced. At that time they were certainly in the public domain, quoted and referred to in the public press. When the author of this book sought access to the entire record, especially the record of the public trial (usually available in a democracy), he received the French version of the run-around—diplomatic, suave, even seemingly co-operative, but, nonetheless, adamantly negative.

The first approach was made in 1947 through the U.S. Embassy. It was flatly turned down because, said a spokesman for the French Government, a book on the intimate details of the crimes of Petiot might prompt others to engage in similar mass liquidations. (Did the many books on Landru based on records available after World War I then invite more Landrus?) Some five years later another request was rejected, this time on the grounds that the Petiot trial, with all its cruel and intimate revelations of immorality and collaboration, involved many people still alive who might be damaged by publication. The record, therefore, would be sequestered for fifty years—until 1996—when most, if not all, of the people mentioned would be dead, as provided in an old French law.

But still a final effort was made in Paris in 1966. The author was able to arrange through a cabinet member friend an appointment with M. Jean Foyer, Minister of Justice of the French Republic. But the Honorable M. Foyer did not keep his appointment. Instead he delegated a deputy, M. Michel Taupignon, to fend off his visitor. M. Taupignon was faultless in his manners at a meeting at 2 P.M. on Thursday, April 28, 1966, and offered every evidence of willingness to help. The records had been sequestered? He had no knowledge of such a thing. He listened with a careful and attentive ear as promises were made to omit or exclude any material that might be deemed embarrassing to the French Government and he noted with sympathy that the author had put in over twenty years of part-time research and had interviewed over two hundred people, had even secured Gestapo and French police records from the German Occupation authorities through U.S. Army secret agents. The book, he was told, would be forthcoming in any case. Both sides would benefit, therefore, from co-operation. Much of the record had already been examined and photographed when it was accessible to the public and before sequestration. This, too, the suave gentleman had not known and seemingly did not believe. But rest assured, he would look into the matter with the utmost urgency. There would be an answer within a few days. Of a certainty, not more than a week. There was no answer—in a week, in a month, in years. Telephone calls were fruitless. Letters and telegrams went unacknowledged. The French Government at that time positively did not want a book to be written on the Petiot case, nor were they anxious evidently to go on record with a turndown. The records remained locked away. Fortunately a way developed, or had already been used, for getting the full details of the public trial without official access to the sequestered and now classified official records.

But the veil the government drew around the case and its extreme sensitivity to publication of any of the record of the Petiot case did not cover the official record alone. A number of books about the case were published in France but most of them were quickly but quietly suppressed or the publishers were discouraged to print many copies.

René Nezondet, Petiot's bachelor companion at Villeneuve, wrote a book. It was published under the title of Petiot "le Possédé" (Petiot "the Possessed"). This book was promptly suppressed by the police and the shop that printed it closed up.

Later, two newspaper reporters, Jacques Perry and Jane Charbert, wrote a lively and authentic book called L'Affaire Petiot, which was published by Gallimard in 1957. But even at this late date the government could not tolerate any publicity on the Petiot affair. The police descended upon the publisher and many of the parties mentioned in the book threatened litigation. The book was finally abandoned by agreement of the authors and publishers. By 1966 not a single copy could be found to purchase nor could one be found in any library.

Then there entered into the Petiot case, eleven years after it had officially closed, another figure of mystery. A number of copies of L'Affaire Petiot had, of course, reached the bookstores, but nearly all were systematically bought up by a strange, unidentified woman. Her description did not fit any of the women who had been close to Petiot. Then who was it who wanted this slate washed so clean?

The mysterious woman was to appear again, when another book on Petiot (described as "semi-fiction") was published in Belgium. Copies of this book, too, disappeared and now no one can even name it or identify the author. Not a copy is to be unearthed anywhere in Europe. The few bookstores that recall stocking such a book also tell of a mysterious lady who quietly came and gathered them all up. Another book, title now forgotten, has been spoken of. This reportedly "unmasked" Petiot even before his arrest and said that Petiot was protected by the French police under pressure from rue Lauriston (Lafont and Bonny). The book was published in Belgium and was for sale in Brussels and Antwerp and Liege. In all three cities, booksellers tell of a mysterious and attractive lady who took every last copy from their shelves. Another book on the Petiot case, published in Paris by a major publisher, written by Claude Barret, was withdrawn and disappeared. Years later, while admitting the publication of this book, the publishers had no copies, nor could they even suggest where a copy could be found.

One book did achieve circulation, however. That was *L'Enquete Petiot* by George Massu, head of the Homicide Squad in Paris under the Occupation. This volume, published in 1959 by Arthème Fayard, purports to be an inside story of the whole Petiot case, beginning with the discovery of the charnel house. Actually, it is a self-serving account to justify Massu's own dilatory behavior in pursuing Petiot. It does not, unhappily, do a particularly good job of that, for it makes it painfully obvious that Massu seized on any excuse not to start in pursuit of the owner of 21 rue Le Sueur until the man had a good head start. He knew where he was, even knew his telephone number, but he did not send officers to arrest him until the morning after he had fled from number 21. Massu explained:

"By order of the German authorities, I was directed to proceed to arrest Dr. Petiot, a dangerous madman." Yet no German record could be found matching this statement. All Gestapo records evaluated Dr. Petiot as "not mentally responsible for his acts, but harmless."

Apparently Massu was trying in the book to indicate that he had no zeal for co-operating with the Germans and that he believed the Germans wanted Petiot alive. Had this true fact been featured in the press perhaps the "monster" tag would not have been affixed so quickly to Petiot. Perhaps—who knows?—he might even have had a fair trial as another overzealous resistant. It is doubtful, however, that he could ever have proved himself either the innocent victim of a frame-up or the gallant leader of a resistance unit. He could only have proved himself mad.

Among the many rumors that have arisen in the last ten years in Paris is that some of the victims of Petiot have reappeared— very much alive. Also, that many discoveries have been made to prove that Petiot was innocent of the murders he denied but he may well have liquidated scores of Germans and collaborators for patriotic reasons. However, more than thirty years of private investigation and contacts with hundreds of people and the Paris police by the author have failed to turn up a single Petiot victim . . . either the twenty-seven listed in the trial or many others who were missing after contact with the doctor.

An English version of the Petiot case in a collection of *Famous European Crimes* by David Rowan, published by Frederick Muller Ltd., of London, in 1956, had this to say: "Petiot was found guilty of twenty-four of the twenty-seven murders for which he stood accused. It was perhaps fortunate that he was cleared of the others for one of the three in question, a Mme. Hotin, was found by the Paris police very much alive three weeks after Petiot's execution." Of course, Petiot was convicted of twenty-six of twenty-seven murders, and while not convicted of murdering Mme. Hotin, she was never found alive by the Paris police or anyone else in Paris or anywhere else. An additional and special search was made for her in 1966 without result.

In the United States in *True* magazine of March 1952, Petiot was featured in an article by Alan Hynd, crime writer, entitled "The Super Bluebeard." The article gave the impression that Petiot's victims were mostly women and asserted he was another Landru and that he rode about Occupied Paris in a red motorcycle, notwithstanding German curfews and gasoline rationing. Of course, the real Petiot was far more efficient and gruesome. He pedaled silently on a green bicycle with a two-wheeled trailer trunk filled with cut-up cadavers (license No. 3866RD7). *True* tells about "Bluebeard Petiot" taking over 21 rue Le Sueur from a Russian princess instead of a French charity worker married to a titled German-Czech. Twenty-one rue Le Sueur, instead of being located in the finest residential neighborhood in Paris, was described as a corner house in an abandoned neighborhood and next to a lumberyard—all incorrect.

Perhaps the most tantalizing of all the Petiot mysteries was the disappearance of the treasure. Mme. Petiot was known to have some valuable jewelry, including pieces that Petiot had purchased and some that came, presumably, from his victims. When he was released by the Germans and when he apparently feared that he might be quickly arrested by the Paris police, he urged his wife to gather her jewels together, along with other valuables, and turn them over to him. But where did he hide them?

An anonymous letter to the Paris police in 1948 reported that two young men named Schipiglouz, with a jewelry store at 95 rue de Provence, had sold jewelry given them by Gerhardt Petiot. The police, acting promptly on this tip, found that the Schipiglouz were a Jewish family who had lived at 66 rue Caumartin and were, indeed, friends of the Petiots. The Schipiglouz mother and father had often been urged by Petiot to accept his help in escaping to South America, but they chose to remain in Paris, were shortly thereafter arrested and deported by the Gestapo and died lingering deaths in a concentration camp. (Still another example that Petiot's claim about giving a quick death to the already condemned may have been true.) But the police could find no clue whatever to indicate that any of the Petiot jewels had passed through the hands of the younger Schipiglouz. As for Gerhardt, he had already left France to hide himself—in South America.

Of course, some of the money Petiot took in through his various enterprises was safely invested, largely in real estate, and it seems certain in the name of his father-in-law, Nestor Lablais, who died leaving all his wealth to his only daughter, Georgette Petiot. Brother Maurice must certainly have taken a large share, too, for he was able to purchase properties far beyond the reach of even a successful operator of a radio shop. Petiot purchased a number of buildings (including 21 rue Le Sueur) in the name of his son, who, of course, eventually took title. Real estate values in Paris, just as Petiot foresaw, spiraled wildly upward after the war and undoubtedly these investments made his wife, his son, and his sister-in-law, Mrs. Maurice Petiot, and his nephew, Daniel, wealthy.

While justice would seem to require that this fortune in real estate should be divided somehow among the unwilling contributors to Petiot's fortune, there is no way in which this could be accomplished. To sort out righteous money from sinful money has never seemed practicable, and French justice, in the Petiot case, has long since been appeased. The rather penurious civil awards made at the trial were not settled as far as can be ascertained by Mme. Petiot or by Gerhardt Petiot so any settlement did not reduce what might be called the Petiot estate. The later spoils of the Dr. Eugène travel agency in cash, gold, jewelry, and furs, estimated at $14 million, has never been found.

So the legend persists that somewhere—perhaps in a numbered account in a Swiss bank, perhaps in a hole in the ground, perhaps in some distant land—the Petiot treasure is hidden. And many, even up to 1966, were still hoping to come upon it buried somewhere or sealed into a wall. The Petiot property in Villeneuve, at 56 rue Carnot, now owned and occupied by a Dr. Le Maître, has quite obviously been combed over through the years. In 1966, the brick walks in the garden and patio showed clear signs of having been dug up and replaced. The owner will proudly show visitors the badly repaired cement floor of the garage which was torn up— as were the walks—not once but several times. The police dug first for bodies, but later they dug more deeply, looking for buried loot.

All the Petiot properties (and his family owned fifty-one of them) have been searched and their basements and foundations dug into without success. The two adjoining apartment buildings he owned at 52 rue Reuilly have been torn down to lay deeper foundations for a new Catholic church and the workers on this project enlivened their days by watching every moment to see a cache of gold or jewels brought to light by bulldozers or drills.

Naturally the most obvious place to search was 21 rue Le Sueur. On July 5, 1952, this building was purchased by a well-known architect who undertook at once to remodel it completely. Cellar, court, passageway, and foundations were all uprooted and, along with the lime pit, reduced to rubble with hand picks. Yet not a single gold napoleon was ever found, not a piece of jewelry. It has since become a seven-story office building with a small apartment building in the rear of the court and it is worth probably in excess of $2 million.

It would not be fair, of course, to insist that Petiot's crimes are entirely what left his family wealthy. But the proceeds of his crimes were never recovered. Gerhardt Petiot, now in business with his cousin Daniel Petiot in South America, undoubtedly has worked hard to build their own fortunes but some nest egg provided by their father and uncle may well have provided a very good start.

The Petiot family, however, never would grant that Petiot was guilty of any crimes except—as he might have put it—"loving France too much." While Georgette Petiot would not claim her husband's body and, at the advice of her priest, prayed for her husband at home rather than going to Ivry Cemetery on All Souls' Day, she knew then which grave her husband lay in. She made no great effort at any time to hide her identity and, when interviewed in 1957, still maintained that her Marcel was innocent. A large framed photograph of Petiot was displayed on her dressing table. On December 28, 1966, Georgette Petiot remarried. Her new husband was a reportedly well-to-do retired civil servant who owns many houses in the South of France. Real estate as usual clung to Georgette Petiot.*

The younger Petiots—Gerhardt and his cousin Daniel—living comfortably in South America, quite properly escaped most of the publicity surrounding the Petiot case. It was reported, however, that for a long time they were subject to close surveillance by unidentified persons and that their homes as well as their offices were under close watch. By whom? No one could say. Perhaps by the police seeking leads to the Petiot treasure—perhaps by representatives of the victims' families—perhaps by the survivors of Fly Tox.

There was talk that the Petiot loot had gone directly to the Communist Party, confirming the hint dropped by Lieutenant l'Héritier that Petiot was actually working for the party, which had to disown him for political reasons.

One writer, it is true, argued, in a book published in London, that Petiot was indeed perhaps a dedicated Communist who went to the guillotine rather than betray the party secrets and that his Fly Tox operation was actually a Communist terrorist unit with the special mission of raising funds to finance a Communist takeover of France, with a preference for preying on both Germans and Jews.

The killing of both Nazis and Jews, as an incidental means of collecting billions of francs, was welcome to both the Communist underground and its organizers, the Soviet intelligence and propaganda services. It will be remembered that when Russia and Germany, as allies, invaded Poland, there was no difference in the liquidation of the Jewish population in both the German and Russian sectors. Anti-Semitism has been more cruel and more continuous in Russia than anywhere else.

The author of this Petiot book, Ronald Seth, described himself

---

* One rather significant fact is that the legal papers and deeds of the Petiot properties reveal the fact that as far back as August 1941, Dr. Petiot and his wife had renounced all rights to their properties in favor of their son, Gerhardt, perhaps as a means of protecting it from seizure based on criminal prosecution.

as a former British secret agent in Paris in 1944, during the latter part of the Occupation. In another book, Seth claims he was a secret agent for the British in Estonia and was captured by the Germans and was in jail for some time in 1942. He further states he revealed himself as a British agent to Soviet agents while in the Gestapo prison. If so—what was wrong with German security and the Gestapo in Paris? Could they not recognize a British agent they had apprehended before?

Seth's book on Petiot, called *Petiot, Victim of Chance*, was published in 1964 by Hutchinson & Co., deliberately echoing in its title Petiot's own book, *The Conquest of Chance*, and suggesting that Petiot lost that battle, too.

Despite many convincing arguments, Seth, who has a number of spy stories to his credit, makes some serious errors in his text. He describes 21 rue Le Sucur, for instance, as a large house on a corner (a mistake first made by the shadowlike Charles Rolland in his alleged letter to *Résistance*). Seth was in the house, he said, on March 12, 1944, which would be the day after the charnel house was discovered. But 21 rue Le Sueur is buried between two other buildings and not even in the nighttime could it be imagined that it stood at an intersection of two streets. Besides, when the police and firemen withdrew from the building in the early morning of March 12, the house was sealed off to all but official visitors while French police and German Gestapo both kept careful records of everyone who went in and out. In fact, a careful record was preserved. Examination of these records shows no Ronald Seth, nor anyone with another identity, who could possibly have been Ronald Seth.

There are other mistakes: Seth misplaces 66 rue Caumartin, showing an ignorance of Paris geography when he does so. He also says that Mme. Khait received injections from Petiot "in her arm," whereas all witnesses and the official record report the shots were in her thigh. Mme. Khait's own physician confirmed, in 1966, that he had seen the hypodermic scars on her thigh.

But Seth's worst error, and one that casts the gravest doubts on his claim to have been working in Paris as a British agent, is his report that Maître Floriot produced in court, as a witness for Petiot, Lafont, the head of the French Gestapo, who testified that Mme. Kahan had indeed been an agent of the Gestapo. The trial of Petiot began on March 18, 1946. Lafont was executed by a firing squad on December 27, 1944. Inasmuch as Lafont was one of the most important and most hated figures in the Occupation forces, it is unbelievable that anyone active with underground operations or intelligence should not have known that his death was over fourteen months prior to Petiot's trial.

It is true that Lafont, after being sentenced to death, recanted previous testimony and said that he recognized Mme. Kahan by a picture. However, both the police and the investigating judge agreed that he clearly changed his testimony in hopes that he might be called as a witness in the Petiot trial and thus receive a stay of execution.

Seth, notwithstanding his claim of being a British secret agent, apparently did not realize that Jacques Yonnet, editor of *Résistance* and intelligence officer of the Resistance, had the code name of Lieutenant Ybarne. Seth treats these names as being those of two persons. Seth's basic premise, however—that Petiot killed to gather funds for the Communist underground—is a very tenable theory and it might explain Petiot's stern refusal to make any confession whatever, even in arm's reach of the guillotine. His remarks to Desvaux could have been significant and Lieutenant l'Héritier's testimony all too true. Petiot's devotion to his family exceeded in strength every other motive, and he certainly would have gone to his death in silence rather than have harm befall them. (Seth's book on Petiot, incidentally, cannot be ordered or found in London. The publisher says it is out of print. All copies, like the other books on Petiot, have disappeared.)

But Ronald Seth has a very logical explanation or theory on Petiot that would, in a way, explain many things and once more prove Petiot's devotion to his family. He would rather be guillotined as a murderer than explain that he was a Communist patriot for a Communist France and have his family liquidated by the Communist underground he worked for.

The authors of *L'Affaire Petiot*—perhaps the best early book written on the case with the little material then available to the press—also question Petiot's guilt and motivations and suggest that there might well have been an explanation other than any of those advanced at the trial.

In the last ten years, however, very many more books have, with no government interference, been published in France and some in Germany about Petiot. Among these are: *Dr. Petiot* by René Tavernier, who quite obviously gathered his material many years after the case. The editor of this book was interestingly enough the son of Judge Leser. Beyond nit-picking, it had only one serious error: It ascribed the murder of Petiot's dairy-manager mistress to being knifed to death whereas her head was beaten in by a hammer. Due to the author's visit to Villeneuve and his study of the autopsy and conversations with many witnesses there, he notified the publisher of the error and a checkup at Villeneuve convinced both the publisher and author of their error. Another book appeared in 1974 entitled *The Abominable Dr. Petiot* by Jean-Marc Varaut, published by Balland, but none of these books demonstrates over thirty years of research and investigative procedures, beginning when Petiot was still alive.

As a further proof of the extraordinary differences between Petiot and the ordinary or even the extraordinary mass murderer is that over thirty years after his execution the New York *Times*, in an obituary on the death of his defense counsel, printed an unusual error about Petiot. The New York *Times* of December 23, 1975, states that Petiot was found guilty of only twenty-four out of twenty-seven murders that he was accused of committing. This was later supported and repeated by a feature story by the Paris *Jour* of January 21, 1977. Yet the established facts are that Petiot was found guilty of twenty-six out of twenty-seven murders for which he was charged!

One more item of great interest after over thirty years is what part, if any, of the $436,522.30 costs and damages assessed to the estate of Petiot by the court and by French law were paid. This is particularly important, for French law puts a limit against any further prosecution or collection of such assessments after thirty years, namely, after 1976.

Based on several sources, the nonguaranteed conclusion is that less than 12 per cent of the assessments were ever recovered. When you consider the elements of the estate—its known ownership of some fifty-one real estate holdings from Paris apartments to vineyards and farms and the considerable plunder of Eugène's travel agency—Petiot must be rated as a highly efficient criminal. He did leave a final note which he demanded to be used but destroyed. In a way, it was written by "fingers from the grave." It was used in the preparation of this book, but added little to the many mysteries or to the location of the millions of dollars of spoils. Whatever the explanation may be, the world will never hear it, for Petiot, grim traveler, is on the same route to which he committed so many others.

However, Petiot did establish a record in criminology: What other murderer has an unknown record as a successful spy or intelligence informer in a world war . . . what other mass murderer left a considerable, unrecoverable, and undiscovered fortune . . . or is it somehow in the possession of a less guilty party or parties?